Designing Quality Databases with IDEF1X Information Models

Designing Quality Databases with IDEF1X Information Models

DH

Thomas A. Bruce

Foreword by John A. Zachman

DORSET HOUSE PUBLISHING
353 West 12th St., New York, NY 10014

Library of Congress Cataloging in Publication Data

Bruce, Thomas A., 1946-
  Designing quality databases : practical information
management & IDEF1X / by Thomas A. Bruce.
      p.   cm.
  Includes bibliographical references and index.
  ISBN 0-932633-18-8 :
    1. Data base design. 2. IDEF1X
  I. Title.
  QA76.9.D26B78 1991   91-18092
  005.74--dc20   CIP

Trademark credits: All trade or product names are either trademarks or registered trademarks of their respective companies, and are the property of their respective holders. Intelect™ is a trademark of AI Corp. Apple® and Macintosh® are registered trademarks of Apple Computer, Inc. IDMS® is a registered trademark and Computer Associates™ is a trademark of Computer Associates International, Inc. DACOM® and Leverage® are registered trademarks and ModelPro™ is a trademark of D. Appleton Co. DEC® and VAX® are registered trademarks of Digital Equipment Corp. SQLBase™ is a trademark of Gupta Technologies. Excelerator™ is a trademark of Intersolv. IBM®, OS/2®, and PS/2® are registered trademarks, and AD/Cycle™, DB2™, IMS/ESA™, MVS/ESA™, MVS/XA™, OS/2 Extended Edition™, OS/2 Data Manager™, QMF™, Repository Manager™, Repository Manager/MVS™, REXX™, SQL/DS™, TIRS™, and VM™ are trademarks of International Business Machines Corp. Logic Works® is a registered trademark, and ERwin™, ERwin/ERX™, and ERwin/SQL™ are trademarks of Logic Works, Inc. Lotus® and 1-2-3® are registered trademarks of Lotus Development Corp. Metaphor® is a registered trademark of Metaphor Computer Systems. Microsoft® is a registered trademark, and MS-DOS™ and Windows™ are trademarks of Microsoft Corp. Ontos® is a registered trademark of Ontologic, Inc. Oracle® is a registered trademark of Oracle Corp. INGRES® is a registered trademark of Relational Technology, Inc. Gemstone® is a registered trademark of Servio Corp. SYBASE® is a registered trademark of Sybase, Inc. Unisys® is a registered trademark and Semantic Information Manager™ is a trademark of Unisys Corp. Versant® is a registered trademark of Versant Open Technology Corp.

Cover design by Jeff Faville, Faville Graphics

Distributed in the English language in the United Kingdom, Ireland, Europe, and Africa by John Wiley & Sons Ltd., Chichester, Sussex, England. Distributed in the English language in Singapore, the Philippines, and Southeast Asia by Toppan Co., Ltd., Singapore; and in the English language in Japan by Toppan Co., Ltd., Tokyo, Japan.

Printed in the United States of America

Library of Congress Catalog Number 91-18092
ISBN: 0-932633-18-8   12 11 10 9

To Robert M. Underhill

a wise man
who would have understood

FOREWORD

As I re-read Tom Bruce's book *Designing Quality Databases with IDEF1X Information Models* in preparation for writing this Foreword, I was even more impressed with the book than I was at my initial reading. Although the ideas that constitute the theoretical foundation for data-driven design have been around for many years, it is only recently, in my experience, that its actual practice has become a reality. It seems that for most of the years that I have attempted to articulate the data premise, the interest in the subject has been more intellectual than practical. Now, of late, it is seldom that I walk into an enterprise that is not aggressively pursuing the concepts. The questions are no longer "Why should we be interested in this?" but "How can we do this better and faster?"

This for me is awe-inspiring to say the least! Because, in this frame of reference, it becomes painfully obvious that there are data models . . . and there are *data models!* That is, building a data model is not sufficient in itself. If an enterprise is actually going to use these models successfully, they will have to be *good* data models! Furthermore, you can't send data designers to a three-day data modeling school and expect them to come away competent data modelers any more than you can send programmers to a three-day COBOL programming school and expect them to come away competent COBOL programmers. Nowhere have I seen an authoritative work that puts some definition around what constitutes a *good* data model until I read *Designing Quality Databases with IDEF1X Information Models.*

This book has been written by a man who has been there. Tom Bruce started out with Bob Brown, one of the real giants of the discipline, back in the late 1970s and has earned his stripes in the crucible of real-world implementations. He has designed databases, implemented them, and had to go back and fix the mistakes he made. He learned it from the bottom up and has written this book to give you the benefit of his real-life experiences.

Some people might read this book as a handbook of IDEF1X syntax (which it is), but actually what Tom has done is used IDEF1X as the vehicle to demonstrate the criticality of key data design decisions and their impact on the *enterprise* itself. Yes, this is a book on IDEF1X, but more importantly, it is a book on the "right" way to design data. This is what separates the good ones from the not-so-good ones. Here we find definitive criteria for *quality* data structures. I believe that some day, the book will be looked back on as the base reference point for measuring data structure quality.

As if that is not enough, the book is filled with giant tidbits of systems wisdom. How do you like this one for example: "What is often missed is that each denormalization of a data structure changes the business rules stated by the structure." Wow! What seems so obvious as it is stated, completely eluded me until I read the statement. I have always accepted denormalization as an inevitable consequence of performance tuning without ever contemplating the enormous business impact of such an obvious, merely technical decision!

Or, how about the frank discussion of reverse engineering?

Or, how about the clear and explicit differentiation between the ANSI, ISO, and IBM repository standards? And, I even enjoyed the case study!

Tom's book is loaded with insight and wisdom, quite over and above the very technical discussion of IDEF1X syntax, foreign key migration, attribute unification, normalization rules, and so forth.

Actually, I wish I had written the book myself . . . for three reasons.

FIRST, it is a very competently written technical book that speaks, virtually on every page, of a depth of professional experience that few could match. Unfortunately, I could not even begin to compare with Tom in this respect. His actual use of the precursor of IDEF1X at Bank of America before the IDEF languages were even a gleam in the Department of Defense's eyes is a testimony to his authority on the subject.

SECOND, to my knowledge, it is the first commercially available book on IDEF1X, which potentially could become the world standard language for data structure. Considering the fact that the Department of Defense has expended enormous sums of money defining and establishing standard function and data languages and considering their intent to drive manufacturing quality and productivity to unheard-of levels in the continuing battle to reduce defense expenditures dramatically, it does not take too much imagination to suspect that the 25,000 manufacturers around the world that market to DoD might catch on to the significance of IDEF. Already, there are more than forty CASE-type methods and products that support the IDEF0 (function) and IDEF1X (data) languages.

THIRD, referring to my earlier comments about the book being the first definitive work I've seen that qualifies a "good" data model, it is a very useful mixture of the theory and practice of data design. It is a book that will satisfy both those who want to understand the "why," and those who want to know the "how" of data driven design.

Consequently, this book can be expected to have more than some lingering relevance in the context of the Information Age, a context far beyond the usual conceptual boundaries attributed to data-driven design. In any case, these are some of the reasons I wish I could say I wrote the book. Last among them is the conviction that you will learn from, use, and above all enjoy the book.

Glendale, California   John A. Zachman
September 1991

PREFACE

I prepared my first information model using IDEF1X in 1981. It wasn't called IDEF1X then. It was called ADAM. But it was more or less the same thing.

I remember the afternoon quite well. I spent a couple of hours in my office on the sixteenth floor of Bank of America's data center in San Francisco drawing boxes and arrows with a fellow named Bob Brown and getting confused about which way the arrows went. I kept seeing pointers and asking, "How do we . . . ?" And Bob kept answering, "Is it there?"

By the end of that session in 1981, I couldn't think straight, and it took me a while to learn to do so. I had been developing data processing systems for about fifteen years and was trapped in a certain mode of thinking. To develop an information model, I needed to stop thinking "how" and start thinking "what." An information model doesn't show *how* something is done. It shows *what* information is needed to do it. As you work through the material in this book, you may also need to make this mental shift.

IDEF1X HISTORY

Robert G. Brown initially conceived of IDEF1X (pronounced "eye-deaf-one-ecks") in 1979 while he was employed as a consultant at Lockheed. It was based on evolving relational theory, and early work by Chen [1], Codd [2, 3], Smith and Smith [4], and others. Its first public appearance was at IBM's 1980 GUIDE-51 meeting in Miami, Florida. That year, Bob brought his ideas to Bank of America. In those days, the Bank was struggling with the issue of how to design its delivery and database applications to support an ever-increasing volume of electronic transactions. Data-centered design concepts were beginning to take hold, and an information modeling technique was needed for improving the quality of database designs. What Bob had developed was attractive, and evolved into what was known internally at the Bank as ADAM. Outside the Bank, ADAM was known simply as the Data Modeling Technique, or DMT.

At about the same time, other organizations were beginning to recognize the need for a semantic data modeling method. The Integrated Computer Aided Manufacturing (ICAM) studies conducted by the U.S. Air Force in the late 1970s identified a set of three graphic methods for defining the functions, data structures, and dynamics of manufacturing businesses. These three methods came to be known as the IDEF (*ICAM DEF*inition) methods, with IDEF0 being the *function* method (a technique for recording models of functions and information flows); IDEF1 being the original *data* method (developed by Hughes Aircraft and the D. Appleton Company (DACOM)); and IDEF2 being the *dynamics* method (a technique for describing the behavior of a system) [5].

When Bob left the Bank in 1985, his company, the Data Base Design Group, retained the rights to the ADAM product. Through arrangements with DACOM, the mainframe-based modeling tool was made commercially available, first under the name Janus, and later as the Leverage product.

One of the major users of the IDEF techniques is the U.S. Air Force. In 1985, DACOM approached the Air Force with a proposal to extend IDEF1 to add capabilities available in ADAM. Rather than extending IDEF1, DACOM replaced IDEF1 with ADAM and it was labeled IDEF1X (the X stands for eXtended). IDEF1X was accepted as an Air Force standard and, as such, became part of the public domain. To this point, the only IDEF1X descriptions available to the public have been a short document entitled IISS—Information Modeling Manual, Extended [6], and a summary included in Loomis' *The Database Book* [7].

I have been involved with IDEF1X since its early days, sometimes as a developer, but more often as a practitioner. People often ask me about reference material for the modeling language, but little has been available in book form to date. My decision to write this book and the viewpoint taken in it stem from the perspective of a *practitioner* of information management techniques. The book reflects experience I have gained in supporting many design efforts, both large and small, over a number of years. I hope you will find it to be a practical guide to using the very powerful information modeling language that is IDEF1X.

Berkeley, California   T.A.B.
July 1991

REFERENCES

[1]   Chen, P.P-S. "The Entity-Relationship Model—Toward a Unified View of Data," *ACM Transactions on Database Systems,* Vol. 1, No. 1 (March 1976), pp. 9-36.

[2]   Codd. E.F. "A Relational Model of Data for Large Shared Data Bases," *Communications of the ACM,* Vol. 13, No. 6 (June 1970).

[3]   _____. "Extending the Relational Model to Capture More Meaning," *ACM Transactions on Database Systems,* Vol. 4, No. 4 (December 1979), pp. 397-434.

[4]   Smith, J.M., and D.C.P. Smith. "Database Abstractions: Aggregation & Generalization," *ACM Transactions on Database Systems,* Vol, 2, No. 2 (June 1977).

[5]   SofTech, Inc. *Integrated Computer Aided Manufacturing (ICAM) Architecture, Part II,* Report No. AFWAL-TR-81-4023, Vols. I-XI, AFWAL/MLTC and AFTC. Wright-Patterson Air Force Base, Ohio, 1981.

[6]   D. Appleton Company, Inc. *Integrated Information Support System—Information Modeling Manual—IDEF1X Extended,* ICAM Project, Priority 6201, Subcontract No. 013-078-846, U.S.A.F. Prime Contract No. F33615-80-C-5155, Air Force Wright Aeronautical Laboratories, U.S. Air Force Systems Command, Wright-Patterson Air Force Base, Ohio, 1985.

[7]   Loomis, M.E.S. *The Database Book.* New York: Macmillan, 1987.

ACKNOWLEDGMENTS

No one writes a book without the help of others. The contributions may be large or small, but all are important. Many have contributed to this work, and I greatly appreciate their efforts.

Some of this material is derived from a methods guide I wrote for Logic Works, Inc., of Princeton, New Jersey, in early 1989. I would especially like to acknowledge Dr. Benjamin Cohen, president of Logic Works, for his help in preparing that early material. Many of the figures in this book were prepared using his company's ERwin product.

Many thanks also to Bill Fujimoto and Monterey Foods of Berkeley, California, for use of their produce model. It's nice to have a friend with a business large enough to be the basis for a case study. We have known each other for more than thirty years, and Bill pays me in bananas for systems work I do for him. For his efforts, he got a design for his market system. I got a case study.

Many people were kind enough to review the draft manuscript. Their contributions have been significant. My sincere thanks go to Bob Brown, John Zachman, Keri Anderson Healy, David Pollock, Rick Gaspard, Anne Giansiracusa, Bob Binder, Michael Silves, Gary Schuldt, and Harriet Serenkin.

Thanks also to my editor at Dorset House, Wendy Eakin, and to the many friends who put up with me during the two years this took to complete. It has been a long road, and more tedious than I ever could have imagined. But I have managed to have fun.

One individual deserves credit for the basic foundation of the material covered here, the modeling language itself, and its evolution to support object-oriented concepts. During the early 1980s, I had the pleasure of working with Bob Brown on the early development and use of the IDEF1X language and the mainframe-based tool needed to support it. Bob has been instrumental in developing what I believe is the best information modeling technique available for supporting top-to-bottom, high-level-to-detailed representations of data structures. His critical review of and contributions to the material in this book are much appreciated. Bob is the one who got this particular language started. He would, of course, pass the credit to the early database pioneers.

CONTENTS

CONTENTS

LIST OF FIGURES

Designing Quality Databases with IDEF1X Information Models

INTRODUCTION

Designing Quality Databases with IDEF1X Information Models is a book on information modeling, but it is not just for information modelers. It is intended for anyone who needs to understand data-centered design techniques. Such techniques improve the quality of the resulting system. Although a specific information modeling language is described here, the general principles can help you understand and use any such graphic language.

IDEF1X is a language. Not a natural language, or a programming language, but a specification language for describing data structures. The capabilities of this language surpass those of many others.

THE POWER OF LANGUAGE

The idea that the language we use determines what we can think is not new. Those who study primitive cultures and societies often find behavior and thought heavily influenced by language. If our language has no word for a concept, we cannot think about it. Try, for example, to consider what it would mean if your language had no word for the concept of *self,* and what that would imply. There is a science fiction story by Samuel R. Delany called *Babel-17* about just this thought [1].

IDEF1X lets us think about complex data structures and business rules without being concerned about the characteristics of the database management system that will be used to implement these structures and rules. It forces us to clearly define keys (attributes that identify entities) and to be specific about the relationships that exist among the entities. The language lets us generalize information structures, that is, recognize similarity among detailed structures, and form general structures that consolidate the detailed ones. The precision

3

in the language lets us be specific about the rules that govern what is related to what. All of these features are needed if we are to accurately specify what must be built in order to satisfy a business need.

The language can be used not only to define business information requirements and business data structures, but also to specify structures used to store the specifications of our information systems. There is an important component of the information management environment, known as the information repository, that will, in time, store these specifications. IDEF1X can be used to define the structure of the information in a repository and many of the rules that govern its behavior and use. With the recent introduction of IBM's AD/Cycle and Repository Manager products, we will see more emphasis on defining system development information requirements as well as business information requirements. IDEF1X is well suited to these tasks.

But what the book is about and who it is written for are as important as understanding the power of language.

THE AUDIENCE

This text is intended for use by three audiences: managers, systems professionals, and students. *Managers* will find the introductory sections useful as a review of database and information management concepts and approaches, and are urged to spend a bit of time with the technical sections. The techniques covered here are not simply academic. They describe the application of sound, theoretical concepts to the business world.

The technical sections and the case study examples are oriented toward *technical systems professionals,* including systems developers, the data administrator, and the database administrator who will be putting these techniques into practice. *Students* learning about the data processing field will find an overview of information systems planning and design and can begin to develop an understanding of how to apply these, and other, information management concepts.

ORGANIZATION

The book is divided into three parts. The three chapters of Part One provide background material, as follows: Chapter 1 reviews general database concepts. Chapter 2 introduces the practice of information management, and discusses information modeling in the context of John Zachman's "A Framework for

Information Systems Architecture" [2]. Chapter 3 describes the basic concepts behind information modeling, defines different types of information models, and explores the methods used to develop them.

Part Two consists of Chapters 4-12, which, along with Appendix D, provide a full description of the IDEF1X language. In Chapter 4, the graphic symbols are introduced, and examples help you understand the syntax and semantics of IDEF1X diagrams. The importance of good definitions of model objects is discussed in Chapter 5. Chapters 6, 7, and 8 present the details of the language. Chapter 9 examines the subject of normalization in a somewhat informal manner; Chapter 10 discusses reverse engineering and re-engineering, and presents an example of how IDEF1X can be used to describe current data structures. Chapter 11 is the crystal ball chapter, in which I speculate about the future of information management in general. Chapter 12 provides a first look at the evolution of IDEF1X to support the object-oriented approach to developing systems.

Part Three's three chapters contain a case study based on a produce market in Berkeley, California. The models are simplified, but represent a real business. The structures developed in the case study are designed to help you understand the concepts discussed in the rest of the book.

The book concludes with eight Appendices, a Glossary, and an Index. Appendices A, B, and C describe Zachman's Framework, data administration functions, and information modeling sessions, and support the introductory material of Part One. Appendix D contains a listing of referential integrity rules that can be stated with IDEF1X constructs, along with SQL queries for finding integrity violations in physical databases. Appendix E provides information on commercial product support for IDEF1X. Appendix F contains additional detail supporting the case study in Part Three.

Appendix G reviews the information modeling language introduced in 1990 by IBM for use with its Repository Manager product. Translations are provided between the IBM and IDEF1X languages. Appendix H provides answers to the exercises associated with the first ten chapters. I urge you to try them, as they enforce the basic concepts, and introduce some that are more advanced.

NOTATION CONVENTIONS

Conventions are used throughout to highlight certain terms, although I have tried not to clutter the text excessively with them when no particular emphasis is needed. The notations follow:

- *Italics are used for emphasis and often signify defined terms.*

  Example: We will be discussing *entities, attributes,* and *relationships.*

- **Bold type in a shaded box highlights definitions.**

> **Definition: An attribute is a property of an entity.**

- ENTITY-NAMEs appear in UPPERCASE in a reduced size.

  Example: A CUSTOMER is described in the model as ...

- "attribute-names" appear in lowercase in literal-type quotation marks.

  Example: A "salary" is recorded for each EMPLOYEE.

- Entity and attribute names consisting of multiple words are hyphenated.

  Example: SERVICE-BUREAU, "customer-name"

- The plural of an entity is indicated by appending an s (ignoring spelling).

  Example: A COMPANY operates in many CITYs (rather than CITIES).

- The plural of an attribute is indicated by appending an s (ignoring spelling).

  Example: "batch-prioritys" are recorded for BATCHs.

- Relationship verb phrases appear inside brackets.

  Example: A STATE <contains> one or more CITYs.

REFERENCES

[1]   Delany, S.R. *Babel-17.* New York: Ace Books, 1966.

[2]   Zachman, J.A. "A Framework for Information Systems Architecture," *IBM Systems Journal,* Vol. 26, No. 3 (1987), pp. 276-92.

PART ONE

Designing Quality Databases is primarily a book about how to use IDEF1X information models to specify business information requirements, policies, and rules, and how to use these specifications to design and build database applications. The discussion, however, cannot start there. Information modeling is done in a business environment in which other things, like making a profit, are considered more important. To be viewed as adding value to a business, information modeling must be conducted in the larger context of an information management environment.

The three chapters of Part One examine what database applications are, how they are designed, and how the information they contain can be managed. Chapter 1 reviews the evolution of database technology and design techniques. Chapter 2 expands the discussion by examining where information modeling fits in the larger arena of information management and the architectural representations of information systems. Chapter 3 focuses on information modeling, providing a generic overview of the concept and describing the specific types of models supported by the IDEF1X language, and completes the background discussion by identifying the purposes of these models and describing different approaches used to develop them.

1

DATABASE INTRODUCTION

In the beginning, there was no database. Computers were the expensive toys and tools of engineers and scientists in the back room. Computer systems staff were not often involved in the analysis of the business. In fact, there was little in the way of computer systems staff, and often there was little analysis.

But, despite its early inaccessibility, the computer made it out of the back room and became one of the mainstays of the business world. As time went on, computer capabilities rapidly increased and the cost of applying computer resources in a business situation dramatically decreased. As a result, new methods of exploiting the computing environment were needed. Some of these needs were met by the emergence of database technology.

The evolution of database concepts and technology has driven the need for information systems developers to find ways to manage the effect of changes in the structure and use of data. As a discipline, information modeling has followed as a way to better understand the structure and meaning of that data. Moreover, information modeling, by capturing more of the meaning of the data structure, that is, its semantics, helps to control costs of information systems development, and improve the quality of the resulting system.

This chapter provides a bit of the history of database. It introduces schemas and describes three reference models used to depict the logical structure of data. The chapter presents different approaches to designing database applications and shows how information modeling helps us construct integrated information systems.

1.1 DATABASE COMES OF AGE

Definition: Database

An organized collection of data values.

Database technology has evolved rapidly. By the early 1960s, a situation had developed in which thousands of programs needed to access information held in external files. New ways were needed to control program development and maintenance costs, and it became clear that a set of utility functions placed between the programs and the data could help to control such costs. These utility functions, called *access methods,* were a first step toward removing responsibility for managing data from the application program.

Increasing availability of inexpensive storage and computing capacity then led database technology through a series of steps in which each achieved a further separation of program functions from data access functions. Using utility data access functions simplified the job of the programmer (the device-dependent code did not have to be rewritten each time), but also forced the programmer to give up some control.

Each step in the evolution of the database concepts and techniques also introduced new ways of conceptualizing the structure of data, and of specifying the physical storage characteristics of that data. The evolution has gone from simple files (in which the application program maintained the linkage among records), to the use of network and hierarchical database management systems (in which the application code was less tied to the intricacies of the data structures), to today's relational systems (in which the code no longer needs to navigate through the data structures).

We might expect things to get easier as the technology becomes more capable, but it doesn't seem to work that way. The applications that use the evolving technology have a way of becoming more complex.

1.1.1 Three Schemas

Definition: Schema

A representation of the structure of data.

The first computing systems had no schema, that is, no representation of the structure of data (see Fig. 1.1). There was no data storage, so there was no need to describe the data structure. Old programmable calculators were like this. They had no nice user interface and couldn't store data. We could plug in values in certain locations, compute, and get results from other locations. These calculators were early computing machines, and were difficult to use.

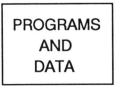

Figure 1.1.   No-Schema Architecture.

Eventually, storage devices were added, creating a need for a description of the structure of the data so that a program could store and retrieve data, and make it available to algorithms. The description of the physical data structure is called an *internal schema*.

> **Definition: Internal Schema**
>
> **A description of the physical structure of data.**

At first, programs manipulated data storage devices directly; the code to control those devices was part of the application. In time, programs were able to use the basic access methods provided by early operating systems to control those devices, and a degree of separation between the processing functions and the physical data structure was achieved. In both situations, however, programs needed to know how the data was arranged (the access methods simply removed the burden of manipulating the storage devices). The programs needed a "view" of how the data was stored. An internal schema is often referred to as a *storage view*.

In early applications, there was a single view, a one-schema architecture (Fig. 1.2). The physical data structure was managed by the program code. The user was an algorithm. The user's view of the data was the same as the storage view of the data. To get a feeling for this single internal schema, think of a file dump. You see the data exactly the same way the code sees it. Unless you are a programmer, that's not useful. Although several programs were often able to use the same internal schema to access the data, changes in the structure of the stored data required changes in the programs. Likewise, changes in the structure of the programs often required changes in the structure of the data.

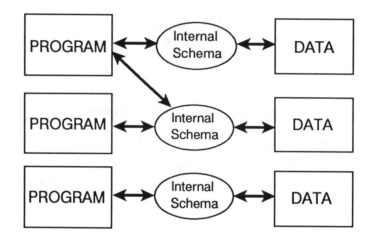

Figure 1.2. One-Schema Architecture.

As people other than scientists and programmers began to look at the data, a division in views developed. Business users didn't care about the physical structure of the data. They weren't interested in seeing data as it was stored in the storage devices. Business users had their own user views; they wanted forms and reports. It thus became the responsibility of the programs to stand in the middle, translating user views into storage views and vice versa. This responsibility led to the concept of an *external schema,* that is, a representation of the data structure in a form appropriate to a user of the data. An external schema is often referred to as a *user view.*

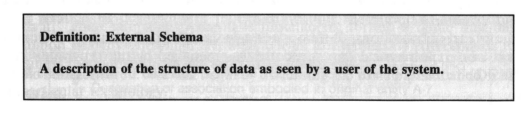

Definition: External Schema

A description of the structure of data as seen by a user of the system.

Applications constructed using this concept had a two-schema architecture, as illustrated in Fig. 1.3. Data was arranged on reports or display screens in a form that was convenient for the user. Data input forms or screens were designed so that entry of data was efficient for the user. Data from several files was often merged by the programs to create the reports or screen displays, and different pieces of data entered on a single screen or form were often stored in separate files. Users then only needed to understand the external schemas (the layouts of the screens, forms, and reports). The programs needed to understand both the external and internal schemas.

Although two-schema architecture applications were easier for users to work with than one-schema architecture applications, the programs remained complex because the mapping between the code and the data structure was the same as in the one-schema architecture. Whenever the external or internal schemas changed, many of the programs had to change as well in order to maintain the mapping between the external (user) and internal (storage) views.

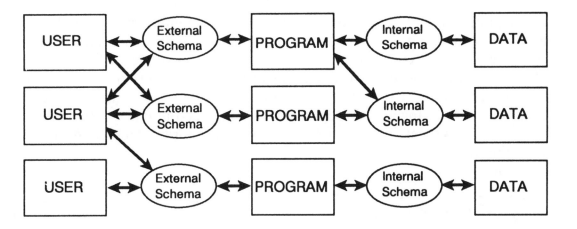

Figure 1.3.   Two-Schema Architecture.

As data processing applications became more complex, programs needed more internal schemas and users needed more external schemas. Moreover, if data was shared among programs, the same internal schemas were needed by more and more programs. As the physical data structures changed, the cost of maintaining two-schema systems escalated rapidly. Every time a schema changed, programs had to change. Every time a program needed a change in an internal schema, all other programs that used the schema had to change as well, even if those programs were functioning fine from the perspective of their users. Sharing data among multiple processing applications became more and more expensive.

To make data sharing maintainable and economically feasible, designers added a new view between the programs and the storage views. Applications constructed using this so-called *conceptual view* employed a three-schema architecture [1]. A *conceptual schema,* illustrated in Fig. 1.4, defines the data structure in a form that is independent of all storage views and user views but with a scope that spans them all.

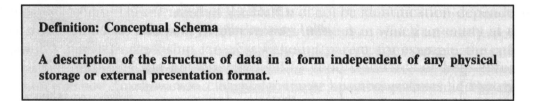

Definition: Conceptual Schema

A description of the structure of data in a form independent of any physical storage or external presentation format.

In the three-schema architecture, a database management system (DBMS) manages the mapping between the conceptual schema and the internal schemas while the programs continue to manage the mappings between the external schemas and the conceptual schema. The programs and users no longer need to understand the intricacies of data storage. When the structure of the underlying data changes, the programs no longer need to change; their view of the data is completely separate from the storage representations. At least, that's the theory.

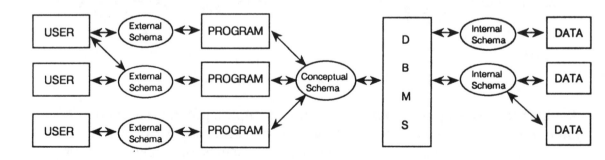

Figure 1.4.   Three-Schema Architecture.

1.1.2 Keys, Pointers, and Record Identification

Individual pieces of data are often referred to as fields or data elements. These fields are gathered into groups called records. Records, in turn, are organized into files. In any database system, there must be some way to identify the stored records, that is, there must be some record identifier. The record identifier is often called the *primary key* (or simply, key). Keys are handled differently in conceptual and internal schemas, and by different types of database management systems.

At the physical storage level, keys usually correspond to addresses on disk drives containing the data. These physical keys may be stored as pointers in database records to establish relationships among the records, and are represented as such in the internal schema.

At the conceptual schema level, primary keys correspond to fields in logical records (logical collections of data elements) that carry information that distinguishes one logical record from another. For example, a logical record describing a customer might be constructed with customer-number as the logical key. This type of key is also used to tie records together in a physical file, for example by storing the logical key of a contract record in a record for a customer involved with that contract.

Physical keys are normally found at the internal schema level. Logical keys are found in the conceptual schema and external schemas (the user views). In external schemas, additional fields may be used to identify data the user wants to store or retrieve.

1.1.3 Hierarchical and Network Representations

Database Management Systems developed in the late 1960s through the early 1980s generally used one of two models to represent the conceptual schema —either the hierarchical model or the network model. Both of these models were oriented toward the characteristics of the data storage structures as seen by the programs. DBMS products such as IBM's Information Management System (IMS) use a hierarchical model of the data structures. The programs see data as a hierarchical collection of records, while the DBMS oversees the physical location of data within storage blocks and across the physical storage with address and relative block pointers. The hierarchical conceptual schema is an attempt to accommodate all user views by integrating them into a single hierarchical structure.

As an example, consider a situation in which customers buy many products and products are sold to many customers, with each sale recorded by a contract. Further, assume there is a business policy that says a contract can involve several customers and products at the same time. With a hierarchical model, we might draw a picture like that shown in Fig. 1.5 to represent the relationships. The programs that access the database must know to look at records below the customer record to find pointers to the contracts for the customer, to look at records below the contract record to find pointers to the products and customers for the contract, and so on. These pointers can be maintained by either the programs or the DBMS, depending on the level of sophistication of the DBMS and the degree of overhead acceptable for DBMS pointer maintenance.

DBMS products like Computer Associates' IDMS represent the conceptual schema as a network of interconnected records according to the CODASYL model [2]. As with hierarchical systems, the DBMS manages physical storage but the programs see the data structures as webs of interconnected records and sets that represent relationships among records. Figure 1.6 shows the same example as in Fig. 1.5, but presented as a network model.

In the structure represented by Fig. 1.6, customer and product record types own sets of relationships to associated contracts (participation and sale). Contract owns sets of relationships back to customers and contracts.

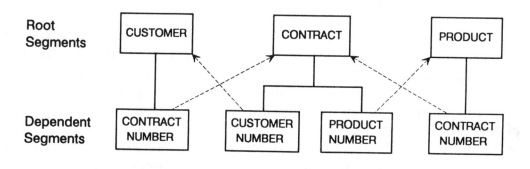

Figure 1.5. Hierarchical Conceptual Schema.

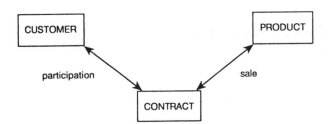

Figure 1.6. Network Conceptual Schema.

In DBMS products built according to both the hierarchical and network models, the application code must understand how to maneuver through the data structure, and must supply the proper navigation information to the DBMS. Individual record keys and relationship structures must be understood by the application code. When the structure of the data changes, the programs still must change, but not as much as in a two-schema system. Information modeling techniques that were developed to support hierarchical and network DBMS installations tended to reflect a hierarchical or network view of the data.

1.1.4 Relational Representations

By the mid-1970s, network and hierarchical DBMSs had removed a great deal of the burden of data structure access from the programs, but the programs still needed to know how to navigate the data structures. The programs still had to determine how to retrieve or insert a set of records and be aware of the sequence in which records were stored. Thus, they remained sensitive to changes in the internal schemas.

Network and hierarchical DBMSs removed a part of the dependence of the programs on the structure of the data, but not all of it. Internal schema changes, therefore, still resulted in expensive changes to programs.

During the 1970s, a relational model [3, 4] for representing the conceptual schema level of the three-schema architecture was introduced. This third model has made a tremendous impact on the way in which data structures can be conceived, as well as the degree to which the application code must understand the data structure. In the relational model, data is represented as a collection of tables, with relationships (the structure) represented by shared foreign keys (a logical key of one record held as data in another record). Database management systems built according to this model separate the programs from the data structures much more than do hierarchical and network systems. Because of the data manipulation capabilities inherent in this model, programs no longer need to be as concerned with the way the DBMS manages the mapping between the conceptual and internal schemas.

Applications that use a relational DBMS are different from the hierarchical and network applications in a fundamental way. In network and hierarchical systems, application programs deal with one record at a time. The DBMS receives a request for a record and processes that request; the application program sequences the processing of the records. In the relational system, the interaction between the programs and the DBMS is set processing. Rather than instructing the DBMS to perform an operation on a record, the application program requests processing on a set, or group of records.

In a record-at-a-time system, to increase the credit limit of every customer in a file by ten percent, a program must pass through the entire file, reading one record at a time, creating the new limit, then writing the record back. In a set-at-a-time system, the program makes a single call to the DBMS, specifying the parameters of the request (in this example, select all of the customer records and increase the limit by ten percent). The DBMS then carries out the processing against each individual record. That's one application program instruction, as opposed to perhaps hundreds required to control the reading, updating, and writing in a record-at-a-time system.*

Figure 1.7 provides an example of a relational model and the underlying tables for our contract example. Participation and sale are representations of the relationships between many customers, products, and contracts. Although a program must know that customers and contracts are related through participation, and that contracts and products are related through sale, it need not know how to sequence operations needed to create, read, update, or delete records.

---

*The most common data manipulation language (DML) used by application programs to communicate with a relational DBMS is Structured Query Language (SQL). There is a basic standard that describes SQL [5], but it is viewed by many as incomplete and is usually extended by each vendor. The SQL for IBM's DB2 in the large mainframe (MVS) environment is different from the SQL for IBM's SQL/DS product for the mid-size mainframe (VM) environment. These are both different from the SQL used by the Oracle DBMS from Oracle Systems, RDB and others for the DEC VAX environment, the SQL server from Microsoft, and even the OS/2 Extended Edition Data Manager from IBM. They all look alike, but the differences are enough to drive a database administrator nuts.

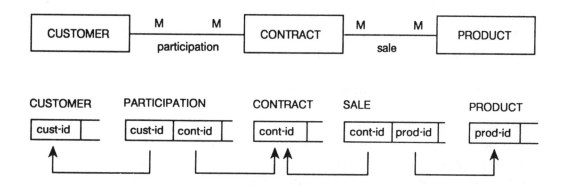

Figure 1.7.   Relational Conceptual Schema.

The IDEF1X information modeling technique discussed in this book is based on the relational model and represents relationships among records with shared keys rather than physical pointers. It is ideally suited to development of a neutral conceptual view of the data, which will satisfy all external user views and shelter the application code from changes in the internal storage views.

1.2 DATABASE DESIGN TECHNIQUES

Techniques for designing databases continue to evolve, driven by the increasing complexity of the systems being developed. A technique tends to mirror the objective of an effort. As the use of database technology has grown and shifted from simple stand-alone systems to complex integrated systems, the design techniques have had to grow as well.

1.2.1 Design for a Specific Technology

Many of the databases developed during the 1970s were constrained by earlier technology decisions intended to standardize the hardware and software placed in central data processing centers. Physical constraints had a large impact on the way database requirements were specified. The underlying thought was "why bother with a logical view of the data structures if we already know that we must eventually translate it into, say, a hierarchical DBMS, and tune it for maximum performance?" In addition, no one had much experience with logical design techniques for the data.

Early database systems were fairly small; a few transactions a second was pushing the limits. Moreover, many of the systems were specifically tuned toward response time for particular functions, and the data design problem was generally simple. But the problems got more complex.

1.2.2 Logical, then Physical, Design Approach

Structured development techniques for data processing began to emerge in the mid-1970s. These techniques emphasized the need to separate logical design (what the system is to do) from physical design (how that is to be done), and provided methods of doing this for the functions of the system [6, 7, 8]. The emphasis shifted toward stating requirements and transforming them into technology-independent designs. This approach helped to ensure that the right problems were being addressed and that the resulting logical design could be segmented into parts that could be implemented separately but could function together smoothly.

Logical design for function has become fairly standard. Logical design for data can have benefits similar to those of logical function design. A precise statement of information requirements can be created, and the resulting picture can be segmented so that the separately implemented pieces can fit together smoothly.

The shift toward the logical, then physical, design approach has been considerably slower for data than for function. The need for the function disciplines became apparent long before the need for the data disciplines arose. Therefore, although the roots of the data disciplines are older, the function disciplines evolved more rapidly. In addition, logical function design techniques are somewhat more intuitively obvious than are the data techniques. People are more used to thinking about how something is done, than about what that something is being done to.

1.2.3 Design for a Single Purpose

Many early database systems were designed without much consideration for sharing data beyond the first application (the one that paid for the initial development work). In these systems, the structure of the data was heavily influenced by the response-time requirements of a single application. Much of this application-specific tuning made it difficult, if not impossible, to use the same database to support additional applications. Moreover, the underlying hardware and system software were usually not fast enough to make data sharing by multiple applications realistic.

We continue to see these single-purpose database systems today. But there is much less justification for them, at least in a centralized high-performance environment. In the early systems, it could reasonably be argued that the response-time requirements and relatively slow performance of the DBMS and supporting hardware left no alternative but to design the database for the single purpose.

There have been tremendous increases in the capabilities of DBMS software and the hardware on which it runs, and there will be continued performance improvements in the future. Specifically, the increasing ability of the DBMS and supporting hardware to accommodate high transaction volumes without the degree of function-specific tuning previously needed will enable us to realize the benefits of operating database systems as a shared resource.

1.2.4 Designing a Shared Resource

The alternative to single-purpose tuning of databases is general sharing of the data. In theory, this means the design of the database should represent a compromise among all the tunings that might be done for specific access. To achieve the benefits that common access to shared data can bring, careful attention must be paid to the design of the data structures.

Just as it is more difficult to construct a logical design for a database before constructing a physical design, it is more difficult to design shared databases than it is to design single-purpose databases. Designing for multiple purposes requires not only that the logical, then physical, approach be taken, but also that a broad view of the requirements for the database be developed and that this view be segmented into parts that can be installed incrementally. Designing a database for a single purpose focuses on tuning for high performance. Designing shared databases requires a fundamental shift—from a focus on data access to a focus on the structure and semantics of the data. The tuning activity must be postponed to a later time.

Shared databases do not happen by accident. The second, third, and fourth applications that need the data will not fit well with the first application if the first has not been designed in the context of the whole. To develop wide views of requirements demands techniques that recognize all views as equally important and will not permit a design to emerge that allows early implementations of a part of the data structures to prevent later requirements from being met. The information modeling techniques discussed in this book provide a way to develop the specifications for shared databases.

1.3 TRADITIONAL SYSTEM DESIGN

Systems developers have been designing and installing computer applications for more than thirty years. Many of their traditional approaches have become ingrained in the culture of development organizations, and in the thinking of the developers. The introduction of database technology has led to the realization that some of the old approaches no longer serve well.

1.3.1 Function-Centered Design

Those who entered the data processing field during the 1960s, 1970s, and early 1980s grew up with a *process* perspective. We were taught to use flowcharts to design program logic and to use dataflow diagrams to specify information flows. We were taught, or learned through experience, that if we worked backward from the required outputs of a system—generally from the reports it was to produce—we could determine what inputs were needed and how the process (code) we were developing could be specified as a conversion of the required inputs into the desired outputs. We were taught that data flowed in the dataflow diagrams and was stored in the data stores. But no one bothered to tell us that the data stores were actually views into a model of data, or how to decide what that model of data should look like. If a data element was not defined as part of some data store, it would not end up in the final database design. There were no techniques available for looking at information in its own right.

1.3.2 Data as Unplanned Byproduct

Data was very much an unplanned byproduct of these early function-centered design approaches. Although we generally got workable designs for our databases, at least for the functions on the dataflow diagrams, it was not because of engineering but rather because of the skills of a few experienced artists. When things worked, it was usually because of the significant efforts of a lot of dedicated people. These approaches were process driven as opposed to data driven.

1.3.3 Database Management Systems as Storage Mechanisms

In many early database systems, the DBMS was primarily a substitute for previous access methods. For example, in some of these early systems, the database design looked remarkably like the sequential file design used in tape-oriented batch-processing systems. It has taken a while for database system designers to understand and apply the concept of data as a shared resource. It has taken even longer for techniques to evolve that will allow us to develop such designs rapidly.

1.4 DATA-CENTERED DESIGN

Data-centered design approaches began to emerge in the mid-1970s. While function-centered design approaches treat data subsidiary to the processing, data-centered design approaches treat the structure and semantics of data as the fundamental underpinnings of the system. They concentrate on the things (data entities) that must be managed, their properties (attributes), and the relationships among these things. Models of the data structure are developed by first determining what data is required in order to support the major functions, then developing a consensus structure that supports all functions. The functions are then restructured around the use and maintenance of the data.

One argument for data-centered design is that if you know what the data is, you can describe most of the function of the system as creating, replacing, using, and deleting that data. When used correctly, this approach works well. But shifting one's orientation toward the data is not an easy thing to do, and requires a great deal of restraint. The tendency is often to return to analysis of the function. It is easier to think *how* than it is to think *what*—that is, until we have developed some experience with the techniques and have begun to trust them.

Function-centered design approaches often can lead to systems that are not well integrated. Function-based techniques tend to divide a system into separate pieces and organize the pieces in a hierarchical form. This often results in systems that concentrate on organizing information around the separate functions, making it difficult to share that information without building interfaces to exchange data among low-level pieces of the system. Each piece tends to own its data.

Data-centered design techniques, on the other hand, yield highly integrated systems. Data structures are designed to be shared across many separate functions, without the need for bridging data from one function to another. No function owns the data. The focus on integration can also suggest structures for functions that can be shared across multiple business applications.

As businesses recognize the need for integrated information resources, they often encounter the dilemma of how to create an atmosphere in which sharing can occur. Most organizations in the western world are hierarchical in nature, and their cultures enforce the "I'll do it my way, you do it yours, and maybe some day we will need to put the pieces together" mentality. To shift the orientation toward cooperation, rather than independent contribution, requires fundamental cultural change. That change can only occur when integration is not viewed as a threat.

1.5 NEED FOR MANAGEMENT INFORMATION

In most organizations, management information services (MIS) is an information-driven function. It needs to see data differently from the way the data is organized in the day-to-day operating functions. Supporting the MIS function often requires solutions different from those used to support the operations functions of the business.

1.5.1 Consolidating Information

As the complexity of information has increased and as the number of solutions to managing that information has grown, MIS professionals have had to find ways to consolidate views of information held in many separate systems. This turns out to be a significant challenge.

Models can provide some assistance in developing consolidated information views, but creating models for existing systems is difficult. Two models are needed—a model of what exists and a model of what is wanted. The process of creating models of existing systems is called *reverse engineering* and is covered in Chapter 10. Creating models of what is wanted is the major topic of Parts Two and Three of this book.

Models of existing systems help to identify where data is currently stored, and can point out redundancies in current databases. Models of what is needed to support MIS describe the way that existing data must be consolidated. Separate processing applications are often constructed to provide the required consolidations.

1.5.2 Integrating in the Back End

In many businesses, there is little opportunity to change the database design for existing operational systems. Organizations have spent time and money building database applications that, to varying degrees, meet the day-to-day operating needs of the organization. The design of these existing databases often constrains what can be added to the system, and how it can be added. Sometimes, a clearly conceived, broad scope information model cannot be implemented in a current operational data processing environment. Consider the following example.

Suppose that during a requirements gathering and logical design phase for a new application, we discover that much of the information that must be recorded about a customer is similar to the information that must be kept about an employee or a supplier. Each has a name and address, and participates in a contract with the business. Suppose further that a single individual may be involved in multiple relationships with the business—for example, a person might be both a customer and an employee—and that it is necessary to understand the overall relationship between a person and the business not as a collection of separate relationships, but as a single relationship.

Also suppose that the environment in which the requirements of this project are to be satisfied is one in which there are separate employee, supplier, and customer databases, and that common information has not been separated out from these databases. When a customer is also an employee, information about that person is stored in two different databases (name, address, telephone number, and so on)—once in the customer database, and once in the employee database. Finally, suppose that the existing environment took fifteen years to build and cost $500 million.

It's not difficult to guess that the chance of changing the current database structure to recognize the commonality of suppliers, employees, and customers is about zero. The question then is, What good has it done to discover the integration requirement in the first place?

One answer has to do with knowing what is needed. Another has to do with the needs of an organization to extract information from its front-end operational systems for use in a back-end MIS or decision-support environment. In many organizations, this separate extract environment is not constrained to the same degree as is the operational environment and may be an appropriate place to provide the wide, interconnected information structures described in an enterprise-wide information model. This approach has been adopted by many companies, and it works.

It is against this consolidated view of the information used by the business that the decision-support systems will find their most valuable use, at least in the foreseeable future in large organizations in which existing systems are meeting the majority of day-to-day operating needs. Databases that cannot be integrated in the front-end operational systems can often be integrated in the back-end MIS systems.

1.5.3 Guiding the Front End

Even if the operational systems of the business are constrained in their ability to change, they are probably not completely rigid. As opportunities present themselves, a well-conceived information strategy, supported by logical models of the information, can be helpful in making decisions about design alternatives. In the employee and customer example, the addition of relationship data to each operational system could provide an appearance of integration, even if there is actually very little. It might be possible to hold a common identifier of the person as additional data about the customer and employee, and use the identifier to tie the structure together in a different environment, or to allow processing functions to extract information from both of the systems to produce a consolidated picture.

1.6 SUMMARY

The requirements for database applications are becoming evermore complex. Information modeling enables us to uncover requirements that we could not previously see. It is an appropriate technique for determining requirements and specifying designs of information systems. It is a fundamental part of data-centered design, an approach that leads to more highly integrated systems. Evolving technology has made data sharing a realistic alternative, and it is just in time.

1.7 REVIEW EXERCISES

Answers to boldface questions appear in Appendix H.

1. **What is a database?**

2. Why are there three schemas?

3. **Which schema does information modeling address?**

4. How many schemas are there in a spreadsheet package like Lotus 1-2-3 or Excel?

5. **Are there schemas for function as well as for data? If so, what are they?**

6. **Why are schemas threatening? Whom do they threaten?**

7. What is the difference between a record-at-a-time DBMS and a set-at-a-time DBMS?

1.8 REFERENCES

[1] Tsichritzis, D., and A. Klug, eds. "The ANSI/SPARC DBMS Framework Report of the Study Group on Database Management Systems," *Infosystems,* Vol. 3 (1978).

[2] CODASYL. *Data Description Language Committee Journal of Development, 1978.* Ottawa: Material Development Management Branch, Canadian Federal Government, 1978.

[3] Codd, E.F. "A Relational Model of Data for Large Shared Data Bases," *Communications of the ACM,* Vol. 13, No. 6 (June 1970).

[4] _____. "Extending the Relational Model to Capture More Meaning," *ACM Transactions on Database Systems,* Vol. 4, No. 4 (December 1979), pp. 397-434.

[5] Date, C.J. *A Guide to the SQL Standard,* 2nd ed. Reading, Mass.: Addison-Wesley, 1989.

[6] DeMarco, T. *Structured Analysis and System Specification.* Englewood Cliffs, N.J.: Prentice-Hall, 1978.

[7]   Yourdon, E., and L. Constantine. *Structured Design.* Englewood Cliffs, N.J.: Prentice-Hall, 1979.

[8]   Gane, C., and T. Sarson. *Structured Systems Analysis: Tools and Techniques.* Englewood Cliffs, N.J.: Prentice-Hall, 1979.

2

CONTEXT FOR INFORMATION MODELING

Information modeling is a technique that supports many of the activities needed to manage information as an asset. In Chapter 1, we discussed the evolution of the database, and looked at approaches that have emerged to support the development of database applications. In this chapter, we review the general arena of information management and the architecture of information systems.

The chapter begins with a definition of information and a brief discussion of several aspects of information management, and then discusses how John Zachman's concept of an architecture *framework* can help identify the role that information modeling plays in the overall design and development of a system. Using Zachman's definitions, we see how information models are architectural representations of data and how they relate to other dimensions of a system, specifically, its functions and the distribution of the functions and data across a geographically distributed business. An understanding of Zachman's Framework will help put the modeling language introduced in Part Two in context. The Framework discussion here is limited to essentials; additional information is provided in Appendix A.

Many organizations have established formal data administration (DA) functions responsible for developing and applying information management principles. The chapter concludes with a brief discussion of areas in which DA can use information models to manage corporate information.

2.1 INFORMATION MANAGEMENT ENVIRONMENT

Information management involves planning for effective use of the data carried in data processing systems and for building and controlling the environment needed to turn that data into information. An information management environment (IME) is comprised of the hardware and software base chosen for delivery of information, the standards and guidelines selected for enabling tools and techniques, an appropriate organizational structure, and a culture that recognizes the need to manage information as an asset. Information management also involves developing approaches for achieving consensus on what information is important enough to manage, and how information can be reused. Much of the work is technical, but the most difficult work is political. And much of that involves education.

2.1.1 Information

Definition: Information

Data in a context.

To understand information management and modeling, we must first understand what information itself is. We can start by defining information as data in a context. The following four tables demonstrate the necessity of context. Look first at Table 2.1, which presents data but nothing more. We have no idea what the data means.

Table 2.1.
Data.

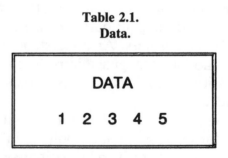

DATA

1   2   3   4   5

We can add more data, as in Table 2.2, but we still haven't a clue as to what the data means.

Table 2.2.
Still Data.

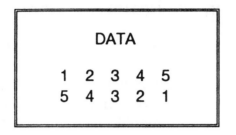

DATA

1 2 3 4 5
5 4 3 2 1

Once we add some context—the definition of the data as in Table 2.3—we begin to get information. We now know there are at least five valid zip codes and that using a zip code has an effect on the time it takes to deliver a letter.

Table 2.3.
Information.

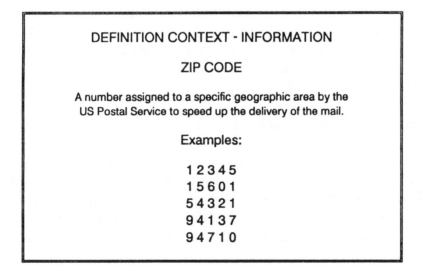

DEFINITION CONTEXT - INFORMATION

ZIP CODE

A number assigned to a specific geographic area by the
US Postal Service to speed up the delivery of the mail.

Examples:

1 2 3 4 5
1 5 6 0 1
5 4 3 2 1
9 4 1 3 7
9 4 7 1 0

Table 2.3 is still basically data, but when we relate that data to some other data we get more information (Table 2.4).

Table 2.4.
More Information.

MORE CONTEXT (STRUCTURE) --- MORE INFORMATION		
ZIP CODE	CITY	STATE
1 2 3 4 5	Schenectady	New York
1 5 6 0 1	Greensburgh	Pennsylvania
5 4 3 2 1	Green Bay	Wisconsin
9 4 1 3 7	San Francisco	California
9 4 7 1 0	Berkeley	California

From the example, we see that to get useful information we need both the definition of the data and the definition of the structure. This is the context that makes the data useful. Without the definition of the data, we know that 12345 is related to Schenectady and that Schenectady is related to New York, but we don't know how to use the information. Without the relationships, we only know what a zip code is and that there are (at least) five of them. When we know both the data definition and the relationship structure, we know that if we put the number 12345 on a letter to Schenectady, New York, it will get there faster. The definitions and structure provide the context to turn the data into information. The definitions of the data and the structure are often called *meta-data*, that is, data about data.

2.1.2 Information Management

With our understanding of information, we can characterize information management as the practice of giving context to data. The giving of context consists of developing and applying techniques and standards for the areas of information planning, data definition, data structure definition, meta-data access, and context presentation. Each is briefly discussed in the sections that follow.

Information Planning   Determining what data and structure are important to analyze and share, as well as when and how.

Data Definition	Determining what data needs definition, the components of those definitions, and when and how to obtain them.
Data Structure Definition	Determining what structural information to capture, when to capture it, and how (that is, the choice of modeling techniques and tools).
Meta-Data Access	Determining how to use a data dictionary or repository to hold the meta-data and defining mechanisms to ensure the quality of this meta-data.
Context Presentation	Determining when and how to make the context evident.

Information management is important in every stage of business planning and systems development. Some organizations refer to it as a data management or data administration function. Others refer to it as information resource management (IRM). Information modeling is a technique used to understand and document the definition and structure (context) of data.

2.1.2.1 *Information planning*

Information on technology trends, competition, and business needs are necessary elements in forming an Information Management Plan for an enterprise. Information planning can be considered a front-end activity that precedes the development of any system. It is based on the concept of determining where you are, determining where you want to go, and developing a plan to get there. Sometimes it helps to lay it out; Fig. 2.1 provides an example of how to present the process of information planning [1].

The process begins at the left of the figure with an articulation of the vision of those who run the business and a description of the environment that will allow the vision to be realized. This desired environment description is developed top-down and described in terms of business needs, the information systems architecture (ISA) required to satisfy those needs, and the necessary information management environment. Many factors influence that vision, including the current needs of the business and its customers, trends in technology (an enabling factor in many cases), the actions of competitors, and the amount of change that the organization can tolerate.

To move to the assessment step in the center of the figure, one must also have a description of what currently exists. The current environment description is developed bottom-up, that is, we determine what the environment looks like, infer what information systems architecture supports it, and guess what needs are being satisfied and what needs the current ISA is intended to satisfy.

The assessment step compares the description of the current environment to the description of the desired environment in order to develop plans and budgets for the next cycle of change. The priorities and strategies of the business are important since the actions that can be taken are limited by the investment plan of the organization. The direction for future efforts emerges. It may, for example, be that the current ISA and IME can support required functionality, but business needs are not well supported because the functionality is not available in the application portfolio. On the other hand, current needs may be well supported, but the existing environment and architecture might be in such a state that future support is severely limited. Assessment takes place both from a business perspective—what does the business need to make money—and from a systems perspective—what is needed to help the business make money.

The third step, represented at the right of the figure, leads to a realization of the vision, or at least to an attempt to do so. Based on the results of the assessment step, an information management plan and a set of strategies and priorities are developed. The plan describes the hardware, software, communications mechanisms, human resources, and operating environment to be constructed, identifies required standards and guidelines, and describes any organizational changes needed to allow the vision to be realized. Strategies and priorities are established that will yield a development plan for applications and will result in a well-controlled allocation of resources.

And the cycle begins again.

2.1.2.2 Data definition and data structure definition

To manage information, we must first define the data and the structure that gives that data meaning. As we learned above, neither the data definitions nor the definition of the structure alone can provide the needed context.

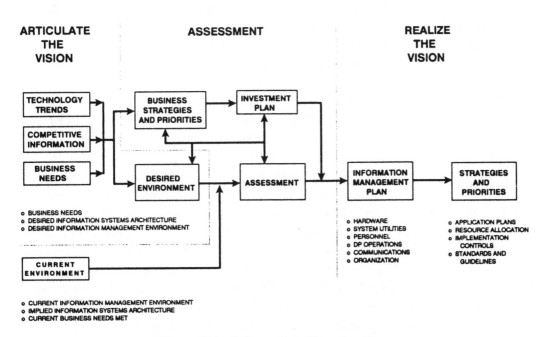

ARTICULATE THE VISION

ASSESSMENT

REALIZE THE VISION

TECHNOLOGY TRENDS

COMPETITIVE INFORMATION

BUSINESS NEEDS

BUSINESS STRATEGIES AND PRIORITIES

INVESTMENT PLAN

DESIRED ENVIRONMENT

ASSESSMENT

INFORMATION MANAGEMENT PLAN

STRATEGIES AND PRIORITIES

o BUSINESS NEEDS
o DESIRED INFORMATION SYSTEMS ARCHITECTURE
o DESIRED INFORMATION MANAGEMENT ENVIRONMENT

o HARDWARE
o SYSTEM UTILITIES
o PERSONNEL
o DP OPERATIONS
o COMMUNICATIONS
o ORGANIZATION

o APPLICATION PLANS
o RESOURCE ALLOCATION
o IMPLEMENTATION CONTROLS
o STANDARDS AND GUIDELINES

CURRENT ENVIRONMENT

o CURRENT INFORMATION MANAGEMENT ENVIRONMENT
o IMPLIED INFORMATION SYSTEMS ARCHITECTURE
o CURRENT BUSINESS NEEDS MET

Figure 2.1. Information Planning Steps.

Most of the material in this book is concerned with defining data and describing its structure. In a development organization, standards are needed both for the modeling language that will be used and for the components of the definitions of the data. Each standard must also specify when it should be applied, and when and how exemptions will be granted.

Data structure standards include the choice of a modeling language and techniques for using it, a description of the types of models that are needed and when and how to develop and maintain them, and conventions for where these models are to be stored. Data definition standards include a specification of the components of the data definition (what the definition should and should not include), naming and abbreviation conventions, and methods for storing these definitions. Both data structure and data definition standards also must include procedures for managing change, that is, designating who can change the definition and structural information, and specifying the processes that will be used to coordinate and control the changes.

2.1.2.3 Meta-data access

As defined above, meta-data is data about data. It is the definition of the data and the structural context. Models and data definitions must be stored somewhere, and the usual place is in a data dictionary or information repository.

A dictionary or repository is itself a database application. However, its data is a bit different from data used in the day-to-day operation of a business. For example, the dictionary does not include information about any individual customer. Rather, it includes a definition of what a customer is, a specification of the data that must be maintained about a customer, and descriptions of how a customer is related to other important concepts in the business.

A meta-database must be designed just as carefully as any database. If we want to be able to store the definition of an information model, we must first understand the parts that make up such a model, and create a model of models. If we want to be able to relate a logical design for the data (the model) to the physical implementation of that data (in an operational database), we must first understand what makes up a physical database (for example, files, records, and data elements) and how these parts relate to the parts of the logical model of that database. If we want to be able to use our meta-database to manage changes in operational systems, we must understand how data is related to the programs that use it, how these programs are related to various parts of the organization (for example, those that use or maintain them), and who is responsible for defining and approving changes to the programs. If logical design techniques are used to describe the functions of a system, we need to understand how the parts of a logical function description interact (that is, we need a model of function models) and how the function description relates to the data descriptions. And so on. The meta-model of the dictionary is a model of the information needed by those who manage information. It is a large and complex model.

Once a dictionary model has been developed, a dictionary product must be built or acquired, and standards developed for its use. Just as in business database applications, controls are needed to ensure the quality and accuracy of the contents of the dictionary.

2.1.2.4 Context presentation

We must then define a method of storing the context (definitions and structure) and we must devise mechanisms for making it available to those who need it. Defining these mechanisms involves decisions on who can access the dictionary, how that access will be provided, what information to provide, the presentation form of the information (for example, detailed reports or summaries), general approaches to presenting or summarizing the information for those who do not directly use the dictionary, and so on. A fully populated dictionary contains a great deal of information. Many views of this information are needed, each tailored to the needs of the viewer.

2.1.3 Information Systems Architecture

"Architecture" was one of the most overused buzzwords of the 1980s. It took on so many meanings that it retained little value other than to communicate such broad concepts as strategy, structure, and flexibility. Architecture came to simply represent some general type of unifying structure.

In 1987, John Zachman published a useful framework for discussing the architecture of an information system [2]. Developed using analogies from the construction and manufacturing businesses, Zachman's Information Systems Architecture Framework provides a context for describing different views of a system to be developed. These views reflect the perspectives of the owners, designers, and builders, and focus on the dimensions of data, function, and network.

Many parties have a stake in the outcome of a systems development effort, and these parties play different roles in relation to the system. Each of the stakeholders (owners, designers, builders) views the system from a different perspective. These perspectives are represented by the rows in Fig. 2.2. Furthermore, each stakeholder may focus on different aspects of the system, that is, the data, the processes performed (function), and the location of the data and processing (network). The focus is represented by a column in the Framework. The simplest form of a view corresponds to a cell (that is, a row/column intersection).

Zachman defines an architecture as a representation of the final product (in this case, an information system) as seen by one of the stakeholders. Thus, there is not one architecture but a *set* of architectures. Depending on who you are (owner, designer, builder) and on your focus (data, function, network), you see the architecture of the system differently. If you are a programmer, for example, you may see the intersection of the Technology Model row and the Function column as the architecture (that's your view). If you are a data modeler working at the business requirements stage of systems development, you may see the intersection of the Model of the Business row and the Data column as the architecture. In either case, you are correct. Each view (architectural representation) is distinct from other views in content and presentation form.

INFORMATION SYSTEMS ARCHITECTURE - A FRAMEWORK

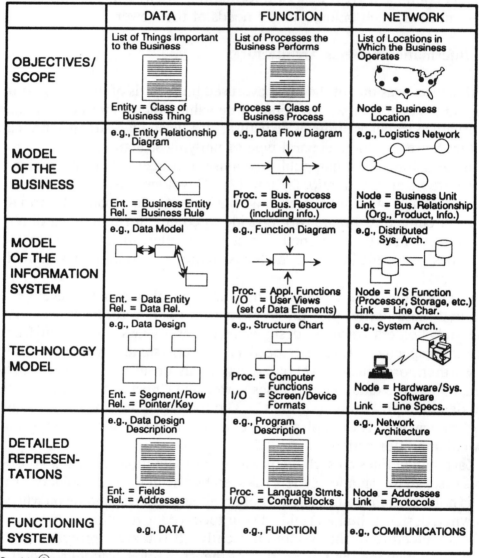

Figure 2.2. The Zachman Framework.

2.1.3.1 *The perspectives*

Perspectives reflect the values and areas of responsibility of the stakeholders. The owners' views concentrate on the overall strategic and tactical considerations a business must face. As such, they may be very wide in scope (the whole business as opposed to a part of it), and may not always be defined precisely. They correspond to the top two rows in Fig. 2.2: Objectives/Scope and Model of the Business. Initial business planning and analysis usually define the first level of detail for these views. Detailed business objectives and statements of business requirements for a system will then fill out the full detail for each view.

The designers' views, although they describe the same system, are fundamentally different from the owners' views, not simply additional detail. They describe the system as seen by those who must design solutions to requirements described by the owners' views. Many of the designers' views add precision needed by those who will build the system, but the owners' and designers' views remain independent of the technology that will eventually be used. Structured analysis and design, information modeling, and some types of prototyping are techniques that can be used to develop the designers' views. Designers' views correspond to the Model of the Information System row of the Framework.

Systems development projects are most successful when the Function, Data, and Network components of each technology-independent perspective (the top three rows) are designed at the same time by a team with a good blend of business, application development, network, and data administration expertise. Although each participating area may represent a different perspective (owner or designer) or have a different focus (data, function, or network), each brings a set of skills and knowledge which, when combined, can yield good overall pictures of the system that is needed. To some degree, the designers need to understand the owners' perspective, and the owners need to understand the designers' perspective. Neither group (owners nor designers) can develop their views independently.

Physical solutions to logical requirements depend on the characteristics of the hardware and software base chosen for the system. Although desired logical relationships are not influenced by physical constraints, realizable relationships normally are. Thus, it is necessary first to know what we want before assuming that something is impossible. Technology constrains solutions, not requirements.

It is in the perspective represented by the builders' views in Fig. 2.2 that technology considerations come into play. Owners' and designers' views represent statements of business requirements. Builders' views represent statements of solutions, constrained by technology, time, and cost. Builders' views correspond to the Technology Model and Detailed Representation rows of the Framework. Again, these are not simply another level of detail of the designers' views. They represent a shift in perspective from logical (requirements) to physical (solutions).

In the physical world, an organization may adopt standards that specify hardware and utility software for use in various geographic locations. Depending on the characteristics of that hardware and software, standard structures may be specified for function and data within the capabilities of the technology. Instead of calling these standards views or architectures, consider them as *templates* for building *architectural systems.* These templates emerge over time and constrain the shape of the builders' views.

Although Zachman does not break it out separately, there is another possible perspective, that of the operators of the system. The operators' views support day-to-day system operation and monitoring. There are two types of operators: the computer operations and systems support staff (who need run-time documentation and exception procedures to keep the information system running smoothly), and the business operations staff (who are processing the daily work). Operators' views are represented by the Functioning System row of the Framework.

It is important to remember that the rows of the Framework represent different perspectives, not different levels of detail. Within each cell, descriptions may be provided at many levels of detail. It is also important to recognize that there may be situations in which a view can span many cells of the Framework (for example, focusing on both data and function at the same time), but only cells in the same row. A different concept connects the rows. Views that represent one perspective will generally require some *transformation* to represent another perspective.

2.1.3.2 The focuses

The three focuses in the Framework in Fig. 2.2 lead to distinct architectural representations for each of the perspectives. The focuses correspond to the *what, how,* and *where* descriptions of the final product (the information system). Different representation techniques are appropriate for each focus.

The Data column represents the "what." In the building industry, for example, the what corresponds to the bill of materials listing the parts to be assembled to form buildings and describing the relationships among those parts. The focus is on what buildings are made of, not on how they are assembled or where they are located. For information systems, the what is described in terms of data entities and their relationships.

The Function column represents the "how." It describes how the individual parts of the system work. In information systems, functions are normally described by inputs (data elements), processes (transformations), and outputs (data elements). The focus is no longer on the individual parts and their relationships, but on how these parts are manipulated to accomplish a complete task.

The Network column represents the "where." Architectural representations in this column describe where the individual components of the system are located and the mechanisms needed to move things from one location to another.

Information modeling supports the Model of the Business, Model of the Information System, and Technology Model cells in the Data column of the Framework. Different types of information models are used for descriptions in different cells.

The Framework can be extended to describe cross-cell views, and additional focuses (as Zachman puts it, "the who, when, and why," as well as "the what, how, and where"). For additional information, see Appendix A.

2.1.4 Methods, Tools, and Templates

Agreed-upon methods, tools, and standards are needed to ensure consistency across a development organization, although these must not be so rigid as to become overly burdensome or constraining. Adopting the Zachman Framework as a context for developing systems can provide some basic consistency. The Framework can then help us choose methods and tools that produce the architectural representations required to support each perspective. Methods applicable in different development situations are needed. Classes of methods include

- systems development life cycle descriptions
- business analysis methods
- business planning methods

- information planning methods
- functional decomposition and analysis methods
- information modeling methods

Tools, both automated and manual, are needed to speed development, and to manage and control the development process. Many computer-aided software engineering (CASE) tools are available, and, at least in the near term, the challenge is to find individual tools or sets of tools that work together well. At a minimum, the following tools are needed, along with such traditional ones as editors, compilers, and so on.

- functional decomposition and recording tools
- information modeling tools
- reverse engineering tools (for both function and data)
- data dictionary/repository
- project management tools

Design standards are needed to ensure consistent system solutions. Standards must evolve over time and be flexible enough to accommodate changing business situations. They are needed for the form and content of the various architectural representations. The techniques and information modeling language described in this book can be the basis for standards covering a large part of the Data column of the Framework.

Once we shift our orientation from building separate systems to building integrated systems, templates for reusable building blocks can emerge as the development of the logical and physical designs proceeds. A template is an architectural representation that can be used again to describe some other system. For example, if we develop a logical model of relationships between customers and products for one part of the business, large parts of it may be applicable to another part of the business. If we design a security layer for access to a database for one system, much of that design may be reusable for another system. The more we think about common solutions, the more common the solutions become.

2.2   ADDING VALUE TO THE BUSINESS

From what we have seen, an information management environment is one in which the information systems architecture is driven by business information needs. Moreover, we have seen that understanding information management is important because to understand information modeling and how it can add value to a business, the context (that is, the information management environment) must be clear. In other words, the context helps us understand where information modeling is appropriate.

2.2.1 Where Information Modeling Helps

The information management discipline is often practiced and taught by a data administration function. DA is a business within a wider business and must focus on meeting the information management needs of its clients. Appendix B develops the idea that there are different markets for DA services and that these markets each has a set of needs. Figure 2.3 shows a matrix that results from mapping data administration services against the needs of its markets. Each row represents a general area of opportunity for DA. The following sections describe how information modeling can help in each area.

2.2.1.1 Education

A logical information model is a specification of the data structures and business rules needed to support a business area. A physical information model represents a solution to these requirements. As such, information models are useful in educating the employees of a business by describing the business and information systems to them. The process of developing an information model can allow staff in different areas to understand how their responsibilities are related to those in other areas.

2.2.1.2 Business planning support

An important part of business planning is to decide what your business is. The process of developing a model can help with both short-term tactical planning and long-term strategic planning. High-level information modeling focuses discussion on the most important data the business needs to manage. More detailed models describe the policies and rules that must be enforced throughout a business area.

NEEDS	Business Clients	Application Development	Database Administration	Systems Programming	Telecommunications	Data Processing Operations	Audit
EDUCATION	X	X	X	X	X	X	X
BUSINESS PLANNING SUPPORT	X						
BUSINESS REQUIREMENTS ANALYSIS	X	X					
DATABASE REQUIREMENTS DEFINITION	X	X	X				
REQUIREMENTS DOCUMENTATION	X	X	X				X
LOGICAL AND PHYSICAL DESIGN		X	X				
DATABASE GENERATION			X				
"COPY CODE" GENERATION		X					
DATA OBJECT STANDARDIZATION		X	X				
EXISTING SYSTEM AND "PACKAGE" ANALYSIS		X	X				
SYSTEM DOCUMENTATION	X	X	X			X	X
INVENTORY/CHANGE MANAGEMENT		X	X	X	X	X	X
STANDARDS/POLICY ENFORCEMENT				X	X	X	X
SPEED	X	X	X	X	X	X	X

Figure 2.3. Data Administration Opportunities.

2.2.1.3 *Business requirements analysis and database requirements definition*

The process of developing a model draws out requirements for both the business functions to be supported and the data that will need to be stored in a database. Information models capture precise statements of requirements and can be used to describe how the requirements are to be satisfied within a particular technology.

2.2.1.4 Requirements documentation

A detailed logical information model is a precise statement of information requirements. It documents requirements for those who must satisfy them.

2.2.1.5 Logical and physical design

The logical design of a system is represented in Fig. 2.2 by the Model of the Information System row in the Framework. The physical design is represented by the Technology Model row. For the Data column, different types of information models are used for each row. Using separate but related models for logical requirements and physical solutions emphasizes the need to first concentrate on what needs to be built before concentrating on how to build it, and can allow the solution to be traced back to the requirements.

2.2.1.6 Database and copy code generation

As used here, copy code means schemas stored in sharable libraries for use by application programs. Generation means the automated production of the schemas, for example, of the data definition language needed to create a relational database, and file definitions (record layouts) needed by COBOL programs that access that database. If the information modeling process is supported by the necessary repository and diagramming tools, it can provide the necessary source information.

2.2.1.7 Data object standardization

Developing and using standard data object names and connecting various manifestations of a data object to the standard are fundamental parts of information management. This is directly supported by development of a model. All data objects in an information model are precisely named and defined, and many of them are reusable in subsequent models.

2.2.1.8 Existing system and package analysis

Most organizations have existing computer systems, and many consider the purchase of off-the-shelf application packages to support their business.

Models developed by reverse engineering (see Chapter 10) can be used to analyze and evaluate these existing and proposed applications.

2.2.1.9 Systems documentation and inventory and change management

As we discussed, different models represent requirements, technology-independent designs, and technology-dependent designs. When stored in a repository, these models provide the documentation of a system and become a basis from which to manage changes in the environment. Information modeling is not limited to traditional business applications. It is applied to the technology itself and is a primary means of designing and extending information repositories such as the IBM Repository Manager product.

2.2.1.10 Standards and policy enforcement

Information models do not directly lead to good standards or help enforce policies. They can, however, clearly document business policies and provide reusable designs for parts of information systems. In time, reusable designs tend to become standards.

2.2.1.11 Speed

If done well, information modeling can speed the development of shared database systems. If done poorly, it can slow things and lead to disaster. There is no magic, and modeling, like any discipline, must be applied in only the right situations.

2.2.2 Making Right Choices

For a data administration function, choosing which opportunities to address is not easy, and often has little to do with technical considerations. If we are working in a business organization, the choices must be based on business principles, not technical principles.

A balance must always be struck between addressing current needs and addressing perceived future needs. The needs and opportunities will change over time as an organization begins to understand the value that can be added by information modeling. The best strategy is to address the now needs now, and lay the foundation for addressing future ones. Pay attention to the politics.

Information management professionals must be prepared to push ideas and to fight for them, but must also be prepared to back off. If the choices the organization makes seem irrational, look further at the needs. People don't often do irrational things. If two intelligent people come to different conclusions based on the same facts, there must be a difference in values. Be prepared to move the value system of the organization and accept that these values will not change overnight.

2.3 REVIEW EXERCISES

Answers to boldface questions appear in Appendix H.

1. **For each of the following systems development products, processes, and tools, identify the cells of the Zachman Framework in which they are most commonly represented.**

    PRODUCTS
    - Preliminary Requirements
    - Initial System Solutions
    - Detailed Requirements
    - Functional Specifications
    - Hardware / Software Specifications
    - Application Software / Job Control Language
    - Area Information Models
    - Project Information Models
    - Physical Database Specifications
    - Design Templates

    PROCESSES
    - Systems Development Life Cycle
    - Business Systems Planning
    - Functional Analysis
    - Information Modeling
    - Structured Design
    - Structured Programming
    - Prototyping
    - Project Planning and Control

TOOLS
- Activity / Function Modeling
- Information Modeling
- Data Dictionary / Repository
- Programming
- Prototyping
- Source Code Library Maintenance
- Project Planning and Control
- Reverse Engineering
- Re-Engineering
- Editors
- Compilers

2.   Identify the cells in the Zachman Framework representing each of the markets shown in Fig. 2.3.

3.   **Two white spots on a black background are provided as *data*. What is a context that will turn this data into *information*?** Hint: It is the night of April 18, 1775, in Boston, Massachusetts.

4.   In the Zachman Framework, what is the difference between a perspective and a focus?

5.   **Why is it important to develop architectures starting at the top of the Zachman Framework and working downward?**

2.4 REFERENCES

[1]   Moriarty, T. *Strategic Planning.* Unpublished communication to the author, July 1989.

[2]   Zachman, J.A. "A Framework for Information Systems Architecture," *IBM Systems Journal,* Vol. 26, No. 3 (1987), pp. 276-92.

3

INFORMATION MODELING BASICS

Chapters 1 and 2 provided a context for discussing the application of information modeling techniques to the development of database applications. They established that an information model is a representation of the data structures of an information system, that is, a data architecture. They led to the conclusions that different types of information models are used to document different perspectives of information systems and that these models provide statements of business requirements, information system requirements, and technology-constrained solutions.

This chapter begins with a discussion of information modeling in general, presenting an overview of the components of any information model—that is, entities, attributes, and relationships. From there, it moves on to look at various types of IDEF1X models and identifies where those models fit into the overall Zachman Information Systems Architecture Framework described in Chapter 2. Zachman's Framework is useful for guiding our application of the modeling techniques because it helps us understand what kind of model is appropriate in various situations. The chapter concludes with a discussion of which approach works when and provides references for other information modeling techniques.

Some of the definitions in this chapter are intentionally informal. The objective is to get general ideas across without burying them in overly precise terminology. Formal definitions, as specified in IDEF1X, will be introduced in the detailed material in Part Two.

3.1 INFORMATION MODELS

Information modeling is a technique for describing information structures. Logical models specify business information requirements, policies, and rules.

Physical models specify solutions. As such, information modeling can be viewed as a way to develop information system requirements and solutions. Models are used to design a physical system database that represents a balance between the specific needs of a particular implementation project and the general needs of the business area in which that project is being conducted.

Most information models (those developed with IDEF1X or any other modeling language) are representations of things (entities), properties of things (attributes), and associations among things (relationships). The models are pictures of how these things are related.

3.1.1 Information Model Components

Entities in information models are abstractions of real-world things. It is important to distinguish between the real-world thing and the abstraction. An information model, for example, might include an entity named CUSTOMER that represents the information a business wants to keep about its customers. Individual customers of the business are not shown in the model—the CUSTOMER entity is an abstraction of the real-world concept of a customer.

A way to think about entities and abstractions is to consider an entity as a drawer in a filing cabinet. Suppose there is a drawer labeled CUSTOMER. Inside the drawer, we expect to find files for each of our customers. In each file, we find information about a specific customer, not an abstract generalization of a customer. The collection of files, along with the description of what we should find in each file, is the abstraction.

Next, consider *attributes*. Let's continue with our analogy. If we open the filing cabinet drawer, we find many files. Inside each file, we find pieces of data that describe a specific occurrence (instance) of the entity. These individual pieces of data are called *attributes*.

Any filing system (manual or automated) needs to have a convention for what detailed data will be stored. We need to specify what should be in each of the files in our filing cabinet. Each individual piece of data that could be in the file is a description of some property of the individual occurrence (instance) of the entity. In our CUSTOMER drawer example, we might specify that each file should contain the name of the customer, his or her birth date, a credit rating, and so on. The concepts of name, birth date, and credit rating are, again, abstractions.

Expanding on our example, suppose we have another drawer labeled PRODUCT. In it we expect to find a file for each of our products. Each file might contain the name of the product, a description of the product, and pricing information. This drawer represents another entity, one that has attributes that are different from those of our CUSTOMER entity.

Entities and attributes are abstractions. Single instances of an entity along with the values of the attributes of that instance represent the real-world things. Our CUSTOMER drawer represents our customers. The PRODUCT drawer represents our products.

If we have customers and products, chances are we are in some type of business in which we sell those products to customers. Selling is a business function that associates the customers and products. The general concept of selling can be represented by a *relationship* between the abstract concept of a CUSTOMER and the abstract concept of a PRODUCT. Depending on our purpose, we might leave it at that or specify the information we want to keep about each sale. If we stop here, we have two entities (CUSTOMER and PRODUCT) and one relationship (selling). This might be exactly what we need if we are trying to identify the major *things* that are important to the business.

To represent our simple example, we can draw either Fig. 3.1 or 3.2. Although they do not include much precision, they are information models. Figure 3.1 depicts a Chen model [1]. Figure 3.2 shows an IDEF1X model. Both figures say the same thing, that products and customers are involved in a selling relationship.

Figure 3.1. Basic Chen Diagram.

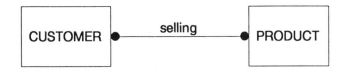

Figure 3.2. Basic IDEF1X Diagram.

Let's add more precision to our picture of the business. Suppose that when a sale occurs, there is a contract that specifies exactly what has occurred or is to occur to satisfy the conditions of the sale. The general concept of a sale might be made more precise by recognizing a new entity (CONTRACT) as the representation of another real-world thing. We could have another drawer in which all of the individual contracts are stored. Each contract in the drawer might identify the customer and the product involved in the sale. Customers, products, and contracts are therefore related in some way.

Figures 3.3 and 3.4 add this detail to the earlier diagrams. Again, they both say the same thing—that customers, products, and contracts are related in some way.

Figure 3.3. Simple Chen Diagram.

Figure 3.4. Simple IDEF1X Diagram.

We keep adding detail until all of the precision we need is shown in the figures. In Chapter 1, we used a similar example, in which *many* customers and products could be involved in the same contract. Figures 3.5 and 3.6 show these extensions.

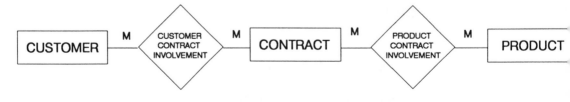

Figure 3.5. Extended Chen Diagram.

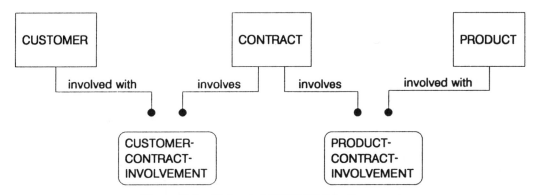

Figure 3.6. Extended IDEF1X Diagram.

3.1.2 Types of Information Models

When adding precision to an information model, there comes a point at which the characterization of an entity as an abstraction of a real-world thing breaks down. We must, therefore, extend the entity concept to cover abstract things (like concepts) in addition to real-world things. This is often the dividing line between the Model of the Business perspective in Zachman's Framework and the Model of the Information System perspective.

To illustrate this concept, Fig. 3.6 contains entities named CUSTOMER-CONTRACT-INVOLVEMENT and PRODUCT-CONTRACT-INVOLVEMENT. These are abstractions of concepts, not real-world things. Although the business may recognize the concept of involvement, it is unlikely that it has other file drawers containing involvements; more likely, involvements are thought of as properties of contracts.

Information system designers need to understand the abstract involvement concept if they are to represent the business rules that govern involvements [2]. To an information system designer, involvement is an entity that needs to be included in the model. The designer's view must be specific. The owners, on the other hand, can view the information system in general. Both views are equally important. The designer must understand the owner's view to know what needs to be designed, and the owner must verify the designer's view to be certain that what is being designed is what is needed. That understanding can only emerge if the owner and designer work together to construct the appropriate views.

Beyond the models that support the owners' and designers' perspectives of the information system lie the models that support the builders' perspectives.

These are solution models rather than requirements models. They are described in Section 3.2.3.

3.1.3 Relationship to Function Models

As we saw in Chapter 2, the design of data structures is only one part of developing a system. Analysis of processes, that is, of the functions, is equally important. IDEF1X is coupled with a function modeling technique called IDEF0, but does not require any particular process modeling style. IDEF1X works well in conjunction with many process modeling techniques.

Function models describe how something is done. They can be presented as hierarchical decomposition charts, dataflow diagrams, HIPO diagrams, and so on. In practice, it is important to develop the function and information models at the same time. Discussion of the functions to be performed by the system uncovers many of the data requirements; discussion of the data uncovers additional function requirements.

Where to start—function or data—is not terribly important. In fact, the starting point for the information model is often a list of high-level business functions to be supported. Thus, developing an overall information model to match the function list is a place to start. As the data is examined, it is likely that the functions will be better understood. The function and data descriptions can be taken together to any level of detail.

3.1.4 Information Modeling Benefits

Structured system development approaches in general, and data-centered design approaches in particular, invest heavily in front-end planning and requirements analysis activities. Information modeling is used by many of these top-down design approaches as a technique for identifying and documenting the portion of system requirements that relates to data. Other models (for example, dataflow diagram sets, distribution models, event/state models) are used to document processing requirements. Different types of models are used during different development phases.

When an information model is created with the full participation of business and system professionals, it can provide many benefits. These benefits fall into two classes—those associated with the model (the product of the effort) and those associated with the process of creating the model (the effort).

3.1.4.1 Product benefits

The following are some of the product benefits provided by an information model:

- An information model defines a context for turning data into information. This context—data definitions and the description of the structure of the data—allows an organization to understand the role of each piece of data in relation to the rest.

- A requirements model provides an unambiguous specification of what is wanted, not what currently exists. It describes the information a company needs to operate various parts of its business and specifies the business rules that must be enforced by the information system. This specification is not constrained by assumptions about what the underlying hardware and software can or cannot provide.

- The model is business-user driven. The content and structure of the model are controlled by the business client, not the system developer. The emphasis is on requirements, not constraints or solutions.

- The terms used in the model are stated in the language of the business, not in that of the system development organization. As such, the model is a description of requirements stated in business, not technology, terms.

- The model provides a context to focus discussions on what is most important to the business.

3.1.4.2 Process benefits

The product of our modeling efforts—the diagrams, descriptions, and accompanying definitions—can be of significant assistance to a company. The process by which the model is created can provide additional benefits. These are often as important as the benefits that accrue to the model itself. Some of the process benefits that can be derived from the information modeling effort follow:

- During early project phases, model development sessions bring together individuals from many parts of the business, and provide a highly structured forum in which business needs and policies are discussed. During these sessions, business staff may, for the first time, meet others in different parts of the organization who have the same or similar needs. Common understandings of business issues, directions, and priorities can therefore emerge, sometimes quite apart from the modeling effort.

- Modeling sessions lead to development of a common business language with consistent and precise definition of terms. Communication among participants is greatly increased, and the common terminology can become the basis for improved communications throughout the company.

- Early phase sessions provide a mechanism for exchanging large amounts of information among business participants and for transferring business knowledge to the system designers and developers. Later phase sessions continue that transfer of knowledge to the staff who will implement the solution.

- Session participants can more clearly see how their activities fit into a larger context. Parts may begin to be seen in the context of the whole. The emphasis is on cooperation rather than separation. Over time, this can lead to a shift in values and the reinforcement of a cooperative philosophy.

- Efforts contribute a pool of reusable structures, with each model adding to the overall information systems architecture. These structures are often useful in future development efforts.

- Sessions foster consensus and build teams.

3.2 IDEF1X INFORMATION MODELS

There are numerous types of IDEF1X information models. The overview provided in the balance of this chapter introduces many new terms, all of which are defined in Part Two and included in the glossary. (If most of the terms are unfamiliar to you, you may wish to reread this material after you have read Part Two.)

IDEF1X is an information modeling technique that can be used with many system development methodologies. Its general model types are outlined in the basic IDEF1X standard and described below. It is important to note again here what was stated in the Introduction: That although IDEF1X is not a standard as in an ANSI or ISO standard, the basic components of an IDEF1X information model are specified in the D. Appleton Company's base reference document and have been adopted by the U.S. Air Force [3].

Using the different model types for different purposes can be very helpful throughout the process of developing a system. In practice, it's useful to expand or contract the number of types to fit individual situations. The model types presented here are best suited to a top-down system development life cycle approach in which precision is added during each project phase. (Note that in some IDEF1X documents, the term "level" is used to designate a "type" of IDEF1X model. This is a bit unfortunate since level generally connotes "level of detail." Different IDEF1X model types are not necessarily decompositions that add detail.)

The area covered by a model is its *scope*. The amount of precision included is its *level of detail*. Scope and level of detail are independent variables. Models with a wide scope may include all detail, or little detail. The same is true for models with a narrow scope. Wide-scope models are normally called *area* models because they cover a wide area. Narrow-scope models are normally called *project* models.

IDEF1X model types range from a not-too-detailed wide-scope view of the major things important to a business down to a level of precision required to specify a database design in terms that are understandable by a particular database management system. Some of the models are technology-dependent; for example, a physical model for an IMS database will look very different from a physical model for a DB2 database. Some models are technology-independent, and may represent some information that is not stored in any automated system.

The area models come in two forms. The *entity relationship diagram* (ERD) identifies major business entities and their relationships. The *key based model* (KBM) sets the boundaries of the business information requirement (all entities and keys are included) and begins to expose the detail. These are logical models.

The project models also come in two forms. The *fully attributed model* (FAM) contains all of the detail for a particular implementation effort. The *transform* or *transformation model* (TM) represents a conversion of the fully attributed model into a physical structure that is appropriate for the DBMS chosen for implementation, and is an addition to the basic IDEF1X standard. Whereas the fully attributed model is a logical model, the transformation model is a physical model. Its structures are optimized based on the capabilities of the DBMS, the data volumes, and the expected access patterns and rates against the data. The TM is an IDEF1X picture of the eventual physical database design.

The physical database design for a system contains the *DBMS model* (DB-MSM). Depending on the degree of integration of a company's information systems, the DBMSM may be for a single implementation project or may cover the entire integrated system area.

These model types are illustrated in Fig. 3.7, and are further described in the sections following the figure.

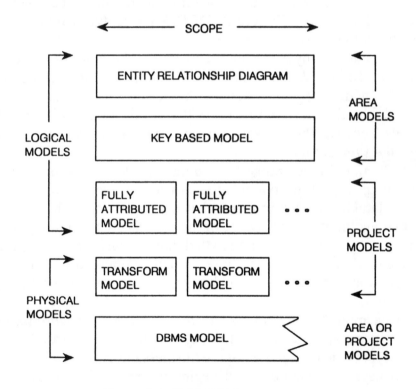

Figure 3.7. IDEF1X Model Types.

3.2.1 Area Information Models

> **Definition: Area Information Model**
>
> An information model that covers a wide business area.

An *area information model* covers a broad business area that usually is larger than the business chooses to address with a single automation project. Two area models are the entity relationship diagram and the key based model, which are described in the following subsections.

3.2.1.1 Entity relationship diagram

> **Definition: Entity Relationship Diagram**
>
> An information model that shows the major entities and relationships that support a wide business area.

The entity relationship diagram is a model of the major entities and relationships that support a wide business area. The diagram can include some attributes as examples of the information kept about the major entities. The objective of the ERD is to provide a wide view of business information requirements sufficient for broad planning for the information system. It is more a presentation or discussion model than it is a design model. As such, it is usually not very detailed. In addition, many-to-many relationships are allowed, and keys are generally not included.

There are many methods available for developing the ERD, ranging from formal modeling sessions to interviews with business managers responsible for wide areas. Formal sessions are called *business view sessions.* An IDEF1X *business view* covers a wide business area.

The entity relationship diagram is most often used to support the initial Objectives/Scope and Model of the Business data perspectives of the Zachman Framework. It represents a high-level owner's view of the business.

3.2.1.2 Key based model

> **Definition: Key Based Model**
>
> **A third normal form information model that describes the major data structures that support a wide business area.**

A key based model is a third normal form information model that describes a wide business area. All entities and primary keys are included, along with sample attributes. As we will see in Chapter 4, primary keys are attributes or groups of attributes that enable us to distinguish among instances of an entity; Chapter 9 provides further discussion of the third normal form.

The objective of the key based model is to provide a view of all entities and keys needed to support the wide business area. It can cover the same scope as the ERD, but includes more of the detail. The model provides a context in which to construct detailed implementation-level models.

Several methods are available for creating the key based model. One method is to conduct formal sessions called *user view sessions*. Interviews and periodic reviews with business users can be substituted in some situations. An IDEF1X *user view* describes a major area of the business and covers one or more closely related business functions. The key based model is generally used to describe Model of the Business and Model of the Information System data perspectives of the Zachman Framework.

3.2.2 Project Information Models

> **Definition: Project Information Model**
>
> **An information model that describes a portion of an overall data structure intended for support by a single automation project.**

A *project* is a distinct effort to build part of an information system. The scope of a project is determined by time and available resources. A *project information model* describes a portion of an overall data structure intended for support by a single automation effort. There are two types of project models, the fully attributed model and the transformation model, which will be defined below.

3.2.2.1 Fully attributed model

> **Definition: Fully Attributed Model**
>
> A third (or higher) normal form information model that includes all entities, attributes, relationships, and integrity rules needed by a single project.

A fully attributed model includes all entities, attributes, relationships, and integrity rules needed by a single project. The model includes entity instance volumes, access paths and rates, and expected access patterns against the data structure. These terms are defined below.

> **Definition: Integrity Rule**
>
> A rule that specifies a valid state of a database.
>
> **Definition: Entity Instance Volume**
>
> An estimate of the number of instances that an entity can be expected to have.
>
> **Definition: Access Path**
>
> A specification of the primary key, alternate key, and inversion entry attributes that will be used to obtain instances of the entity.
>
> **Definition: Logical Transaction**
>
> A transaction that accomplishes a single logical function.
>
> **Definition: Access Pattern**
>
> A specification of the sequence in which a logical transaction creates, replaces, uses, and deletes instances of entities.
>
> **Definition: Access Rate**
>
> A specification of the frequency with which instances of the entity will be accessed.

The objective of the fully attributed model is to provide a view of project data structures, volumes, and access patterns needed to design an efficient physical database. It is a detailed model and usually represents a smaller area than that covered by the key based model.

The fully attributed model contains all attributes and specifies those that will be used to identify and access each entity. It includes expected volumes and change frequencies for entity instances and examines logical transactions that will operate on the data structure to determine their access patterns. Since all of the data detail is included in this model, the processes that create, replace, use, and delete each attribute and group of attributes can be described in terms of algorithms that implement the business rules of the model.

The fully attributed model represents the lowest level of the logical design of the information structures, and contains all of the logical information needed by the database administrator (DBA) to create and maintain one or more physical system databases. The volumes and access patterns allow the DBA to decide which structures can be implemented in their fully normalized form, which structures need to be collapsed for processing efficiency, which attributes to employ as indices into the data structures, when to use application code or DBMS functions to enforce integrity rules, how to anticipate growth requirements, and so on.

The techniques used to create a fully attributed model will vary by project. Often, enough detail will have been included in the key based model to allow the data modeler and the application team to work out the rest and bring it to the business client for validation. Sometimes, formal sessions called *local view sessions* are used. An IDEF1X *local view* corresponds to one or more closely related logical transactions.

The fully attributed model is most often used to present a Model of the Information System data perspective of the Zachman Framework.

3.2.2.2 Transformation model

Definition: Transformation Model

A transformation of a fully attributed model into a structure that is appropriate for the expected access patterns and the database management system chosen for implementation.

The transformation model provides a way to trace the physical design back to the logical design and, potentially, in the future, to assist this transformation with expert system tools. The transformation model is an IDEF1X picture of the physical database design.

The objective of the transformation model is to give the DBA a way to document the database design in a form that can easily be used by application programmers and business users. The model provides a context in which to define the data elements and records that form the database, and can help the application team choose a physical structure for the programs that will access the data.

The model can also provide the basis for comparing the physical database design against the original business information requirements. It can be used to show how well the physical database design supports those requirements, to document physical design choices and their implications (for example, what is satisfied and what is not), and to identify database extension capabilities and constraints.

The Transformation Model is developed jointly by a team representing the data administration, database administration, and application development areas. It can be used to present the Technology Model data perspective of Zachman's Framework.

3.2.3 Database Management System Model for Relational Systems

---

Definition: Database Management System Model

A specification of the detailed structure of the database that includes the transformation model, and any other information needed to describe the intended use of the database management system.

The database management system model describes the data structure in a way that is consistent with the data definition language (DDL) for that DBMS. For a relational DBMS, each entity in the transformation model becomes a relational table. Primary keys may be declared in some systems, and may become unique indices in others. Alternate keys and inversion entries may also become indices. Cardinality and constraint rules may be enforced by the referential integrity capabilities of the DBMS, application logic, or after-the-fact detection and repair of violations.

We will treat this terminology in greater detail beginning in Chapter 4. The case study in Chapters 13 through 15 provides examples of each of the model types we have discussed in this section. Appendix C provides an overview of how to conduct an information modeling session.

3.3 INFORMATION MODELING APPROACHES

There are several approaches to developing an information model. While the most effective is to work top-down with the business owners to develop views of what must be built to support the business, information modeling must sometimes involve bottom-up or middle-out approaches. These three approaches are discussed below.

3.3.1 Top-down, Bottom-up, and Middle-out Approaches

Developing a system from the top down involves a sequenced process of gathering requirements, developing a logical design, developing a physical design, and transforming that physical design into a functioning system. Top-down information modeling is effective for the requirements definition phase of most system development projects. It is not the only approach, and it may not be possible or appropriate to proceed in an entirely top-down manner in all situations.

There are times when it is not possible to work with the business staff to develop top-down models, or when the environment into which the system must be installed is so heavily constrained by existing systems and data structures that little change to the databases is realistic. In these situations, other approaches are needed. The models that result will be the same types (ERD, KBM, FAM, and TM) as for top-down efforts, but will represent requirements described in the context of existing system constraints.

Bottom-up information models (see Chapter 10) represent inferences from existing documentation of how the physical system is structured and how the data might be logically described. Inference of the logical structures of the data and the requirements that these structures appear to address is somewhat risky—the models show what exists, not necessarily what is wanted—but can be of some benefit. Models of current databases can be useful in assessing the impact of change on the existing environment.

Middle-out modeling takes a narrow set of requirements for a business area, drives them downward into a physical design, and, at the same time, attempts to lift them into the context of the business as a whole to see how the design should recognize the wider scope of the business. Middle-out modeling can help but doesn't often work well, as we shall see next.

3.3.2 When to Begin

Knowing when to begin and when to become involved with an effort (or let the opportunity pass) is a judgment that must be made very carefully. Becoming involved too late or trying to use the wrong technique or tool at a certain point will not work.

Choosing the appropriate model types and development approach is fairly straightforward for a top-down project. It is considerably more difficult for a bottom-up effort, such as installing a software package, or for a middle-out project, such as a revision or extension of an existing system in which the physical design will be highly constrained by the current design.

Figure 3.8 summarizes where construction of the various types of models we have reviewed can be useful for a top-down development project. It also indicates the types of models appropriate at different points in the development life cycle. Areas of activity are represented by the rows; the development phases in which these activities occur are represented by the columns.

Two critical points are shown on each line in the figure. The > symbol shows the point beyond which further information modeling may not provide additional value in the completion of the activity. The * symbol indicates the point at which it is too late to start to apply information modeling techniques to support the activity. This is the point beyond which beginning information modeling will likely be perceived as being disruptive (and is the point at which modeling often starts for middle-out efforts). For example, attempting to assist the Database Generation activity with a transformation model during Phase 4 (Physical Design) of the system development life cycle will be of benefit only if logical models were prepared during earlier project phases. Starting the modeling activities during Phase 3 or 4 is extremely difficult. By this point, a project is often committed to a design. Starting a modeling activity here will likely slow down or stop the project.

VALUE AREA	←—— SDLC PHASE ——→					
	1	2	3	4	5	6
BUSINESS PLANNING SUPPORT	E--	-K-*-A->				
BUSINESS REQUIREMENTS ANALYSIS	E--	-K-*-A->				
DATABASE REQUIREMENTS DEFINITION	E--	-K-*-A-	-X->			
REQUIREMENTS DOCUMENTATION	E--	-K-*-A-	-X->			
LOGICAL DESIGN	E--	-K-*-A->				
PHYSICAL DESIGN		*	A-	-X--	D--	D->
DATABASE GENERATION			*	X--	D--	D->
COPY CODE GENERATION			*		D--	D->
DATA OBJECT STANDARDIZATION	E--	-K-*-A-	-X--	D--	D->	
SYSTEM DOCUMENTATION		K-*-A-	-X--	D--	D->	
INVENTORY / CHANGE MANAGEMENT	E--	-K-*-A-	-X--	D--	D->	

Information Model Type:
- E: Entity Relationship Diagram (ERD)
- K: Key Based Model (KBM)
- A: Fully Attributed Model (FAM)
- X: Transformation Model (TM)
- D: Database Management System Model (DBMSM)

System Development Life Cycle Phase:
- 1: Business Planning
- 2: Requirements Definition
- 3: Logical Design
- 4: Physical Design
- 5: Code / Test / Install
- 6: Maintenance

Figure 3.8. Critical Modeling Points.

3.4 INFORMATION MODELING LANGUAGES

IDEF1X is one of several information modeling languages. Many others have been developed during the last fifteen years. A few of the major ones are referenced in the paragraphs that follow.

Chen: The Chen modeling language [1] was introduced in 1976 by Peter Chen, one of the first to describe how the concepts of entities and relationships might be applied to describing business requirements. Chen's work has been the basis for several extensions and dialects, including the modeling methods described by Matt Flavin in 1981 [4].

Bachman: Charles Bachman is one of the originators of the network model of information: The Bachman diagram [5] has been around since the late 1960s. Although originally developed to support network databases, Bachman modeling techniques have been extended to support relational modeling.

Information Engineering (IE): Originally developed by Clive Finkelstein and James Martin, Information Engineering diagrams [6] were first introduced in the late 1970s. In many respects, they look much like IDEF1X models. A second version of IE diagrams, with notation which is similar, is credited to James Martin [7] and has diverged a bit from the original work. This version is seen in several computer-aided software engineering tools.

NIAM: The Nijssen Information Analysis Method (NIAM) is based on development work done by G.M. Nijssen [8]. Of the techniques listed here, NIAM is probably the most powerful in its precision, although there can be some difficulties using it in a business environment. It is used most frequently in scientific areas.

MERISE: Although not often used in the United States, the MERISE style of describing information structures is used in France and Canada [9].

Associative Data Modeling: The Associative Data Modeling technique [10, 11], also known as the Curtice-Jones technique, was developed in the late 1960s by Paul Jones and Robert Curtice. The resulting diagrams look very different from those which result from using methods more oriented toward the relational view of information.

Semantic Information Modeling: Based on the work of Hammer and McLeod, Semantic Information Modeling [12] is often used to design databases to operate with the Unisys Semantic Information Manager DBMS.

IBM's Repository Modeling Language: The IBM Repository Manager product [13] announced in 1989 and first released in June 1990 includes yet another modeling language. A short description of this language is provided in Appendix G, along with information on ways to translate between IDEF1X and IBM models.

3.5 REVIEW EXERCISES

Answers to boldface questions appear in Appendix H.

1.   Describe the types of IDEF1X models.

2.   **Identify the row(s) of the Zachman Framework supported by each of the IDEF1X model types.**

3.   **What factors influence how well information modeling benefits are realized?**

4.   Draw a diagram similar to Fig. 3.7 for a system development effort you know. Label each of the models with its scope and describe the area covered by each.

5.   What are the two types of benefits derived from an information modeling effort? Provide examples of each. Which type is more important?

3.6 REFERENCES

[1]   Chen, P.P-S. "The Entity-Relationship Model—Toward a Unified View of Data," *ACM Transactions on Database Systems,* Vol. 1, No. 1 (March 1976), pp. 9-36.

[2]   Appleton, D.S. "Business Rules: The Missing Link," *Datamation,* October 15, 1984, pp. 145-50.

[3]   D. Appleton Company, Inc. *Integrated Information Support System—Information Modeling Manual, IDEF1X Extended.* ICAM Project, Priority 6201, Subcontract No. 013-078846, U.S.A.F. Prime Contract No. F33615-80-C-5155, Air Force Wright Aeronautical Laboratories, U.S. Air Force Systems Command, Wright-Patterson Air Force Base, Ohio, 1985.

[4]   Flavin, M. *Fundamental Concepts of Information Modeling.* New York: Yourdon Press, 1981.

[5]   Bachman, C. "Data Structure Diagrams," *Communications of the ACM SIGBDP, Database,* Vol. 1, No. 2 (1969).

[6]   Martin, J., and C. Finklestein. *Information Engineering* (Vols. 1 and 2). London: Savant Institute, 1981.

[7]   Martin, J. *Strategic Data-Planning Methodologies.* Englewood Cliffs, N.J.: Prentice-Hall, 1982.

[8]   Nijssen, G.M. *Conceptual Schema and Relational Data Base Design.* Englewood Cliffs, N.J.: Prentice-Hall, 1989.

[9]   Tardieu, H., H. Heckenroth, D. Pascot, and D. Nanci. "A Method, a Formalism, and Tools for Data Base Design: Three Years of Experimental Practice," *Entity-Relationship Approach to Systems and Analysis,* P.P-S. Chen, ed., Elsevier North-Holland, 1980.

[10]   Jones, P.E. *Data Base Design Methodology—A Logical Framework.* Wellesley, Mass.: QED Information Sciences, 1976.

[11]   _____ , and R.M. Curtice. *Logical Data Base Design.* Wellesley, Mass.: QED Information Sciences, 1988.

[12]   Hammer, M., and D. McLeod. "The Semantic Data Model: A Modeling Mechanism for Database Applications," *Proceedings of the ACM, SIGMOD International Conference on Management of Data,* May 31-June 2, 1978, Austin, Tex.

[13]   IBM Corporation. *Repository Manager/MVS: Repository Modeling Guide,* Document No. GC26-4619, 1990.

PART TWO

Part One provided the overall context for our discussion of IDEF1X. In the nine chapters of Part Two, we will explore how to use this language to develop descriptions of information structures for a system.

Chapter 4 presents a broad-brush overview beginning with the basic terminology and diagram components. Then, since good names and definitions are essential to constructing an information model, Chapter 5 takes a break from the details of the language itself, and discusses names and definitions for entities and attributes.

To understand what the language can do, we must be aware of the problem areas. That way we will not be surprised when IDEF1X does not support everything. Chapters 6, 7, and 8, therefore, present the limitations as well as the details of the language.

Chapter 9 discusses normalization of data structures. Normalization continues to be a somewhat controversial topic, and the discussion in this chapter suggests that ensuring that correct business rules are stated in the diagram is far more important than technical normalization. Chapter 10 covers reverse engineering, the construction of an information model for a current system. Part of the objective here is to point out the dangers.

Chapters 11 and 12 conclude the language description with thoughts about the future and the challenges that lie ahead, not only for information modeling languages like IDEF1X, but also for techniques for designing and building database applications. Chapter 12 briefly describes an emerging next evolutionary step for IDEF1X that will address some of its current limitations and extend it in the direction of object-oriented systems.

4

IDEF1X OVERVIEW

Now that we have a context in which we can use IDEF1X, we are ready to examine the basic parts of the language. Chapter 4 presents a definition of the building blocks of an IDEF1X model—entities, attributes, and relationships. It then extends that discussion to different types of entities (independent and dependent), attributes (keys of many types and non-keys), and relationships (identifying and nonidentifying); it also discusses how to read a model. Each of these topics is examined in more depth in subsequent chapters.

As a review, recall the definitions of information model and information modeling provided in Chapter 3. They are repeated below so that you will be reminded to think about them as you read this chapter.

Definition: Information Model

A specification of data structures and business rules.

Definition: Information Modeling

A technique for describing information structures and capturing information requirements, policies, and rules.

4.1 JOURNEY THROUGH A SAMPLE MODEL

Figure 4.1 presents a simple information model prepared using IDEF1X. It is a key based model that describes a mythical small business that rents video tapes to customers. The figure and definitions of its objects make the following *assertions,* statements declaring that something is true or false:

- A MOVIE is in stock as one or more MOVIE-COPYs. Information recorded about each MOVIE includes its name, rating, and rental rate. Information recorded about each MOVIE-COPY includes its general condition and remaining life.

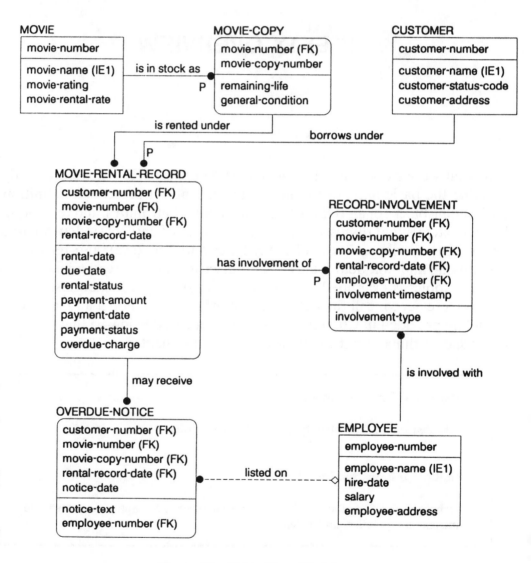

Figure 4.1. Video Store Model.

- CUSTOMERs rent the MOVIE-COPYs. The store keeps track of the name and address of each CUSTOMER. It also assigns each CUSTOMER a status code. The status code depends upon the CUSTOMER's previous relationship with the store and indicates whether the store should accept checks and credit cards for payment, or take only cash.

- A MOVIE-RENTAL-RECORD contains information about the rental of a MOVIE-COPY by a CUSTOMER. The same MOVIE-COPY may, over time, be rented to many CUSTOMERs. Each MOVIE-RENTAL-RECORD includes a rental date, a due date for the movie, and a rental status indicating whether the MOVIE-COPY is overdue.

- Each of the store's EMPLOYEEs can be involved with many MOVIE-RENTAL-RECORDs, as specified by RECORD-INVOLVEMENTs. The type of involvement is designated by an involvement type. There must be at least one EMPLOYEE involved with each MOVIE-RENTAL-RECORD. Since the same EMPLOYEE might be involved with the same rental record several times on the same day, involvements are further distinguished by an involvement timestamp.

- A CUSTOMER's payment for a rental is recorded in the MOVIE-RENTAL-RECORD. An overdue charge is sometimes collected.

- OVERDUE-NOTICEs are sometimes sent out to remind a CUSTOMER that a tape needs to be returned. An EMPLOYEE may be listed on an OVERDUE-NOTICE. This is the EMPLOYEE who must follow up on the notice.

- The store records the hire date, salary, and address for each of its EMPLOYEEs. It sometimes needs to look up CUSTOMERs, EMPLOYEEs, and MOVIEs by their names rather than by their assigned numbers.

This small model provides a great deal of information about the video store. From it, we not only get an idea of what a database for the business should look like, we also get a good picture of the business. Let's look a little closer at some of the business rules.

- The business has decided that the only MOVIEs it wants to keep track of are the ones it has available to rent to its CUSTOMERs, not every movie ever made.

- For every rental of a MOVIE-COPY, there must be at least one involved EMPLOYEE.

- Some EMPLOYEEs may not be involved with any MOVIE-RENTAL-REC-ORDs, although all are permitted to be.

- Some EMPLOYEEs may not be listed on any OVERDUE-NOTICEs, although all are permitted to be.

- The store only keeps records about CUSTOMERs who have rented at least one MOVIE-COPY.

- The store has chosen not to accept reservations for movies, that is, a copy will not be held for any single CUSTOMER. (We can see this in the absence of a structure to support reservations.)

- There is exactly one MOVIE-COPY included on each MOVIE-RENTAL-REC-ORD. If a CUSTOMER wishes to rent several movies at a time, a separate MOVIE-RENTAL-RECORD is required for each.

- The store has decided not to keep track of the borrowing of movies by its EMPLOYEEs. For such a borrowing, an EMPLOYEE is treated as a CUSTOMER; there need be no way to know that the CUSTOMER is an EMPLOYEE.

- There is only one store; the store does not wish to make provisions in its database design for additional outlets.

Figure 4.1 contains several different types of objects. Its entities, attributes, and relationships, along with its other symbols, describe the video store's business rules. An IDEF1X information model consists of a diagram like the one shown as Fig. 4.1, definitions of the objects, and textual description of the topic being covered. We will begin by discussing the basic parts of an IDEF1X diagram.

4.2 BASIC DIAGRAM COMPONENTS

An IDEF1X diagram is made up of three main building blocks—entities, attributes, and relationships [1]. We can view IDEF1X as a graphic language for expressing statements about a business. The entities act like nouns, the attributes act like adjectives or modifiers, and the relationships act like verbs. Creating an IDEF1X model is generally a matter of finding the right collection of building blocks and putting them together. The statements that result describe many of the rules that control the business and are often referred to as assertions.

4.2.1 Entities and Attributes

> **Definition: Entity**
>
> **Any distinguishable person, place, thing, event, or concept about which information is kept.**

An *entity* is any distinguishable person, place, thing, event, or concept about which information is kept. More precisely, an entity is a set or collection of like things called *instances*. Entities are named by nouns, such as customer and employee. They are represented by capital letters with hyphens between words.

An *instance* is a single occurrence of an entity. Each instance must have an identity distinct from all other instances. For example, we might say that the entity CUSTOMER represents the set of all customers of a business. Each individual customer—for example, Ben, Margaret, or Tom—is an instance of the CUSTOMER entity.

> **Definition: Instance**
>
> **A single occurrence of an entity.**

As you will recall from Chapter 1, IDEF1X is based on the relational model. From the standpoint of the relational model, an entity corresponds to a table in which each row represents an instance of the entity. In the more precise relational formalism, the correct term for the set of instances is *entity type,* and an *entity* (referred to here as an instance) is a member of the set represented by the entity type. In practice, the terms entity and instance are commonly used. In this text, we use the term entity for the set and the term instance for a member of the set, as this is the terminology most often used by those who work with IDEF1X.

Examples prepared to demonstrate the meaning of an IDEF1X model are often shown as tables. These are called *sample instance tables,* because they provide samples of entity instances displayed as rows in a table. A sample instance table for the CUSTOMER entity in Fig. 4.1 is shown as Table 4.1.

Table 4.1.
Sample Instance Table.

CUSTOMER

customer-number	customer-name	customer-status-code	customer-address	(etc.)
1	Ben	A	Princeton NJ	
2	Margaret	P	New Brunswick NJ	
3	Tom	N	Berkeley CA	
4	John	F	New York NY	
5	Leon	A	Princeton NJ	

In the video store example, certain facts (properties) must be kept about each CUSTOMER. We must know, among other things, the customer's name and address. In a relational database, such facts would be stored as the values of data elements represented by the different columns of a table. Each column stores the value of a certain property. These properties are called the *attributes* of the entity.

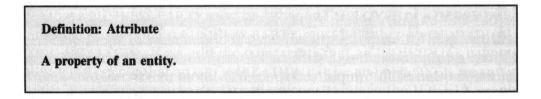

Definition: Attribute

A property of an entity.

4.2.2 Diagram Syntax for Entities and Attributes

In an IDEF1X diagram, an entity is represented by a closed box with the name
of the entity at the top and the attributes of the entity listed inside the box.
This is shown in Fig. 4.2.

Entity names are always singular. For example, we use CUSTOMER not
CUSTOMERS, MOVIE not MOVIES, and EMPLOYEE not EMPLOYEES. Singular
nouns provide a consistent naming standard and, as we will see, ensure the
ability to read the diagram as a set of declarative statements (assertions) about
entity instances. When we name an entity, we are actually naming an instance.
In Fig. 4.2, each instance represents a customer, not multiple customers.

```
CUSTOMER
 ┌─────────────────────┐
 │ customer-number     │      <--- PRIMARY KEY AREA
 │                     │           (Primary Key Attributes)
 ├─────────────────────┤
 │ customer-name       │
 │ customer-status-code│      <--- DATA AREA
 │ customer-address    │           (Non-primary-key Attributes)
 └─────────────────────┘
```

Figure 4.2. Entity with Key and Data Areas.

In an IDEF1X entity, the horizontal line divides the entity attributes into two
sets: primary key attributes and data attributes. The area above the line is
called the *primary key area* (often referred to simply as the *key area),* and the
area below the line is called the *data area.*   In Fig. 4.2, the primary key
attribute of CUSTOMER is "customer-number". The data attributes are "customer-name", "customer-status-code", and "customer-address".   In this text,
IDEF1X attributes are represented by words spelled in lowercase letters
enclosed in literal quotation mark symbols, and are hyphenated when more
than one word is used.

4.2.3 Keys

To use an entity such as the CUSTOMER entity in our video store model, we
must be able to identify instances uniquely, that is, we must be able to distinguish one customer from another. The set of attributes that uniquely identifies
an entity is called its key. As we saw in Fig. 4.2, primary key attributes are

placed above the line in the key area. Each attribute in the key area is called a *primary key attribute*. In practice, the terms *key* and *key attribute* are often used to signify "primary key" and "primary key attribute." As we shall see, there are other types of keys, such as candidate keys, alternate keys, foreign keys, and surrogate keys. These will be discussed later in the book. Non-key attributes (also called *data attributes*) are placed in the data area.

One way to identify a CUSTOMER instance may be to use "customer-name" as the key. Another may be to assign a unique number to each instance of CUSTOMER, that is, a "customer-number". The latter is the choice that is recorded in Fig. 4.2.

Definition: Primary Key

An attribute or group of attributes that has been chosen as the unique identifier of the entity.

Definition: Primary Key Attribute

An attribute that, either by itself or in combination with other primary key attributes, will form the primary key.

Definition: Non-key Attribute

An attribute that has not been chosen as a part of the primary key of the entity.

Whenever someone proposes an entity for a model, one of the most important questions you need to ask is, How do we identify instances? A maxim to help remember this is, No entity without identity. Entity instances in an IDEF1X model are always identified by primary key attributes.

4.2.4 Candidate and Primary Key Attributes

There may be several attributes, or groups of attributes, which could be used as primary keys. These are called *candidate keys*. For a candidate key to be accepted as the primary key, the candidate must uniquely identify each instance of the entity. In IDEF1X, if any part of the candidate key may be null, that is, empty or missing, the candidate must be disqualified as the primary key.

It is also important to make sure that each attribute of the entity is dependent on the whole key and nothing else.

The concept of dependency is fundamental to the relational theory on which IDEF1X is based. Dependency has to do with determining the values of attributes: An attribute is said to be fully functionally dependent on another attribute, or group of attributes, if its value will be determined based on the value or values of the other attribute or attributes. This does not mean that a functionally dependent attribute can be computed from the other attributes; rather, it means that if the values of the other attributes are known, the value of the dependent attribute can be determined—that is, we can look it up by supplying the values of the others.

> **Definition: Candidate Key**
>
> **An attribute or group of attributes that might be chosen as a primary key.**

Consider the example in Fig. 4.3. Here the entity EMPLOYEE has the following attributes:

- employee-number
- employee-sex
- employee-social-security-number
- employee-birth-date

- employee-name
- employee-hire-date

- employee-bonus-amount

EMPLOYEE

employee-number
employee-name employee-sex employee-hire-date employee-social-security-number employee-birth-date employee-bonus-amount

Figure 4.3. Identifying Candidate Keys.

The attribute "employee-number" has been chosen as the primary key. The first step toward this choice was to find the candidate keys. The analysis might have been as follows:

- Suppose we know from the definition of the attribute that only some EMPLOYEEs of the company are eligible for annual bonuses. Therefore, "employee-bonus-amount" can be expected to be null (empty, not zero) in many cases. Because this attribute may be null, it cannot be part of the primary key (it can be part of a candidate key, but that candidate cannot become the primary key). In addition, "employee-bonus-amount" could not, by itself, serve as a primary key since many EMPLOYEEs might get the same bonus.

- The "employee-number" attribute is a candidate key since it is unique for all EMPLOYEEs. It is never null (empty).

- Assuming the federal government never issues the same social security number (SSN) to different people, each "employee-social-security-number" will be unique, and will designate a specific EMPLOYEE. This attribute might be a candidate key if the assumption about the uniqueness of social security numbers is correct. Since we cannot guarantee this, and cannot guarantee that all EMPLOYEEs will have a social security number, we will put the attribute aside.

- The attribute "employee-name" does not look like a good choice. There may be two or more people in the company with the same name.

- The combination of "employee-name" and "employee-birth-date" might serve as a primary key. Let's assume that this combination does designate a specific EMPLOYEE. Let's also assume that the name of an EMPLOYEE never changes. In that case, we have a second candidate key—the combination of "employee-name" and "employee-birth-date".

We have two candidate keys, "employee-number" and the group of attributes containing "employee-name" and "employee-birth-date". To choose the primary key, we must remember that the model represents statements of business information requirements, and business policies and rules. The choice of the primary key of EMPLOYEE represents a policy statement on how the business will identify its EMPLOYEEs. The business must make this choice, but the information modeler must make a recommendation.

4.2.5 Rules for Choosing Primary Keys

There is a certain amount of discretion involved in selecting primary keys, but care must be taken in choosing them and they must always be unique. Imagine what might happen if, for instance, the government identified each taxpayer by name only, and you happen to be Jane Smith or John Jones. You could spend your entire life trying to straighten out whose taxes and benefits were whose. It just wouldn't work. Choosing the primary key of an entity is an important step, and requires serious consideration. Here are some rules.

- First, and most important, try to find an attribute that will not change its value over the life of each instance of the entity. An instance takes its identity from the value of the primary key. If the primary key changes, it's a different instance.

- Second, look for a reasonably small key. If you can find a single attribute for the key (or invent one), you will often have a good primary key. When a candidate key consists of more than one attribute, make sure that, for every instance of the entity, all parts of the key will have values (none will be null). If this cannot be guaranteed, do not chose the candidate as the primary key.

- Third, avoid the use of intelligent keys such as situations in which the structure of the digits in an identifier indicates groupings, loca-tions, classifications, dates, and so on. If a key is not intelligent, there will be no reason to change its value (violating the first rule).

- Fourth, when you must, use keys to enforce constraints that govern the existence of entity instances. To do this, form a composite key that includes the primary keys of other entities. Make sure, however, that each part of the key adheres to the first three principles. We will return to the topic of constraints in later chapters.

- Fifth, consider substituting single attribute surrogate keys for large composite keys. As we will see in Chapter 9, this can sometimes lead to problems, but is often worth the inconvenience.

4.2.6 Alternate Keys and Inversion Entries

> **Definition: Alternate Key**
>
> **A candidate key that has not been chosen as the primary key.**

A candidate key that is not chosen as the primary key is called an *alternate key*. To indicate an alternate key in a model, place the symbol (AKn), where n is an integer, after those attributes that form the alternate key. If the alternate key consists of several attributes, place the (AKn) after each. This notation is shown in Fig. 4.4. The combination of "employee-name" and "employee-birth-date" is designated as alternate key 1 (AK1).

> **Definition: Inversion Entry**
>
> **An attribute or group of attributes that will frequently be used to access the entity but may not result in finding exactly one instance.**

An *inversion entry* specifies another way in which the business plans to access an instance of the entity. When using an inversion entry, however, we may not find exactly one instance. Moreover, there may be several inversion entries for an entity. For example, in Fig. 4.4, both "employee-name" and "employee-social-security-number" are designated as inversion entries. By supplying "employee-social-security-number", we can find a single EMPLOYEE (assuming a U.S. citizen with a valid SSN), but we will not be able to find any EMPLOYEE without an SSN. By supplying "employee-name", we may find zero, one, or more EMPLOYEEs (remember there may be many people with the same name).

To indicate an inversion entry, place the symbol (IEn), where n is an integer, after the attribute name. If the inversion entry consists of several attributes, place (IEn) after each of the attributes that form the inversion entry.

Figure 4.4 indicates that there are two inversion entries for the EMPLOYEE entity. Note that "employee-social-security-number" could also have been designated as an alternate key (AK2) if we were sure that it would be unique for all EMPLOYEEs who have a social security number.

Alternate keys and inversion entries are often useful to identify different ways in which the business needs to access the information represented by the model. Note that in Fig. 4.4, the symbols and lines beside the entity (A1, I1, and I2) are an extension to the basic IDEF1X diagramming standard. They do not point to the alternate key and inversion entry attributes. Rather, they bring the viewer's attention to the entity and indicate that, in this case, it has one alternate key and two inversion entries. To find the attributes that form the alternate key and inversion entries, we must look inside the entity shape. Table 4.2 is a sample instance table for the EMPLOYEE entity.

EMPLOYEE

```
                    |  employee-number                               |
                    |------------------------------------------------|
A1 ----->           |  employee-name (AK1) (IE1)                      |
I1 -------          |  employee-sex                                   |
I2 -------          |  employee-hire-date                             |
                    |  employee-social-security-number (IE2)          |
                    |  employee-birth-date (AK1)                      |
                    |  employee-bonus-amount                          |
```

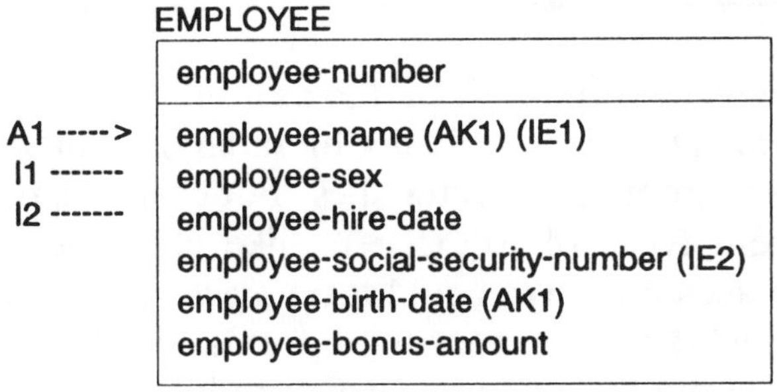

Figure 4.4. Alternate Keys and Inversion Entries.

Table 4.2.
EMPLOYEE Sample Instance Example.

EMPLOYEE

employee-number	employee-name	employee-sex	employee-hire-date	employee-social-security-number	employee-birth-date	employee-bonus-amount
1	T. Adams	M	01-01-89	123-456-7890	12-04-42	1,000
2	J. Smith	M	12-15-90	012-345-6789	03-01-46	null
3	J. Smith	F	06-15-91	901-234-5678	09-11-47	1,000
4	B. Jones	M	04-30-91	null	09-30-49	null
5	J. Glynn	F	03-22-91	789-012-3456	07-13-38	2,000
6	R. Brown	M	10-17-89	678-901-2345	10-22-36	null

4.2.7 Generalization Hierarchies

Definition: Generalization Hierarchy

A hierarchical grouping of entities that share common characteristics.

Definition: Generalization Entity (Generic Parent)

The entity at the top of any level of a generalization hierarchy.

Definition: Category Entity

A subset of the instances of an entity (referred to as the generalization entity, or generic parent) that share common attributes or relationships distinct from other subsets.

A *generalization hierarchy* (often referred to as a subtype hierarchy, a category or subcategory hierarchy, or an inheritance hierarchy) is a hierarchical grouping of entities that share common characteristics. For example, in a bank we might find several different types of ACCOUNTs, like checking accounts, savings accounts, and loan accounts. We could form a *generalization entity* (a *generic parent)* called ACCOUNT to represent the information that is common across the three types of accounts, yielding a structure like that in Fig. 4.5.

There are various terminologies used to designate the entities in a generalization hierarchy. IDEF1X uses the term *category entity* to refer to a subtype of the *generic parent.* Therefore, this book will use the terms *category entity,* or simply *category,* and *generic parent.*

4.2.8 Category Discriminators

Definition: Category Discriminator

An attribute that determines to which category a generic parent instance belongs.

A *category discriminator* is an attribute that indicates how we can tell (discriminate) one category entity from another. In the banking example in Fig. 4.5, "account-type" is the discriminator. An ACCOUNT (the generic parent) is either a CHECKING ACCOUNT, a SAVINGS-ACCOUNT, or a LOAN-ACCOUNT (the categories). Each category *is* an ACCOUNT and inherits the properties of ACCOUNT. The three different categories of ACCOUNT are mutually exclusive. We cover generalization hierarchies and category discriminators in Chapter 7.

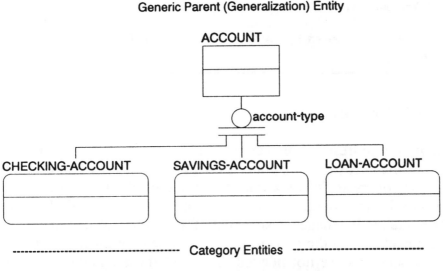

Figure 4.5.   **Generalization Hierarchy.**

4.3 RELATIONSHIPS AND FOREIGN KEY ATTRIBUTES

In Chapter 1, we saw that one of the main differences between the relational model and the hierarchical and network models is the representation of relationships. The hierarchical and network models represent relationships by inter-record pointers at the physical level. The relational model captures relationships with shared keys at the logical level.

The IDEF1X modeling language represents relationships with shared keys. Although IDEF1X certainly can be, and is, used to describe information stored in nonrelational database management systems, its treatment of keys has a relational bias.

Whenever entities are connected by a relationship, the relationship contributes a key (or set of keys) to the child entity. *Foreign key attributes* are primary key attributes of a parent entity contributed to a child entity across a relationship. The contributed keys are said to migrate or propagate from parent to child. Foreign key attributes are designated in the model by an (FK) following the attribute name.

> **Definition: Relationship**
>
> **A connection between two entities.**
>
> **Definition: Foreign Key**
>
> **A primary key of an entity that is contributed to another entity across a relationship.**

4.3.1 Relationships

Relationships represent connections, links, or associations between entities. They are the verbs of a diagram showing how entities relate to each other. Relationships in an information model are used to represent some of the business rules that describe the area being modeled. IDEF1X, unlike some other modeling languages, insists that all relationships be binary; that is, that they connect exactly the two entities. This does not mean that three, four, or n-ary associations are not needed, only that these situations are adequately addressed with another construct—the *associative entity.*

Following are some relationship examples. The words inside the < > brackets are called a *verb phrase.*

A TEAM <has> many PLAYERs.
A PLANE-FLIGHT <transports> many PASSENGERs.
A DOUBLES-TENNIS-MATCH <requires> exactly 4 PLAYERs.
A HOUSE <is owned by> one or more OWNERs.
A SALESPERSON <sells> many PRODUCTs.

In each of these examples, the relationships are chosen so that the connection between the two entities is what is known as *one-to-many.* This means that one and only one instance of the first entity is related to or connected to many instances of the second entity. The entity on the one end is called the *parent entity,* and the entity on the many end is called the *child entity.*

4.3.2 Diagram Syntax for Relationships

In the information model, relationships are displayed as a line connecting two entities, with a dot on one end and a verb phrase written along the line. The many end of the relationship is the end with the dot. Figure 4.6 shows a one-to-many relationship between PLANE-FLIGHTs and PASSENGERs on those flights.

4.3.3 Notion of Many

The notion of many does not mean there *must* be more than one instance of a child entity connected to a given instance of a parent entity. The *many* in one-to-many, unless otherwise qualified, means that there *can be zero, one, or more* instances of the child associated with each instance of the parent.

Figure 4.6. Simple Relationship.

There can also be relationships in the reverse direction between child and parent, but this is not implied by saying that a parent/child relationship is one-to-many. When there are one-to-many relationships in *both* directions between two entities, a *many-to-many* relationship exists, and the classification as parent and child loses its meaning. Many-to-many relationships (also known as *nonspecific)* relationships are drawn as a line with dots at both ends, as illustrated in Fig. 4.7. These relationships are used only in a preliminary stage of diagram development.

In the many-to-many example in Fig. 4.7, a PERSON uses many ADDRESSs and an ADDRESS is used by many PERSONs. Neither entity is parent nor child. One of the goals in developing detailed IDEF1X diagrams is to eliminate many-to-many relationships by converting each into a pair of one-to-many relationships with an associative entity between them.

The number of entity instances to be expected at each end of the relationship is called the *cardinality* of the relationship. Various symbols are used to specify how many entity instances may or must be present at the end with the dot. "P" (positive) is used for one or more, nothing for zero or more, "Z" for zero or one, and "N" for exactly N. There are always zero or one entity instances at the end without the dot. Cardinality declarations record business rules and influence the precise ways in which we read relationships.

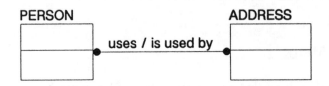

Figure 4.7. Many-to-Many Relationship.

4.3.4 Reading a Model

If we choose our verb phrases correctly, we can read a relationship from the parent to the child (toward the end with the dot) using an active verb phrase and thereby come up with a reasonably meaningful English statement. The example in Fig. 4.6 can be read as follows:

A PLANE-FLIGHT <transports> many PASSENGERs.

Figure 4.8 is read as

A CUSTOMER <borrows under> many MOVIE-RENTAL-RECORDs.

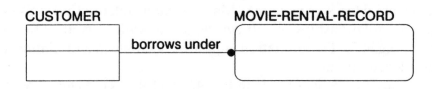

Figure 4.8. CUSTOMER to MOVIE-RENTAL-RECORD **Relationship.**

Figure 4.9 reads

A MOVIE <is in stock as> many MOVIE-COPYs.

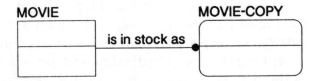

Figure 4.9. MOVIE to MOVIE-COPY **Relationship.**

Figure 4.10 reads

A PERSON <may own> many PETs.

Figure 4.10. PERSON to PET Relationship.

The example in Fig. 4.11 involves an *associative entity* (ADDRESS-USAGE) that represents a many-to-many relationship between PERSON and ADDRESS. These relationships tend to be more difficult to read, and the pattern appears to break down. We will come back to this example in Chapters 5 and 6. Using our standard pattern for reading the relationships in the figure results in

A PERSON <may use> many ADDRESS-USAGEs.
An ADDRESS is <used by> many ADDRESS-USAGEs.

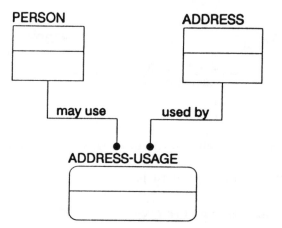

Figure 4.11. Resolved Many-to-Many Relationship.

Verb phrases can describe a relationship from the perspective of either or both of the participating entities. It is common practice to use verb phrases that describe the relationship only from the perspective of the parent entity. Most of the examples in this book have been prepared in this way. Sometimes, however, it is useful to include the child perspective as well. When the verb phrases are read from the perspective of a child entity, the actions are generally passive. For example, Figs. 4.12, 4.13, and 4.14 show the examples in Figs. 4.8, 4.9, and 4.10, respectively, with both verb phrases included. The reverse relationship for Fig. 4.12 is

A MOVIE-RENTAL-RECORD <records borrowing by> exactly one CUSTOMER.

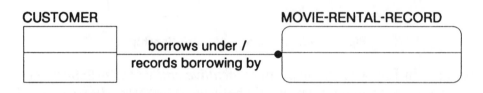

Figure 4.12. Complete CUSTOMER to MOVIE-RENTAL-RECORD Relationship.

The reverse relationship for Fig. 4.13 is

A MOVIE-COPY <is a copy of> exactly one MOVIE.

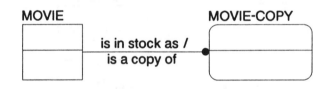

Figure 4.13. Complete MOVIE to MOVIE-COPY Relationship.

The reverse relationship for Fig. 4.14 is

A PET <is owned by> exactly one PERSON.

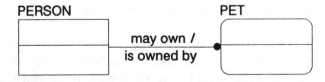

Figure 4.14. Complete PERSON to PET Relationship.

Verb phrases and cardinality statements provide a brief summary of the business rules embodied by the relationship. Although they do not precisely describe the rules, they allow the person looking at the model to get an initial sense of how the entities are connected. It is therefore a good practice to make sure that reading the model gives valid statements. Reading a model back to those who participated in its development is a primary method of verifying that the business rules have been correctly captured. Using sample instance tables to verify the model is also a good idea.

4.3.5 Key Migration and Relationship Types

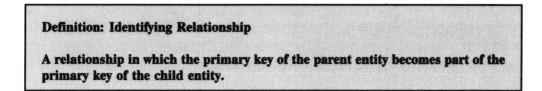

Definition: Identifying Relationship

A relationship in which the primary key of the parent entity becomes part of the primary key of the child entity.

An *identifying relationship* connects a parent entity to a child entity and causes all primary key attributes of a parent entity to become primary key attributes of a child entity. Identifying relationships are indicated by a solid line connecting the entities, with a dot on the many end. All of the relationships we have seen so far have been identifying relationships. A *nonidentifying relationship* also connects a parent entity to a child entity, and is denoted by a dashed line. Parent entity keys migrate across nonidentifying relationships but do not automatically become part of the primary key of the child entity.

As shown in Fig. 4.15, foreign keys contributed to an entity by identifying relationships migrate to the primary key area of the entity, that is, above the line. Those contributed by nonidentifying relationships normally migrate to the data area, that is, below the line.

4.3.6 Identifying Relationships

Figure 4.16 provides an example of an identifying relationship. Table 4.3 represents a sample instance table for it. The double line in the sample instance table separates the key attributes from the non-key attributes. Notice that there are two parts to the primary key of MOVIE-COPY, and that the first part is the migrated primary key of MOVIE. In the sample instance table we can see that there are five copies of *Batman,* one copy of *Bambi,* and two copies each of *Alien, Putney Swope,* and *Rocky XVII.*

Identifying Relationship

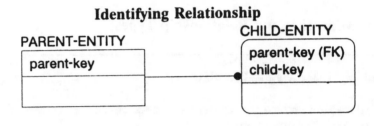

Nonidentifying Relationship

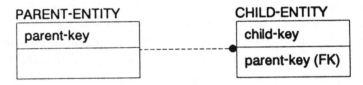

Figure 4.15. Identifying and Nonidentifying Relationship Syntax.

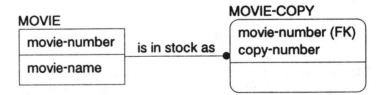

Figure 4.16. Identifying Relationship.

Table 4.3.
Identifying Relationship Sample Instance Example.

MOVIE

movie-number	movie-name
1	Batman
2	Bambi
3	Alien
4	Putney Swope
5	Rocky XVII

MOVIE-COPY

movie-number	copy-number
1	1
1	2
1	3
1	4
1	5
2	1

movie-number	copy-number
3	1
3	2
4	1
4	2
5	1
5	2

An identifying relationship carries with it a business rule, which says that an intentional choice has been made to include the primary key of the parent entity as part of the primary key of the child. In the example of MOVIE and MOVIE-COPY in Fig. 4.16, we could have chosen to identify the copy by its own unique number. Instead, we decided to use the key of the MOVIE and add a second part ("copy-number") to tell one copy from another. We *decided* that the relationship would be identifying. It didn't happen by itself, and we didn't assume it.

The relationship is called identifying because the key of the parent becomes part of the key of the child. The child is *dependent on the parent for its identity;* it cannot be identified without knowing the key of the parent. The child is also dependent on the parent for its existence. If the parent does not exist, part of the primary key of the child will be missing, so the child cannot exist.

As you will find, there are advantages to contributing primary keys via identifying relationships. For one, it tends to make some physical system queries more straightforward. But there are also some disadvantages; for example, the number of attributes that form the primary key can tend to get quite large. Some advanced relational theory suggests that primary key attributes should not be contributed by relationships, and requires not only that each entity be identified by its own primary key, but that the key be a single attribute called a surrogate key, never to be seen by the user of the system. There is a strong theoretical argument for this and those who are interested are urged to review the work of E.F. Codd [2] and C.J. Date [3]. The use of surrogate keys corresponds to IDEF1X models in which all primary keys are single attributes, and all relationships are nonidentifying.

4.3.7 Nonidentifying Relationships

Recall from Section 4.3.5 that *nonidentifying relationships* connect a parent entity to a child entity. However, unlike identifying relationships, foreign key attributes contributed by nonidentifying relationships are placed in the data area, not in the key area.

Since the migrated keys in a nonidentifying relationship are not part of the primary key of the child, the child is not identified by the parent and the relationship may, from the perspective of the child, be optional. As we shall see in Chapter 8, this difference is important when we must maintain the integrity of the relationship between parent and child under the operations of insert, replace, and delete.

In nonidentifying relationships, the child still may be *existence-dependent* on a parent, but will not be *identification-dependent* on the parent. If the relationship is mandatory from the perspective of the child, then the child is existence-dependent on the parent. If it is optional, the child is not existence-dependent on the parent.

In Fig. 4.17, an airline has chosen to identify an instance of SEAT-RESER-VATION by a combination of "flight-number", "flight-date", and "seat-number". It has also chosen to record the identifier of the PASSENGER who holds the reservation, but cannot guarantee that each reservation will be held by some-one. A sample instance table for the figure is shown in Table 4.4.

Because a seat might not be reserved, the identifier of the PASSENGER who holds the SEAT-RESERVATION cannot be part of the primary key of SEAT-RESERVATION, and, from the perspective of SEAT-RESERVATION, the relationship can be considered optional. However, when a passenger does hold a reservation for a seat, we want to know who the passenger is. Therefore, a nonidentifying relationship is required to allow us to record the key of the PASSENGER who holds the reservation in SEAT-RESERVATION, or leave this key empty (null) if there is no current holder. The diamond on the relationship says that it is proper to have a SEAT-RESERVATION for which there is no current PASSENGER, that is, an open reservation.

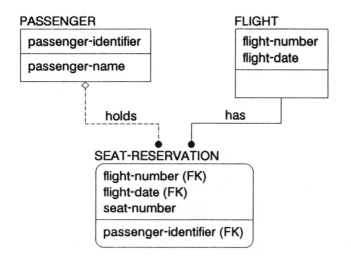

Figure 4.17. Mixing Identifying and Nonidentifying Relationships.

Table 4.4.
Mixing Identifying and Nonidentifying Relationships.

PASSENGER

passenger-identifier	passenger-name
1	J. Fox
2	W. Wolf
3	T. Bair
4	T. Hawks
5	R. Dere

FLIGHT

flight-number	flight-date	
101	01Mar89	
202	04Mar89	
303	15Apr89	

(continued)

SEAT-RESERVATION

flight-number	flight-date	seat-number	passenger-identifier
101	01Mar91	1	1
101	01Mar91	2	2
101	01Mar91	3	null
202	04Mar91	1	1
202	04Mar91	2	3
202	04Mar91	3	null
303	15Apr91	1	null
303	15Apr91	2	4
303	15Apr91	3	null

4.3.8 Independent and Dependent Entities

Entities are designated as either *independent entities* or *dependent entities*, depending on how they acquire their keys. *Independent entities* do not depend on any other entity for their identification. *Dependent entities* depend on one or more other entities for their identification. These two types of entities are shown in Fig. 4.18.

Independent entities are represented by square-corner boxes. These are sometimes referred to as square boxes, a bit of a misnomer since they are usually rectangles. In Fig. 4.1, since each CUSTOMER instance is identified by a unique "customer-number", CUSTOMER is an independent entity.

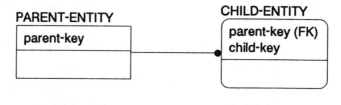

Independent Entity   Dependent Entity

Figure 4.18. Independent and Dependent Entities.

> **Definition: Independent Entity**
>
> An entity that does not depend on any other for its identification.
>
> **Definition: Dependent Entity**
>
> An entity that depends on one or more other entities for its identification.

Dependent entities are represented by boxes with rounded corners. These are sometimes referred to as rounded boxes, roundy boxes, puffy boxes, and so on. In the video store example, the store has many copies of the same MOVIE. In constructing the model, the business had two choices—either to identify each MOVIE-COPY individually with its own unique "movie-copy-number" (which would make it an independent entity) or to identify the copy by a combination of "movie-number" and "copy-number" (the chosen alternative). Because "movie-number" is an identifier of the MOVIE (not the copy), MOVIE-COPY is said to be dependent on MOVIE for its identification and is therefore a dependent entity.

Relationships usually result in dependencies between parent and child. The dependency can be *existence-dependency,* whereby the dependent entity cannot *exist* unless its parent does. Or it can be *identification-dependency,* whereby the dependent entity cannot be *identified* without using the key of the parent. Identifying relationships always result in both existence- and identification-dependency.

4.4 ROLE NAMES

> **Definition: Role Name**
>
> A new name for a foreign key attribute or group of foreign key attributes, which defines the role that it plays in the child entity.

Role names are new names for foreign key attributes contributed by relationships. A role name declares a new attribute whose name and definition are intended to connote the business statement embodied by the relationship that contributes the foreign key or keys. The new attribute must be given a definition, like any other attribute; its definition is said to be based on the definition of the original foreign key or keys. The original foreign keys are therefore classified as base attributes. When a role name is assigned to a single foreign key, the values that this new attribute may have must be either the complete set of values allowed for the original foreign key, or a subset of these values. When a role name is assigned to a group of foreign keys, the question of allowed values is more complex. We'll return to this topic in Chapter 5.

Figure 4.19 shows a simple role-name example. Notice that one primary key attribute of PLAYER reads

player-team-id.team-id (FK)

This shows the syntax for defining and displaying a role name. The first half (before the period) is the *role name*. The second half is the original name of the foreign key, sometimes called the *base name*. The syntax is

role-name.base-name (FK)

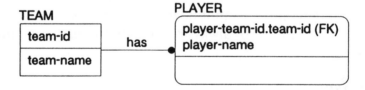

Figure 4.19. Role Name.

Key attributes with role names are still attributes, and their role names migrate across relationships like the names of any other key attributes. For example, let's extend Fig. 4.19 to record which PLAYERs scored in various GAMEs. Figure 4.20 shows the extension; and Table 4.5 is a sample instance table for Fig. 4.20.

In Fig. 4.20, we could have chosen to create new role names for the primary key attributes of SCORING-PLAY but did not do so. Figure 4.21 shows the result if we do provide new role names.

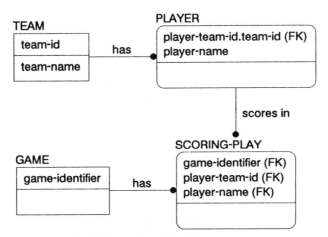

Figure 4.20. Migrating Role Named Primary Key Attributes.

Table 4.5.
Migrating Role Named Primary Key Attributes.

TEAM

team-id	team-name
A	Gnarlers
B	Crushers
C	Bruisers

PLAYER

player-team-id	player-name	
A	Jones	
A	Smith	
B	Wong	
B	Wang	
C	Michael	
C	Scott	

GAME

game-identifier	
1	
2	
3	
4	
5	

SCORING-PLAY

game-identifier	player-team-id	player-name	
1	A	Jones	
1	B	Wong	
2	B	Wong	
5	A	Smith	
5	C	Scott	
5	C	Michael	

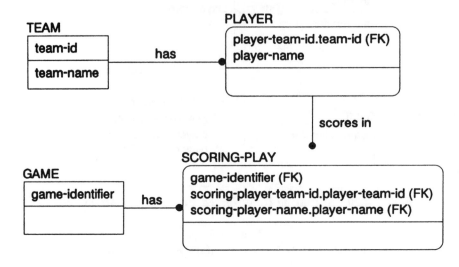

Figure 4.21. Additional Role Names.

The chain of role names reaches from SCORING-PLAY all the way back to TEAM. Notice, however, that the role name displayed in each entity reaches back across only one link of that chain. As we will see in Chapter 5, the definitions of attributes with role names are based on the definitions of the base attributes.

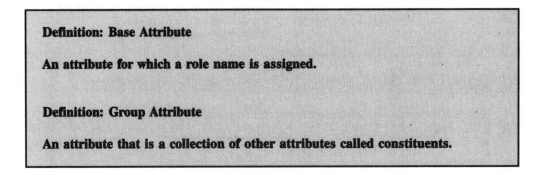

Group attributes can also be declared. A *group attribute* is an attribute that is a collection of other attributes, called *constituents*. A group attribute name *is* a role name. We will cover group attributes in more detail in Chapters 5 and 6. Group attributes are declared in a form similar to single attributes with role names, that is,

group-attribute-name.(constituent-1,constituent-2, . . . constituent-n)

This chapter provided a broad look at the IDEF1X language. There are many more details. We will return to the language after a short chapter on the importance of definitions.

4.5 REVIEW EXERCISES

Answers to boldface questions appear in Appendix H.

1. A set of business rules for the video store example is listed in Section 4.1. Explain how each rule can be seen in the model shown in Fig. 4.1. For example, how does the model specify that for every rental of a MOVIE-COPY, there must be at least one involved EMPLOYEE.

2. **Name and define the three main building blocks of an IDEF1X model.**

3. **Classify each of the following as an entity, entity instance, attribute, or relationship.**

animal	vegetable	mineral
cabbage	dog	the dog named Spot
selling	car engine type	car type
car door	salesperson	employee
John the salesperson	Sally the employee	

4. Draw a sample instance table for the following entity:

PRODUCT

product-id
product-name
product-description
product-price

5. **Why can no part of a primary key be null? Show, with a sample instance table, an example of what would happen if this were allowed.**

6. What are the differences among candidate keys, primary keys, alternate keys, and inversion entries?

7. **Review the following diagram and write down what it tells you.**

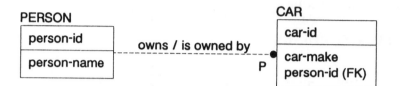

8. Draw a diagram that represents the following statements: A customer has many names and addresses and must have at least one of each. A customer can also have an account but need not.

9. What is the difference between an *identifying relationship* and a *nonidentifying relationship?*

10. What is the difference between an *independent entity* and a *dependent entity?*

11. Write down the business rules stated by these three diagrams. What are the differences?

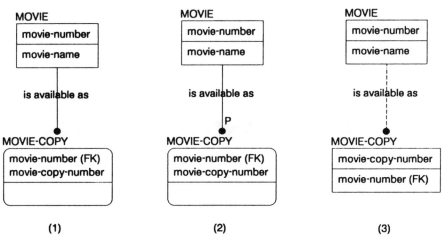

(1)   (2)   (3)

4.6 REFERENCES

[1]   Brown, R.G., and the Data Base Design Group. *Logical Database Design Techniques,* 2nd ed. Mountain View, Calif.: Data Base Design Group, 1984.

[2]   Codd, E.F. "Extending the Relational Model to Capture More Meaning," *ACM Transactions on Database Systems,* Vol. 4, No. 4 (December 1979), pp. 397-434.

[3]   Date, C.J. *Relational Database: Selected Writings.* Reading, Mass.: Addison-Wesley, 1986.

5

NAMES AND DEFINITIONS

Chapter 4 introduced one component of the information model: the model diagram. This chapter presents a second component: the names and definitions of entities and attributes. As we saw, the diagrams provide a context to help us understand the meaning of the data. But the data must be defined before the model is complete. Although the diagrams show us how entities and attributes are related, we still need to know what the entities and attributes represent.

The chapter begins with a section on choosing good names. Clear and meaningful names are essential if the information model is to be understood. It then describes a structure for writing definitions and discusses attribute domains. IDEF1X does not currently specify full domain support so the chapter extends the idea of a domain to show a way to capture value constraints outside the context of the model diagram. Treating domains in this way is not pure and sometimes generates controversy, but can be a pragmatic way to increase the value of the models.

The chapter continues with a discussion of data types and role names, definition references, and group attributes. It concludes with a selection of examples from the case study in Part Three.

5.1 CHOOSING A NAME

In information modeling, and in system development in general, it is important to choose clear and well-thought-out names. This is often given little emphasis because it tends to be tedious and not as much fun as working with the logic of relationship structures. It is, however, the subject of data analysis, and deserves recognition as being just as important as developing the structures.

5.1.1 Singular Names

Always give entities names that are singular. Singular names let us read a model with declarative statements such as "A FLIGHT <transports> zero or more PASSENGERs" and "A PASSENGER <is transported by> one FLIGHT." When we name the collection of instances represented by the entity, we are assigning a name we will use to refer to an instance. Each instance of the PASSENGER entity is a single passenger, not a collection of passengers.

Similarly, always make attribute names singular, such as "person-name", "movie-number", and "employee-bonus-amount". We do so partly for consistency and partly to avoid certain kinds of normalization errors. If you saw an attribute name like "person's-hobbies", you might have an intuitive sense that something was amiss. How many hobbies are the How do we tell one from another? How would we represent them in a sample instance table? Your intuition would be right—there would be something wrong. We will discuss this further in Chapter 9.

Before we proceed further with this chapter, we need to clarify our system of notation: You will have noticed a style throughout this book in which certain terms within the text are set off, as follows: Uppercase letters designate entities, and lowercase letters within literal quotation marks designate attributes. Using such conventions and notation within the textual definitions of entities and attributes makes it unnecessary to define terms each time they are used, since readers will know that if a term is presented according to these rules, it can be looked up in the information model glossary whenever needed. Using the conventions in written descriptions of models, like those provided throughout the book, is intended to help you better follow the descriptions.

5.1.2 Clear Names

IDEF1X entity and attribute names may be up to 65 characters long. It is important to choose a name that will clearly communicate what the entity or attribute represents, as well as distinguish it from other entities and attributes with similar names. For example, consider the names PERSON, CUSTOMER, and EMPLOYEE. We get a clear sense that there are differences among each of these. Although they all may represent some individual, each has distinct characteristics or qualities.

It's also important not to call two different things by the same name when they are not the same thing. For example, in dealing with a business area that insists on calling its customers "consumers," don't force or insist on the name CUSTOMER. You might have an alias, another name for CUSTOMER, or you might have a new concept, CONSUMER, that is distinct from, although similar to, CUSTOMER. Perhaps a CONSUMER is a category of CUSTOMER that may participate in relationships not allowed for other categories of CUSTOMER.

Sometimes it is difficult to name an entity or attribute without first defining it. Developing the definition first helps clarify the concept behind the entity or attribute, and can help us find a good name. Providing a good definition is as important as providing a good name. The ability to find meaningful names comes with experience and a fundamental understanding of what the model represents.

5.1.3 Naming Associative Entities

Finding meaningful names for associative entities can present significant challenges. Let's look at the example shown as Fig. 5.1 (and seen previously as Fig. 4.11). Note that the association between PERSON and ADDRESS has the name ADDRESS-USAGE. Although that is a fairly good name, it could be better. The question is, How can we choose a better name?

Our first inclination might be to call this associative entity PERSON-AD-DRESS. The problem is that the entity represents neither a PERSON nor an ADDRESS, and the name PERSON-ADDRESS could lead us to believe that this entity is some sort of PERSON or some sort of ADDRESS. What the entity really represents is the use of an ADDRESS by a PERSON as well as any information we want to keep about that use. The name ADDRESS-USAGE captures most of this idea, but it is a bit short. PERSON-ADDRESS-USAGE would have told us more.

Remember, an information model describes a business. Therefore, choose meaningful *business* names wherever possible. However, suppose there is no business name for an entity like this (the business probably doesn't consciously think about things like person address usages). In such situations, it is best to simply give the entity a name that fits its purpose in the model, and be done with it. There are times when it is futile to try to find a name that has a common business meaning. However, if an entity directly corresponds to a business *thing*, it should have a business *name*.

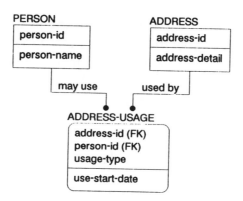

Figure 5.1. Naming Associative Entities.

5.2 DEFINING ENTITIES

All entities in a model must be defined. Writing a good definition is more difficult than it might initially seem. We all know, for example, what a PERSON is. Now try to write a definition of PERSON that will hold up to scrutiny. Attorneys have had a good time with that issue for years. Developing and using a standard structure for definitions can help.

5.2.1 Entity Definition Structure

For consistency, most organizations and individuals develop a convention or standard for the format and content of definitions. In practice you will find that definitions can be structured in a way that helps readers understand the concepts being defined. IDEF1X does not provide standards for definitions, but here is a structure to use as a starting point.

5.2.1.1 Description

A description is a clear and concise statement from which we can determine whether an object is or is not the thing that is described. It can be short and even a bit cryptic. Be careful, however, that the description is not too general, and does not use terms that have not themselves been defined.

An example of a good description is

A COMMODITY is something that has a value that can be determined in an exchange.

We might wonder what an exchange is and might need to understand more about value, but we can know that something is a COMMODITY if someone is, or would be, willing to trade something for it. If, for example, someone is willing to give us three peanuts and a stick of gum for a marble, we know a marble is a COMMODITY. And so are peanuts and sticks of gum.

Here is a poor description:

A CUSTOMER is someone who buys something from our company.

This description raises several questions. First, can a "someone" be another company? Second, must a CUSTOMER already have bought something from us to be considered one? What about potential for sales in the future, even if there are none now? And so on.

5.2.1.2 Business examples

It is a good idea to provide examples of the thing being defined, and to avoid defining things by example. Examples, such as our peanuts and marbles example for a COMMODITY, help readers understand a definition. The description said that a COMMODITY had value. The example shows that value is not always money.

5.2.1.3 Comments

General comments should be included for a definition, such as who is responsible for it, what condition it is in (preliminary, under review, approved, and so on), when it was last changed, and what its source was. It is also helpful to comment about how something similar to the entity being defined is not exactly the same (distinctions) and about any restrictions placed on the entity that are different from those placed on similar entities. For instance, a CUSTOMER might be distinguished from a PROSPECT by including a comment that a PROSPECT might someday become a CUSTOMER. Another comment might restrict the relationships in which a PROSPECT may participate to a subset of the relationships in which a CUSTOMER may participate. The point is that PROSPECT and CUSTOMER might at first look like the same thing, but if the business considers them to be different, they require different definitions.

5.2.2 Defining Associative Entities

An associative entity records intersection data. It pairs the keys of the entities being associated, and can hold information about that association. Defining an associative entity can be difficult. Therefore, let's look again at Fig. 5.1 and define ADDRESS-USAGE. A first try might be

An ADDRESS used by a PERSON.

But this is not an ADDRESS. Therefore, we might try to define ADDRESS-USAGE as

Information about an ADDRESS used by a PERSON.

This is closer, but still not correct. Information about an ADDRESS is recorded as a set of attributes of ADDRESS. Now, how about

Information about the use of an ADDRESS by a PERSON.

This last definition is fine. Associative entities often represent many-to-many relationships that have been resolved into a pair of one-to-many relationships with the associative entity in the middle.

Definition patterns like this one for associative entities are useful, but it is important not to fall into the trap of using them without thinking about the resulting definitions. Some associative entities have direct business meaning. We probably wouldn't want to use the same definition pattern for a CONTRACT, and define it simply as information about a relationship between a PRODUCT and a CUSTOMER. Although CONTRACT might be an associative entity connecting PRODUCT and CUSTOMER, there are better ways to define it.

5.3 DEFINING ATTRIBUTES

As with entities, it's important to develop clear definitions for all attributes. The same rules apply: By comparing a thing to a definition, we should be able to tell if it fits and is the defined attribute. Again, this is more difficult than it may first sound.

To illustrate the difficulty, let's try to construct a definition for the attribute "person-name". We could start with "A title by which a PERSON is known," with a distinction between a PERSON's name and his or her nickname. The trouble here is with the word "title." If we know that Your Honor is a title by which we must address a judge in a court of law, we might argue that Your Honor is a name. Clearly it is not.

We could try defining "person-name" as "the string of text that appears on the Name line of the birth certificate for a PERSON." The trouble with this is that, if your birth certificate lists a formal name (like Thomas), and you use an informal one (like Tom), the informal one does not qualify as "name." Changing your "name" also presents problems for this definition. In addition, by definition, you have no name if you have no birth certificate.

There comes a time in writing a definition at which it doesn't make sense to try to be any more precise. Our first definition for name would be sufficient if we added comments to prevent the wrong interpretation of the word "title." Including the concepts contained in our second definition as comments might also help readers distinguish among different types of names.

The point here is that writing good definitions requires a delicate balance between precision and practicality. The definition must be precise enough to allow us to understand the term being defined, but not so precise as to cause the kind of problems we found in our two examples for "person-name". However, beware of situations like "account-open-date", defined as "The date on which the ACCOUNT was opened" because they include terms that themselves need further definition. Now, what do we mean by "opened"?

In summary, attribute definitions should have the same basic structure as entity definitions, that is, description, business examples, and comments. The value of description and comments is clear. Business examples are often useful and lead us to the topic of domains.

5.4 DOMAINS

A *domain* is a set of values an attribute may have. These values have meanings in both an abstract and a business sense. In physical systems, domains are reflected as field types and edit rules that govern the values of data elements.

> **Definition: Domain**
>
> **A set of values that an attribute is allowed to take.**

For example, if "person-name" is defined as "the preferred form of address chosen by the PERSON," it has as its domain the set of all character strings (although, in actuality, its domain is usually constrained to a finite length in a physical system). The concept of "all character strings" is important here. People could choose to call themselves by phrases, numbers, descriptions, or other such things, as well as more conventional names like Jonah, or Tom.

One way to think of a domain is to think of two attributes coming from the same domain if it makes sense to compare them. It makes sense to compare two dates or two colors. It might make sense to compare two character strings (unless, for instance, one is the name of a city and the other is the title of a text on database design). It doesn't make sense to compare a date with a color.

In the formal description of relational theory, an attribute is said to be defined over a domain. The formal theory separates the attribute name concept from the domain concept, leading to two distinct things. IDEF1X does not specify how to treat domains. Therefore, the comments in this chapter are provided not as a formal treatment of domains, but as a way to include information about them in the definitions of attributes.

5.4.1 Domain Specifications

Specify the domain for each attribute. For some attributes, like codes, identifiers, amounts, and so on, it is difficult to provide good business examples. However, including a description of the attribute's domain communicates additional information about its meaning.

When specifying a domain, it is good practice to go beyond listing the values that an attribute can take. For example, suppose we define the attribute "customer-status" as follows:

> customer-status: A code that describes the association between the CUSTOMER and our business.

The following domain specification would not be too helpful:

> Domain: A, P, F, N

It would be better—that is, more complete—to specify a domain by including a meaning and description for each allowed value of "customer-status".

Domain: A: Active

               The CUSTOMER is currently involved in a purchasing
               relationship with our company.

               P: Prospect

               The CUSTOMER is someone in whom we have an
               interest, but with whom we have no current purchas-
               ing relationship.

               F: Former

               The CUSTOMER relationship has lapsed, that is, there
               has been no sale in the past 24 months.

               N: Never (do business with this person)

               The company has decided (for reasons we might go
               on to describe) that no business will be done with this
               CUSTOMER.

Attribute values have meanings, and domain descriptions are an important part
of the definition of the attribute. The eventual implementation of the data
structures described by the model must include provisions for ensuring that
all attributes can take values only from their domains.

5.4.2 Domain Declarations and Explicit Entities

In the "customer-status" attribute example, it could be argued that since the
codes have values, meanings, and descriptions, we should create an entity to
explicitly show the information we want to keep about each code. To do so
would result in Fig. 5.2. There are four instances of STANDARD-CUSTOM-
ER-STATUS. The code values for "customer-status" are A, P, F, and N. The
meanings and descriptions for these values were listed above in Section 5.4.1.

   If we were to create an entity like STANDARD-CUSTOMER-STATUS in Fig.
5.2 for each attribute in the model, the result would be that every attribute
would become a foreign key to an entity representing its domain. This would

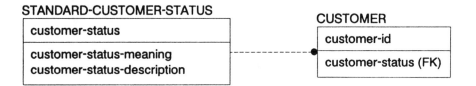

Figure 5.2. Entity Representing an Attribute Domain.

not be helpful in most models. Therefore, the question is, When should a domain be exposed as an explicit entity, and when should it simply be documented in the dictionary definition of the attribute?

There is no cookbook answer for this question. It depends on the purpose of the model. A guideline, however, is that a domain should be shown as an explicit entity only if the business intends to keep domain information about the attribute that will be used in day-to-day operations. In the example, if the meaning or description of the "customer-status" attribute needs to be available for presentation on screens or reports, the entity should be included to capture this information. If it will be sufficient to look up meanings in the dictionary when they are needed, the explicit entity should not be included in the model.

5.4.3 Logical and Physical Domain Distinction

There is a fairly picky point that needs to be made about the values that make up a domain. In practice, we are likely to see definitions and domain specifications like the one for "customer-status". We could, however, argue that the definition of "customer-status" has introduced *physical* characteristics to an attribute in a *logical* model. If the model containing this definition is a key based or fully attributed model, we could argue that introducing the physical representation of the attribute (a one-character alphabetic code) is premature.

This argument is correct in theory but counterproductive in practice. Declaration of the physical characteristics of a data element can often wait for the point of physical design. But if the decision has already been made to adopt a certain coding scheme for an attribute, it would be silly to fail to capture this information. In the "customer-status" example, the logical domain is represented by the meanings of the codes; the physical domain is represented by the values of the codes. There is a one-to-one correspondence between the logical and physical values.

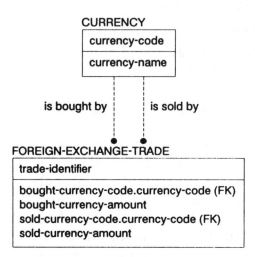

CURRENCY

currency-code
currency-name

is bought by ⋮   ⋮ is sold by

FOREIGN-EXCHANGE-TRADE

trade-identifier
bought-currency-code.currency-code (FK) bought-currency-amount sold-currency-code.currency-code (FK) sold-currency-amount

Figure 5.3. Role Names.

5.5   DATA TYPES AND ROLE NAMES

Several attributes in an information model will often be defined over the same domain, meaning that they will have the same allowed values but not the same definitions. This is common in cases in which foreign keys are contributed to an entity by a relationship. IDEF1X handles this situation by providing *role* names to allow different occurrences of the same underlying attributes to play different roles.

Consider the example in Fig. 5.3. It shows a FOREIGN-EXCHANGE-TRADE with two relationships to CURRENCY. The key of CURRENCY is "currency-code" (the identifier of a valid CURRENCY we are interested in tracking). We see from the relationships that one CURRENCY is bought by, and one is sold by, each FOREIGN-EXCHANGE-TRADE. We see also that the primary key of the CURRENCY ("currency-code") is used to identify each CURRENCY in the trade. The key of the one that is bought is named "bought-currency-code" and the key of the one that is sold is named "sold-currency-code". These are the *role names*. IDEF1X declares the "bought-currency-code" and "sold-currency-code" as *data types** of "currency-code".   They are not at all the same thing as "currency-code".

It would be silly to trade a CURRENCY for the same CURRENCY, at least at the same time and exchange rate. Thus, for a given transaction (an instance of FOREIGN-EXCHANGE-TRADE), the values of "bought-currency-code" and "sold-currency-code" may be different. By giving role names and definitions to the two different occurrences of "currency-code," we can capture the difference between these two attributes. Thus, we have the following:

currency-code: The unique identifier of a CURRENCY.

bought-currency-code: The identifier ("currency-code") of the CURREN-CY bought by (purchased by) the FOREIGN-EX-CHANGE-TRADE.

sold-currency-code: The identifier ("currency-code") of the CURREN-CY sold by the FOREIGN-EXCHANGE-TRADE.

The definitions and domains of the bought and sold codes are based on "currency-code". Thus, "currency-code" is called a *base attribute*. The bought and sold codes are said to be *data types* of this base attribute. If we wish to state a constraint that the "bought-currency-code" and the "sold-currency-code" cannot be the same, we can do so with a specific business rule.

Figure 5.4 shows another example using role names. It is our familiar address example, but this time role names have been assigned in the AD-DRESS-USAGE entity. Here are the definitions:

person-id: The unique identifier of a PERSON.

address-id: The unique identifier of an ADDRESS.

usage-person-id: The identifier ("person-id") of the PERSON for which the use of the ADDRESS is recorded.

---

*In relational database management systems, the term *data type* is often used to represent the physical format of a data element. In IDEF1X, data type is used for a different concept. To avoid confusion, I will therefore refer to the physical representation of an IDEF1X attribute as its *format*.

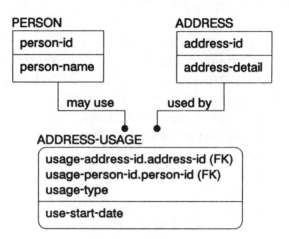

Figure 5.4. Using Role Names for Clarity.

usage-address-id: The identifier ("address-id") of the ADDRESS for which
the use by a PERSON is recorded.

The use of role names to add clarity is not strictly required in IDEF1X models,
but can sometimes be helpful. In the foreign exchange example, the role
names were *required* to distinguish between the two occurrences of "currency-
code". In the address example, the role names were not needed for that reason
(without the role names, "person-id" and "address-id" each would appear only
once in the ADDRESS-USAGE entity). However, outside the context of Fig. 5.4,
it is impossible to know that the attribute "person-id" is playing an identification
role in the ADDRESS-USAGE entity. By assigning the role names, we now have
attributes ("usage-person-id" and "usage-address-id") whose names tell us more
about the roles they play in the model.

5.6 DEFINING GROUP ATTRIBUTES

Definition: Group Attribute

An attribute that is a collection of other attributes called constituents.

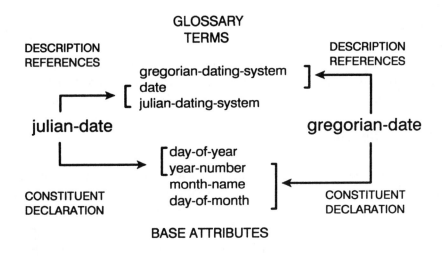

GLOSSARY
TERMS

DESCRIPTION
REFERENCES

DESCRIPTION
REFERENCES

gregorian-dating-system
date
julian-dating-system

julian-date

gregorian-date

day-of-year
year-number
month-name
day-of-month

CONSTITUENT
DECLARATION

CONSTITUENT
DECLARATION

BASE ATTRIBUTES

Figure 5.5. Defining Group Attributes.

As we saw in Chapter 4, a group attribute is an attribute that has been declared to consist of a collection of other attributes. Group attributes are declared with role names. For example, we might *describe* a "julian-date" as "a "date" recorded in the "julian-dating-system" and a "gregorian-date" as "a "date" recorded in the "gregorian-dating-system," with "date", "julian-dating-system", and "gregorian-dating-system" defined as common business terms in a glossary. We could then *declare* that "julian-date" is a group containing the attributes "year-number" and "day-of-year", and that "gregorian-date" is a group containing the attributes "month-name", "day-of-month", and "year-number". Figure 5.5 shows this arrangement. Together, the description (what it is) and the declaration (what it consists of) make up the definition.

5.6.1 Group Attribute Descriptions

A group attribute has an identity and definition distinct from the identities and definitions of its constituents. In the example, "gregorian-date" and "julian-date" are *described* not as combinations of their constituents, but as concepts in and of themselves. They are points on different calendars and are represented in different ways. They are *declared* to have constituents, but the descriptions do not refer to the constituents. The way in which it is represented is a fundamental part of the definition of each attribute but is not part of its description.

This may at first seem like an unnecessarily fine distinction, but describing a group attribute in terms of its constituents is like describing an individual attribute by examples of its use. Description by use tells us what an attribute is used for, but does not tell us what it is. Description by constituents tells us what an attribute group contains but, again, doesn't tell us what it represents.

5.6.2 Composite Domains

Preparing business examples for a group attribute can be challenging. For instance, what is a good example of a group consisting of three colors? One way to give examples is to list valid combinations of the constituents of the group. Therefore, we might use "red, green, and blue" as an example of a color group. This is often helpful and points to the importance of another aspect of the group, the concept of a composite domain. Here are two date examples.

    julian-date: 90 366
    gregorian-date: June 31, 1990

These dates are obviously incorrect. The problem is not with the constituents—they all lie within their respective domains. The problem is that there were only 365 days in 1990, and only 30 days in June. Specifying the composite domain of a group attribute, that is, the allowed combinations of constituent values, is an important part of its definition.

To specify a composite domain for a group attribute, we declare the group and add a constraint over the valid combinations of constituent values. The constraint can be stated directly, for example, "the value of "day-of-month" may be from one to 30 when "month-name" is June," or indirectly, for example, "for each year where "year-number" is evenly divisible by four and is not equal to 2000, "day-of-year" must be from one to 366; for all other values of "year-number", "day-of-year" must be from one to 365."

5.6.3 Domains and Business Rules

Business rules represent constraints on the content of the database and are an integral part of an information model. Some of these business rules are found in relationships and others are found in entity, attribute, and domain definitions. It is important to understand the basic principles involved here. Domains need to be addressed in the definitions of attributes since they are not directly specified or given a standard treatment by the IDEF1X language.

For example, the CURRENCY entity in Fig. 5.3 could be defined to include either the set of all currencies recognized anywhere in the world, or the subset of these currencies that the company has decided to use in its day-to-day business operations. This is a subtle but important distinction. In the latter case, there is a business rule involved, a policy statement if you will. This rule restricts the general domain of all "currency-codes" to the subset of those we will use. Maintaining the business rule then becomes a task of maintaining the CURRENCY entity. To permit or prohibit trading of CURRENCYs, instances are created or deleted.

The domains of "bought-currency-code" and "sold-currency-code" are similarly restricted by the business rule. One of them may be restricted even further by forming a group attribute consisting of the two currency codes and including a constraint that says the values of the two codes cannot be the same.

5.7 DEFINITION REFERENCES

It is often convenient to make use of common business terms when defining an entity or attribute. We did this in our example of Julian and Gregorian dates. "Date", "gregorian-dating-system", and "julian-dating-system" were not entities or attributes; rather, they were business terms. Here is another example. The business terms are highlighted with italics.

A CURRENCY-SWAP is a complex agreement between two PARTYs in which they agree to exchange *cash-flows* in two different CUR-RENCYs over a period of time. Exchanges can be fixed over the *term* of the swap, or may *float*. Swaps are often used to *hedge* currency and interest *rate-risks*.

When using a business term in a definition, be sure to define it. One way to do this is to define each term every time it is used. However, if these business-term definitions appear in many places, they will have to be maintained in many places; the probability that a change will be made to all of them at the same time is very small. A separate glossary of commonly used terms is a better solution. Such a glossary can serve several purposes. It can become the basis for modeling definitions, and can, by itself, help people to communicate more effectively.

5.7.1 Circularity

When we look in a dictionary, we often find a situation like this:

CIRCULAR:	Moving in a cycle . . .
CYCLE:	Any round of operations or events . . .
ROUND:	Circular.

The individual descriptions look good, but when we look at them together they are circular. Without some care, this can happen with entity and attribute descriptions.   For example,

CUSTOMER: Someone who buys one or more of our PRODUCTs.

PRODUCT: Something we sell to CUSTOMERs.

With care we can avoid such circularity. In this example, we could change the description of PRODUCT to "something we offer for sale." That would cure the circularity problem but would still not give us a good description: We have described what we do with a PRODUCT, not what it is. "A tangible thing, created by our company, and from which we expect to derive a profit" would be a better description for PRODUCT.

5.8 SYNONYMS, HOMONYMS, AND ALIASES

> **Definition: Synonym**
>
> **A word with the same or nearly the same meaning as another word.**
>
> **Definition: Homonym**
>
> **A word that is like another in sound and perhaps in spelling, but with a different meaning.**
>
> **Definition: Alias**
>
> **Another name for something, used in a different context.**

We do not all speak the same language. And even when we do, we are not always precise in our use of terms. We often use, and confuse, synonyms, homonyms, and aliases. A *synonym* is another name for an object that already has a name. A *homonym* is a name that is or sounds the same or nearly the same for two different objects. An *alias* is another name for an object, usually one which is common throughout a business area.

Because entities and attributes in an IDEF1X information model are *identified* by their names, we must have a systematic way of dealing with synonyms, homonyms, and aliases. At the logical level, each entity and attribute in a model must be assigned a unique name, and each must have exactly one identifying name. IDEF1X does not formally describe the declaration and handling of synonyms, homonyms, or aliases, but we need to find a way to do so. A good place to start is to include a list of synonyms, homonyms, and aliases in a definition.

5.9 DEFINITION EXAMPLES

Learning to name and define entities and attributes is a most crucial aspect of IDEF1X practice. Therefore, we present good examples of entity and attribute definitions as the final section of this chapter. These examples have been taken from the case study in Part Three. Note that because the definitions are designed to be read out of context (that is, without always referring to other definitions), they may seem redundant. For more examples, refer to the case study.

Comments and examples are provided when they help to clarify the description. Components of a definition need not be present if they add no value.

CASHIER

Description:	A job function in which an EMPLOYEE is assigned as the operator of a CASH-REGISTER.
Comment:	In this role, the EMPLOYEE is involved with SALEs to CUSTOMERs.
Example:	EMPLOYEE Judy is assigned to CASH REGISTER 123 from 1:00 October 17 to 5:30 October 17.

CUSTOMER-CLASS

Description: A grouping of CUSTOMERs formed to track buying trends and preferences.

Comment: Each class includes a description of the general type of CUSTOMER to be included.

Example: Berkeley Gourmands.

CUSTOMER-CLASSIFICATION

Description: A record of the inclusion of a CUSTOMER in a CUSTOMER-CLASS.

Example: Customer Alvyn is included in the Berkeley Gourmand class.

HOUSE

Description: A general part of a MARKET where produce is sold.

Comment: A MARKET is like a shopping mall, with each HOUSE a department store in the mall. A HOUSE can also represent a farm, where the MARKET represents the farming region.

MARKET

Description: A wholesaler of produce.

Comment: A MARKET can cover several city blocks and contains HOUSEs where the produce is sold. A MARKET is like a shopping mall, with each HOUSE a department store in the mall. A MARKET can also cover a geographic region, like Sonoma County.

Example: San Francisco Produce Market, Northern California.

5.9.1 Attribute Definition Examples

The following attribute definitions include the standard description, comment, and example sections as well as domain (as applicable) and physical system characteristics, including a relational column name and format. When an attribute is based on (that is, is a role name for) another attribute, its values must come from the same domain as the base and its physical representation must be the same as the base. This is indicated by naming the base attribute in a data type entry for the role named attribute, and as needed, constraining its domain in the domain entry. Group attributes are treated in a similar way. Group names the constituents, and domain constrains allowed combinations of constituent values.

address

Description:	A place at which someone can be contacted.
Comment:	This is a group attribute established for two purposes. First, it is used in high-level models to leave a place mark for future extension. Second, it explodes into the constituents of all types of addresses and is used in low-level models to distinguish between a situation in which a generic (able to accommodate any kind) as opposed to specific type of address is needed.
	It is clear that only some combinations of cities, states, and zip codes are allowable. This additional detail may be needed at some point.
Example:	A street address or a post office box.
Col Name:	addr
Group:	address-po-box
	address-street-number
	address-street-name
	address-street-extension
	address-city
	address-state
	address-zip-code

address-city

Description:	A part of an address containing the name of a city.
Example:	Berkeley
Domain:	Any nonblank character string up to length 30.
Col Name:	addr_city
Format:	VARCHAR (30)

cashier-end-timestamp

Description:	The date and time at which a CASHIER assignment ends.
Example:	17OCT8917040000
Domain:	Any valid time and date after 1/1/89, or NULL (designated by zero) if the CASHIER is still assigned.
Col Name:	csh_end_ts
Data Type:	timestamp

cashier-id

Description:	The identifier of the EMPLOYEE is serving as CASHIER.
Data Type:	employee-id
Col Name:	csh_id

cashier-start-end-constraint

Description:	A group attribute formed for the purpose of declaring the composite domain of the attributes "cashier-start-time-stamp" and "cashier-end-timestamp".
Group:	cashier-start-timestamp
	cashier-end-timestamp
Domain:	When recorded, the end timestamp must be later than the start timestamp, but by no more than 5 hours.

cashier-start-timestamp

Description:	The date and time at which a CASHIER assignment begins.
Example:	17OCT8916300000
Domain:	Any valid time and date after 1/1/89.
Col Name:	csh_strt_ts
Data Type:	timestamp

family-membership-type

Description:	A specification of the type of relationship between the CUSTOMER and the FAMILY.
Domain:	B: Buyer for the establishment represented by the FAMILY.

G: General membership, no specific type recorded.

M: Manager of the establishment represented by the FAMILY.

O: Owner of the establishment represented by the FAMILY.

Col Name: fam_mbr_typ
Format: CHARACTER (1)

house-address

Description: The mailing address of the HOUSE.
Example: 123 4th Street, Berkeley CA 94703
Domain: Any valid address, either a street address or a post office box.
Col Name: hs_addr
Data Type: address

5.11 REVIEW EXERCISES

Answers to boldface questions appear in Appendix H.

1.   Why are the names of entities and attributes always singular?

2.   **Provide good names for the following:**

a.   A record of a request by a customer to purchase a product that is not in stock.

b.   A record of a request by a customer to purchase a product that was not originally in stock, but that was acquired and delivered to the customer.

c.   Something that is mechanical and generally is used to transport people or things from one place to another.

d.   A building in which one or more people can or do live.

e.   A record of a relationship between a mazerkaf and a quantu.

3.   Write a good definition for each of the things named in Exercise 2.

4.   **Name and define the associative entities in the following diagrams.**

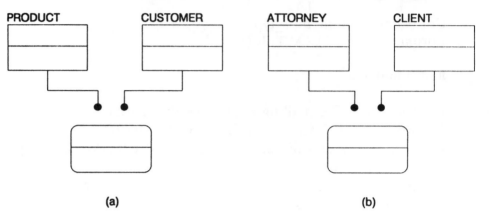

              (a)   (b)

5.   Name and define the associative entities in the following diagrams.

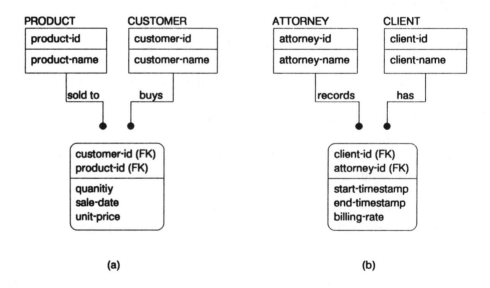

              (a)   (b)

6.   **Write definitions and domain specifications for the following attributes:**

a. telephone-area-code
b. customer-name
c. **account-currency-code**
d. **account-balance**
e. **account-balance-currency-code**
f. employee-social-security-number
g. social-security-number
h. employee-gregorian-birth-date
i. age (a derived attribute)
j. weather-reading (a group attribute)

6

ENTITIES, ATTRIBUTES, AND RELATIONSHIPS

Chapters 4 and 5 introduced basic concepts and notation used in IDEF1X models. In this chapter, we provide a more detailed look at dependent entities, derived and group attributes, and relationships, including cardinality, recursive relationships, and the concept of many-to-many. The chapter concludes with a discussion of n-ary relationships, that is, associations among three or more entities.

To begin, let's review the concepts introduced so far:

Entities are the basic building blocks of the information model. They have properties called *attributes* and are connected by *relationships*. An *instance* is a single occurrence of an entity. As needed, entities can be collected into *generalization hierarchies*. All entities and attributes have definitions.

Primary key attributes identify entities. Attributes have *domains,* which specify values that the attribute is allowed to take.

A *relationship* connects two entities and has a *cardinality* that indicates how many instances of each of the two entities may or must be involved. Relationships contribute *foreign keys* from the *parent entity* to the *child entity.* Foreign keys may be assigned *role names.*

6.1 ENTITIES

Chapter 4 introduced *independent* and *dependent* entities, and provided the following definitions:

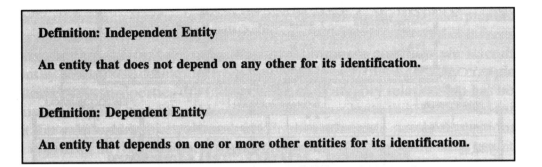

Chapter 4 also introduced *sample instance tables* as an aid to understanding what the entities and attributes represent. Sample instance tables are used extensively throughout this and subsequent chapters.

The following paragraphs define and discuss the three types of dependent entities—characteristic, associative, and category.

> **Definition: Characteristic Entity**
>
> **A group of attributes that occurs many times for an entity, and is not directly identified by any other entity.**

As defined, a *characteristic entity* is a group of attributes that occurs many times for an entity and is not directly identified by any other entity. A characteristic entity is a dependent entity with exactly one identifying parent. An example of a characteristic entity is shown in Fig. 6.1 with a its sample instance table provided as Table 6.1. The diagram tells the reader that a PERSON <may own> many PETs, and that a PET is owned by exactly one PERSON. In this situation, the PET entity is said to be a characteristic of the PERSON entity.

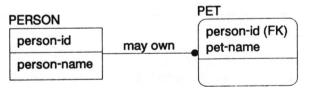

Figure 6.1. Characteristic Entity.

Table 6.1.
Characteristic Entity Sample Instance Example.

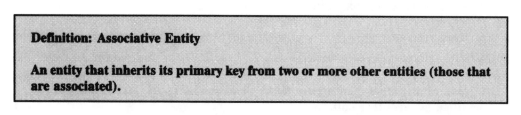

PERSON			PET		
person-id	person-name		person-id	pet-name	
P1	Tom		P1	Felix	
P2	Ben		P1	Malcomb	
P3	Marilyn		P1	Avis	
			P2	Sandy	
			P2	Brutus	
			P3	Sierra	

Definition: Associative Entity

An entity that inherits its primary key from two or more other entities (those that are associated).

Associative entities record multiple associations (relationships) between two or more entities. In Chapter 5 (Fig. 5.1), we saw an example of an association between a PERSON and an ADDRESS; it is repeated here as Fig. 6.2. In this example, ADDRESS-USAGE is an associative entity because it has more than one identifying parent. Associative entities carry information about the association of two or more entities (in this case, two).

The difference between a characteristic and an associative entity is the number of identifying relationships to the entity. A characteristic entity has only one. An associative entity has more than one.

Definition: Category Entity

A subset of the instances of an entity (referred to as the generalization entity, or generic parent) that share common attributes or relationships distinct from other subsets.

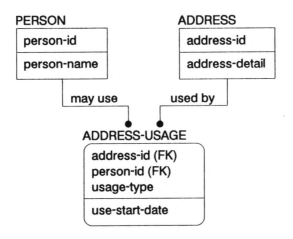

Figure 6.2. Associative Entity.

The category entity is the third type of dependent entity. Category entities and generalization hierarchies are discussed in Chapter 7.

6.2 ATTRIBUTES

Chapter 4 described various types of attributes. Here is a summary of their definitions:

A *primary key* is an attribute or group of attributes that has been chosen as the unique identifier of an entity.

A *primary key attribute* is an attribute that, either by itself or in combination with other primary key attributes, will form the primary key.

A *candidate key* is an attribute or group of attributes that might be chosen as a primary key.

An *alternate key* is a candidate key that has not been chosen as the primary key.

An *inversion entry* is an attribute or group of attributes that will frequently be used to access the entity but may not result in finding exactly one instance.

A *non-key attribute* is an attribute that has not been chosen as a part of the primary key of the entity.

Now we will look at two other types of attributes: derived attributes and group attributes.

6.2.1 Derived Attributes

Derived attributes are attributes, such as totals, that can be computed from other attributes and therefore need not be stored directly. As we will see in Chapter 9, recording a derived attribute in a model is a normalization error. There are, however, business situations in which it makes sense to record derived attributes in a model.

Definition: Derived Attribute

An attribute whose value can be computed based on the values of other attributes.

First, let's briefly consider the issue of normalization. A goal of normalization is to ensure that there is only one way to know each fact recorded in a database. If we know the value of a derived attribute, the algorithm by which it is derived, and the values of the attributes used by the algorithm, there are *two* ways to know the fact: Look at the value of the derived attribute, or derive it from scratch. If we can get an answer two different ways, it is possible to get two different answers to the same question.

   As an example, consider what could happen if we were to record both a "birth-date" and an "age" attribute for an EMPLOYEE, but only update the "age" attribute during an end-of-month maintenance job. When we asked the question, How old is such and such EMPLOYEE? we could access "age" directly and get an answer, or we could subtract "birth-date" from the current date. If we did the subtraction, we would always get the right answer. If we accessed "age" and it had not been updated recently, it might give us the wrong answer. This might cause problems depending upon why we wanted to know the employee's age.

   In discussions with business people, it can sometimes be useful to include derived attributes in a model. This is common practice in physical models of current or planned databases that contain such derived data. Although some modeling theory says never include derived data, I suggest you break the rules when you must. But always record the fact that the attribute is derived and state the derivation algorithm.

An example of a situation in which it makes sense to record derived data is an account that tracks receivables from a customer. A balance attribute, which is derived, would be appropriate. Although balance can be determined by adding the amounts of all transactions, computing discounts and other variable factors from time zero, and so on, it is difficult to argue that this tedious process makes any sense. The cost of deriving the balance each time it is needed may be too high, and it will not be possible to get wrong answers as long as the balance attribute is updated at the time of each transaction.

Another example of a situation in which derived attributes are appropriate is a management information services database that is separate from the operations support databases in a company. MIS databases often contain large amounts of derived data and the data is frequently refreshed from the operations systems. The reason that this process can work is that data that is a few days or weeks old is sufficient to meet business needs. The cost of computing some answers in real-time is too high.

Including derived attributes in a model must be considered with great care. If you find that you are adding entities to a model simply to house derived data, you have probably crossed the line from a business model (the conceptual schema) to defining user views (the external schemas).

6.2.2 Group Attributes

As first presented in Chapters 4 and 5, a *group attribute* is an attribute whose constituents themselves are attributes or group attributes.   In an IDEF1X model, a group attribute behaves almost exactly like any other attribute.

Definition: Group Attribute

An attribute that is a collection of other attributes called constituents.

We can draw an IDEF1X diagram to represent the definition of a group
attribute. It involves a generalization hierarchy (see Chapter 7) and is shown
as Fig. 6.3. It is read as follows:

> An ATTRIBUTE is either a GROUP-ATTRIBUTE or a BASE-ATTRIBUTE.
> A GROUP-ATTRIBUTE <is a> ATTRIBUTE. A GROUP-ATTRIBUTE <has
> two or more> CONSTITUENTs. A CONSTITUENT <is a> ATTRIBUTE.
> A CONSTITUENT <is part of> one GROUP-ATTRIBUTE. An ATTRIBUTE
> is used as zero or more CONSTITUENTs. A BASE-ATTRIBUTE <is a>
> ATTRIBUTE (one that has no constituents, and is therefore not a group).*

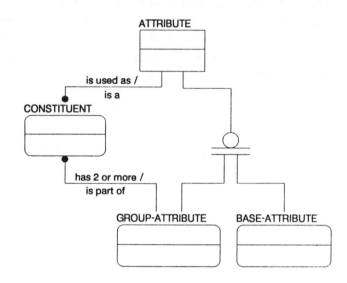

Figure 6.3. Group Attributes.

Chapter 5 gave the examples of "gregorian-date", with constituents "month-
name", "day-of-month", and "year-number"; and "julian-date", with constituents
"day-of-year" and "year-number". These are natural groups we can recognize
almost immediately once we think about definitions and examples for dates.
Other groupings are not so obvious. For example, a model for a bank might
contain an attribute "loan-account-number" which, on closer examination,
breaks down into a "branch-number" plus a "statement-cycle-number" plus a
"loan-number" plus a "transposition-check-digit".

---

*This structure is the classic bill of materials structure, where a "thing" can be made up of other
"things," some of which themselves are made up of other "things."

Group attributes such as dates do not always need to be declared in the model as "groups." Sometimes, it is sufficient to list the constituents in the definition of an attribute. At other times, it is best to take advantage of the capability of IDEF1X to display the declarations of group attributes graphically. But be careful. For example, without closely inspecting our "loan-account-number", we might not discover the entity BRANCH, the general concept of a "statement cycle", the presence of derived data (the check digit), and the possible distinction between a loan and an account.

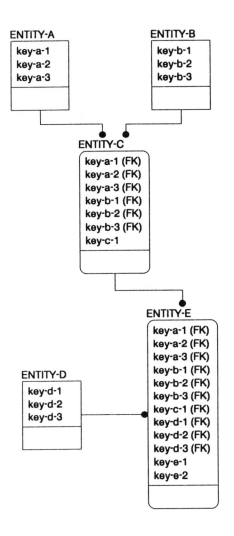

Figure 6.4. Large Entity Keys.

Group attributes can also be used for convenience. One area where group attributes are frequently used is in declaring a role name for a group of foreign keys. In Fig. 6.4, for example, there is a multi-part key for ENTITY-A and another for ENTITY-B. If we add an associative entity (ENTITY-C), the key of the associative entity gets even larger. ENTITY-E becomes somewhat difficult to manage and the presence of so many key attributes begins to obscure the message of the diagram, that of possible connections among entities A, B, and D. This is a situation in which a group attribute is a convenient way to simplify the diagram.

Figure 6.5 introduces a group attribute in ENTITY-C containing the entire set of foreign keys. Notice that ENTITY-E now has a shorter key. The name assigned to the group attribute can convey a sense of what the structure means. The knowledge that part of the key of ENTITY-E consists of a large number of group constituents, however, is hidden. You can still see the constituents, but you must trace back from ENTITY-E to ENTITY-C to find them.

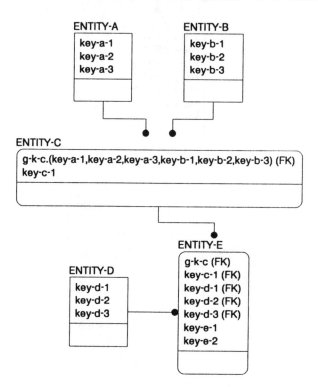

Figure 6.5. Migrating Group Attributes as Keys.

Using role names for groups of attributes in this way can be helpful but is sometimes misleading. There can be situations in which the overuse of groups can hide business rule errors; this is covered in Chapter 9.

6.3 RELATIONSHIPS AND CARDINALITY

Relationships carry a great deal of information. In fact, they can be considered the heart of the information model, because, to a great extent, they describe the rules of the business. Information modeling techniques place a great deal of emphasis on relationships. In high-level business models (for example, the ERD type of IDEF1X model), discussion of relationships brings out important policies and rules and provides the essential context in which a business chooses to view the world. In detailed information models (such as the key based and fully attributed model types), relationships represent constraints that govern the behavior of the data structure, that is, rules that specify valid states of the data.

The term *relationship* means different things in different information modeling techniques. Some techniques treat relationships as things that connect entities and represent them with a distinct symbol. In languages derived from the work of Peter Chen, for example, a relationship is represented by a diamond symbol. In some languages, relationships are allowed to have attributes, and can connect other relationships as well as entities.

IDEF1X takes a different approach. It defines a relationship as a directed association between two entities. The more loosely defined relationship becomes an IDEF1X associative entity if it has any attributes (which it must have if it is representing a many-to-many association) or if it must participate in other relationships.

Discussions of whether relationships can have attributes, participate in relationships, and so on, generally boil down to matters of preference. IDEF1X prefers to make the distinction clear. By definition, any *thing* we want to keep information about is an entity. Therefore, a relationship with attributes or one that participates in other relationships is a *thing* and must, by definition, be represented as an entity.

6.3.1 Cardinality

As we saw in Chapter 4, relationships have a property called *cardinality* that defines how many instances of each participating entity may or must participate. Cardinality statements designate how many instances of the parent entity are connected to how many instances of the child.

The relationship graphic (the solid or dashed line with the dot on the end) displays most of this as an annotation at the many end. Remember that the solid line represents an identifying relationship, that the dashed line represents a nonidentifying relationship, and that the dot represents the many. The notation is summarized in Fig. 6.6.

For nonidentifying relationships, cardinality is further designated by the presence or absence of a diamond at the end of the relationship without the dot. Without the diamond, the cardinality is one-to-something. With the diamond, it is changed to zero-or-one-to-something.

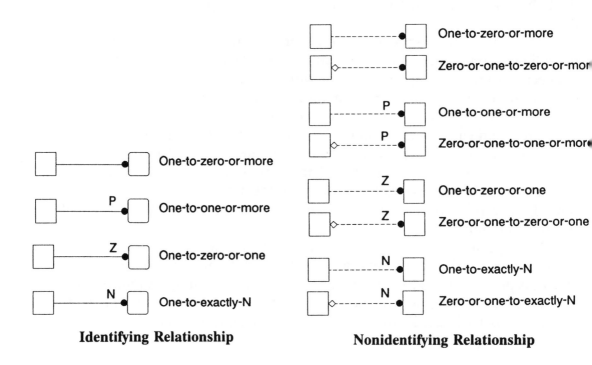

Identifying Relationship   **Nonidentifying Relationship**

Figure 6.6. Cardinality Notation.

6.3.2 One-to-Many Relationships

There are two types of one-to-many relationships: those that contribute primary key attributes to a child entity (identifying), and those that do not (nonidentifying).

6.3.2.1 One-to-many—Identifying

Chapter 4 contained many examples of identifying relationships. Let's look again at Fig. 4.9, the MOVIE / MOVIE-COPY example. It is repeated here with a slight modification as Fig. 6.7:

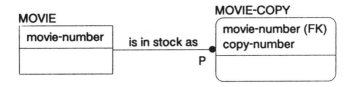

Figure 6.7. One-to-One-or-More Identifying Relationship.

One of the basic principles of relational modeling, as supported by IDEF1X, is that an instance of an entity cannot exist if it cannot be uniquely identified. In the example, a MOVIE-COPY cannot be identified unless the primary key of the MOVIE (the "movie-number") is known. The identifying relationship contributes this foreign key ("movie-number") to the primary key of MOVIE-CO-PY. MOVIE-COPY is therefore existence-dependent on MOVIE.

Existence-dependency means something to the cardinality statement. It means that, on the end of the relationship without the dot, there will be exactly one MOVIE. How about the MOVIE-COPY end (the one with the dot)?

In the video store example, we defined a MOVIE-COPY as one of perhaps several reproductions of an original that was available for rent. It is possible that only the original (the MOVIE) exists or that the store has no copies. The business has decided to exclude such movies from its database. Therefore, this is a one-to-one-or-more relationship. The "P" symbol (you can think of P as Positive) next to the dot says this. To record a MOVIE in the database, at least one MOVIE-COPY must also be recorded.

Suppose there is another video store and it has a different policy regarding MOVIEs it keeps track of. It does care to know about all of the MOVIEs in the world, even those for which it has no copies. So the business rule for this store is that for a MOVIE to exist (be recorded in the database), there need not be at least one copy. To record this business rule, the "P" would be removed, and the relationship would become a one-to-zero-or-more relationship.

One-to-zero-or-one is specified with a "Z" (for example, a person has zero or one spouse at any given time), and one-to-exactly-n is indicated with a number near the dot (say, for each financial transaction there are exactly two entries to a double-entry bookkeeping system).

6.3.2.2 One-to-many—Nonidentifying

As we saw in Chapter 4, nonidentifying relationships also contribute keys from a parent to a child. The keys, however, do not become part of the primary key of the child. This means that the child will not be identification-dependent on this parent. In addition, there can be situations in which an entity at the many end of the relationship can exist without a parent, for example, the entity is not existence-dependent on a parent.

If the relationship is mandatory from the perspective of the child, the child is existence-dependent on the parent. If it is optional, the child is neither existence- nor identification-dependent with respect to this parent (although it may be dependent on other parents). IDEF1X uses a diamond to indicate the optional case. Let us look at a simple example: In Fig. 6.8 (the reservation example from Chapter 4), "passenger-identifier" is a foreign key attribute of SEAT-RESERVATION. It doesn't identify the reservation; it identifies the PASSENGER who holds the reservation. A SEAT-RESERVATION could be Open (not held by any PASSENGER). When the reservation is Open, the "passenger-id" foreign key will be empty (null). If, by business policy, this can be allowed to happen (or in this case, by necessity, since the airline cannot force passengers to reserve every seat on every flight), the relationship is, from the perspective of the child entity, optional. The diamond at the parent end of the relationship signifies this.

Diamonds can only exist for nonidentifying relationships (since an identifying relationship contributes one or more primary key attributes, and no part of a primary key can be null). A nonidentifying relationship with a diamond is a zero-or-one-to-something relationship.

Aside from the diamond, the cardinality graphics for nonidentifying relationships are the same as those for identifying relationships; no symbol at the many end for zero or more, "P" for one or more, "Z" for zero or one, and "N" for exactly that number.

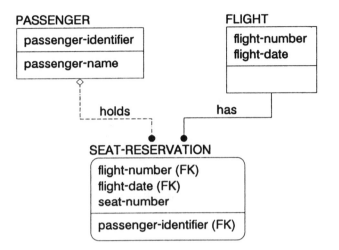

Figure 6.8. Zero-or-One-to-Many Nonidentifying Relationship.

6.3.3 Recursive Relationships

An entity can participate in a relationship in which it is both the parent and the child. Such a relationship is called a *recursive relationship*. Any recursive relationship must be nonidentifying.

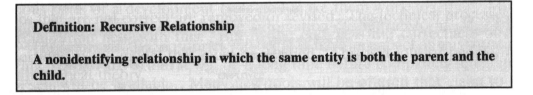

Definition: Recursive Relationship

A nonidentifying relationship in which the same entity is both the parent and the child.

Figure 6.9 shows a recursive relationship. In it, a COMPANY <owns> other COMPANYs. As with all nonidentifying relationships, this one brings the key of the parent entity into the data area of the child entity as a foreign key. In this case, however, both parent and child are the same entity.

Notice two other things in Fig. 6.9: First, the name of the contributed foreign key is changed when it appears in the data area. Rather than being "company-id (FK)", it is "owner-id.company-id (FK)", where "owner-id" is a role name. Second, there is a diamond on the relationship; it is optional from the perspective of the child.

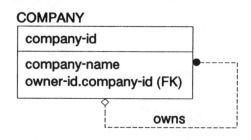

Figure 6.9. Recursive Relationship.

One of the basic principles of IDEF1X is that if two things have the same name, they are the same thing. In Fig. 6.9, the role name is required since an attribute cannot appear twice in the same entity under the same name. If it did, there would be no way to tell the occurrences apart. Furthermore, the identifier of a COMPANY, "company-id", is not the same thing as the identifier of the COMPANY that owns the COMPANY. It is not defined the same, and although its values come from the same domain, it will have a different value ("company-id" identifies the COMPANY, and "owner-id" identifies the COMPANY that is the owner). Definitions and the sample instance table shown in Table 6.2 will help clarify the point.

company-id: The unique identifier of a COMPANY.

owner-id: The "company-id" of the COMPANY that owns this COM-PANY. Not all COMPANYs have an owner.

The diamond is needed on the relationship since a COMPANY may or may not have an owner. From the sample instance table, we can see that Big Monster Company owns Small Monster Company and Other Small Company. Small Monster Company, in turn, owns Big Subsidiary and Small Subsidiary. Independent Company does not own any other company and has no owner. Big Monster Company also has no owner. Figure 6.10 illustrates the relationships shown in Table 6.2.

Table 6.2.
Recursive Relationship Sample Instance Table.

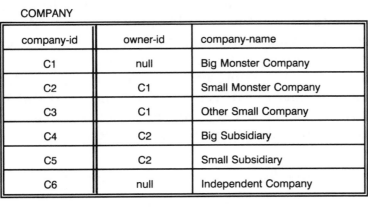

COMPANY

company-id	owner-id	company-name
C1	null	Big Monster Company
C2	C1	Small Monster Company
C3	C1	Other Small Company
C4	C2	Big Subsidiary
C5	C2	Small Subsidiary
C6	null	Independent Company

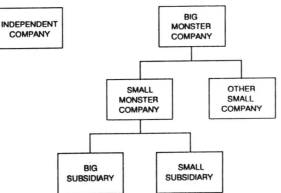

Figure 6.10. Recursive Relationship Example.

The diamond on the relationship in this example was required so that a COMPANY could have no owner. Diamonds are not required on all recursive relationships, but it is common to see them. The absence of a diamond indicates there must be a cycle of foreign keys in the database.

Recursive relationships are sometimes called fish hooks. For one thing, they look a bit like them. For another, in early versions of IDEF1X, the dot designating the many end of a relationship was an arrowhead making the relationship look even more like a fish hook. Arrows, however, caused people to try to read the models as flow diagrams, or to see pointers, which led to confusion. Thus, arrowheads became dots (to indicate the *heavy* end of the relationship).

6.3.4 Nonspecific Relationships

To this point, all of the relationships we have seen have been one-to-many relationships. We can use one-to-many relationships to associate a single parent entity instance with many child entity instances. As we have seen, however, there are situations in which many instances of one entity must be associated with many instances of another entity.

Consider Fig. 6.11, first presented in Chapter 4 as Fig. 4.7. It shows a many-to-many relationship between a PERSON and an ADDRESS. Moreover, because the relationship line is a solid line not a dashed line, it seems to say that the relationship is identifying in both directions. That's a bit strange.

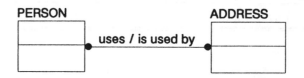

Figure 6.11. Nonspecific Relationship.

There is nothing wrong with this relationship from a conceptual point of view, provided we simply are saying a PERSON <uses> many ADDRESSs and an ADDRESS <is used by> many PERSONs. Indeed, there is an IDEF1X model, the entity relationship diagram, in which this relationship is allowed, and often encouraged. In an ERD, we aren't concerned about keys; we are striving to capture broad concepts. This many-to-many relationship, graphically represented as a solid line with dots on both ends, is called a *nonspecific relationship*.

> **Definition: Nonspecific Relationship**
>
> **A presentation style relationship in which no foreign keys are contributed, and in which many instances of one entity are related to many instances of another entity.**

In the world of keys, nonspecific relationships don't make sense. If we apply what we know about identifying relationships and independent entities to Fig. 6.11, we discover that the key of PERSON must be part of the key of ADDRESS and the key of ADDRESS must be part of the key of PERSON. But ADDRESSs are identified by their own keys, and likewise for PERSONs (the entity shapes have square corners). We therefore have an illogical statement.

Nonspecific relationships are allowed only in an entity relationship diagram. In key based and fully attributed models, all relationships are (zero-or)-one-to-something. Nonspecific relationships are not allowed. Nevertheless, in key based and fully attributed models, we still must be able to record multiple associations between two entities. We saw how to do this in Figs. 4.11 and 5.1; let's review it in more detail using Fig. 6.12.

6.3.5 Resolving Nonspecific Relationships

In Fig. 6.12, we have added an associative entity called ADDRESS-USAGE and turned the many-to-many relationship into a pair of one-to-many relationships. Let's follow the keys. The key of PERSON ("person-id") migrates to the associative entity, as does the key of ADDRESS ("address-id"). These are not the only key attributes of ADDRESS-USAGE. Notice the third part, "usage-type".

Nonspecific relationships often hide meaning. To illustrate, in Fig. 6.11, we see that PERSONs use many ADDRESSs, but cannot see *how* the ADDRESSs are used. In the expanded structure in Fig. 6.12, we can see how; the attribute "usage-type" tells us. A question now is, Why is this attribute in the key area, and not in the data area?

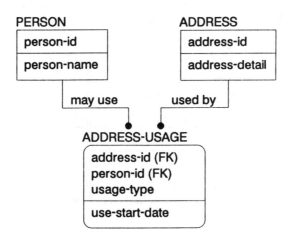

Figure 6.12. Resolved Nonspecific Relationship.

To answer, we must know what business rules the model represents. If a single PERSON can use a single ADDRESS in only a single way, then "usage-type" can be in the data area and we still can tell how the address is used. But if a PERSON can use the same ADDRESS in many ways (for example, both as a mailing address and as a residence address), and if "address-usage" is in the data area, there is no way to record this information. The sample instance table in Table 6.3 and definitions following it illustrate this point.

Table 6.3.
Resolved Nonspecific Relationship Example.

PERSON

person-id	person-name
P1	Ben
P2	Margaret
P3	Tom
P4	John
P5	Leon

ADDRESS

address-id	address-detail
A1	Princeton
A2	New Brunswick
A3	Berkeley 1
A4	Berkeley 2
A5	New York City

ADDRESS-USAGE

person-id	address-id	usage-type	use-start-date	0 0 0
P1	A1	business	01 Jun 88	
P1	A2	residence	15 Sep 86	
P1	A2	mailing	15 Sep 86	
P2	A1	business	01 Jan 89	
P3	A1	business	01 Feb 89	
P3	A3	residence	15 May 75	
P3	A3	mailing	01 Jun 75	
P3	A4	mailing	01 Mar 89	
P4	A5	residence	30 Sep 87	

<------------------------------- Key Area -------------------------------> <-------------- Data Area -------------->

PERSON:	Someone we want to keep track of.
ADDRESS:	A place at which a PERSON can be contacted.
ADDRESS-USAGE:	The recording of a way in which a PERSON uses an AD-DRESS along with information about that use.

We see from the ADDRESS-USAGE section of Table 6.3 that Ben uses two addresses: Princeton and New Brunswick. We also see that he uses New Brunswick in two different ways: as residence and mailing addresses. Tom has a similar situation for Berkeley. If "usage-type" is not part of the key of ADDRESS-USAGE, there can only be a single instance that pairs Ben with New Brunswick (P1/A2). That means only one use of the New Brunswick address can be recorded for Ben. The question is, Which one, residence or mailing?

We might argue that if residence is indicated, mailing can be assumed. But that doesn't seem to be the case for John in New York (P4/A5). If we want to allow a PERSON to use an ADDRESS in more than one way, we must place the "usage-type" attribute in the key area of ADDRESS-USAGE.

6.3.6 Reading Many-to-Many Relationships

Let's return to Fig. 6.12 and read the relationships. Recall that in Chapter 4 we had trouble reading them. When we choose verb phrases for relationships from parent entities to child associative entities, we must use a consistent style and pattern for reading the relationships. The standard pattern of reading directly from the parent to the child can be used, but becomes tedious. The style used in Fig. 6.12 is different from this standard pattern.

Many IDEF1X modelers adopt the style shown in Fig. 6.12, preferring to read *through* the associative entity, especially at the higher levels of detail. If you read the relationship *through* the associative entity to the entity on the other side, you come up with reasonable statements, in this case, "An ADDRESS is <used by> zero or more PERSONs (through ADDRESS-USAGEs)," and "A PERSON <may use> zero or more ADDRESSs (through ADDRESS-USAGEs)."

The standard pattern of reading directly from parent to child is theoretically more correct than reading through, but it is also more cumbersome. The structure of the model is exactly the same when the standard pattern is used, but the verb phrases are different. Figure 6.13 shows the address example using the standard pattern.

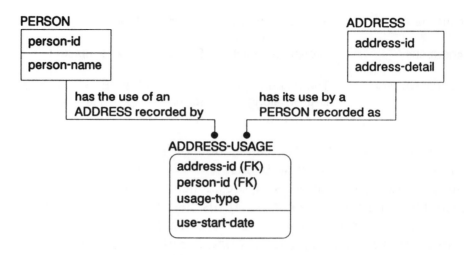

Figure 6.13. Standard Verb Phrases.

Notice that the verb phrases have become fairly long. They are read as,

A PERSON <has the use of an ADDRESS recorded by> zero or more AD-
DRESS-USAGEs.

An ADDRESS <has its use by a PERSON recorded as> zero or more AD-
DRESS-USAGEs.

As you become familiar with the modeling techniques described in this chapter
and apply them to real projects, you will undoubtedly develop your own style
for choosing verb phrases. Whatever style you choose, be consistent. Deciding
how to record verb phrases for relationships is not too difficult when the
structures are fairly simple, as in the examples, but can become difficult when
the structures become more complex. Often the entities on either side of an
associative entity are themselves associative entities, which represent other
many-to-many relationships. Try constructing consistent verb phrases in different styles for Figs. 6.14 and 6.15 in the next section.

As we will discuss further in Chapter 8, a textual description is normally
presented along with an information model diagram and its entity and attribute
definitions. This is the third part of the information model (along with the
diagram and definitions), and is a translation of the model structure into
natural language. The description can be precise or imprecise, depending on
the audience and the purpose of the model. It is called a view description and
provides a guided tour through the rules and constraints. View descriptions

help an audience read the relationships in the model. Several are provided in the case study in Part Three. The discussion following the introductory video store example in Chapter 4 is a view description.

6.3.7 Associative Entities and N-ary Relationships

IDEF1X, unlike some modeling languages, insists that all relationships be binary, that is, they must connect exactly two entities. This does not mean that three, four, or n-ary relationships are not needed, only that these situations are addressed with another construct, the associative entity.

To understand associative entities, we need to be clear on the meaning of the term *relationship;* it is important to distinguish between the line that connects two entities and the general concept of a way that two things are *related.* The concept of "relationship," as used in IDEF1X, means the line, along with the cardinality statement, verb phrase, and any other constraints that can be stated. This line is sometimes referred to as an arc connecting two nodes on the diagram (where the nodes are the entities). In IDEF1X, the general concept of relationship, meaning a way in which two things are related, is represented by the associative entity when the relationship is information bearing and therefore needs attributes. When the relationship requires no attributes, it is represented by the IDEF1X relationship line.

All of the relationships we have been discussing have been IDEF1X binary relationships, that is, the line has connected exactly two entities. We separate many-to-many relationships into pairs of one-to-manys. Associations among three or more entities are represented in a similar way. The relationship line does not connect the three or more entities. Rather, the n-ary relationship is represented as a set of n binary relationships to an associative entity.

As an example, consider the business rules in Fig. 6.14. The figure shows that a CONTRACT represents a three-way association among COMPANY, PRODUCT, and CUSTOMER. The structure indicates that many COMPANYs sell many PRODUCTs to many CUSTOMERs.

Associations among four or more entities can be constructed in a similar way. When we see such a structure, however, business questions need to be asked; the rules need to be clarified. For example, must a PRODUCT be offered by a COMPANY before it can be sold? Can a CUSTOMER establish a single CONTRACT including PRODUCTs from several different COMPANYs? Must we keep track of which CUSTOMERs belong to which COMPANYs? Depending on the answers, the structure may change.

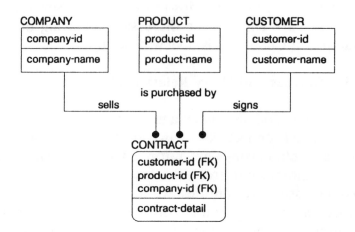

Figure 6.14. Representing a Three-Way Relationship.

If, for example, the answer to the first question is yes and the answers to the second and third are no, we must change the structure to that shown in Fig. 6.15. Notice that the single three-way association has been replaced by two two-way associations.

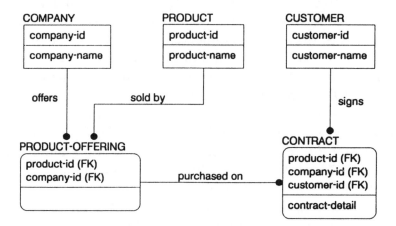

Figure 6.15. Decomposed Three-Way Relationship.

By asking these kinds of business questions, we can break most n-ary associations into a series of binary ones. It is rare to see a real three-way associative entity in a detailed IDEF1X model. It is even more rare to see fours, fives, and so on.

6.4 REVIEW EXERCISES

Answers to boldface questions appear in Appendix H.

1. Figure 6.3 depicts a structure that can be used for the classic bill of materials problem. Create a diagram and a sample instance table that show how a PART (either an ASSEMBLY or a BASE-PART) can be represented as a grouping of other parts, which themselves have parts, and so on.

2. **Some modeling languages do not have separate graphic symbols for relationships that have no attributes and relationships that have attributes. IDEF1X uses different symbols for these situations. What are the different symbols?**

3. Figure 6.9 allows a company to be owned by only one other company. Draw a diagram that allows a company to be owned by more than one other company. Show with sample instance tables how it supports the following ownership structure.

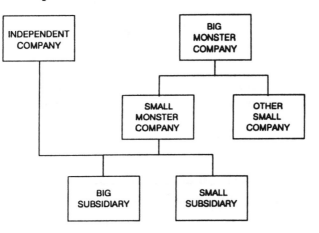

4. **Create a model from the following list of attributes:**

    *   salesperson-id   *   customer-id
    *   salesperson-name *   territory-sales-target
    *   order-customer-id *   territory-salesperson-id

- customer-name
- customer-rating
- territory-id
- quota
- size

- territory-name
- order-number
- order-status
- order-salesperson-id

5. What business questions does the structure shown here raise? Draw different structures that provide different answers to the questions.

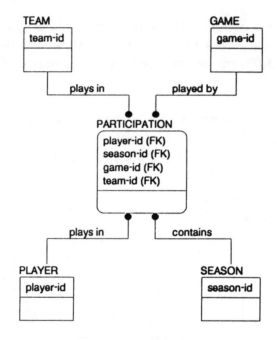

6. **For each of the following diagrams, explain why the primary key of entity A must be an alternate key of entity B.**

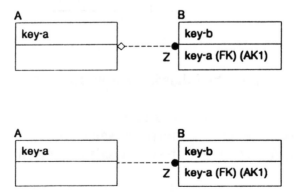

7

GENERALIZATION

When we look at an object in the physical world, we almost immediately classify it as something more abstract. If we see a sparrow or an eagle, we classify it as a bird. If we see a Ferrari, we classify it as a fast car. We tend to see objects as types of something we already know. This classification allows us to infer more about the object at hand.

Our sparrow, for example, might be sitting in a cage or on the branch of a tree. But because we know it is a bird and know birds can fly, we know the sparrow can fly. Even though we might not see the Ferrari's engine, we know that because a Ferrari is a car and cars have engines, it must have one. Sparrows and Ferraris, being types of some other general concept, inherit the properties of that generalization.

One of the most powerful features of the IDEF1X language is its treatment of generalization, the notion that some things are types of other things, and the inverse, categorization. Categorization is the notion that a thing comes in various types. This is a rich part of the language used to simplify data structures and declare business rules that constrain the allowed associations among entities.

So far we have discussed several types of IDEF1X entities. We have discussed independent entities and two types of dependent entities, characteristic and associative. We have also discussed identifying and nonidentifying relationships, and classified relationships by their cardinality, that is one-to-one, one-to-many, and many-to-many (nonspecific). There are two other types of entities: the category entity and the generic parent (generalization) entity; and one other relationship: the category relationship.

This chapter discusses these remaining entity and relationship types. It begins with a discussion of how to form a generalization hierarchy and how to simplify one that has become unmanageable. Overcoming problems with constraints stated in generalization hierarchies is covered next and the chapter ends with a caution about not taking the generalization concept too far.

7.1 FORMING A GENERALIZATION HIERARCHY

Definition: Generalization Hierarchy

A hierarchical grouping of entities that share common characteristics.

A brief introduction to generalization hierarchies was provided in Chapter 4 and illustrated in Fig. 4.5, repeated here as Fig. 7.1. In the discussion in Chapter 4, we concluded that an ACCOUNT (the generic parent) is either a CHECKING-ACCOUNT, a SAVINGS-ACCOUNT, or a LOAN-ACCOUNT (the categories). Each category is an ACCOUNT and inherits the properties of ACCOUNT. The three different categories of ACCOUNT are mutually exclusive.

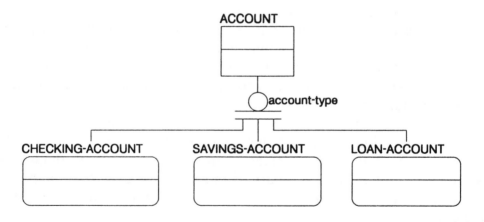

Figure 7.1. Generalization Hierarchy.

To see how category and generic parent (generalization) entities and category relationships are used in information models, let's look at the process by which the hierarchy was formed. We start with some definitions.

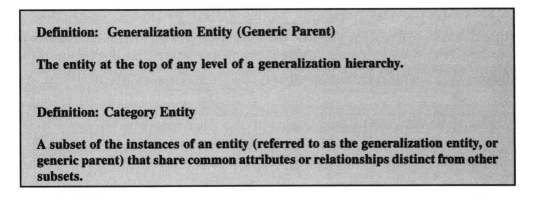

Definition: Generalization Entity (Generic Parent)

The entity at the top of any level of a generalization hierarchy.

Definition: Category Entity

A subset of the instances of an entity (referred to as the generalization entity, or generic parent) that share common attributes or relationships distinct from other subsets.

7.1.1 Collecting Common Attributes

Let's assume that in developing a model, we have found the three entities in Fig. 7.2. As we develop descriptions of the different types of ACCOUNTs, we will recognize similarities among the independent entities. To form a generalization hierarchy, the first thing we do is find attributes common to all three types of accounts. Then, we move these common attributes into a higher-level entity called the generic parent. Attributes specific to the individual account types will remain in the category entities.

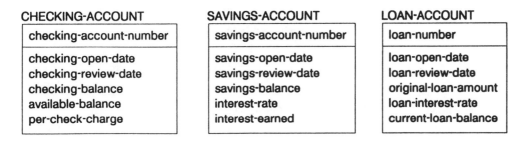

CHECKING-ACCOUNT

checking-account-number
checking-open-date
checking-review-date
checking-balance
available-balance
per-check-charge

SAVINGS-ACCOUNT

savings-account-number
savings-open-date
savings-review-date
savings-balance
interest-rate
interest-earned

LOAN-ACCOUNT

loan-number
loan-open-date
loan-review-date
original-loan-amount
loan-interest-rate
current-loan-balance

Figure 7.2. Separate ACCOUNT Entities.

Now, we need a primary key for our generic parent, ACCOUNT. Let's assume we have not yet chosen the physical system keys for the three types of accounts. (If we have, another similar structure is needed, which we will examine in Chapter 8.) Here, we are working at a logical, or conceptual, level. We give ACCOUNT the key "account-number". The new "account-number" attribute takes the place of the original "checking-account-number", "savings-account-number", and "loan-number" attributes.

Next, we need an attribute, called a *category discriminator,* that will distinguish one type of ACCOUNT from another. The attribute needs to be common to all three category entities and have a value that discriminates one category of ACCOUNT from the others.

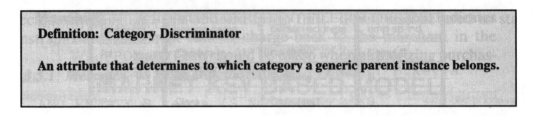

Definition: Category Discriminator

An attribute that determines to which category a generic parent instance belongs.

For the three types of ACCOUNT, there is no such common attribute—balances, open dates, and account numbers aren't suitable; therefore, we must create one. We create the attribute "account-type" as the category discriminator. It is an attribute of ACCOUNT. Next, we add the three categories, CHECKING-AC-COUNT, SAVINGS-ACCOUNT, and LOAN-ACCOUNT. Each category is an ACCOUNT and inherits all of the properties of ACCOUNT. To this point, our diagram looks like Fig. 7.3.

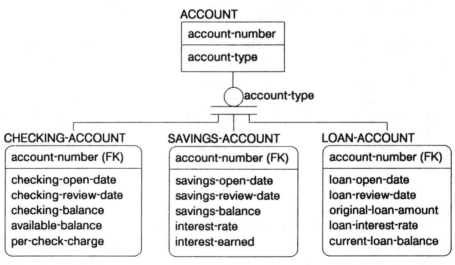

Figure 7.3. Partially Completed Generalization Hierarchy.

In our example, ACCOUNT is the generic parent. CHECKING-ACCOUNT, SAV-INGS-ACCOUNT, and LOAN-ACCOUNT are the category entities. Thus, we have the two remaining types of IDEF1X entities. A category entity is always a dependent entity since it inherits its key from the generic parent. A generic parent can be either a dependent or independent entity.

Generalization hierarchies also contain the final type of IDEF1X relationship, the category relationship. This relationship connects the generic parent to the category and, from the perspective of the generic parent, is a one-to-zero-or-one relationship with the implicit verb phrase *is a*. We sometimes hear this referred to as an *is a* relationship. Each instance of the generic parent either *is a* instance of the category or it's not. Each instance of the category entity *is a* instance of the generic parent. Category discriminators, as we will see in the following sections, declare constraints over the allowed combinations of instances of the category entities.

To complete the generalization hierarchy, we compare the attributes of the three categories. Each has an "open-date". If and only if the definitions of the three kinds of "open-date" are the same, we move them to the generic parent and drop them from the categories. For this example, we will assume that the definitions are the same. The three attributes *unify* into "account-open-date". By similar analysis, we get an "account-review-date". Each of the three categories of ACCOUNT, therefore, has an "account-open-date" and an "account-review-date". However, we will no longer see these attributes in the categories; they are inherited from the generic parent.

Continuing the analysis, we see all three categories have some sort of balance. CHECKING-ACCOUNT has two (checking and available), SAVINGS-ACCOUNT has one, and LOAN-ACCOUNT has two. The question now is, Should we move the balances up to the generic parent? Again, the answer lies in the definitions. Assuming we have good definitions, we might find "checking-balance", "savings-balance", and "current-loan-balance" mean almost, but not quite, the same thing. In that case, they would stay with the category entities. Or, perhaps we find that "checking-balance" and "savings-balance" are the same but "current-loan-balance" is very different.

In cases in which almost all of a set of attributes are the same but a few are different, there are two options: Either leave the attributes with their categories, or move up the ones that are the same and leave the others behind.

If we leave the attributes where they are, we must make sure they have unique names but can base the definitions of those that are the same on a common base attribute or glossary term that does not appear on the model diagram. This base attribute or glossary term is given a name that will be meaningful from the perspective of the attributes remaining in the categories.

Suppose in our account example we determine that "savings-balance" and "checking-balance" have identical definitions (for example, the amount of funds recorded in the account, including immediate credit for deposits, even if those deposits have not yet been verified). We could then define a base attribute named "account-balance" (which includes the distinction regarding unverified deposits) but not include it on the diagram. We would then define the category attributes named "savings-account-balance" (or, simply, "savings-balance") and "checking-account-balance" (or "checking-balance") based on the definition of "account-balance". This would mean that we would not have to include the concept of unverified deposits in the definitions of the savings and checking balances. Each would simply be defined as an "account-balance" for the checking or savings category.

If we move the attributes up to the generic parent, the value of the generic parent attribute will be null when the value of the category discriminator specifies a category from which the attribute was not moved (in this case, for the LOAN-ACCOUNT category). Non-key attributes, unlike key attributes, may be allowed to be null.

Which alternative to choose depends on how many of the categories share the common attribute and the purpose of the diagram. If most categories share an attribute, it is good practice in a high-level model to move it up. If few categories share the attribute, it is best to leave it where it is. In more detailed models, it is often appropriate to leave all attributes in their categories (with unique names).

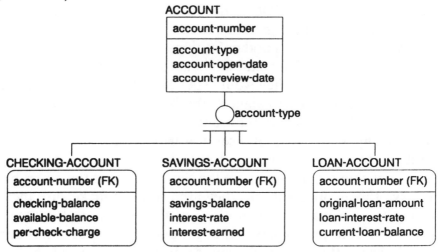

Figure 7.4. Account Generalization Hierarchy—First Alternative.

For this example, if we leave the balances where they are, we end up with Fig. 7.4 and its sample instance table, Table 7.1. Let's assume we decide to leave the rest of the attributes in the categories by determining from their definitions that they are, indeed, different things.

Table 7.1.
Account Generalization Hierarchy—
First Alternative Instance Example.

ACCOUNT

account-number	account-type	account-open-date	account-review-date
1	check	1/15/76	12/1/91
2	check	6/10/82	10/5/91
3	save	7/22/82	10/1/92
4	save	3/30/88	11/5/92
5	loan	4/15/80	10/1/91
6	loan	9/15/88	10/1/92

CHECKING-ACCOUNT

account-number	checking-balance	available-balance	per-check-charge
1	12,000	11,500	.15
2	500	500	.20

SAVINGS-ACCOUNT

account-number	savings-balance	interest-rate	interest-earned
3	45,000	6.5%	1,443
4	1,225	5.0%	85

LOAN-ACCOUNT

account-number	original-loan-amount	loan-interest-rate	current-loan-balance
5	80,000	8.8%	52,447
6	25,000	12.2%	21,339

If we had decided to move the balance attributes up to the generic parent, we would have ended up with Fig. 7.5 and its sample instance table, Table 7.2. Note the null values of the "account-balance" attribute when the account represents a loan.

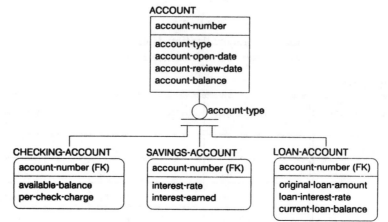

Figure 7.5. Account Generalization Hierarchy—Second Alternative.

Table 7.2.
Account Generalization Hierarchy—
Second Alternative Sample Instance Example.

ACCOUNT

account-number	account-type	account-bal-ance	account-open-date	account-review-date
1	check	12,000	1/15/76	12/1/91
2	check	500	6/10/82	10/5/91
3	save	45,000	7/22/82	10/1/92
4	save	1,225	3/30/88	11/5/92
5	loan	null	4/15/80	10/1/91
6	loan	null	9/15/88	10/1/92

CHECKING-ACCOUNT

account-number	available-balance	per-check-charge
1	11,500	.15
2	500	.20

SAVINGS-ACCOUNT

account-number	interest-rate	interest-earned
3	6.5%	1,443
4	5.0%	85

LOAN-ACCOUNT

account-number	original-loan-amount	loan-interest-rate	current-loan-balance
5	80,000	8.8%	52,447
6	25,000	12.2%	21,339

7.1.2 Using Ands and Ors

The category structure we just reviewed was an *or* structure. Each ACCOUNT was a CHECKING-ACCOUNT *or* a SAVINGS-ACCOUNT *or* a LOAN-ACCOUNT. No ACCOUNT could be more than one type at a time. The *or* structure generally reflects a view of accounts that was common in the financial sector until the 1980s.

Over time, the view of accounts has changed. Financial institutions have seen that it is to their advantage to combine the features of multiple account types into a single account. The new view of ACCOUNT is fundamentally different from the *or* situation depicted in Figs. 7.4 and 7.5. The new business rule is that an ACCOUNT might be a CHECKING-ACCOUNT, a SAVINGS-AC-COUNT, and a LOAN-ACCOUNT, *all at the same time.* A different structure, shown in Fig. 7.6, is used to represent this situation. This is an *and* structure. Notice that there are now three category discriminators, and three category symbols. Figure 7.6 says that an ACCOUNT may be simultaneously a CHECK-ING-ACCOUNT *and* a SAVINGS-ACCOUNT and a LOAN-ACCOUNT. The three category discriminators will tell us whether the ACCOUNT has checking, savings, and loan characteristics.

Ands and *ors* can be mixed. For example, in Fig. 7.7, each ACCOUNT must be either a CHECKING-ACCOUNT or a SAVINGS-ACCOUNT and at the same time may be a LOAN-ACCOUNT (an overdraft protection feature perhaps). The attributes of the various types of accounts are still placed in the categories and common attributes are moved up to the generic parent, but the category structure gives us a new *and plus or* business rule.

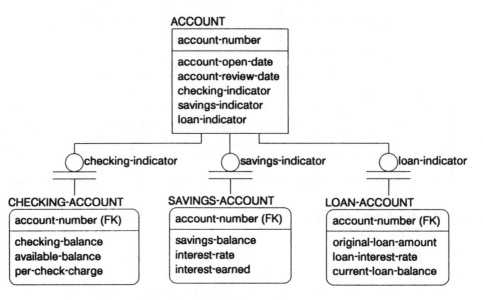

Figure 7.6. The *And* Category Structure.

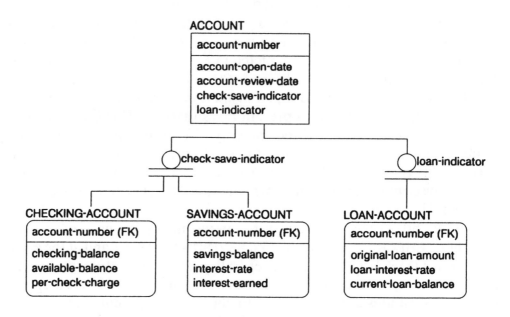

Figure 7.7. The *And Plus Or* Category Structure.

7.1.3 Specifying Complete and Incomplete Category Structures

Category structures are specified as either complete or incomplete. A complete structure displays all of the possible categories. An incomplete structure displays only some of the possible categories. Different notation is used to specify whether the set of categories is complete or incomplete. A single line at the bottom of the category symbol specifies an incomplete structure. A double line specifies a complete structure. This notation is shown in Fig. 7.8.

INCOMPLETE
CATEGORY
STRUCTURE

COMPLETE
CATEGORY
STRUCTURE

Figure 7.8. Category Notation.

In Fig. 7.9, an EMPLOYEE can be a CONSULTANT, a FULL-TIME-EMPLOYEE, or something else. The single-line notation at the bottom of the category symbol indicates the structure is incomplete. In other words, there may be categories that are not included on the diagram.

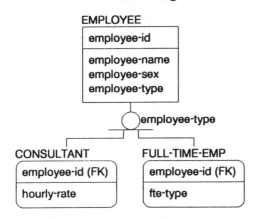

Figure 7.9. Incomplete Category Structure.

In contrast, Fig. 7.10 shows a complete structure. Notice the double-line notation at the bottom of the category symbol. In Fig. 7.10, an EMPLOYEE is either a MALE-EMPLOYEE or a FEMALE-EMPLOYEE. There are no other kinds.

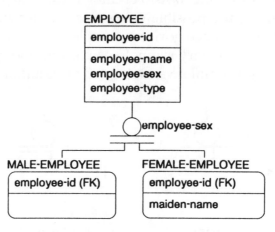

Figure 7.10. Complete Category Structure.

Figure 7.11 shows a combination of complete and incomplete category structures. In this example, the EMPLOYEE may be either a FULL-TIME-EMP or a CONSULTANT *and, at the same time,* must be either a MALE-EMPLOYEE or a FEMALE-EMPLOYEE. The implication is that there may be other undiscovered or hidden categories beyond CONSULTANT and FULL-TIME-EMP, but there are no undiscovered nor hidden sexes.

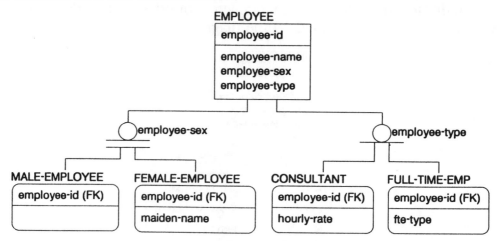

Figure 7.11. Mixed Category Structure.

Figure 7.12 extends the structure. Another level of categories below FULL-TIME-EMP, as well as BENEFIT-ACCOUNT and its categories, are added. As the structures become more complex, they make more explicit statements about the allowed combinations of the instances of the category entities. It is wise to test complex structures with sample instance tables to ensure that they are meaningful. Table 7.3 shows a set of sample instance tables for Fig. 7.12. Note that the tenth employee has an "employee-type" that designates neither full-time nor consultant, which is consistent with the incomplete category constraint stated in the diagram. Note also that no CONSULTANT has a BENEFIT-ACCOUNT.

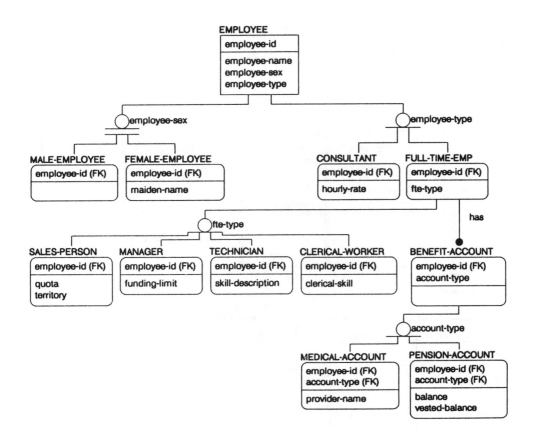

Figure 7.12. Mixed Multi-Level Category Structure.

Table 7.3.
Mixed Multi-Level Category Structure Example.

EMPLOYEE

employee-id	employee-name	employee-sex	employee-type
1	John Smith	M	C
2	Lisa Underhill	F	C
3	Tad Turner	M	F
4	George Jensen	M	F
5	Arlys Watson	F	F
6	Bob Jones	M	F
7	Karen Brown	F	C
8	Randy Andrews	M	C
9	Cathy Norton	F	F
10	Alice Bookend	F	S

MALE-EMPLOYEE

employee-id
1
3
4
6
8

FEMALE-EMPLOYEE

employee-id	maiden-name
2	Foote
5	Johnson
7	Jones
9	Lawrence

CONSULTANT

employee-id	hourly-rate
2	100
7	75
8	50

FULL-TIME-EMP

employee-id	fte-type
1	C
3	S
4	T
5	C
6	M
9	S

SALES-PERSON

employee-id	quota	territory
3	10,000	USA
9	8,000	Europe

MANAGER	
employee-id	funding-limit
6	100,000

TECHNICIAN	
employ-ee-id	skill-des-cription
4	database

CLERICAL-WORKER	
employ-ee-id	clerical-skill
1	office
5	accounting

BENEFIT-ACCOUNT

employ-ee-id	account-type
1	M
1	P
3	M
3	P
4	P
5	M
5	P
6	M
9	M
9	P

MEDICAL-ACCOUNT

employ-ee-id	account-type	provid-er-name
1	M	Blue X
3	M	Blue S
5	M	Kaiser
6	M	Blue X
9	M	Blue S

PENSION-ACCOUNT

employ-ee-id	account-type	balance	vested-balance
1	P	18,000	18,000
3	P	3,000	600
4	P	13,000	7,500
5	P	5,000	2,000
9	P	20,000	6,000

7.1.4 Collecting Common Relationships

As we have discussed, one reason to form a generalization hierarchy is to collect attributes common to a set of entities and move the attributes into a higher-level entity called a generic parent. Another reason to form a generalization hierarchy is to collect common relationships from category entities and convert the relationships into a single relationship from a generic parent. Relationships specific to the categories remain with the categories; those that are common move up.

For example, Fig. 7.12 includes a relationship between FULL-TIME-EMP and BENEFIT-ACCOUNT. This relationship does not come from the EMPLOYEE entity (a generic parent), but from one of its categories (which is itself the generic parent for the second level of the hierarchy). The business rule captured by this relationship is that it is only FULL-TIME-EMPs who may have BENEFIT-ACCOUNTs. An EMPLOYEE who is a CONSULTANT is not permitted to have a BENEFIT-ACCOUNT.

Recall that each of the categories of ACCOUNT presented in Fig. 7.4 (loan, checking, or savings) *is* an ACCOUNT and inherits all of the properties of ACCOUNT, for example, the attributes "account-open-date" and "account-review-date". Category entities also inherit the relationships in which their generic parents participate. Therefore, in Fig. 7.12, each of the categories of FULL-TIME-EMP inherits the relationship to BENEFIT-ACCOUNT. This means that any SALES-PERSON, MANAGER, TECHNICIAN, or CLERICAL-WORKER can have a BENEFIT-ACCOUNT.

Just as with attributes shared by some but not all of the categories, we have a dilemma as to what to do with relationships shared by some but not all categories. We must choose either to move them up (giving null relationships in some cases) or to leave them behind. In Section 7.1.6, we will look at ways to make the choice.

7.1.5 Deciding When to Form a Generalization Hierarchy

There are three reasons to form a generalization hierarchy. First, the entities share a common set of attributes. This was the case in the ACCOUNT examples (Figs. 7.4, 7.5, 7.6, and 7.7). Second, the entities share a common set of relationships, which is important to show on the diagram. This was the case with the FULL-TIME-EMP to BENEFIT-ACCOUNT relationship in Fig. 7.12.

Third, categories of an entity should be shown in business models—the entity relationship diagram and initial key based model—if the business situation requires it (usually for communication or understanding) even if the categories have no attributes that are different and even if they participate in no relationships distinct from other categories. Remember, one of the major purposes of a model is to help communicate information structures; if showing categories does so, then show them. Be careful, however, not to overdo it and lose the meaning of the model in a web of detailed category structures and relationships among the categories.

7.1.6 Collapsing Relationships Among Categories

Chapters 4 and 5 introduced the group attribute and discussed the concept of a composite domain. A composite domain can be used to simplify diagram structures in some models while retaining the business rules that must be enforced. One common use of a composite domain is to collapse relationships among category structures,

The diagram in Fig. 7.13 is a bit overwhelming. It appears to be almost entirely a description of the allowed relationships among the categories of two generalization hierarchies. It says, for example, that category CA-1 may be related to category CB-1 (via the relationship embodied in the associative entity A-1), that category CA-1 may also be related to category CB-2 (via A-2), and so on.

Figure 7.13 might be useful to a programmer writing code to ensure the integrity of the database, but would not be very effective to communicate the general concept that certain categories of GP-B can be linked to certain categories of GP-A. To communicate this general concept, Fig. 7.14 and Table 7.4 do a better job.

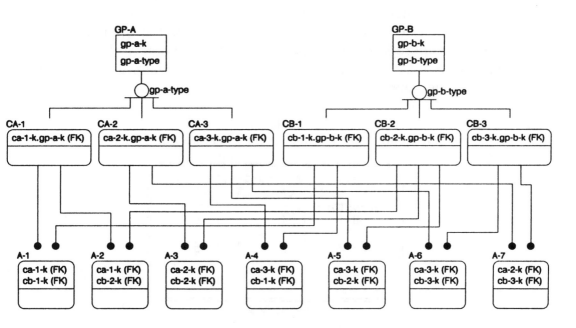

Figure 7.13. Specific Relationships Among Categories.

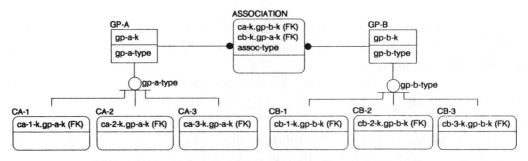

Figure 7.14. Generalized Relationship Among Categories.

Table 7.4 is not a sample instance table. Rather, it shows the categories of the GP-A and GP-B entities as the rows and columns. These rows and columns correspond to the allowed values (domains) of the category discriminators "gp-a-type" and "gp-b-type".

The row/column intersections (cells) marked with the "-" designate combinations of values of the category discriminators not allowed when GP-A instances are paired with GP-B instances in the ASSOCIATION entity. The numbers in the other cells designate allowed combinations of the category discriminators and correspond to entries in the legend at the bottom of the table. The legend represents the domain of the third part of the primary key group of the ASSOCIATION entity, the "assoc-type" attribute. The text descriptions specify the meanings of the allowed associations.

Table 7.4.
Generalized Relationship Among Collapsed Categories.

	← gp-a-type →		
gp-b-type	CA-1	CA-2	CA-3
CB-1	1	–	4
CB-2	2	3	5
CB-3	–	7	6

assoc-type:

1: Description of association embodied in original entity A-1
2: Description of association embodied in original entity A-2
• • •
7: Description of association embodied in original entity A-7
etc.

Table 7.4 represents a composite domain. It specifies constraints governing the allowed combinations of values of the three attributes "gp-a-type", "gp-b-type", and "assoc-type". Figure 7.14 along with Table 7.4 state exactly the same constraints as Fig. 7.13. The detail, however, is no longer seen in the diagram; it is provided in the table.

Collapsing category structures in this way, especially in high-level models and especially if the categories being collapsed exist only to show the allowed relationships, can significantly improve the communication aspects of diagrams. The information model is described by both the diagram and the definitions of its objects. It is sometimes best to limit the structure of the diagram to what is most important to communicate to an audience and capture the detail in other ways, for example, by declaring a composite domain.

7.2 OVERCOMING GENERALIZATION HIERARCHY PROBLEMS

There are some situations in which IDEF1X graphics aren't able to state a business rule, and these are areas of continuing development of the language. Two of these situations relating to generalization hierarchies are Boolean constraints and key substitution. This section discusses these situations and provides ways to handle them until a systematic treatment is adopted by IDEF1X.

7.2.1 Boolean Constraints

As we have seen, IDEF1X provides good support for simple generalization structures. Figure 7.15 shows a simple Boolean constraint (an exclusive *or*) in which a BUSINESS-PARTY can be either an EMPLOYEE or a DEPARTMENT, must be one or the other, and cannot be both.

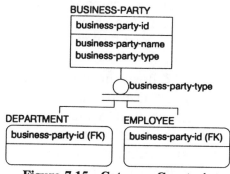

Figure 7.15. Category Constraint.

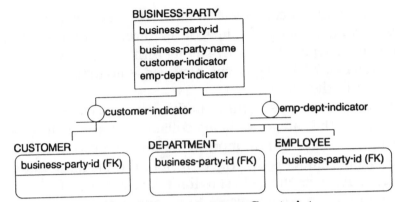

Figure 7.16. Additional Category Constraint.

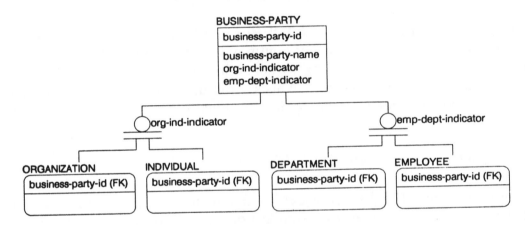

Figure 7.17. Erroneous Category Constraint.

We have also seen that more complex category structures are possible, such as that shown in Fig. 7.16. The figure shows an *and* and *or* combined; in addition to being an EMPLOYEE or a DEPARTMENT, a BUSINESS-PARTY might also be a CUSTOMER.

A situation such as Fig. 7.17, however, poses a problem. Figure 7.17 still states that a BUSINESS-PARTY must be either an EMPLOYEE or a DEPARTMENT. In addition, it says that a BUSINESS-PARTY must be either an INDIVIDUAL or an ORGANIZATION. If we add the constraints that an INDIVIDUAL cannot be a DEPARTMENT but that an ORGANIZATION can be an EMPLOYEE, we run into trouble. There is no way to declare these constraints in the IDEF1X graphics (if you disagree with the business statements implied, turn it into a theoretical problem by substituting A, B, C, D, and E for the entity names).

What the language needs is a more complete way to handle constraints. For example, a structure like Fig. 7.18, in which a category entity can have more than one generic parent, has been considered as a possible extension, but formal treatment of constraints will probably evolve differently.

Thus, until the language is extended, one way to capture the missing constraints is through the addition of text notes. But keep in mind that doing so limits the ability to use automated tools to transform the specification represented by the model to a physical implementation. Constraints must be enforced in the physical system, and transformation tools cannot read, understand, or use constraints stated in text.

Another possible language extension is to add constructs to the graphics to capture the missing constraints. A third is to state the constraints as rules governing the insertion of instances of the various category instances. The choice is not entirely clear. To continue to add symbols to the graphics will eventually lead to diagrams that try to show so much information that they are too complex to use. Deciding where to stop extending the graphics is at the moment a judgment call. The point to keep in mind is, we must be attentive to situations like this, in which current decisions on how to capture specifications will determine how well we will be able to use them further down the road.

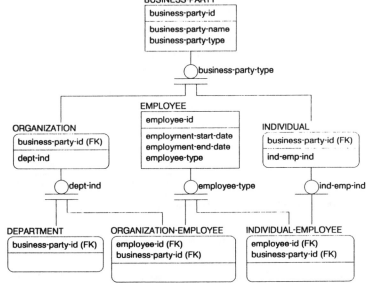

Figure 7.18. Possible Language Extension.

7.2.2 Key Substitution

IDEF1X handles alternate keys well but does not allow them to migrate across relationships. One area in which this presents a problem is in substituting alternate keys for category entities in a generalization hierarchy. For example, look at Fig. 7.19, which extends the BUSINESS-PARTY, EMPLOYEE, DEPART-MENT, and CUSTOMER example. None of the category entities contain name attributes; each inherits the attribute "business-party-name" from BUSI-NESS-PARTY. Each category entity also inherits its primary key from BUSI-NESS-PARTY, specifying the same key must be used to identify BUSINESS-PARTY in each of its roles (EMPLOYEE, DEPARTMENT, and CUSTOMER).

Suppose, however, that the business has decided to identify the CUSTOMER manifestation of BUSINESS-PARTY by an attribute called "customer-id", the EMPLOYEE manifestation by "employee-id", and the DEPARTMENT manifesta-tion by "department-id", and that each of these attributes will have a value that is not necessarily the same as the value of "business-party-id". Also assume that the three identifiers (for EMPLOYEE, DEPARTMENT, and CUSTOMER) will have different physical representations. These conditions mean we cannot simply assign new identifiers as role names for "business-party-id". If we did, the values and physical representations of the new identifiers would be inherited from the original "business-party-id".

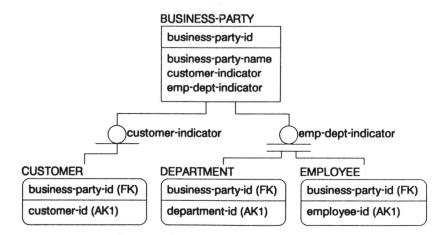

Figure 7.19. Alternate Keys in Category Entities.

Figure 7.19 says the primary identifier of each category entity is "business-party-id", while "customer-id", "department-id", and "employee-id" are alternate keys.

The primary key of a generic parent *always* becomes the primary key of each of its categories. We cannot substitute alternate keys as primary keys without losing the inheritance quality of the hierarchy. If we break the hierarchy and substitute the alternate keys, the categories will no longer inherit the "business-party-name" attribute.

Figure 7.20 shows the migration of the keys when an associative entity is used to represent a relationship between CUSTOMER and EMPLOYEE. The primary key of CUSTOMER-SUPPORT contains a pair of "business-party-id"s, which will unify into a single key attribute unless we assign them role names. If we want to see a "customer-id" and an "employee-id" in CUSTOMER-SUPPORT, not a pair of "business-party-id"s, we must abandon the generalization hierarchy structure.

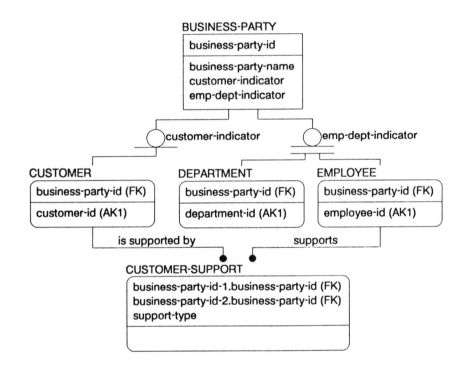

Figure 7.20. Migration of Category Keys.

If we abandon the generalization hierarchy, we can approximate it by substituting nonidentifying one-to-zero-or-one relationships for each category relationship. This will allow us to substitute the alternate keys and migrate them into CUSTOMER-SUPPORT. Figure 7.21 shows the approximation. It is a commonly used solution to overcome this problem of migrating alternate keys.

Our approximation must give up the constraint that a BUSINESS-PARTY cannot be both an EMPLOYEE and a DEPARTMENT. In addition, since CUS-TOMER, DEPARTMENT, and EMPLOYEE are no longer category entities, they no longer inherit the attributes and relationships of the original generic parent. We will need to specify application functions to enforce the rules we had originally recorded with the category structure, and we will need to record these rules somewhere outside the diagram, perhaps as text notes.

This approximation in Fig. 7.21 shows how category relationships must be implemented in a state-of-the-art 1991 relational DBMS. Even if we could state the correct constraints in the diagram, we would still have to implement the categories as separate tables structured as in the figure. The language deficiency is another issue that will eventually be addressed by a more powerful constraint language. The implementation issue will likely be addressed by the introduction of inheritance capabilities to DBMSs. Some early versions of inheritance can be seen in object-oriented systems.

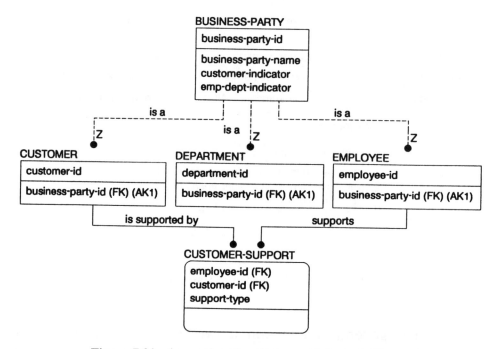

Figure 7.21. Approximating Category Alternate Keys.

7.3   RIGHT AMOUNT OF GENERALIZATION

When we construct an information model, we try to find general structures to replace several similar but independent structures. Section 7.1.6, for example, showed a complex structure (Fig. 7.13) and a less complex alternative (Fig. 7.14). The simpler diagram substituted one general associative entity for seven specific associative entities. There are situations, however, in which generalization can go too far.

Consider, for instance, the set of BUSINESS-PARTY roles described in Section 7.2.2. We could argue that the structure in Fig. 7.20 could be generalized into a two-entity structure, containing a PARTY entity and a general relationship between two parties (PARTY-ASSOCIATION). Such a solution, as shown in Fig. 7.22, might be appropriate if we are simply trying to decrease the level of detail of the diagram and are not concerned with the differences in keys in the original categories or the specific relationships that are and are not allowed. But the diagram doesn't tell us much.

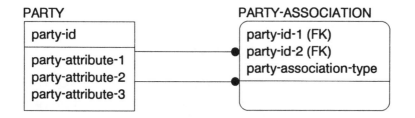

Figure 7.22.   Too Much Generalization.

It might also be useful to simplify a structure like Fig. 7.23 into one like Fig. 7.24. Again, the reason might be to make the model more suitable for a certain audience or to provide a high-level summary. It would, however, be difficult to argue that PARTY and ANIMAL are sufficiently alike as to suggest a further generalization to the structure shown in Fig. 7.25. The point is to be careful when applying the concept of generalization. Specifically, be leery of the two-entity solution.

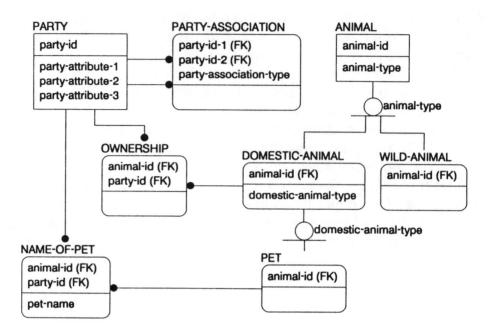

Figure 7.23. Explicit Structure.

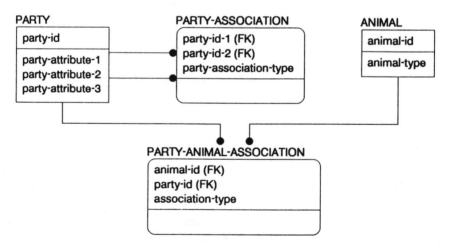

Figure 7.24. Reasonable Generalization.

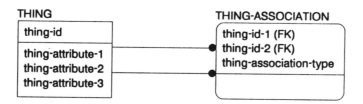

Figure 7.25. Two-Entity Solution.

How much generalization is appropriate is determined by many factors. One is the level of precision expected from the model: Do we want to record all the detail or only the general rules? Another factor is the flexibility desired in the system being described. General structures are usually more resilient to changes in the functions of the system. They are, however, more difficult to construct and maintain, and the resulting diagrams can only show some of the operative business rules. The rest of the rules must be supported by some additional method of recording constraints.

7.4   REVIEW EXERCISES

Answers to boldface questions appear in Appendix H.

1.   When should you use a generalization hierarchy in a model?

2.   **What is lost in substituting a mandatory nonidentifying "is a Z" relationship for a category relationship?**

3.   **Create a model based on the following business rules:**

   •   An account can be a deposit account and, at the same time, a loan account. There are no other types of accounts

   •   An account can have a loan balance if it is a loan and can have a deposit balance if it is a deposit account.

   •   There are at least three types of deposit accounts: checking accounts, savings accounts, and time deposits.

- There are exactly two types of loan accounts: credit lines and term loans.

- A term loan has a due date and can be either secured or unsecured.

- Secured loans require collateral, and the type of collateral must be known. One possible type of collateral is a time deposit. A time deposit may be used as collateral for at most one secured loan.

- A credit line may provide overdraft protection for any number of checking accounts.

- A credit line has a credit limit.

- The amount of available credit for a credit line must be known.

- A savings account can receive automatic transfers from only one checking account, but the same checking account can be the transfer source for any number of savings accounts.

- A savings account can be the source of automatic payments for any number of credit lines.

4. The solution to Exercise 3 involves a complex generalization hierarchy. Using the following structure, define a composite domain of the attribute group containing "account-association-type" and the five non-key attributes of each of the two involved accounts. Explain how the composite domain makes the same assertions about allowed relationships as the original generalization hierarchy.

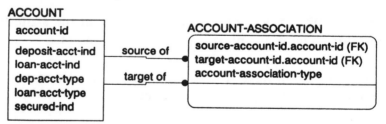

5. The following model allows us to record multiple hierarchies involving the same instances of OBJECT. Three examples are shown. Create the sample instance table from which the three given hierarchies can be derived.

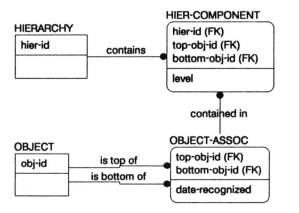

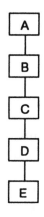

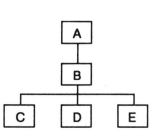

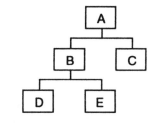

OBJECT

OBJ-ID	
A	
B	
C	
D	
E	

OBJECT-ASSOC

TOP OBJ-ID	BOTTOM OBJ-ID	DATE-RECOGNIZED

HIER-COMPONENT

HIER-ID	TOP OBJ-ID	BOTTOM OBJ-ID	LEVEL
A			
B			
C			
D			
E			

HIERARCHY

HIER-ID	
H-1	
H-2	
H-3	

8

EDGE OF THE LANGUAGE

As we have seen, IDEF1X is a powerful language for describing information structures. In this chapter, we discuss some of the language's advanced features, and a few more of its limitations.

Much of the power of IDEF1X lies in its handling of constraints. A primary objective of information modeling is to describe the business rules that constrain the allowed states of the data. In earlier chapters, we saw how to record many types of rules. We saw how to use different types of relationships and cardinality statements to declare existence and identification dependencies (constraints) among the entities. We saw how to use generalization hierarchies to limit (constrain) the relationships in which sets of entities may participate. We also saw that, in some cases, alternatives to the graphic notation are needed to record the proper constraints—for example, recall our discussion of composite domain declarations in Chapter 5.

Most of the limitations of IDEF1X also lie in the area of recording complex constraints. Therefore, the chapter begins with a discussion of some of the most difficult constraint areas, and provides suggestions on how to overcome language limitations. It continues with a discussion of how to include history in models, how to use IDEF1X to describe events, and uses of surrogate keys. The chapter concludes with ways to present information models.

8.1 CONSTRAINTS

Constraint statements in a model represent business rules governing the behavior of the data structure. Each constraint must eventually be enforced in the physical system built to satisfy the requirements stated in the information model. Existence and identification constraints that can be specified with identifying, nonidentifying, and category relationships are summarized in Appendix D. These relationship constraints are often referred to as referential integrity constraints and are governed by *insert, replace,* and *delete* rules. Some relational database management systems have evolved to a point at which internal DBMS functions can be invoked to prevent database activity that would violate specific constraints. Examples include the primary key and foreign key referential assertions that can be declared when creating a set of relational tables.

Some constraints cannot be enforced in real-time by the DBMS and must therefore be enforced by application function. Enforcing referential integrity or other constraints in real-time can be expensive in terms of performance of the system, and there may be situations in which the only realistic alternative for ensuring the quality of the data is to detect and resolve violations after the fact. An excellent discussion of this topic is provided by Brown [1].

8.1.1 Insert, Replace, and Delete Rules

In Chapter 6, we looked at several aspects of relationships, including cardinality—that is, how many instances of each entity participate in the relationship—and verb phrases, which let us read the model. Here we will look at another important aspect of recording relationships—insert, replace, and delete rules. There is no formal IDEF1X graphic notation for these rules, but they need to be considered and recorded for each relationship in the model.

8.1.1.1 Insert and replace rules

Insert and replace rules are explicitly stated in the model, but are not evident unless we think about the assertions made by the relationships. These rules are stated by the relationship types and cardinality. For insert, an instance can be added only if all referenced foreign keys match existing instances in the referenced entities, unless the relationship explicitly states otherwise (for example, the diamond on a nonidentifying relationship indicates that the foreign key or keys may be null).

Let's look at an example: We've repeated Fig. 6.7 here as Fig. 8.1 to show that each instance of MOVIE-COPY holds the key of a corresponding MOVIE. Therefore, we cannot insert a MOVIE-COPY for which there is no MOVIE. The "P" on the relationship also tells us that we cannot insert a MOVIE without inserting at least one MOVIE-COPY.

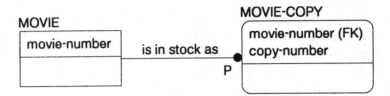

Figure 8.1. One-to-One-or-More Insert Rule.

A replace is, in effect, an insert of an instance with the same primary key (overriding all attributes of the old instance), so it is governed by the insert rules.

8.1.1.2 Delete rules

As we have just seen, insert and replace rules govern what will happen when an instance is added or changed. Delete rules govern what will happen in a database when an entity instance is deleted.

To understand delete rules, look at Fig. 8.2, which shows an identifying relationship between PROJECT and PROJECT-EMPLOYMENT. The primary key of PROJECT becomes part of the primary key of PROJECT-EMPLOYMENT. The cardinality rules say that for each instance of PROJECT-EMPLOYMENT, there is exactly one instance of PROJECT. The identifying nature of the relationship specifies that PROJECT-EMPLOYMENT is existence-dependent on PROJECT.

What would happen if we were to delete an instance of PROJECT? The diagram says we would also have to delete all instances of PROJECT-EMPLOY-MENT that inherited part of their key from the deleted PROJECT. That's because a part of the key of these PROJECT-EMPLOYMENT instances would become null, and null is not allowed as the value of any of the constituent parts of a primary key.

Therefore, when we want to delete an instance of PROJECT, we have two choices: First, delete every instance of PROJECT-EMPLOYMENT that inherited the key of the deleted instance of PROJECT or, second, prevent the deletion of PROJECT if there are any PROJECT-EMPLOYMENT instances that would end up with incomplete keys. These choices are called *cascade* and *restrict* rules, and the decision about which one to use can be recorded.

The cascade rule indicates that all instances of PROJECT-EMPLOYMENT that are affected by the deletion of an instance of PROJECT should also be deleted. The restrict rule indicates that a PROJECT cannot be deleted until all instances of PROJECT-EMPLOYMENT that inherit its key have been deleted. If there are any left, the delete is not allowed—that is, the delete is restricted. A reason to use restrict might be that there are facts recorded about a PROJECT-EMPLOYMENT, such as the "date-started" on the project, that would be lost if we were to cascade the delete. Instead, we might want to restrict the delete and mark the instance of PROJECT obsolete.

Suppose, on further analysis of the business rules governing projects and employees, we discover that PROJECT-EMPLOYMENT instances are neither existence- nor identification-dependent on PROJECT. We would then need to change the diagram by using a nonidentifying relationship between the two entities. The new diagram is shown as Fig. 8.3.

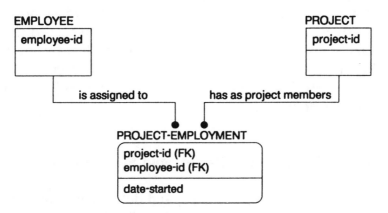

Figure 8.2. Existence-Dependency.

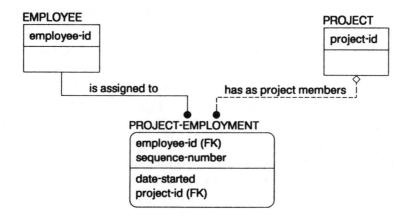

Figure 8.3. Existence-Independence.

In this case, the situation is a bit different. As we know, a foreign key contributed across a nonidentifying relationship is allowed to be null (the diamond notation). Therefore, for a nonidentifying relationship, we have a third delete option called *set null.*

Set null indicates that if an instance of PROJECT is deleted and the key of that PROJECT is held as data about a PROJECT-EMPLOYMENT, the foreign key should be set to null in the PROJECT-EMPLOYMENT instance. The delete does not cascade as in the previous example, and we do not prohibit the delete, as in restrict. We set the foreign keys to null. The advantage of this approach to the relationship is that we may be able to preserve some information about a PROJECT-EMPLOYMENT while effectively breaking the connection between the PROJECT-EMPLOYMENT and the PROJECT.

In summary, rules governing what to do when an instance is deleted are called delete rules. Delete rules are another way to record the rules of the business. Decisions to use cascade and set null reflect business decisions to delete the historical knowledge of relationships represented by the foreign keys.

A complete description of the insert and delete rules for IDEF1X relationships is given in Appendix D.

8.1.2 Referential Integrity Constraints and Structured Query Language

In physical systems, the insert, replace, and delete rules must be enforced by the database management system or the application code that maintains the content of the database. Taken together, the rules are commonly referred to as *referential integrity* rules. A database satisfies referential integrity if and only if it contains no unmatched foreign key values.

Structured Query Language is the most common language used to declare and manipulate data structures in relational database management systems. General referential integrity support is spelled out in the SQL standard [2]. Primary and foreign key assertions declared in an IDEF1X model can be directly declared to some RDBMSs like IBM's DB2 Release 2. For example, Fig. 8.4 is a small model for which the following DB2 data definition language statements will declare and enforce primary and foreign key integrity. Two tables, corresponding to ENTITY-A and ENTITY-B, are created. The declarations also cause the creation of unique indices on the primary keys of the entities and instruct the DBMS to cascade deletes for ENTITY-A.

Figure 8.4. DDL Generation Example.

```
CREATE TABLE ENTITY_A
(
key_a                     INTEGER                NOT NULL,
PRIMARY KEY (key_a)
);

CREATE UNIQUE INDEX X_ENTITY_A
    ON ENTITY_A (key_a);


CREATE TABLE ENTITY_B
(
key_b                     INTEGER                NOT NULL,
key_a                     INTEGER,
PRIMARY KEY (key_b),
FOREIGN KEY  (key_a)
    REFERENCES ENTITY_A
    ON DELETE CASCADE
);

CREATE UNIQUE INDEX X_ENTITY_B
    ON ENTITY_B (key_b);
```

If the integrity constraints for this model are not to be enforced by the DBMS, violations can be detected after the fact. The following are SQL queries that will find violations for the example model.

To find duplicate primary keys in ENTITY_A (a similar query will find them for ENTITY_B):

```
SELECT *
FROM ENTITY_A
GROUP BY key_a
HAVING COUNT(*) > 1;
```

To find foreign key violations in ENTITY_B:

```
SELECT key_b,
       'MISSING parent ENTITY_A',
       key_a
FROM ENTITY_B
WHERE NOT EXISTS
       (SELECT *
        FROM ENTITY_A
        WHERE ENTITY_A.key_a = ENTITY_B.key_a
       )
AND ENTITY_B.key_a IS NOT NULL;
```

The general queries for detecting such violations are given in Appendix D. Similar queries can be developed for detecting violations of constraints that cannot be explicitly stated in the IDEF1X diagram, for example, to detect violations of combinations of allowed attribute values.

8.1.3 Domain and Boolean Constraints

Many constraints can be described directly with the IDEF1X graphic constructs. There are, however, some existence constraints that must be documented outside the graphic model and for which a specific database management system function or application function must be used for enforcement. Here are two examples.

8.1.3.1 Domain constraints

Recall our definition of a domain as the set of values an attribute is allowed to take. Also recall that the modeling language does not directly support the declaration of domains. Domain constraints must therefore be captured as part of the definition of the attribute and recorded in a data dictionary.

8.1.3.2 Boolean constraints

Section 7.2.1 discussed complex category constraints that could not be stated with the IDEF1X language. These Boolean constraints are a special case of a general situation in which we may wish to declare that one thing must exist if another exists, cannot exist if the other exists, must exist if one of two other things exists, and so on. Except for declaring exclusivity of categories in a generalization hierarchy, IDEF1X cannot currently declare such constraints. It can only record them as notes to accompany the model.

These language limitations do not mean we are relieved of the burden of recording all constraints. It simply means that for domains and some types of Boolean constraints, we cannot use the graphic language to do so. Such constraints are common in business and need to be recorded in detailed models. Some DBMSs are able to enforce domain constraints and some types of Boolean constraints in real-time, but in others, a specific application function must be used to enforce the constraints, or to detect and repair violations. Matrices, like the one used to support Fig. 7.14 and treated in Table 7.4, can often be used to represent complex constraints in a convenient form. Queries like those described in Section 8.1.2 can be used to find violations.

8.1.4 Unification

Unification is a method for stating constraints and is controlled by assigning role names. As we learned in Chapter 5, the definition of a role-named attribute is different from the definition of the attribute or attributes on which it is based. We also saw that the role name is intended to describe the role the attribute plays. In addition, role names carry assertions concerning the identity of the entity instance or instances represented by the role name or names.

For an example of how to use role names to make assertions, look at the keys of NEGOTIATION-ASSIST in Fig. 8.5: There, we see two different role names for "employee-id" ("neg-emp-id" and "asst-emp-id"). The assertion is that when there is assistance of some sort, the assisting employee is not (necessarily) the same individual as the negotiating employee. *Because two different EMPLOYEEs may be involved, two separate attributes are required to hold the identifiers.* The role names specify this for us.

There are times when we may wish to assert that two or more foreign key values *must* be different. If we follow the precise IDEF1X standard, we cannot do this directly. We need additional constraint declarations (in this case, the constraint that "asst-emp-id" and "neg-emp-id" *must* hold different values). The concept of a composite domain was introduced in Chapter 5 as one way to record such constraints.

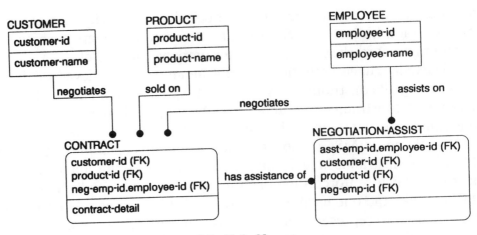

Figure 8.5. Role Names.

There are also times when we may wish to assert that two or more foreign keys must hold the key of the *same* instance. IDEF1X refers to this instance as a *common ancestor*, but does not explicitly specify how to state the constraint in all situations. In this book, we refer to a same-instance assertion as unification. The following discussion is partly an extension to the IDEF1X language, and may not be supported in all tools used to prepare IDEF1X diagrams.

As an example of unification, suppose we are constructing a model for the security function for an on-line transaction processing application. Figure 8.6 shows a case in which OPERATORs and TERMINALs are granted privileges to perform BASIC-TRANSACTIONs. TRANSACTION records the actual occurrence of an OPERATOR using a TERMINAL to perform the BASIC-TRANSACTION.

The subset of all BASIC-TRANSACTIONs allowed for a specific OPERATOR may be different from the subset allowed for a specific TERMINAL. When an actual TRANSACTION occurs, the identifiers of the OPERATOR and TERMINAL are recorded, along with a timestamp for the transaction. The identifier of the BASIC-TRANSACTION being performed is also recorded.

Notice that "base-tran-id" occurs only once in the TRANSACTION entity. The assertion is that the OPERATOR and the TERMINAL must be performing the *same* BASIC-TRANSACTION. The "base-tran-id" in TRANSACTION is a foreign key attribute contributed to the entity twice (once via the relationship from TERMINAL-PRIVILEGE and once via the relationship from OPERATOR-PRIVILEGE). Because the two occurrences of the foreign key have the same name ("base-tran-id"), they *unify* into a single foreign key attribute in the TRANSACTION entity.

We can, if we wish, assign the same role name in the TRANSACTION entity to both occurrences of "base-tran-id"; Fig. 8.7 shows the diagram. The resulting "tran-id" attribute again occurs only once in TRANSACTION. Figures 8.6 and 8.7 both represent correct IDEF1X representations of the unification assertion.

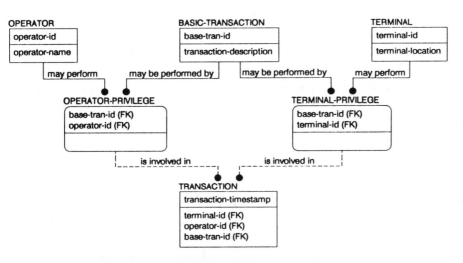

Figure 8.6. Unification Without Role Names.

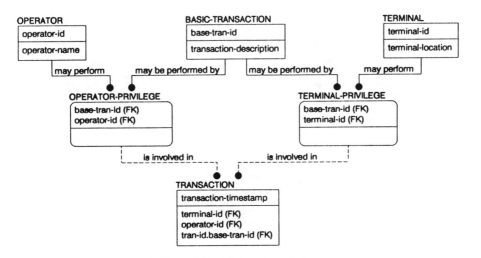

Figure 8.7. Unification with the Same Role Name.

Now, suppose that we decide to assign role names for "base-tran-id" in OPERA-TOR-PRIVILEGE and TERMINAL-PRIVILEGE. Perhaps we are trying to give the attributes names that connote the reasons they appear in each entity. If we do nothing else, the diagram will look like Fig. 8.8, and we will have an incorrect assertion. Two separate occurrences of "base-tran-id" ("term-tran-id" and "oper-tran-id") have been contributed to TRANSACTION as foreign keys. Because there are two separate attributes, they may hold *different* values of the "base-tran-id" foreign key attribute.

That makes no sense. How can the OPERATOR and the TERMINAL be performing *different* BASIC-TRANSACTIONs? To correct the assertion, we must *unify* "oper-tran-id" and "term-tran-id" into a single foreign key attribute. We could stay within the standard IDEF1X syntax and specify, as a note separate from the model, a constraint that the values of the two foreign keys must be the same. Or we can extend the language to state the constraint with a unification assertion. Figure 8.9 shows this extended unification.

In Fig. 8.9, notice the attribute in the TRANSACTION entity that reads "tran-id.(oper-tran-id term-tran-id) (FK)". The role name "tran-id" has been assigned both to "oper-tran-id" and to "term-tran-id". Because of this, "tran-id" occurs only once in the TRANSACTION entity. This is the identifier of the BASIC-TRANSACTION being performed and carries the unification assertion.

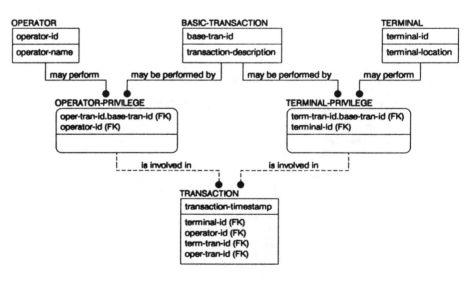

Figure 8.8. Unification Error.

Assigning the same role name to two different foreign key attributes *that have previously been assigned role names* is an extension to the IDEF1X standard. If we choose to use role names for clarity, we will need to adopt this extension to ensure that the models make the correct business assertions.

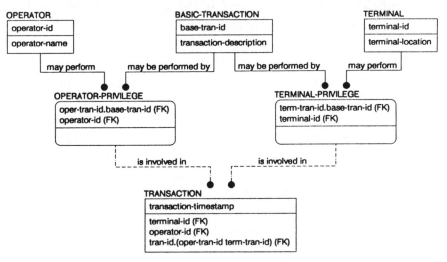

Figure 8.9. Unification of Separate Role Names.

When we choose to cause unification, the assertion is that the instances "pointed to" by the unified foreign keys are the same instance. When we choose not to cause unification, we are declaring that the instances may be different. If you see a situation in which foreign keys contributed by two different relationships have the same name, it is a good idea to closely inspect the structure for possible errors or conflicts in the assertions being made.

8.1.4.1 Rules of unification

The rules of unification are presented below. Note that the italicized entry depicts the extension to the basic IDEF1X standard:

- Two attributes within an entity are considered distinct if they have distinct names, unless one is a role name for another or one is a group attribute containing the other.

- If the same foreign key constituent is contributed to an entity more than once, without the assignment of role names, all occurrences of that constituent unify. (This situation deserves review, however, since unification without the assignment of role names might mean there may be an error of omission in the diagram.)

- Unification does not occur if the occurrences of the foreign key constituent are given different role names.

- If the same foreign key constituent is contributed to an entity more than once and if each one is assigned the same role name, unification will occur.

- *If role names have been assigned previously to the contributed foreign keys, the foreign keys may be unified by assigning them the identical new role name in the receiving entity. The two chains of role names must, however, reach back to a common base attribute for the structure to be meaningful. If the chains do not reach back to the same base attribute, there is an error in the diagram.*

- If any of the foreign key constituents that unify are part of the primary key of the entity, the unified attribute will remain as part of the primary key.

- If none of the foreign key constituents that unify is part of the primary key, the unified attribute will not be part of the primary key.

- If a foreign key is a group attribute and a second foreign key is not a group attribute and the group attribute contains a constituent attribute of the same name as the second foreign key, the second foreign key will seem to disappear; that is, it will unify into the group attribute.

As indicated at the beginning of Section 8.4, the use of extensions to a language can have disadvantages as well as benefits. The unification extension described here can be a powerful addition to IDEF1X, but may not be supported by the modeling tools you use. For example, the practice of assigning the same role name to two different attributes is not currently supported by the Leverage product (described in Appendix E). Leverage will produce output like that shown as Fig. 8.9, but will point out the duplicate role-name assignment, and will not continue with a normalization analysis of the model. Use of the IDEF1X unification extension will disable one of Leverage's other important features.

8.2 SURROGATE KEYS

Definition: Surrogate Key

A single meaningless attribute assigned as the primary key for an entity.

Section 6.2.2 presented the use of group attributes to simplify the key structure of one or more associative entities. Whenever compound keys are encountered, as in Fig. 8.10 (originally shown as Fig. 6.4), it is important to ask whether the keys are meant to be the specific attributes by which each instance of the entity will be identified or whether the key structure has emerged simply as a statement of existence-dependencies among entities.

If the key structure simply reflects existence-dependencies rather than how the entity is to be identified, it is sometimes appropriate to substitute shorter *surrogate keys* in entities with compound keys and enforce the existence-dependencies with mandatory nonidentifying relationships. A surrogate key is an artificial identifier for an entity. It is a meaningless unique number or character string, which is assigned as the primary key. Using surrogate keys will produce an alternative to the original group attribute simplification solution shown in Fig. 6.5. The alternative is shown as Fig. 8.11.

Some modelers contend that all entity keys should be surrogates and that all relationships should be nonidentifying. One argument in favor of this practice is that the use of surrogates tends to remove intelligence (internal hidden structure and meaning) from the keys and to guard against any change in the value of an instance's key to reflect some change in information kept about the instance.

The use of surrogate keys provides a convenient and effective alternative to compound keys in some specific situations, but as we will see in Chapter 9, the careless use of attribute groups and surrogate keys to shorten key structures can lead to unintended changes in the business rules represented by the model.

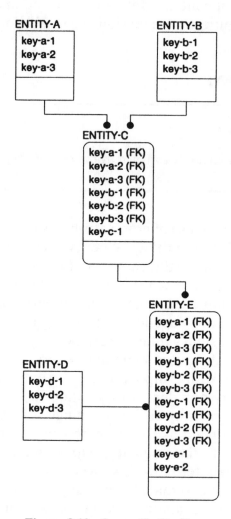

Figure 8.10. Large Entity Keys.

8.3 HISTORY, TIMESTAMPS, AND EVENTS

Our discussion of unification in Section 8.1.4 illustrated a way of recording transactions. An IDEF1X model can be used to provide some information about functions. For example, the BASIC-TRANSACTION entity in the earlier figures contains a set of functions as its instances. If we wished to do so, we could extend the structure in Fig. 8.6 further to record the sequence in which FUNCTIONs are to be performed to complete our BASIC-TRANSACTION.

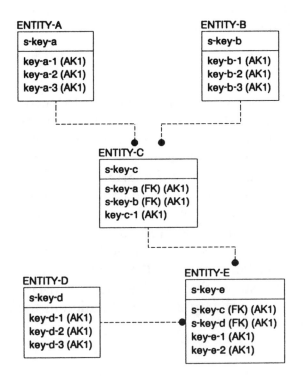

Figure 8.11. Surrogate Key Alternative.

In doing so, however, we would reach a point at which we would cross over from describing the *what* of a system (the Data column of the Zachman Framework) to providing a meta-model for recording the *how* (the Function column). This might or might not be appropriate, depending on the purpose of the model.

We have shown that function and data are important considerations in business and information system modeling. Another major consideration is *timing.* Zachman's work on frameworks suggests that there are other columns beyond data and function to be considered. One of them describes *when* something happens. We can use IDEF1X to describe historical events—that is, when something *did* happen. With extension, we can allow the models to represent when something *is to* happen.

Although the results are cumbersome, we may sometimes need to use a model to describe this historical aspect of a data structure. For example, there may be business rules governing history-keeping and we may need to capture these rules. IDEF1X does not declare a formal way to track events or history, but it provides the tools to do so, as described in the following sections.

8.3.1 Timestamps

Let's look at Fig. 8.12 to see how the requirements for recording history might be addressed. The original structure shown in the figure does not allow us to keep track of changes in the use of ADDRESSs by PERSONs. But we can easily extend the structure to do so, by adding a "timestamp" to the key of the ADDRESS-USAGE entity, as shown in Fig. 8.13.

The general structure in Fig. 8.13 remains the same, and we can now know which ADDRESS-USAGE instance is the most current for any combination of the original keys ("person-id", "address-id", and "usage-type"). In fact, we can know it in one of two ways: We can add an attribute to the entity to explicitly state that an instance of ADDRESS-USAGE is the most current, or we can declare a rule that states that the instance of ADDRESS-USAGE, which carries the most recent timestamp for a combination of the three other keys, is the most current.

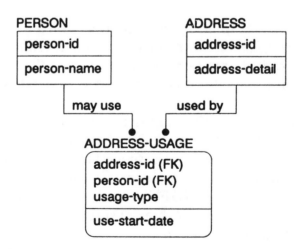

Figure 8.12. No History.

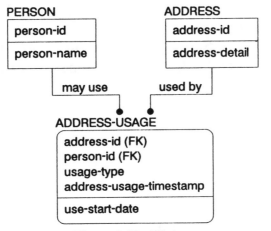

Figure 8.13. History.

Either way, we can keep track of one part of history—the memory of the values of the attributes of an entity instance over a period of time. (Note that this is not an "instance" in the normal sense. Rather, it represents a set of instances of the entity in which the "timestamp" component of their key is the variable and the values of the other components are held constant.) Figure 8.13 allows us to see the changes in the state of the entity, but we still cannot see *what* caused these changes in state to occur.

8.3.2 Events

If we want to see *what* caused change to the state of the entities, we must add an event structure to the diagram. (For the purpose of this discussion, consider an EVENT to be an action that changes the state of entities, and that itself can be initiated by other events.) The diagram now looks like Fig. 8.14.

IDEF1X does not treat the state changes of entities directly, but as we have seen, the language can be used to represent them. Figure 8.14 tells us that an EVENT can affect any entity in zero or more ways. The -ASSOCIATION entities record the details of which EVENTs affected each PERSON, ADDRESS, and ADDRESS-USAGE.

Adding the event layer to a model will increase its size by at least a factor of two; our example shows that a doubling has occurred. Additional structure would be required to show the detailed interactions among the effects of the event on more than one entity. Although this *can* be done, it seldom is in practice.

Whether to include the event layer in a model is, basically, a judgment call. The model represents the rules of the business. Stating which events are to be recorded is a type of business rule and can be useful in detailed models. When the event layer is added, however, it tends to obscure other rules.

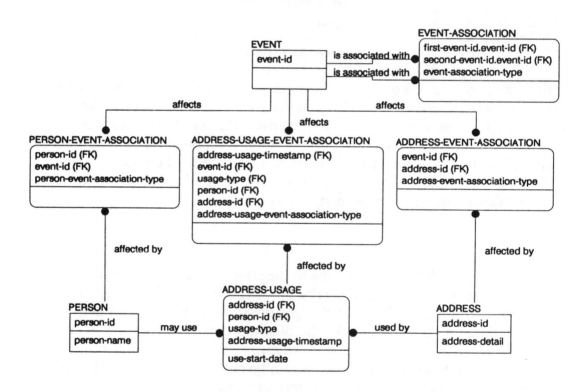

Figure 8.14. Adding an Event Layer.

8.4 PRESENTING A MODEL

Most information models are considerably larger than the ones described in this book. A *composite model* representing the entire structure for even a small business can contain hundreds of entities. This complexity is more than most people, even experienced modelers, want to see on a single diagram. Therefore, it is advisable to divide huge models into smaller pieces—or it will be a major challenge to present them.

Moreover, there are situations in which the IDEF1X graphic language cannot state a business rule, or in which using the language to state the rule results in diagrams that are so busy that the solution is not appropriate for the intended use of the model. Thus, we need to consider how to present the model to an audience, and fill in the missing rules. We have already covered the first two parts of the model: the diagram and the definitions of entities and attributes. The third part of the model is a description of the view provided by the diagram. This is called a view description and can be used to add the missing rules. View and view descriptions are discussed below.

8.4.1 Views

A *view* is represented by a diagram that presents a subset of a model. The diagram view can be constructed so that it corresponds to a specific business function or topic. Large models normally are presented as several views. A function-based view might cover the business function "pay employees" or "establish a customer relationship." A topical view might cover contracts or vendors or employee benefit plans. Depending on the audience, we might use either topical or function-based views, or a combination of the two.

Since views address a specific subject, they are generally much smaller than the composite model. However, to people not experienced with the symbols and structures present in the model, even small views can be confusing. Therefore, when presenting a model, we should provide a *written* description for each view.

8.4.2 View Descriptions

A *view description* is a natural language statement of the business rules carried by a view, and optionally contains comments and examples that explain the view to an audience. Although view descriptions are not specified in the documents that describe the IDEF1X standards, they provide an excellent way to present models. Depending on their purpose, these descriptions can be highly detailed, or presented in summary form.

The reason we use the diagrams to capture the model is that they are more precise than the written language and can say more in a small space. A translation of a view back into natural language can be several pages long, but is often the only way to ensure that the audience will be able to understand the view.

8.5 SUMMARY

This first half of Part Two has provided most of the details of the IDEF1X language. The second half provides additional information that will help you use the language effectively. We move on next to a discussion of normalizing information models, and applying them to existing systems, then look at future directions for information management and modeling.

8.6 REVIEW EXERCISES

Answers to boldface questions appear in Appendix H.

1. **Draw a Venn diagram to show the intersection of the domains of "base-tran-id", "oper-tran-id", "term-tran-id", and "tran-id" in Fig. 8.9. Draw a second diagram to represent the actual instances for a single TERMINAL and a single OPERATOR in which the terminal and operator share at least some common privileges. Draw a third diagram showing this second case but with the unification assertion dropped and having both the "oper-tran-id" and "term-tran-id" present in the TRANSACTION entity (see Fig. 8.8).**

2. Create a model based on the following description. For the business questions it leaves unanswered, state your assumptions. Write a view description for the result.

    Like many, our city has a municipal library system. Each branch of the library lends books to members of the library, residents of the city with valid library cards.

A library can have several copies of the same book title, but because there are more books in the world than would fit in our city hall, our library cannot have every one of them. If someone wants to borrow a book that is not owned by one of our branches, we can often borrow a copy from another library in the area and mail it back later When we get our new computer, we are going to be able to keep track of what books the other libraries have so we can find them faster for our members. Right now we sometimes have to make a lot of phone calls to find a book. I keep a list of contacts for different places. Sometimes, we can find books by name. Other times, all we know is the author, the publisher, or the publication date.

We also take reservations for books we have in the system and keep track of borrowing among our branches just like we do for borrowing from other libraries. If someone needs a book by a particular time, we can often get it for them.

Some of the libraries in the area are known for specializing in certain types of books. Sometimes, different branches have different specialties. For example, our campus branch has a lot of books on computers. When we are looking for a book for someone, we will often start with a library that specializes in the subject.

We don't keep much information about our members, other than their names, addresses, and library-card number. Did I mention that we are about to get those fancy new ones with the magnetic stripe on them? Like credit cards? Most people have paper ones now. Anyway, all we really need to know when someone wants to borrow a book is whether they are a member in good standing.

—Alice Bookend, City Librarian

3. List three types of constraints that cannot be directly stated by the IDEF1X graphics.

8.7 REFERENCES

[1]   Brown, R.G. "Referential Integrity Checking and SQL," *Database Programming &*
Design, Vol. 1, No. 3 (March 1988), pp. 36-45.

[2]   Date, C.J. *A Guide to the SQL Standard.* Reading, Mass.: Addison-Wesley, 1987.

9

NORMALIZATION AND BUSINESS RULES

According to formal mathematical theory, the goal of normalization is to ensure that there is only one way to know a fact. Thus, the technical process of normalizing a model removes all structures that provide more than one way to know the same fact. At the level of physical database design, we can view normalization as a method of controlling and eliminating redundancy in data storage.

From a business perspective, the goal of normalizing an information model is to ensure that the correct business rules are recorded in the model and that rules that are not correct are removed or revised. The technical processes of normalization help with this. But in the end, it is the correctness of the assertions in the model that must be verified. This is a job for people, not mathematical theory.

Here are two useful slogans for summarizing the goals of normalization:

ONE FACT IN ONE PLACE

GET THE BUSINESS RULES RIGHT

This chapter presents what we need to know about normalizing IDEF1X models without getting into a deep theoretical treatment of the subject. It introduces the basic ideas of normalization and examines some examples of obvious, and not so obvious, design problems. It then provides some hints on how to find normalization errors hidden in large models. Formal definitions of the normal forms are not provided. For a more rigorous treatment of the topic, there are several excellent technical discussions, including the works of C.J. Date [1] and M.E.S. Loomis [2]. An excellent short treatment is provided by William Kent [3].

Normalization of data structures continues to be a controversial topic, especially in the design of logical, as opposed to physical, structures. Discussions of whether to introduce redundancy into data structures are often driven by performance issues surrounding physical systems. Discussing performance of *logical* structures is a bit questionable. Moving these discussions to the area of business rules makes them more meaningful.

9.1 COMMON DESIGN PROBLEMS

To begin our discussion of normalization, let's look at some common design errors.

9.1.1 Repeating Attributes

Something is wrong with the model in Fig. 9.1. The sample instance table in Table 9.1 reveals that the problem lies with the attribute "childrens-names".

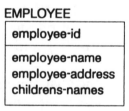

Figure 9.1. Repeating Attribute.

Table 9.1.
Repeating Attribute Instance Example.

EMPLOYEE

emp-id	emp-name	emp-address	childrens-names
E1	Tom	Berkeley	Jane
E2	Don	Berkeley	Tom, Dick, Donna
E3	Ben	Princeton	--
E4	John	New York	Lisa
E5	Carol	Berkeley	--

Recall the discussions of entities and attributes in earlier chapters in which we saw that all names must be singular. Here we see one that is not. The attribute "childrens-names" raises questions, such as, How many children's names do we need to record? How much space should we leave in each row in the database for the names? What will we do if we have more names than we have space? The first of these is a business-rule question. The second and third have to do with how we might use the structure to approximate the business rule.

The design in Fig. 9.1 violates what is called *first normal form*. The repeating attribute ("childrens-names") is the violation. First normal form is a basic definition of the shape of a design. It says that the rows and columns of the data must form a two-dimensional table with no nested structure inside any cell in the table. Every data element in the database must be atomic, with no lists, repeated occurrences, nor internal structure. We can think of each value in a column as a single entry in a cell in a spreadsheet like EXCEL or Lotus 1-2-3. But we must think of it as a literal, or label, not a formula that computes something.

To fix the design, we must remove the list of children's names from the EMPLOYEE entity. The way to do this is to convert the non-first-normal-form entity into the new structure shown in Fig. 9.2. Then, we can represent the names of the children as discrete things, as shown in Table 9.2. In terms of a physical record structure, this may resolve space allocation issues, including wasting space in records for employees who have no children and deciding how much space to allocate for employees with families. That, however, is a physical storage issue, not a normalization issue.

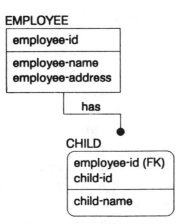

Figure 9.2. No Repeating Attributes.

**Table 9.2.
No Repeating Attributes Instance Example.**

EMPLOYEE

emp-id	emp-name	emp-address
E1	Tom	Berkeley
E2	Don	Berkeley
E3	Ben	Princeton
E4	John	New York
E5	Carol	Berkeley

CHILD

emp-id	child-id	child-name
E1	C1	Jane
E2	C1	Tom
E2	C2	Dick
E2	C3	Donna
E4	C1	Lisa

In our example, we discovered a group of repeating data and dropped it out to a new entity. In doing so, we took the first step toward creating a normalized model. That is, we converted our model into first normal form. We also recorded two new business rules. One says that, for each employee, we must be able to keep track of any number of children (including none). The other says that, for each employee, we must be able to record more than one child with the same name. As with all business rules, these are constraints that govern the allowed values of fields in the database.

9.1.2 Multiple Use of the Same Attribute

Figure 9.3 shows another design with problems. A sample instance table is provided in Table 9.3. In Fig. 9.3, we have a single attribute, "start-or-termina-tion-date", that can represent one of two facts. The first problem here is that there is no way to know which fact it represents. The second problem is that there is no way to record both a start date—the date the EMPLOYEE started work—and a termination date—the date the EMPLOYEE left the company—when both dates are known. These are the business rules issues. C.J. Date refers to this as "overloading" [4].

The solution is to allow separate attributes to carry the separate facts. Figure 9.4 illustrates a first attempt to arrive at that solution, but it's not correct because we still must derive the kind of date from the "date-type" attribute. Although this solution may be efficient in terms of physical database space conservation, it does not let us record both dates and it wreaks havoc with query logic. The business rule is still not correct: It says we have no need to keep track of both a start date and a termination date for an employee.

EMPLOYEE

employee-id
employee-name employee-address start-or-termination-date

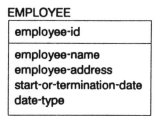

EMPLOYEE

employee-id
employee-name employee-address start-or-termination-date date-type

Figure 9.3.   Attribute Overloading.   **Figure 9.4. More Attribute Overloading.**

Table 9.3.
Attribute Overloading Instance Example.

EMPLOYEE

emp-id	emp-name	emp-address	start-or-termination-date
E1	Tom	Berkeley	Jan 10, 1991
E2	Don	Berkeley	May 22, 1989
E3	Ben	Princeton	Mar 15, 1988
E4	John	New York	Sep 30, 1990
E5	Carol	Berkeley	Apr 22, 1990
E6	George	Pittsburgh	Oct 15, 1990

What we have is a type of error that involves *definition dependency*. This is not a classic normalization error (no normalization rules are violated), but is nonetheless incorrect. These kinds of errors can be easy to spot whenever we see an attribute carrying more than one fact. Figure 9.5 shows the correct solution. All attributes carry separate facts.

The two errors described above resulted in models that did not correctly represent the business rules. The first was a first normal form error. The second was a failure to represent different facts separately. By changing the structures, we made sure each attribute appeared only once in the entity, and each attribute carried only one fact. Here is a working definition for first normal form.

EMPLOYEE

employee-id
employee-name employee-address start-date termination-date

Figure 9.5. No Attribute Overloading.

Table 9.4.
No Attribute Overloading Instance Example.

EMPLOYEE

emp-id	emp-name	emp-address	start-date	termination-date
E1	Tom	Berkeley	Jan 10, 1991	--
E2	Don	Berkeley	May 22, 1989	--
E3	Ben	Princeton	Mar 15, 1988	--
E4	John	New York	Sep 30, 1990	--
E5	Carol	Berkeley	Apr 22, 1990	--
E6	George	Pittsburgh	Oct 15, 1990	Nov 30, 1990

Informal Definition: First Normal Form

An entity is in first normal form if each of its attributes has exactly one value in each instance.

Although not part of the precise definition of first normal form, it is often useful to add the following.

Every attribute must have a single meaning.

If we make sure that all entity and attribute names are singular and that no attribute carries multiple facts, we will have taken a large step toward assuring that a model is in first normal form and correctly represents the business rules.

9.1.3 Multiple Occurrences of the Same Fact

Figure 9.6 provides an example of a structure with another problem. If we were to place the "employee-address" attribute in the CHILD entity, as shown in the figure, we might have an intuitive feeling that something was wrong. The "employee-address" attribute carries information about the EMPLOYEE, not information about the CHILD. The formal way to say this is that the value of "employee-address" does not depend on the *entire* key of CHILD; it depends only on part of it (the "employee-id" part).

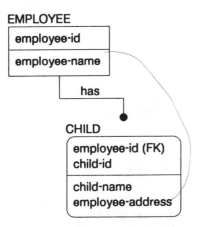

Figure 9.6. Fact in the Wrong Place.

In addition to the normalization error, the business rule is wrong. The rule seems to say that an EMPLOYEE can have as many addresses as he or she has children (including none if there are no children). This is the real problem with the structure. We have recorded an incorrect business rule.

By placing "employee-address" back with EMPLOYEE as we did in Fig. 9.2, we correct the business rule and ensure that the structure is in at least *second normal form*. An informal working definition for second normal form follows.

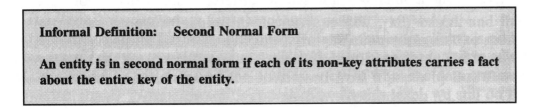

Informal Definition: Second Normal Form

An entity is in second normal form if each of its non-key attributes carries a fact about the entire key of the entity.

The difference between second and third normal form is subtle. An entity violates *second normal form* if a fact can be determined by knowing only part of the key of the entity. It violates *third normal form* if a fact can be determined by knowing the value of some *non-key* attribute of the entity. For example, Fig. 9.5 would contain a third normal form error if the EMPLOYEE entity contained both a "city" attribute (as part of a further detailing of the address) and a "city-tax-rate" attribute. Tax rates for cities are determined by knowing the city and are the same for all residents of that city. Placing a "city-tax-rate" attribute in the EMPLOYEE entity would specify an incorrect rule: It would allow the rate to vary by EMPLOYEE. In addition to the third-normal-form error, we would have another incorrect business rule.

As another example, consider what would happen if we recorded both a "birth-date" and an "age" as non-key attributes in EMPLOYEE in Fig. 9.5. "Age" is dependent on "birth-date". By knowing "birth-date" and today's date, we can derive "age". In addition, today's date is not an attribute of EMPLOYEE, so the derivation of age depends on information not included in the model.

For third normal form, we have the following informal working definition.

> **Informal Definition: Third Normal Form**
>
> **An entity is in third normal form if every non-key attribute of the entity (a) depends on the entity's key, (b) depends on the whole of the key, and (c) does not depend on any key or non-key attribute of any other entity.**

9.1.4 Conflicting Facts

Figure 9.7, along with its sample instance table (Table 9.5), provides an example of another normalization problem. Look at the attribute "emp-spouse-address". From the sample instance table, we see that Don is the parent of Tom, Dick, and Donna. We also see two different addresses for Don's spouse. Perhaps Don has two spouses (one in Berkeley and one in Cleveland) or Donna has a different mother from Tom and Dick. Or perhaps Don has one spouse with addresses in both Berkeley and Cleveland. Or perhaps there is an error. There is no way to know the correct answer from the given model.

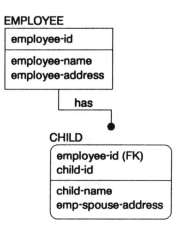

Figure 9.7. Conflicting Facts.

Table 9.5.
Conflicting Facts Instance Example.

EMPLOYEE

emp-id	emp-name	emp-address
E1	Tom	Berkeley
E2	Don	Berkeley
E3	Ben	Princeton
E4	John	New York
E5	Carol	Berkeley

CHILD

emp-id	child-id	child-name	emp-spouse-address
E1	C1	Jane	Berkeley
E2	C1	Tom	Berkeley
E2	C2	Dick	Berkeley
E2	C3	Donna	Cleveland
E4	C1	Lisa	New York

The problem is that "emp-spouse-address" is a fact about the EMPLOYEE's SPOUSE, not about the CHILD. What we have is another incorrect business rule. If we leave the structure as is, every time Don's spouse changes her address, we have to update that fact in several places, that is, in each CHILD instance where Don is the parent. The chance of always getting it right is not good.

The first thing to do is recognize that "emp-spouse-address" is not a fact about a CHILD but about a SPOUSE. We might come up with a rule that says that an "emp-spouse-address" is the same as "emp-address" and derive this information from the EMPLOYEE entity. But there would then be no way to record an address for a SPOUSE not living at the same address as the EMPLOY-EE. Therefore, we must make a change, as in Fig. 9.8 and Table 9.6.

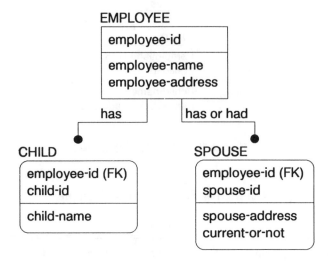

Figure 9.8. Fact in the Right Place.

Table 9.6.
Fact in the Right Place Instance Example.

EMPLOYEE

emp-id	emp-name	emp-address
E1	Tom	Berkeley
E2	Don	Berkeley
E3	Ben	Princeton
E4	John	New York
E5	Carol	Berkeley

CHILD

emp-id	child-id	child-name
E1	C1	Jane
E2	C1	Tom
E2	C2	Dick
E2	C3	Donna
E4	C1	Lisa

SPOUSE

emp-id	spouse-id	spouse-address	current-or-not
E2	S1	Berkeley	Y
E2	S2	Berkeley	N
E3	S1	Princeton	Y
E4	S1	New York	Y
E5	S1	Berkeley	Y

In breaking out SPOUSE into a separate entity, we see that there was no error in the data for Don's spouse's address. There were two spouses, one current, and one not current.

By making sure every attribute in an entity carries a fact about *that* entity, we generally can be sure that a model is in at least second normal form. Transforming a model into third normal form generally reduces the likelihood that the database will become corrupt, that is, that it will contain conflicting information or that required information will be missing. After that, we still need to ensure that the correct business rules are recorded.

9.1.5 Missing Information

When we changed from Fig. 9.7 to Fig. 9.8, we might have lost something we assumed we knew. The reason "emp-spouse-address" was originally placed in the CHILD entity might have been an attempt to represent the address of the other parent of the child (who was assumed to be the spouse). If we do need to know the other parent of each CHILD, we must add this information to the CHILD entity. For our example, let's assume that the only other parents we want to know about are SPOUSEs.

Figure 9.9 might represent a solution. It provides a way to record both parents of a CHILD (the EMPLOYEE and the SPOUSE). It also resolves our problems with the addresses. However, there is still something wrong in Table 9.7, the sample instance table for Fig. 9.9. There is no "spouse-id" entry representing the other parent of Jane.

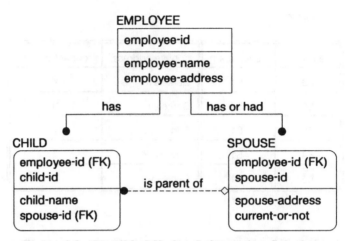

Figure 9.9. Possible Missing Information Solution.

Table 9.7.
Possible Missing Information Solution Instance Example.

EMPLOYEE

emp-id	emp-name	emp-address
E1	Tom	Berkeley
E2	Don	Berkeley
E3	Ben	Princeton
E4	John	New York
E5	Carol	Berkeley

CHILD

emp-id	child-id	child-name	spouse-id
E1	C1	Jane	--
E2	C1	Tom	S1
E2	C2	Dick	S1
E2	C3	Donna	S2
E4	C1	Lisa	S1

SPOUSE

emp-id	spouse-id	spouse-address	current-or-not
E1	S1	Berkeley	Y
E2	S2	Berkeley	N
E3	S1	Princeton	Y
E4	S1	New York	Y
E5	S1	Berkeley	Y

In Table 9.7, we see that Tom is the father of Jane, but we don't have a record of anyone who is Tom's SPOUSE, and we don't have any other way to find Jane's other parent. If we want to know with certainty about relationships between EMPLOYEEs and OTHER-PERSONs, and if we want to know who the parents of the children of EMPLOYEEs are (the business rules), we must record these facts separately.

Figure 9.10 represents a step in the right direction. It allows us to record both parents of a CHILD but does not allow both parents to be EMPLOYEEs. In fact, it says that once a person is an EMPLOYEE, his or her spouse may not also be an EMPLOYEE. Again, this is an incorrect business rule.

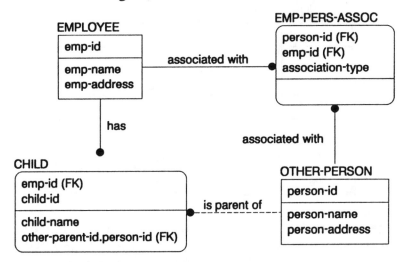

Figure 9.10. Another Possible Solution.

Table 9.8.
Another Possible Solution Instance Example.

EMPLOYEE

emp-id	emp-name	emp-address
E1	Tom	Berkeley
E2	Don	Berkeley
E3	Ben	Princeton
E4	John	New York
E5	Carol	Berkeley

CHILD

emp-id	child-id	child-name	other-parent-id
E1	C1	Jane	P1
E2	C1	Tom	P2
E2	C2	Dick	P2
E2	C3	Donna	P3
E4	C1	Lisa	P5

EMPLOYEE-PERSON-ASSOCIATION

emp-id	person-id	association-type
E2	P2	spouse
E2	P3	former spouse
E3	P4	spouse
E4	P5	spouse
E5	P6	spouse

OTHER-PERSON

person-id	person-name	person-address
P1	Carol	Berkeley
P2	Jean	Berkeley
P3	Clara	Cleveland
P4	Margaret	Princeton
P5	Lynn	New York
P6	Tom	Berkeley

Figure 9.11 depicts another possible way to know about parentage and spouses. However, in preparing a sample instance table for it (Table 9.9), we would discover that, again, a PERSON cannot be both an EMPLOYEE and a SPOUSE (for example, Carol, Ben, Tom) or neither (for example, Jane). These are business rule errors. Moreover, in trying to create the sample instance table, we might finally discover that our test data was incorrect all along. We had a hint that something was wrong in Fig. 9.10, when Tom was the name of both an EMPLOYEE and an OTHER-PERSON and we could not find the other parent of Jane. It turns out that Tom and Carol are both employees of the business and that Jane is their daughter.

9.1.6 Incorrect Business Rules

Let's continue with our example. Figure 9.11 says that a PERSON is either an EMPLOYEE or a SPOUSE, that EMPLOYEEs and SPOUSES may be related, and that another relationship (represented by the CHILD entity) may exist between two PERSONs. From a formal normalization perspective, that is, what an algorithm would find solely from the shape of the model without understanding the meanings of the entities and attributes, there is nothing wrong with this model. A normalization algorithm might recognize the presence of two similar relationships between instances of the PERSON entity (CHILD and EMPLOYEE-SPOUSE-ASSOCIATION) and point it out. But it would have no way to understand that CHILD and PERSON are similar concepts.

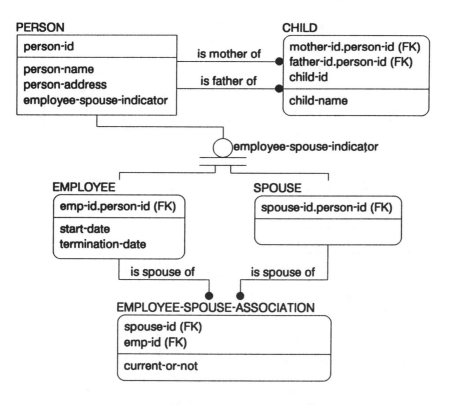

Figure 9.11. Parentage and Spouses (But Wrong).

Table 9.9.
Parentage and Spouses Instance Example (But Wrong).

PERSON

person-id	person-name	person-address	emp-sp-ind
P1	Carol	Berkeley	E and S
P2	Jean	Berkeley	S
P3	Clara	Cleveland	S
P4	Margaret	Princeton	E
P5	Lynn	New York	S
P6	Tom	Berkeley	E and S
P7	Jane	Berkeley	--
P8	Don	Berkeley	E
P9	Ben	Princeton	E and S
P10	John	New York	E
P11	George	Pittsburgh	E

EMPLOYEE

emp-id. person-id	start-date	termination-date
P1	Apr 22, 1990	--
P4	June 1, 1990	--
P6	Jan 10, 1991	--
P8	May 22, 1989	--
P9	Mar 15, 1988	--
P10	Sep 30, 1990	--
P11	Oct 15, 1990	Nov 30, 1990

SPOUSE

spouse-id.person-id
P1
P2
P3
P4
P5
P6

EMPLOYEE-SPOUSE-ASSOCIATION   CHILD

emp-id	spouse-id	current-or-not
P1	P6	Y
P6	P1	Y
P8	P2	Y
P8	P3	N
P9	P4	Y
P10	P5	Y

mother-id.person-id	father-id.person-id	child-id	child-name
P1	P6	C1	Jane
P2	P8	C1	Tom
P2	P8	C2	Dick
P3	P8	C1	Donna
P5	P10	C1	Lisa

Without an understanding of the meanings of the attributes and entities in the model, a normalization algorithm probably could not help any farther (actually, it could not help us find any of the earlier errors unless we supplied it with more information about functional dependencies among attributes). This is the point at which people take over. With experience, people are able to detect and remove what's not necessary, and what's wrong. Removing errors usually has more to do with correcting business rules than it has to do with applying normalization theory.

In the employee model, for example, we can see no way to record two EMPLOYEEs who are SPOUSEs, or a CHILD whose parents are both EMPLOYEEs. Therefore, we might make a change like that in Fig. 9.12 and test the meaning of the structure with the sample instance table in Table 9.10.

In Fig. 9.12, we run into a problem if we try to record more than one CHILD with the same parents (notice that the instances for Tom and Dick both have the same key). If we understood that the EMPLOYEE Tom was the same person as the CHILD Tom, we would see another problem. If he is the same person, his name should appear only once. Again, we have to change the structure.

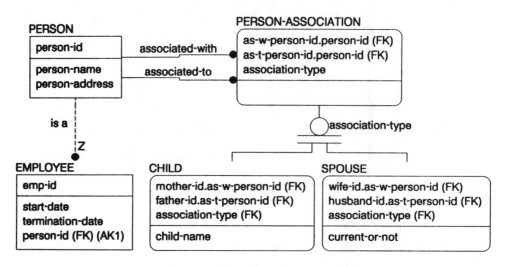

Figure 9.12. Employees and Children.

Table 9.10.
Employees and Children Instance Example.

PERSON

person-id	person-name	person-address
P1	Carol	Berkeley
P2	Jean	Berkeley
P3	Clara	Cleveland
P4	Margaret	Princeton
P5	Lynn	New York
P6	Tom	Berkeley
P7	Jane	Berkeley
P8	Don	Berkeley
P9	Ben	Princeton
P10	John	New York
P11	George	Pittsburgh

EMPLOYEE

emp-id	person-id	start-date	termination-date
E1	P1	Apr 22, 1990	--
E2	P4	June 1, 1990	--
E3	P6	Jan 10, 1991	--
E4	P8	May 22, 1989	--
E5	P9	Mar 15, 1988	--
E6	P10	Sep 30, 1990	--
E7	P11	Oct 15, 1990	Nov 30, 1990

PERSON-ASSOCIATION

as-w-p-id	as-t-p-id	association-type
P1	P6	spouse
P1	P6	child
P2	P8	spouse
P2	P8	child
P3	P8	former spouse
P3	P8	child
P4	P9	spouse
P5	P10	spouse
P5	P10	child

SPOUSE

wife-id.as-w-p-id	husband-id.as-t-p-id	association-type
P1	P6	spouse
P2	P8	spouse
P3	P8	former spouse
P4	P9	spouse
P5	P10	spouse

CHILD

mother-id.as-w-p-id	father-id.as-t-p-id	association-type	child-name
P1	P6	child	Jane
P2	P8	child	Tom ←
P2	P8	child	Dick ←
P3	P8	child	Donna
P5	P10	child	Lisa

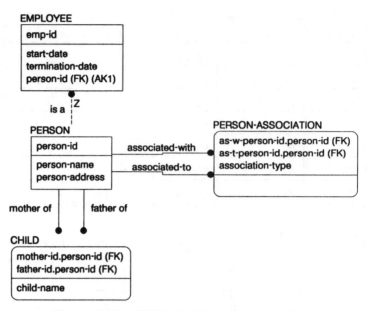

Figure 9.13. CHILD Is Not a Relationship.

Figure 9.13 takes us in the right direction. Using this diagram, we can record multiple CHILDs for a pair of PERSONs. But we still have the problem that a CHILD is not a *relationship* between two PERSONs, like marriage. It is a PERSON.

To correct that error, we eliminate CHILD from the model and record parentage through the relationship between two PERSONs called PERSON-ASSOCIATION. These changes are shown in Fig. 9.14. This, finally, is a good solution.

In this structure, we can record any number of relationships between two PERSONs. We can also record things we had not considered before, such as adoption. We simply add a new value to the domain of "association-type" to represent adopted parentage. If we wish, we can also include categories (by the discriminator "association-type") to record separate information about the different types of associations. The full domain of "association-type" is

as-t-person-id	<is>	Natural Father	<of>	as-w-person-id
as-t-person-id	<is>	Natural Mother	<of>	as-w-person-id
as-t-person-id	<is>	Adopted Father	<of>	as-w-person-id
as-t-person-id	<is>	Adopted Mother	<of>	as-w-person-id
as-t-person-id	<is>	Current Spouse	<of>	as-w-person-id
as-t-person-id	<is>	Former Spouse	<of>	as-w-person-id

We could also add legal guardian, significant other, or other appropriate relationships between two PERSONs later, if needed.

In our final solution, we left EMPLOYEE, the place where this all started, as an independent entity because of a business rule that says we intend to identify EMPLOYEE differently from PERSON. In our solution, EMPLOYEE does not inherit the properties of PERSON, since the category relationship has been removed. Application function will need to approximate this inheritance using the *is a* relationship to PERSON.

Notice the "Z" on the EMPLOYEE and PERSON relationship and the absence of a diamond. It is a one-to-zero-or-one relationship which, as described in Chapter 7, can sometimes be used in place of a generalization hierarchy when the categories require different keys. In our example, either a PERSON *is a* EMPLOYEE, or is not.

If we wanted to use the same key for both PERSON and EMPLOYEE (and the business rule allows it), we could encase the EMPLOYEE entity into PERSON and allow its attributes to be null whenever the PERSON is not an EMPLOYEE, or drop EMPLOYEE out as a category of PERSON. We still could specify that the business wants to look up employees by a separate identifier, but the business rules would be a bit different. The first alternative is shown in Fig. 9.15. It, however, begins to look like the Thing/Thing Association structure cautioned against in Section 7.3.

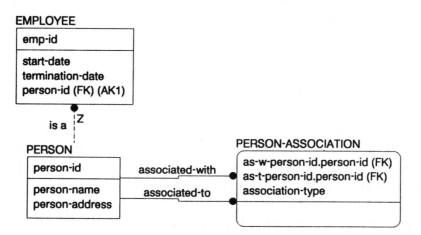

Figure 9.14. Final Solution.

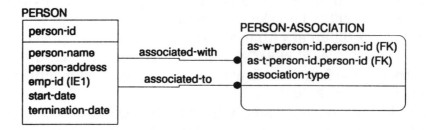

Figure 9.15. Too Much Generalization.

9.2   HIDDEN ERRORS

Business rule and normalization errors in real information models can be far less obvious than those in the examples in this chapter. With experience, we learn how to prevent the obvious ones, such as placing the same attribute in several entities. These normalization steps will become almost automatic. Some errors, however, can be more difficult to find, especially those involving multiple paths to the same fact and single paths to different facts. Such paths are provided by relationships. This section provides hints on discovering and repairing incorrect relationships.

9.2.1   Unwanted Unification

Recall that unification is the merging of two or more contributed foreign key attributes into a single foreign key attribute; it is a way to ensure that different paths arrive at the same fact (as opposed to a way of eliminating multiple paths to a single fact). Figure 8.9, which showed an example of unification, is repeated here as Fig. 9.16.

In Fig. 9.16, the assignment of role names declares that the BASIC-TRANS-ACTION being performed by the OPERATOR is the same one being performed by the TERMINAL. Suppose, however, that we had not assigned role names. This was shown in Fig. 8.6, and is repeated here as Fig. 9.17.

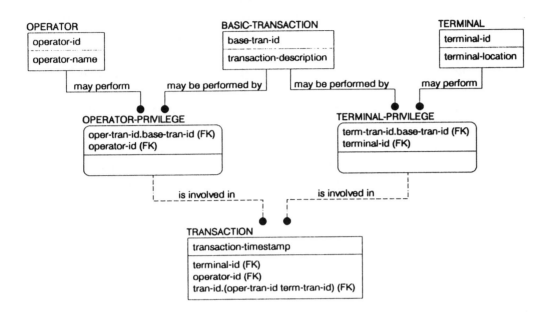

Figure 9.16. Correct Extended Unification.

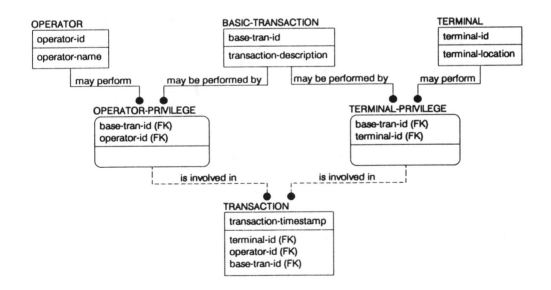

Figure 9.17. Correct Unification.

Notice that the structure is the same and unification has occurred in the TRANSACTION entity.* The unification, however, is not as obvious as in Fig. 9.16. Since we did not specifically declare the unification, we need to ask why it occurred, and whether it is correct. (In this case, it is correct because of our rule that the transaction being performed by the operator and terminal must be the same.)

There are situations in which unification can happen without being noticed by the modeler. For example, Fig. 9.18 (a variation of Fig. 8.5) declares, via role names, that there can be many EMPLOYEEs involved in negotiating a CONTRACT—one who negotiates and some who assist. The foreign keys in NEGOTIATION-ASSIST can identify two separate EMPLOYEES.

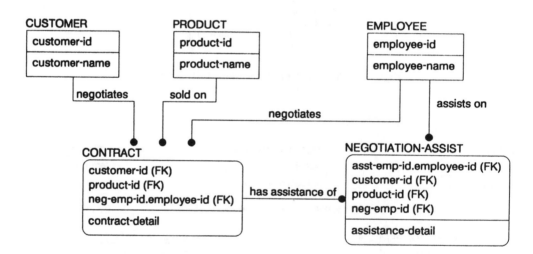

Figure 9.18. No Unwanted Unification.

If we forgot the role names, unification of the two "employee-id"s would occur, and the diagram would appear as in Fig. 9.19. We would then have two paths from NEGOTIATION-ASSIST to the same instance of the EMPLOYEE entity—one

---

*Remember that the unification declaration in Fig. 9.16 is an extension of the basic IDEF1X standard. Figures 8.6 (9.17) and 8.7 represented the only way the correct unification assertion can be stated in the basic standard.

direct and one through CONTRACT. This unnoticed (and unwanted) unification would have created a normalization error in the diagram, and would have *changed the business rule*. The model would state that the assisting employee must be the same individual as the negotiating employee.

Without knowing the intent behind the assertions in the diagram, a normalization algorithm would change it to look like Fig. 9.20. It would do so based on the logic that, in Fig. 9.19, NEGOTIATION-ASSIST has a redundant foreign key to both CONTRACT and EMPLOYEE and the existence constraint (that there can be at most one NEGOTIATION-ASSIST instance per CONTRACT instance) can be preserved with the "Z" cardinality on the relationship between CONTRACT and NEGOTIATION-ASSIST. If NEGOTIATION-ASSIST held no non-key attributes, it might be dropped entirely.

If we did not look closely, we might miss the business rule error in Fig. 9.19, but it would be hard not to notice it in Fig. 9.20. Although the algorithm would not have repaired the business rule, it certainly would cause us to think about it. That's all we can expect from a normalization algorithm.

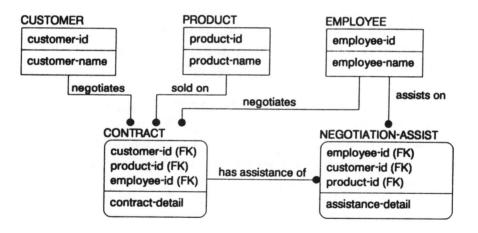

Figure 9.19. Unwanted Unification.

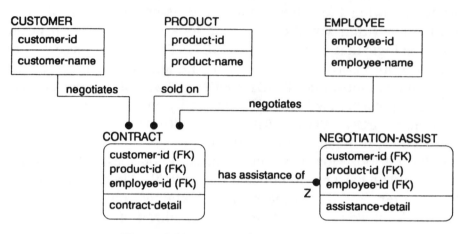

Figure 9.20. Answer from the Algorithm.

9.2.2 Errors Introduced by Surrogate Keys

Surrogate keys, as discussed in Section 8.2, can be useful as substitutes for composite primary keys, but can also lead to business rule errors. To illustrate this, let's return to our TRANSACTION example, and substitute surrogates for the keys of OPERATOR-PRIVILEGE and TERMINAL-PRIVILEGE. Let's also "forget" to use role names. The diagram appears as in Fig. 9.21.

In the TRANSACTION entity, we no longer see the unification of two occurrences of "transaction-id" into a single foreign key. This is correct since the two occurrences are no longer contributed across the relationships. If we wish to make the assertion that the operator and the terminal must both be performing the same transaction (as we did before), we have a problem. The diagram does not say this, even though its structure is generally the same as before, *and there is no way in the current IDEF1X language to make the assertion*. Adding role names for the occurrences of "base-tran-id" would not help.

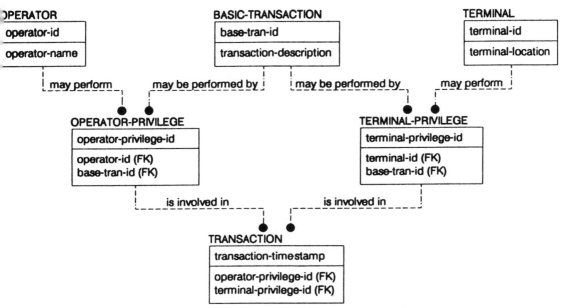

Figure 9.21. Error Introduced by Surrogate Keys.

Substituting surrogate keys can be useful, but must be done with great care. Not only can some errors be hidden by the surrogate keys, some can be introduced that cannot be resolved unless the surrogates are removed or necessary constraint statements are added to the basic IDEF1X language.

9.2.3 Overuse of Groups

Group attributes, like surrogate keys, can often be used to reduce the size of the key area in certain entities in a model. We saw an example of this in Section 6.2.2. Figure 6.4 was collapsed into Fig. 6.5 by the introduction of a group attribute in ENTITY-C. These diagrams are repeated as Figs. 9.22 and 9.23. However, group attributes can also make business rule errors difficult to find.

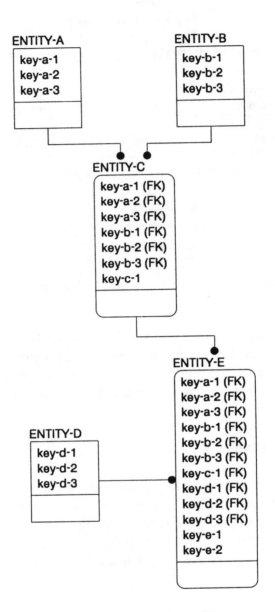

Figure 9.22. Very Large Keys.

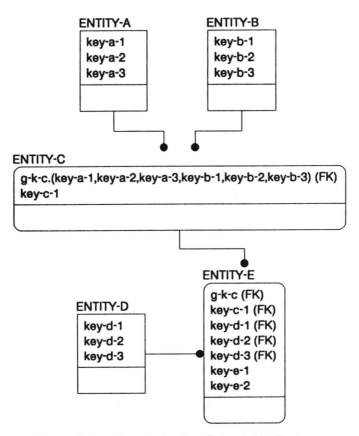

Figure 9.23. Keys Including Groups Attributes.

Unification rules are explicit when it comes to group attributes. If a contributed foreign key has the same name as one of the constituents of the group attribute, it will unify into the group and seem to disappear from the model.

The use of group attributes can obscure unification, and therefore normalization and business rule errors. Therefore, whenever groups are used, it is important to inspect carefully all entities that contain group attributes to ensure that unwanted unification is not occurring in the groups.

9.3 A CAUTION

This chapter tells us that although a model may adhere to the technical rules of normalization, it still may not be a correct representation of the business. Technical normalization is important and is an attempt to have a formal mathematical theory that checks for correctness and consistency of business rules. Using sample instance tables to verify that the model means something, as we have done throughout this chapter, is no less important.

Normalization is a logical design exercise. At the level of physical database design, decisions are often made to denormalize a structure to achieve higher performance in a database. Performance often seems to be the overriding factor in such decisions. What is often missed is that each denormalization of a data structure changes the business rules stated by the structure. Each time this is done, either the rules cannot be enforced (and the user gets a system that doesn't obey the correct rules) or the burden of enforcing the original rules falls to the application code that will operate against the denormalized database.

One of the objectives of using database technology in the first place is to remove much of the processing burden from the application code. Denormalization works directly counter to this objective. Therefore, if you are ever involved in an argument about whether to denormalize a structure, don't argue about performance. Argue about the business rules.

9.4   REVIEW EXERCISES

Answers to boldface questions appear in Appendix H.

1.   List the things wrong with the following model.

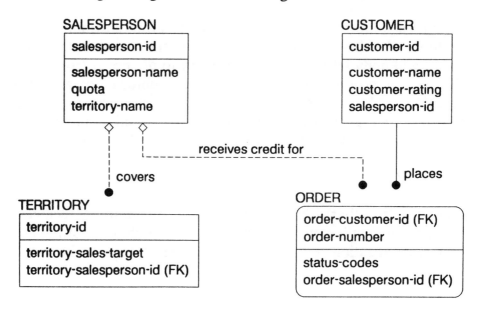

2.   **What, if any, are the technical errors in these diagrams?**

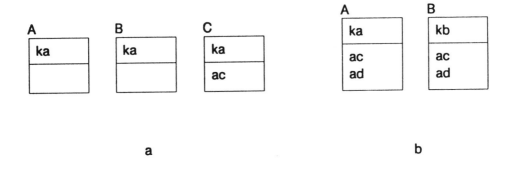

a   b

3.   What, if any, are the technical errors in these diagrams? What revisions
      must be made to remove the errors?

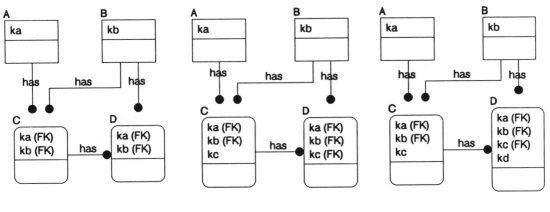

a   b   c

4. **What, if any, are the technical errors in this diagram? What revisions must be made to remove the errors?**

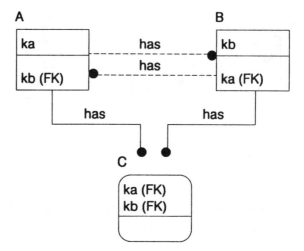

5. What, if any, are the technical errors in this diagram? What revisions must be made to remove the errors?

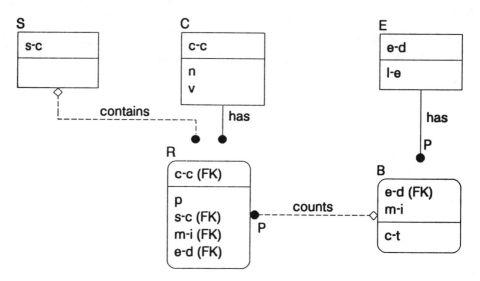

6. **What, if any, are the technical errors in this diagram? What revisions must be made to remove the errors?**

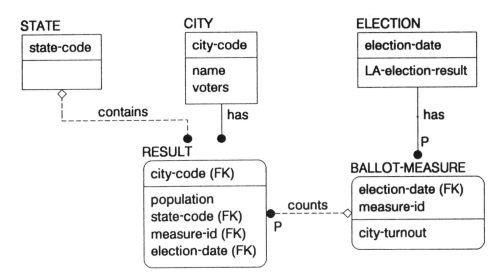

7. Construct a sample instance table for the final solution to the EMPLOYEE, SPOUSE, and CHILD problem shown in the figure below and based on the data in Table 9.10.

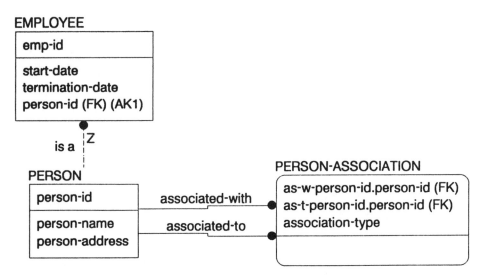

8. **When a fully normalized information model is transformed into a design for a physical database, some denormalization often occurs. What factors**

favor denormalization for the physical database? What factors favor normalization?

9.5 REFERENCES

[1]   Date, C.J. *An Introduction to Database Systems.* Reading, Mass.: Addison-Wesley, 1986.

[2]   Loomis, M.E.S. *The Database Book.* New York: Macmillan, 1987.

[3]   Kent, W.   "A Guide to Effective Data Base Design Using Normal Forms," *Data Resource Management,* Vol. 1, No. 2 (Spring 1990), pp. 34-42.

[4]   Date, C.J. *Relational Database: Selected Writings.* Reading, Mass.: Addison-Wesley, 1986.

10

REVERSE ENGINEERING

To convert an application function from one technology to another requires an understanding of the structure of information in the old system and the design of an information structure for the new one. In some cases, it may not be possible to work top-down on the new design. In these situations, a bottom-up process is needed.

The process involves three steps. First, the current system must be understood and its physical and logical structure documented. This step is called *reverse engineering*. Second, new requirements must be considered, and the logical structure inferred in the first step must be adjusted to satisfy them. Third, the new logical structure must be carried forward into a new physical design. This step is called *forward engineering*. These three steps are shown in Fig. 10.1. Taken together, the entire cycle is called *re-engineering*. The reverse engineering step may also be used simply as a way to obtain an understanding of the current system even if no revisions or conversions are currently planned.

This chapter provides an overview of the reverse engineering of information structures. It illustrates the process with an example of converting an existing set of sequential tape files (described by COBOL record layouts) into a logical design for a new system. The reverse engineering process is tedious and time-consuming, assumptions must be made, and results are always suspect. Pictures of what you have are not necessarily pictures of what you want. A reverse-engineered model of a system only provides a starting point for discussing new requirements.

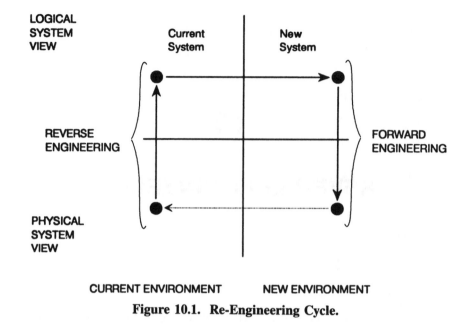

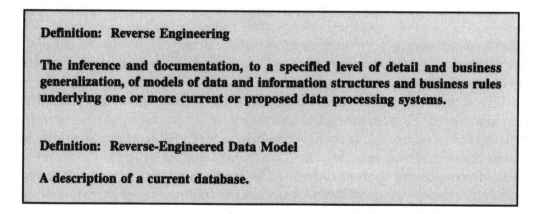

Figure 10.1. Re-Engineering Cycle.

10.1 REVERSE-ENGINEERED MODELS

This section discusses reverse-engineered models. We start with definitions of terms, and discuss the uses of these models. We then introduce the different levels of the models and discuss results that can be expected from a reverse-engineering process.

10.1.1 Definitions

Definition: Reverse Engineering

The inference and documentation, to a specified level of detail and business generalization, of models of data and information structures and business rules underlying one or more current or proposed data processing systems.

Definition: Reverse-Engineered Data Model

A description of a current database.

Definition: Reverse-Engineered Information Model

A description of the information structures and business rules that satisfy a set of business information requirements, constraints, and policies, as implemented in a current system, together with a set of inferences of unstated business directions and needs.

Reverse engineering is the inference and documentation, to a specified level of detail and business generalization, of models of data and information structures and business rules underlying one or more current or proposed data processing systems. For this discussion, we make a distinction between an *information model* and a *data model.* The intent is to distinguish between physical (data) and logical (information) structures.

A *reverse-engineered data model* is a description of a current database. Such a model is comparable to a *transformation model* that has denormalized a top-down information model and shaped it toward an efficient design within the chosen technology.

A *reverse-engineered information model* is a description of the information structures and business rules that satisfy a set of business information requirements, constraints, and policies, as implemented in a current system, together with a set of inferences of unstated business directions and needs.

10.1.2 Usage

Reverse-engineered models represent inferences of what exists and what might be wanted. They describe requirements satisfied by current systems, not necessarily current or future requirements. It is important to be clear on the level of certainty of and the appropriate uses for such models.

10.1.2.1 Data models

Reverse-engineered data models can provide a general understanding of current data structures and applications, and documentation of a current environment. These models present pictures of where we are now and can provide a basis for standardizing physical element characteristics (name, description, format, domain, and so on) before standardizing business information structures. In such cases, data elements (attributes) represented in the model generally will have definitions that are more system-like than business-like.

Reverse-engineered data models can be used to evaluate proposed application software packages (purchased software) to see how well they fit existing environments. If the package has been acquired but not yet installed, a reverse-engineered data model of it can be used to determine how difficult it will be to integrate the package with the existing environment.

Reverse-engineered data models of current systems can provide a basis for best-guess mapping of data among applications, for example, from operations support to MIS systems. This is best-guess in the sense that the correctness of the mapping will depend heavily on business client involvement and current knowledge of the meaning of the elements.

Reverse-engineered data models of current systems can also be used to discuss data structures with application and business personnel. These discussions can lead to a better understanding of current system limitations and future system needs. When this can occur, it is possible to move toward a reverse-engineered *information model*, as described in the following paragraphs.

10.1.2.2 Information models

Reverse-engineered information models can substitute to some degree for top-down business driven requirements models when the top-down models cannot be obtained. In such cases, the likelihood that future developments will move in a consistent business direction will be improved. The extent to which this is the *proper* business direction will vary with the degree of involvement and the quality of input from the business. These models can also provide the basis for identifying major differences between current system designs and desired directions.

Reverse-engineered information models can also be used to identify major differences in business views among large functional units of the organization (for example, the way a specific organizational unit sees CUSTOMER as opposed to the global view or differences between MIS views and operational views).

10.1.3 Levels of Reverse-Engineered Models

Reverse-engineered models can be created at several levels. When beginning a reverse engineering effort, one must clearly define the level to be achieved and understand what to expect from the result. The following assumes that a key based model, rather than a non-key-based (ERD) model is being created. In many cases, an ERD may also be useful and can be abstracted from the key based model.

10.1.3.1 Level 1: Current system documentation (physical DBMS model)

A level-1 model is the documentation, with little inference, of a current data structure. It is very much a physical model. There are at least four sublevels at which this physical model can exist.

1A. Every segment (file record type or DBMS segment type) is represented by an independent entity. Entity keys may be identified, but no relationships among entities are stated. All entity names correspond directly to segment names. Attribute names exactly match data element names.

1B. Category entities are identified and dropped out of the generic parent to represent redefined data areas. Dependent entities may be added to represent multiple occurrence situations. When this is done, a bit of the logical view of the data structure is introduced.

1C. Business-like model names are substituted for each entity and attribute name.

1D. Foreign keys are identified and relationships are established in the model to represent them.

10.1.3.2 Level 2: Inference of application-level model (project data model)

A level-2 model extends the level-1 model to become a logical picture of what the business requirements might have been when the system was developed. At this level, the level-1D model is normalized and, if possible, knowledge of business clients is added to transform the model to a logical statement of what is implemented, and a summary of what requirements were not satisfied. At least two sublevels exist.

2A. At this sublevel, some normalization of the model is done. The amount of normalization is determined on a case-by-case basis. Remaining groups of data are dropped down into dependent entities. Multiple foreign key relationships are pushed out into many-to-many associative entities. Generalization to form category hierarchies is completed, and common attributes are pulled up into the generic parent.

2B. Business knowledge (not necessarily from the business client) is added to test if the correct inferences of structure have been made and to adjust the model to better reflect the business view of what the data structure is all about. Normalization is completed. At this level, we still do not have a model of what is really wanted. Rather, we have a statement of what might have been wanted when the old system was developed.

10.1.3.3 Level 3: Generalization to business-level model (area/composite model)

A level-3 model can serve as a basis (given a general statement of strategic direction) for suggesting structures for future information models. However, there is only so much we can see in the current data structures. To complete the model, we must add business rules. To find out what these business rules are, we must often examine the application code and talk with the business experts.

This level cannot be achieved without direct business client participation. This participation can involve top-down modeling with results compared against the level-2 structures, brainstorming and generalization of the level-2 structures into an existing composite, and serious discussion of the composite and identification of adjustments.

10.1.4 Expected Results

Managers have a tendency to expect reverse-engineered models to be more solid than they usually are. Therefore, it's important to understand up front what can be expected from reverse-engineering efforts and not to oversell the process. These results can be expected.

A level-1 model is guaranteed only to show what *is*. At level 2, generalization to an application-level model depends on how well the application was initially conceived, the availability of good documentation, and access to staff with a good understanding of the current system. We cannot expect these models to be entirely correct, but we can expect them to provide a general description of the requirements currently satisfied.

Generalization to a level-3 business information model depends on business client involvement, and the prior existence of some top-down information model covering the area. It is unlikely that a reverse-engineering process will actually yield a complete level-3 model.

10.2 REVERSE-ENGINEERING EXAMPLE

The following material presents a reverse-engineering example that demonstrates the steps involved in inferring a model from the design of an old system.

The example is simple, but keep in mind that real-life structures usually are far more complex, and that the process is much more difficult than our example illustrates. Because we never have enough information and must make assumptions, results are always suspect.

Assume we work for Express Master Visa Discovery Club Corporation and we are looking at a COBOL batch sequential processing system that accounts for credit card purchases. Also assume that, at the beginning, we have access only to the record layouts (COBOL File Definitions) for the system and nothing else.

10.2.1 Level-1 Model Inferences

We have been given the layouts for two master files in the current system. They contain the record structures shown in Figs. 10.2 and 10.3.

The first step is to create a level-1A model. In this model, every COBOL 01-level structure becomes an entity, so the process basically involves drawing an entity shape around each of the 01 levels. Figure 10.4 shows the result.

Next, we look for repeating groups of data to drop out into characteristic entities and overlapping sets of attributes to arrange into category structures. When we make these changes, we will be at level 1B. In our example, we know that we are dealing with a tape sequential processing system and that many generations of the master file are kept. Therefore, we will also break out a master file entity for each of the files. (We will discard this physical information from the diagram later, although we will need to capture it in the dictionary if our objective is to document the current system.) The level-1B model is shown as Fig. 10.5. The attributes shown in lowercase letters have been inserted to adhere to the rules of the modeling language.

Now, we need to convert from physical system names to business names for the entities and attributes. In some cases, this is easy; but in others, we need more information. For example, we need to know what "DAYS" in MONTH-REC and "IMP" and "WARN" in MERCH mean.

To find this information, we look first for the data dictionary entries that define the data. Unfortunately, we find that our company does not have a data dictionary. Therefore, we must use whatever documentation there is for the current system. Part of it is missing, and what's available is out of date, but we are able to take the process as far as Fig. 10.6. We have not yet been able to find information about the attributes that remain in uppercase letters.

```
000010*************************************************************
000020**          CARD MEMBER MASTER FILE                      **
000030*************************************************************
000040 01  CARD-MEMB-HDR.
000050     05   KEY-AREA.
000060          10   FILLER          PIC X(12).
000070          10   REC-TYPE        PIC 9.
000080               88   H-REC      VALUE IS 0.
000090               88   D-REC      VALUE IS 1.
000100               88   T-REC      VALUE IS 9.
000110          10   SEQ             PIC 9(9).
000120     05   FILE-DESCR.
000130          10   BUS-DATE        PIC 9(6).
000140          10   NEXT-DATE       PIC 9(6).
000150          10   STAT            PIC X.
000160     05   FILLER               PIC X(287).
000170 01  CARD-MEMB.
000180     05   KEY-AREA.
000190          10   ACC-NUM         PIC 9(12).
000200          10   REC-TYPE        PIC 9.
000210               88   H-REC      VALUE IS 0.
000220               88   D-REC      VALUE IS 1.
000230               88   T-REC      VALUE IS 9.
000240          10   SEQ             PIC 9(9).
000250     05   MEMBER.
000260          10   EXP-DATE        PIC 9(6).
000270          10   NAME            PIC X(40).
000280          10   AL-1            PIC X(44).
000290          10   AL-2            PIC X(44).
000300          10   AL-3            PIC X(44).
000310          10   ZIP             PIC 9(5).
000320          10   C-NAME-1        PIC X(40).
000330          10   C-NAME-2        PIC X(40).
000340          10   C-LIMIT         PIC 9(5).
000350          10   MTD-BAL         PIC S9(5)V99.
000360          10   YTD-ACT         PIC S9(6)V99.
000370          10   BAL             PIC S9(5)V99.
000380          10   PMT-AMT         PIC S9(5)V99.
000390          10   PMT-STAT        PIC X.
000400          10   STAT            PIC X(2).
000410     05   STMT-HIST   REDEFINES MEMBER.
000420          10   MONTH-REC   OCCURS 12 TIMES.
000430               15   MONTH      PIC 9(2).
000440               15   CHARGE     PIC S9(5)V99.
000450               15   PAYMENT    PIC S9(5)V99.
000460               15   BAL        PIC S9(5)V99.
000470               15   DAYS       PIC 9(2).
000480     05   CHARGE      REDEFINES MEMBER.
000490          10   CHARGE-DATE     PIC 9(6).
000500          10   CHARGE-AMT      PIC S9(5)V99.
000510          10   MERCH-NUM       PIC 9(7).
000520          10   DESCR           PIC X(52).
000530          10   FILLER          PIC X(228).
000540     05   PAYMENT     REDEFINES MEMBER.
000550          10   PMT-DATE        PIC 9(6).
000560          10   PMT-AMT         PIC S9(5)V99.
000570          10   FILLER          PIC X(287).
000580 01  CARD-MEMB-TLR.
000590     05   KEY-AREA.
000600          10   FILLER          PIC X(12).
000610          10   REC-TYPE        PIC 9.
000620               88   H-REC      VALUE IS 0.
000630               88   D-REC      VALUE IS 1.
000640               88   T-REC      VALUE IS 9.
000650          10   SEQ             PIC 9(9).
000660     05   FILE-DESCR.
000670          10   REC-COUNT       PIC 9(9).
000680          10   HASH            PIC 9(13).
000690          10   HASH-STAT       PIC X.
000700     05   FILLER               PIC X(277).
000710*************************************************************
```

Figure 10.2. Card Member Master File.

```
000010***********************************************************
000020**            MERCHANT MASTER FILE                      **
000030***********************************************************
000040 01  MERCH-HDR.
000050     05  KEY-AREA.
000060         10   FILLER          PIC 9(7).
000070         10   REC-TYPE        PIC 9.
000080         10   SEQ             PIC 9(7).
000090     05  FILE-DESCR.
000100         10   BUS-DATE        PIC 9(6).
000110         10   NEXT-DATE       PIC 9(6).
000120         10   STAT            PIC X.
000130     05  FILLER              PIC X(213).
000140 01  MERCH.
000150     05  KEY-AREA.
000160         10   MERCH-NUM       PIC 9(7).
000170         10   REC-TYPE        PIC 9.
000180         10   SEQ             PIC 9(7).
000190     05  MEMBER.
000200         10   NAME            PIC X(40).
000210         10   FIRST-AD-LINE   PIC X(46).
000220         10   SECND-AD-LINE   PIC X(46).
000230         10   THIRD-AD-LINE   PIC X(46).
000240         10   ZIP             PIC 9(9).
000250         10   IMP             PIC 9.
000260         10   WARN            PIC X.
000270         10   DISCOUNT        PIC 9(3).
000280         10   TD-ACT          PIC S9(8)V99.
000290         10   TD-VOL          PIC S9(6).
000300         10   SIC             PIC 9(4).
000310         10   PHONE           PIC X(14).
000320 01  MERCH-TLR.
000330     05  KEY-AREA.
000340         10   FILLER          PIC 9(7).
000350         10   REC-TYPE        PIC 9.
000360         10   SEQ             PIC 9(7).
000370     05  FILE-DESCR.
000380         10   REC-COUNT       PIC 9(7).
000390         10   HASH            PIC 9(13).
000400         10   HASH-STAT       PIC X.
000410     05  FILLER              PIC X(205).
000420***********************************************************
```

Figure 10.3. Merchant Master File.

```
01  CARD-MEMB-HDR.
    +------------------------------------------+
    | 05  KEY-AREA.                            |
    |     10  FILLER           PIC X(12).      |
    |     10  REC-TYPE         PIC 9.          |
    |         88  H-REC        VALUE IS 0.     |
    |         88  D-REC        VALUE IS 1.     |
    |         88  T-REC        VALUE IS 9.     |
    |     10  SEQ              PIC 9(9).       |
    | 05  FILE-DESCR.                          |
    |     10  BUS-DATE         PIC 9(6).       |
    |     10  NEXT-DATE        PIC 9(6).       |
    |     10  STAT             PIC X.          |
    | 05  FILLER               PIC X(287).     |
    +------------------------------------------+


01  CARD-MEMB.
    +------------------------------------------+
    | 05  KEY-AREA.                            |
    |     10  ACC-NUM          PIC 9(12).      |
    |     10  REC-TYPE         PIC 9.          |
    |         88  H-REC        VALUE IS 0.     |
    |         88  D-REC        VALUE IS 1.     |
    |         88  T-REC        VALUE IS 9.     |
    |     10  SEQ              PIC 9(9).       |
    | 05  MEMBER.                              |
    |     10  EXP-DATE         PIC 9(6).       |
    |     10  NAME             PIC X(40).      |
    |     10  AL-1             PIC X(44).      |
    |     10  AL-2             PIC X(44).      |
    |     10  AL-3             PIC X(44).      |
    |     10  ZIP              PIC 9(5).       |
    |     10  C-NAME-1         PIC X(40).      |
    |     10  C-NAME-2         PIC X(40).      |
    |     10  C-LIMIT          PIC 9(5).       |
    |     10  MTD-BAL          PIC S9(5)V99.   |
    |     10  YTD-ACT          PIC S9(6)V99.   |
    |     10  BAL              PIC S9(5)V99.   |
    |     10  PMT-AMT          PIC S9(5)V99.   |
    |     10  PMT-STAT         PIC X.          |
    |     10  STAT             PIC X(2).       |
    | 05  STMT-HIST  REDEFINES MEMBER.         |
    |     10  MONTH-REC   OCCURS 12 TIMES.     |
    |         15  MONTH        PIC 9(2).       |
    |         15  CHARGE       PIC S9(5)V99.   |
    |         15  PAYMENT      PIC S9(5)V99.   |
    |         15  BAL          PIC S9(5)V99.   |
    |         15  DAYS         PIC 9(2).       |
    | 05  CHARGE      REDEFINES MEMBER.        |
    |     10  CHARGE-DATE      PIC 9(6).       |
    |     10  CHARGE-AMT       PIC S9(5)V99.   |
    |     10  MERCH-NUM        PIC 9(7).       |
    |     10  DESCR            PIC X(52).      |
    |     10  FILLER           PIC X(228).     |
    | 05  PAYMENT     REDEFINES MEMBER.        |
    |     10  PMT-DATE         PIC 9(6).       |
    |     10  PMT-AMT          PIC S9(5)V99.   |
    |     10  FILLER           PIC X(287).     |
    +------------------------------------------+


01  CARD-MEMB-TLR.
    +------------------------------------------+
    | 05  KEY-AREA.                            |
    |     10  FILLER           PIC X(12).      |
    |     10  REC-TYPE         PIC 9.          |
    |         88  H-REC        VALUE IS 0.     |
    |         88  D-REC        VALUE IS 1.     |
    |         88  T-REC        VALUE IS 9.     |
    |     10  SEQ              PIC 9(9).       |
    | 05  FILE-DESCR.                          |
    |     10  REC-COUNT        PIC 9(9).       |
    |     10  HASH             PIC 9(13).      |
    |     10  HASH-STAT        PIC X.          |
    | 05  FILLER               PIC X(277).     |
    +------------------------------------------+


01  MERCH-HDR.
    +------------------------------------------+
    | 05  KEY-AREA.                            |
    |     10  FILLER           PIC 9(7).       |
    |     10  REC-TYPE         PIC 9.          |
    |     10  SEQ              PIC 9(7).       |
    | 05  FILE-DESCR.                          |
    |     10  BUS-DATE         PIC 9(6).       |
    |     10  NEXT-DATE        PIC 9(6).       |
    |     10  STAT             PIC X.          |
    | 05  FILLER               PIC X(213).     |
    +------------------------------------------+


01  MERCH.
    +------------------------------------------+
    | 05  KEY-AREA.                            |
    |     10  MERCH-NUM        PIC 9(7).       |
    |     10  REC-TYPE         PIC 9.          |
    |     10  SEQ              PIC 9(7).       |
    | 05  MEMBER.                              |
    |     10  NAME             PIC X(40).      |
    |     10  FIRST-AD-LINE    PIC X(46).      |
    |     10  SECND-AD-LINE    PIC X(46).      |
    |     10  THIRD-AD-LINE    PIC X(46).      |
    |     10  ZIP              PIC 9(9).       |
    |     10  IMP              PIC 9.          |
    |     10  WARN             PIC X.          |
    |     10  DISCOUNT         PIC 9(3).       |
    |     10  TD-ACT           PIC S9(8)V99.   |
    |     10  TD-VOL           PIC S9(6).      |
    |     10  SIC              PIC 9(4).       |
    |     10  PHONE            PIC X(14).      |
    +------------------------------------------+


01  MERCH-TLR.
    +------------------------------------------+
    | 05  KEY-AREA.                            |
    |     10  FILLER           PIC 9(7).       |
    |     10  REC-TYPE         PIC 9.          |
    |     10  SEQ              PIC 9(7).       |
    | 05  FILE-DESCR.                          |
    |     10  REC-COUNT        PIC 9(7).       |
    |     10  HASH             PIC 9(13).      |
    |     10  HASH-STAT        PIC X.          |
    | 05  FILLER               PIC X(205).     |
    +------------------------------------------+
```

Figure 10.4. Level-1A Model.

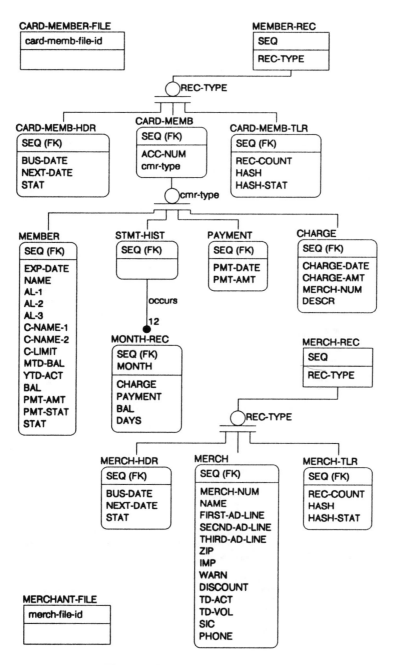

Figure 10.5. Level-1B Model.

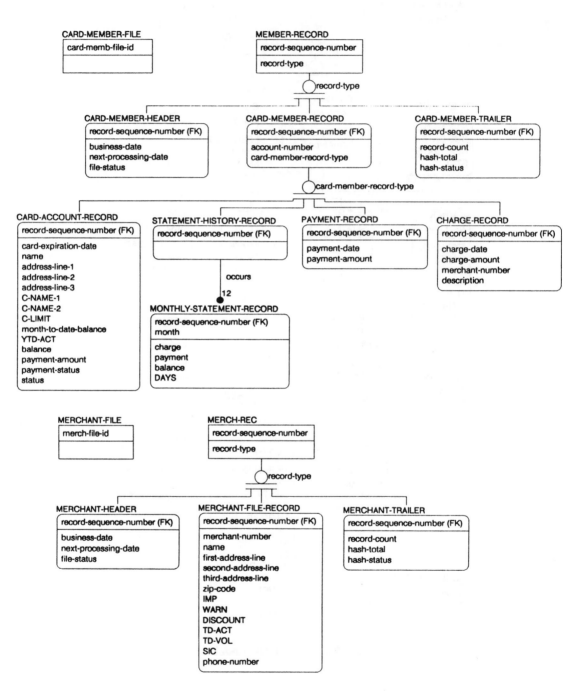

Figure 10.6. Level-1C Model (Almost).

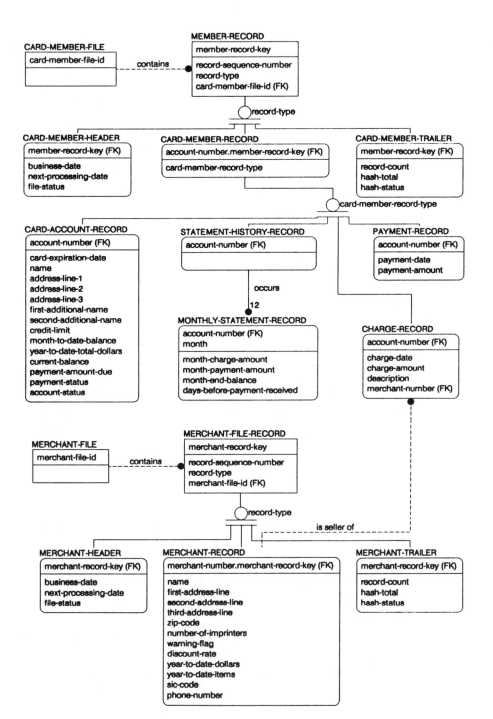

Figure 10.7. Level-1D Model.

With the help of the current programmers, we are able to complete the naming. We now have a level-1C model. This is a good time to write down definitions of the data elements we started with. Here is an example. Note that the element has both a physical name, and a model name.

> **Warning:**   A flag in the MERCHANT-FILE-RECORD that indicates
>   a high rate of charge-back to the merchant in the
>   past. Care should be taken when authorizing purchas-
>   es from this merchant.
>
>   Current element name: WARN

Next, we need to determine how the separate data structures fit together. It's not too hard to find the relationships in our simple example. We know each file contains many records, so there must be one-to-many relationships from CARD-MEMBER-FILE to MEMBER-RECORD and from MERCHANT-FILE to MERCHANT-FILE-RECORD. We provide surrogate keys for MEMBER-RECORD and MERCHANT-FILE-RECORD since we know that the file structure is an artifact of the current sequential processing implementation, and that we will discard the files in the next step. There is only one business relationship between the two files, and we find it represented by the "merchant-number" stored in the CHARGE-RECORD. We now have a level-1D model, which is very much a physical model.

10.2.2 Level-2 Model Inferences

To move to a level-2A model, we must resolve any obvious normalization anomalies and remove the physical system characteristics. Up to this point, our model has represented the physical structure of the current system. Because we are now crossing the boundary into the logical design of the system, we eliminate the implementation characteristics, such as the representation of the physical files.

Dropping the implementation characteristics eliminates both FILE entities and both of the RECORD generic parents as well as their HEADER and TRAILER categories. CARD-MEMBER-RECORD becomes CARD-ACCOUNT and MER-CHANT-RECORD becomes MERCHANT. In this case, aside from assigning unique attribute names, there is little normalization to do. We can see from our level-1D model that each CARD-ACCOUNT should be related to its state-

ments and payments. We therefore decide to allow an unlimited number of
each (by using one-to-many relationships) and remove the limitation of 12
statement records per account. CHARGE replaces CHARGE-RECORD and is
represented as an associative entity.

These changes give us the level-2A model shown in Fig. 10.8. It is still
a representation of the current system, but the physical implementation
characteristics and restrictions have been removed. Notice that we have
retained some derived attributes in our model (and described them as such
in our dictionary). Finding them is left as a chapter exercise.

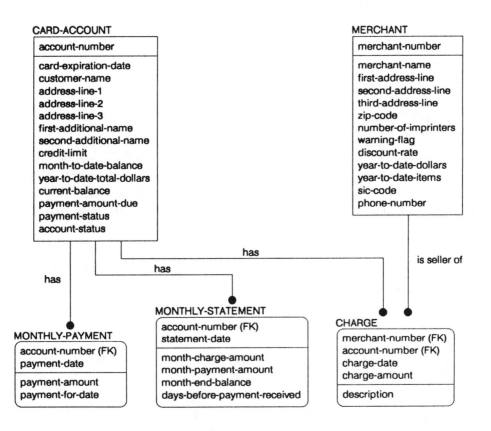

Figure 10.8. Level-2A Model.

To move from level 2A to level 2B, we need to resolve some business issues. In doing so, we attempt to represent the original requirements of the current system. For example, in our research into the meanings of the data elements, we might have learned that "first-additional-name" and "second-additional-name" in CARD-ACCOUNT represent additional individuals who are authorized to use the account. Although separate cards are issued to them in their own names, the individual named by the "customer-name" attribute, not the additional users, has responsibility for the account. We also might have learned that the limit of two additional users was arbitrary and the business requirement actually was for an unlimited number of users. The business would also like to know the addresses of these other users, but the limitations of the current system make this a difficult and expensive enhancement.

Let's assume the only original requirement not met by the current system is the one allowing an unlimited number of additional users of the account. If we extend the model to include this requirement by adding a CUSTOMER and an association between the CUSTOMER and the CARD-ACCOUNT, we end up with Fig. 10.9. Let's deem it level 2B.

10.2.3 Level-3 Model

There is a fine line between the level-2B and level-3 models. A level-2B model represents requirements for the current system. A level-3 model represents requirements for the future. Thus, level 3 is the point at which the model is adjusted to support both current requirements not satisfied by the existing system and strategic considerations of the business.

Taking the model to level 3 is an exercise left to the reader. You might want to consider that a merchant could also be a card member, that the multiple users of the account might like separate accountings, and so on.

10.3 SWEET DREAMS

Reverse engineering is an attractive substitute for developing models of true business information requirements. Too attractive, in fact. At first blush, reverse engineering seems to offer an easy way to gain an understanding of requirements. But in practice, it doesn't work for much of anything beyond documenting a current system. And even that is an iffy proposition. As has been stressed throughout this chapter, a model of what you have is not a model of what you want. If it were, there would be no need to rebuild.

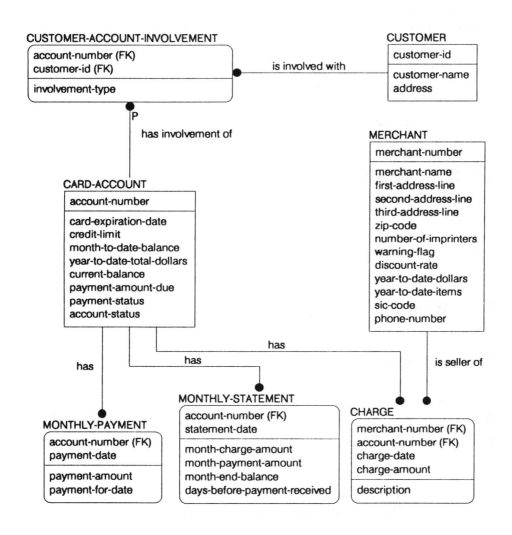

Figure 10.9.   Level-2B Model.

Reverse-engineered models are founded on assumptions, and by now we ought to recognize that assumptions are dangerous. In preparing a reverse-engineered model, there always comes a point when we must guess at what the designers of an old system were trying to do, or what the owners of that system actually want. From the same level-1D model, there will almost certainly be several possible level-2A alternatives corresponding to different sets of assumptions. From any level-2A, there will almost certainly be several possible level-2Bs. And from level-2B, it is impossible to get to level-3 without piling on more assumptions. Remember that the source of reverse-engineered models is the past, including all of the mistakes we made then.

So be extremely careful with reverse engineering. There is no technical process that can substitute for hard work. Except maybe magic. If you believe in magic, then dream your dreams. Quality databases are more properly designed and developed by those who are fully awake.

10.4 REVIEW EXERCISES

Answers to boldface questions appear in Appendix H.

1. What is the difference between reverse engineering and re-engineering?

2. **What are the potential benefits of reverse engineering?**

3. **What are the potential risks of reverse engineering?**

4. **Why is a reverse-engineered model not necessarily a model of what you want? What is required to make it so?**

5. Prepare a reverse-engineered model for a small (very small) database you know about. What assumptions have you needed to make?

6. Prepare a level-3 model for the credit card company example in Section 10.2. What business requirements assumptions have you made?

7. Which of the attributes in Fig. 10.9 represent derived data?

11

FUTURE DIRECTIONS

This chapter looks at several aspects of the future of information management and information modeling. It begins with the business environment in which we will operate, then discusses opportunities for information management in that environment. This leads to a discussion of emerging technologies, including repositories and front ends we will use to access them.

There is only one review exercise for the chapter since my future is your present. I encourage you to do some speculating of your own.

11.1 BUSINESS ENVIRONMENT

Our business world is becoming increasingly competitive. Legislative trends toward deregulation (and in some cases, re-regulation) are spawning innovation in many market sectors. Our focus is changing, the pace is steadily increasing, and challenges are becoming more difficult. The increase in global opportunities and markets provides fertile territory for the introduction of new products and services. These factors combine to suggest that the role of the information management professional will become increasingly important.

11.1.1 Changing Focus

For some time, businesses have been shifting away from a manufacturing focus toward a service focus. Moreover, many services being developed today are information-based, and these are gaining a larger share of the business emphasis. In 1987, for example, American Airlines earned roughly $410 million from flight operations, and $580 million from their SABRE reservations system.

As Charles Bachman has commented, it is interesting to speculate about *which* business American Airlines is actually in [1].

For many businesses, the ability to understand, consolidate, and deliver information in a timely manner will be a determining factor in their ability to survive. People Express founder Donald Burr, for example, cites the cause of the abrupt demise of his airline in 1985 as the inability of its information system to respond to pricing measures taken by United Airlines [2]:

> We were almost as big as American Airlines, and we had half their costs. . . . The airlines decided that the only way to deal with us was to underprice us—but on a spot basis. To do that, they turned to their information systems.

Information-based services require a focus on the structure and meaning of the data that underlies those services. As we have seen, information modeling is a technique for focusing on that data.

11.1.2 Information Delivery

Many new products, especially those in the service and finance sectors, will draw heavily on the ability of an organization to deliver information, both externally to its customers, and internally to its management. Internal business operations will require more real-time information to control the flow of work processed. As products and services become more complex, business management will need more summary and trend information to manage the directions of its products. Therefore, delivery and integration of information from separate systems, often from separate geographic locations, in a manageable and timely form, will be a primary driver of new products and services.

In order to integrate information, managers must know what is available and where it is stored. Top-down or reverse-engineered models of current databases and definitions of the data elements they contain enable rapid identification of the data available for integration. Wide-scope models of integrated information requirements provide an understanding of the mechanisms that must be developed to achieve the integration. The IDEF1X modeling techniques described in this book can be used to develop models satisfying these needs.

11.1.3 Harder Problems

Between 1960 and 1980, most organizations focused computing resources primarily on automating the major repetitive tasks of the business. These tasks, including personnel and payroll systems, procurement, general ledger and accounting, and accounts payable and receivable, posed fairly simple problems. Most of the simple problems have been solved.

Beginning in the 1980s, integration of systems, delivery of electronic services directly to customers, and a rapidly changing business environment created harder problems for data processing. New approaches to addressing information processing needs were required, and the need for them has continued to increase. Information management and information modeling are two such approaches that will be critical to the success, and in some cases the survival, of a turn-of-the-century business.

11.1.4 Short Time Frames

As competition increases, the pressure to develop new products and services quickly also increases. Information management professionals will need the right methods and building blocks to support ever-shortening development cycles. The key is to develop basic product and service building blocks so we can build from inventory rather than building each time from scratch. Wide-scope function and information models, both at a business level and at a technology level, will increase the ability of a company to respond to and lead market movements. Well-structured systems and databases, constructed according to these models, will become increasingly important.

IDEF1X information models can provide many of the building blocks for future systems. The modeling techniques described in this book focus on developing clear requirements both for current systems and for future extensions to these systems. Information structures developed for one application often can be reused in other applications. However, to achieve the future benefits of rapid development of new systems, emphasis must be placed on future directions as well as current requirements. Without such emphasis, shortening of future development cycles will not be achieved.

11.1.5 Decentralization

The availability of inexpensive and powerful small computers is fueling the trend toward distribution of computing and data management functions across decentralized business units. The problems created by uncontrolled distribution of technology are beginning to surface as operators discover that the information maintained in these private systems may be out of sync with information held in the organization's central files and databases. Private system operators are also discovering, as the technology becomes more powerful, that many skills needed to control the central processing environment are needed to control the decentralized environments. In other words, the environments need to be managed.

Personal technology is a double-edged sword. It has the potential to increase the effectiveness of the business. However, it can also be disruptive if the private systems are viewed as the source of basic business information. To prevent chaos in the personal database area, clear standards for the use of private and department-level resources are needed. These standards must be directed toward ensuring an orderly integration of small-scale and large-scale resources. Many of the information management disciplines discussed in Chapter 2 are applicable to small-scale as well as large-scale environments.

11.1.6 Niche Solutions

Advances in technology will continue to provide significant markets for small niche vendors, especially those who provide software to support narrow areas of business operations. There inevitably will be a strong push to adopt niche solutions as many will view them as a way to help a business quickly enter a new market. However, there are potential problems here, especially for companies with large investments in existing application portfolios. Niche products tend to move a business away from a well-integrated set of systems.

Thus, significant challenges will be to rapidly adapt those solutions that are appropriate, and preempt nonintegrable niche solutions; that is, to prevent integration problems from being created. To preempt will require a clear understanding of the impact of niche solutions, and rapid development of in-house alternatives. Reverse-engineered models of potential niche solutions and the availability of strategic models for the business can allow a thorough impact analysis. The modeling techniques and reverse-engineering approaches discussed in this book can be used to develop the material needed for analysis.

11.2 FUTURE OPPORTUNITIES

This environment might seem intimidating, but so it is with any future. We will be presented with opportunities in many forms. To take advantage of the opportunities will require the development and use of new tools and techniques. The opportunities, and supporting tools and techniques, are described in the remainder of the chapter.

11.2.1 Information Management Opportunities

We need to be prepared to manage the future information environment. One goal is to apply the information modeling techniques discussed in this book in the context of a larger, business-driven, information management strategy. To that end, the earlier a data processing organization can become involved with a business area, the better. Participation in the development of information strategies can begin the process of team building and can establish a foundation of business knowledge needed for later work. Do not expect to do a lot of modeling during the early stages. Rather, be prepared to use the techniques we have discussed when the opportunities present themselves. Every chance to assist the business is an opportunity to become more aware of its needs and values, and to advance the partnership.

Another goal is to develop an inventory of existing data definitions and structures. Such an inventory will allow an organization to more rapidly address the needs of its markets with new and innovative products.

11.2.2 New Information Product Opportunities

Understanding its fundamental information structures will enable a business to recognize opportunities for new information-based products and will suggest new ways to package and sell the same basic services. Financial institutions, for example, seek ways to build new products by tying together existing ones or by adding new options. A product that provides an international treasurer with a consolidated view of financial positions across the company can generate revenue and enable the institution that provides the product to develop a wider relationship with the company that uses it.

11.2.3 Information Research Opportunities

We are entering an era in which there will be more information than we know what to do with, an era in which we will have some difficulty finding the information required to make decisions needed to manage a business. One challenge will be to find out what exists, and how to get to it. Thus, an index of what is available and where to find it will be an important component of our environment. Providing such an index will not be easy. An information repository will serve as a basic foundation for this index, but determining how to fit a repository into an existing environment and how to extend or tailor its capabilities to fit the needs of the organization will be significant challenges.

To build an index into the information structures of a business, we will need a detailed analysis of the existing databases and files. This analysis will depend on the availability of good definitions for existing data. Therefore, beginning early to develop an inventory of definitions and data structure descriptions along with the processes needed to manage them will pay dividends in the end. Clear standards for naming and defining data elements, files, programs, systems, and so on, are a must. Many of the techniques discussed in this book address the need to manage the information inventory.

11.2.4 Integration and Bridging Opportunities

Most of today's organizations do not have single, integrated, development and operating environments for all data processing systems. Moreover, few organizations are likely to have such integrated environments in the near future—the trend points in the opposite direction. We often see separate development and production environments, and separate operations-support and decision-support environments. Therefore, at least for the foreseeable future, we need to find effective ways to move or copy (bridge) information from one environment to another so that the environments appear to be integrated, even if they are not.

In many organizations, the only realistic way to respond to internal decision-support needs will continue to be one of extracting information from operational systems and integrating it in back-end decision-support environments. The need to provide improved management information system support will grow as the competitive pace increases. Major challenges for the information manager will be to identify, define, configure, and control the use of decision-support information, and define and develop standard techniques for bridging information from one environment to another.

Information modeling is an effective way to understand MIS needs and to define the information structures needed to address them. Developing a clear set of bridging strategies and tools is something you can do now to prepare for an evermore complex set of future information flows. Many vendor products will attempt to assist the integration of information held in separate environments, but much tailoring of these products will be needed, as existing environments in major companies vary to a large degree.

11.3 TOOLS

Topics like computer aided software engineering, repository, distributed database, object-oriented systems, application development environments, and so on, seem to attract endless discussion. There is promise in these emerging technologies, but they are often surrounded by hype, and much opportunity for confusion.

11.3.1 CASE Tools

CASE tools are directed at automating the transformation of requirements statements into databases and code. They can be viewed as the means to capture information for a cell in the Zachman Framework, reconcile it with information for adjacent cells, and transform it into information for cells in lower rows or, in the case of reverse engineering, to go in the other direction. These tools are still in their infancy.

There are specific tools to fit specific needs, but there is no completely integrated set currently available. Some of the tools allow a more precise specification of system requirements and solutions than do others, but the transformation of these specifications into functioning systems is, for the most part, still human-assisted. Object-oriented systems are beginning to emerge, but we will have to wait until they mature sufficiently for large-scale use.

We must be careful about choosing tools. Every place that a tool cannot capture or enforce a business rule (for example, cardinality and domain enforcement in relational systems, transformation of functional rules into data value dependencies, and transformation and reconciliation of models and object definitions in CASE tools) is a place where code has to be written, and people have to be relied on to do things correctly. Tools that lack basic capabilities for capturing and using necessary information, for guaranteeing its integrity, or for integrating with other needed tools, should be viewed with considerable skepticism.

Information management professionals can play a significant role in helping to choose the right tools, and in ensuring that they will work well together. Mapping your current tool set into the Zachman Framework will help identify areas in which you have inadequate tool support or in which support available from competing tools is incompatible.

11.3.2 Repositories

The area of the information repository (also referred to as an information resource dictionary system, or IRDS) is one in which the integrity of the tool set is critical. The repository, together with its surrounding tools and procedures, is sometimes referred to as an application development environment or an application enabling environment. In time, this will evolve into a business development environment, supporting business as well as information systems professionals. There is, however, considerable confusion about what such environments should look like, and even more confusion about how repository products fit in. Different and competing repository standards have emerged.

The divergence of repository standards and the sometimes divergent objectives of the repository designers both tend to create a great deal of chaos [3, 4, 5]. Specifically, ANSI and ISO repository standards differ from one another; IBM's Repository Manager product follows neither standard.

The ANSI standard [6] defines an information resource dictionary system as "a key computer software tool for the management of data and information resources. It provides facilities for recording, storing, and processing descriptions of an organization's significant data and data processing resources." Neither IBM nor ISO have any quarrel with this. Both the ANSI and ISO standards describe the structure of information in the IRDS according to four levels of abstraction (ANSI calls them layers; ISO calls them levels). IBM uses a similar approach. The ANSI layers are shown in Fig. 11.1.

Physical data—that is, the actual values of such elements as customer names or social security numbers—is represented by the bottom layer of Fig. 11.1, the Production Data Layer. This data is not stored in a repository; rather, it is stored in the databases of the business as elements, records, files, and so on. The abstractions of elements, records, files, information models, entities, attributes, relationships, and so on, and the relationships among these abstractions (for example, records contain elements; information models contain entities) along with the characteristics of the abstractions (such as, records have lengths and elements have allowed ranges or values) are defined to the repository at the IRD Schema Layer.

The IRD Data Layer uses the IRD Schema Layer abstractions to store the conceptual schemas that describe business data, the physical design representations of these conceptual schemas (the internal and external schemas), and the relationships among these schemas. For example, in the data layer, we might discover that "customer-name" is an attribute of the CUSTOMER entity in some specified information model, is implemented as the CUST_NAM column in the T_CUST table in some specified relational database, and is entered in the CUST-NAME field on some specified data entry screen). For the bottom three layers in Fig. 11.1, there is a high degree of correspondence between the ANSI, ISO, and IBM approaches.

Meta-entity Types	Entity Type	Relationship Type	Attribute Type and Attribute Group Type

IRD SCHEMA DESCRIPTION LAYER

Entity Types Attribute Types Relationship Types	Element	Record	Record Contains Element	Length Allowable Range

IRD SCHEMA LAYER

Entities Relationships Attributes	Name SSN	Customer Employee Contract	Customer Record Contains Name	20 Characters Alpha

IRD DATA LAYER

Occurrences	John Sally	Cust Rec 1 Emp Rec 55	Cust Rec 1 Contains "John"	Constraints

PRODUCTION DATA LAYER

Figure 11.1. ANSI Repository Layers.

The major divergence in approaches occurs at the IRD Schema Description Layer. This layer contains the definition of the basic constructs the repository uses to model and store the lower-level data. Specifically, it defines how the concepts of entities, attributes, and relationships are used in the IRD Schema Layer to describe the content of the repository. It defines the repository concepts of repository entities, repository attributes, and repository relationships, and the allowed connections among these concepts.

The ANSI, ISO, and IBM concepts of repository entities, attributes, and relationships are not the same. For example, ANSI and ISO relationships may not themselves participate in relationships, but IBM relationships may. On the other hand, ISO and IBM relationships may not have attributes, but ANSI relationships may. ISO refers to relationships as association-types and entities as object-types. Using IDEF1X as a presentation medium, Figs. 11.2, 11.3, and 11.4 represent the differences between the ANSI, ISO, and IBM structures. Note that the figures illustrate the structure differences, and are not intended to be precise models.

An ANSI RELATIONSHIP-TYPE corresponds to an IDEF1X associative entity with exactly two identifying parents. ANSI standard characteristics follow:

- Relationships may involve only two entities.
- Relationships may not participate in relationships.
- Relationships may have attributes.
- Relationships may be many-to-many.

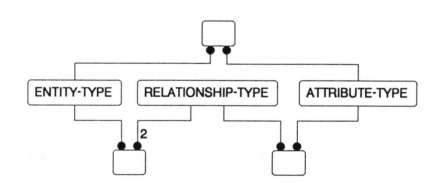

Figure 11.2. ANSI Repository Constructs.

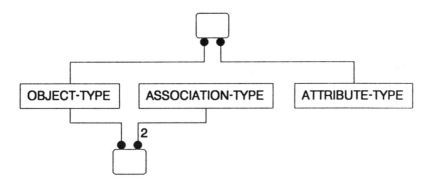

Figure 11.3. ISO Repository Constructs.

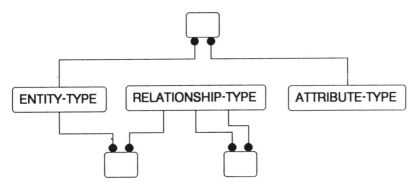

Figure 11.4. IBM Repository Constructs.

An ISO ASSOCIATION-TYPE corresponds to an IDEF1X identifying relationship. Its characteristics are

- Relationships may involve only two entities.
- Relationships may not participate in relationships.
- Relationships may not have attributes.
- Relationships are one-to-many.

An IBM RELATIONSHIP-TYPE corresponds to an IDEF1X associative entity with two parents and no attributes. It has the following characteristics:

- Relationships may involve only two constructs (which may be entities or relationships).
- Relationships may participate in relationships.
- Relationships may not have attributes.
- Relationships may be many-to-many.

It is important to recognize repository similarities and differences as we are likely to see not one but several repositories operating in large companies well into the next century. These repositories will be the basis for our index, containing descriptions of information the business maintains, with instructions for how to retrieve it from the operational and decision-support environments. Front ends to the repositories will be needed to help us find the way through the structures, and the separate repositories will have to be managed carefully.

Information management professionals will need to understand the different repository structures and ensure that compatible repository models are used when different repository standards are used by different areas of the business. We will need to tailor the offered repository structures to our individual needs. Tailoring the repository structures starts with a model of the information that the repository must hold.

IDEF1X can be used to prepare that model, as well as to prepare reverse-engineered models of repository products. IDEF1X also can be used to assess the capabilities of any modeling language supplied with or required by the product.

11.3.3 Intelligent Front Ends

An automated information index will only be effective if it is easy to use. Before the introduction of the personal computer, most interactions between people and systems were provided via character-based interfaces. The personal workstation provides a significant advance in the ease with which information can be presented and manipulated. Icons, pull-down menus, multiple windows, and so on, have become commonplace, and will be the basis for front-end applications that are easier to use than earlier character-based interfaces.

The emergence of expert-system technology can have a similar impact on our interactions with the information resource. Expert systems can assist those who define the architecture of information systems, and eventually may be loaded with rules describing how to access information in the systems. These expert-system rules will help us work through the myriad of detail and alternative sources to find desired information.

Developing queries against normalized data structures can be a trying experience for those who are not experts in languages like SQL. It is not reasonable to expect business professionals to learn such languages. Other ways to make information usable will be required. Some early front-end products attempt to help build queries via the use of natural language translators, while others lead users through the development of queries with point-and-click graphics techniques. The Metaphor product from Metaphor Computer Systems is an early example of a graphics-oriented interface to information. The Intelect product from AI Corp. attempts to be a natural language assist.

Including an expert-system layer around an IDEF1X conceptual schema could help users generate a database definition and develop queries against the resulting database. For example, a summary-level information model might be presented as a starting point for developing a query. Succeeding levels of detail could then be made available as the user selects areas of interest. Finally, point-and-click methods could be provided for forming and initiating queries against the organization's data.

11.3.4 Automation of the Transform

As the precision of specification languages improves, more detail will become available to the tools that help us transform specifications into functioning systems. With more precise specification languages, we can expect to be able to automate more of that transformation. Automation of the transform is a major goal of the emerging CASE technology.

Many current CASE tools are oriented toward a single function or toward small sets of closely related functions. Exchanging information among tools that were not designed to work together has turned out to be somewhat difficult. Thus, a major challenge has been to find products that support various parts of a development cycle and make them work together. More highly integrated tools enable more automation of the transform.

The information repositories will begin to have an impact on this situation during the mid-1990s, but it will be a long time before completely integrated tool sets will be available. Many new tools will be offered that claim to be repository-compliant, or standard. Given the proliferation of repository standards, however, this will continue to be confusing.

11.3.5 Support for Multiple Viewpoints

No single view of information systems can satisfy all audiences and all purposes. Future tools and specification languages will, therefore, need to provide ways of adjusting the view to fit a specific need. This will require an ability to record transformations among different types of models and to select those dimensions of the model needed in a particular situation.

Defining the rules and providing these transformation capabilities will be difficult.   Consider the problem of deriving an ERD model from a fully attributed model. Not only do we need to decide which attributes are important enough to present on the ERD (if any), we also need to make a judgment about each entity to determine whether it is important enough to retain. We must know how to substitute nonspecific relationships for fully resolved relationships, what to do with generalization hierarchies, and so on. The views must then be tailored to the preferences and characteristics of the viewers.

This is a formidable challenge for an algorithm. The algorithm will need to know about the meaning and importance of the structures specified in the model. It will also need to exercise judgment in selecting appropriate areas to highlight. The basic algorithms of future transformation tools and the specification languages we will use to drive them will need the assistance of expert-system rules and human interactions in order to complete the job. When available, these tools will be immensely helpful.

11.4 SPECIFICATION LANGUAGES

A specification language needs to be able to precisely record our understanding of requirements, and make this information available to the tools that will transform the specification into a functioning system. IDEF1X contains much of the required precision. However, as we saw in Chapters 7 and 8, IDEF1X also has its limitations. When we have to resort to notes to record the rules of the business, we give up the ability to have a tool assist with the implementation of those rules. The transformation tools cannot interpret notes unless the notes become a formal part of the language. For each deficiency in a specification language, knowledge is lost. Future specification languages must, therefore, be more complete. They must include the needed precision, and eventually must cover all rows and columns of the Zachman Framework.

11.4.1 Precision

Many information modeling methods and languages are available; some were mentioned in Chapter 3. As information modeling becomes more routine, and as the need for precision become more evident, some current languages are likely to be abandoned, or require significant modification and extension. We can expect languages like IDEF1X, NIAM, Bachman, and perhaps one of the more robust variants of the Chen style to emerge as the most common. Of these, IDEF1X and the Bachman languages do a good job of covering all types of information models. Chen-style languages currently work well at the higher levels of detail, but many lack the required precision to completely support the detailed levels. NIAM is precise at all levels, which may turn out to be a problem, because although the precision is important, the ability to discuss less-than-precise models with business professionals is equally important.

What will cause some languages to survive while others fall away is a combination of precision where required, and presentability where necessary. Languages that lack either of these dimensions will not survive.

11.4.2 Graphic Interfaces and Interactive Assistance

Early information modeling tools were driven by declarative languages. The model was defined by a series of coded statements, and the results looked something like a computer program. During the late 1980s, we began to see interactive graphics-based methods for defining information models. The ability to draw a diagram by point-and-click at a graphics workstation simplifies a modeler's job of entering and maintaining models, and provides a way to organize views so they are aesthetically acceptable to various audiences. Advances in the ability to control the placement of objects, to cluster like things together, to use color for emphasis, and so on, will further help communicate the information captured by the models to those who cannot take the time to learn how to find all the detail.

We are beginning to see these capabilities for some information modeling languages. For example, NIAM is supported by a PC-based product (IAST) available from Control Data Corporation. The Chen style is supported in many CASE tools (although they all seem to support it differently). A somewhat expensive platform is available to support the Bachman style, and IDEF1X has gained graphics support from the ERwin product from Logic Works, Inc. (see Appendix E for information on IDEF1X support products). MERISE and Information Engineering languages are supported by other tools.

Workstation-based modeling tools offer more support to the modeler than did the original coding approaches. When a modeler is required to draw and maintain the diagrams by hand, no assistance is provided. If mainframe-based tools driven by a set of statements that describe the model are used, a great deal of assistance can be provided. However, this assistance is after-the-fact since the tool is basically a batch-processing tool. Process the statements, and the tool will tell you what's right or wrong with the model.

Interactive graphics-based tools can help modelers catch errors before they are made. However, neither the graphics approach nor the "code it up and run it" approach is the complete answer. Each has its place. For small models, or views of a large model, graphics-based tools are extremely attractive. However, it is difficult to imagine maintaining a 500 to 1,000 entity model in a graphics environment. That may be a bit too much to deal with visually, so there is no single answer.

During the next decade, we can expect to see more cooperative solutions emerge, using workstation resources and graphics for some parts of the process, and mainframe power for other parts. We may even begin to move away from two-dimensional diagrams on pieces of paper (or their flat computer screen equivalent) and begin to see three-dimensional models.

11.4.3 Functional Language Integration

Some of the information modeling languages and tools are beginning to support what might be called cross-model validation—that is, they help ensure that separate models are mutually supportive. As we have discussed, neither the function nor the information model alone can completely describe a business area. The function model describes processes and the flow of information from one process to another. The information model describes the structure of the information and the business rules that support the function. When we create separate models of functions and data, it is important that they work together to describe the area being addressed.

When (1) the two models can work together so that the dataflows consist of attributes and attribute groups, (2) the processes create, replace, use, and delete the data, and (3) the data stores, screens, forms, and reports represent views into the information model, then we will have a very solid picture of the business. Add to this the network and rules dimensions, and the composite is even more complete. The languages we use to specify model structures must be able to work together to ensure the pictures they describe are complementary. The tools must help validate that the separate models are synchronized.

It is tempting to try to mix function models, data models, network models, and rules models on the same diagram. In fact, attempts have been made to do this and to add other aspects, such as "behavior" [7]. This can, however, lead to cluttered diagrams that lose their aesthetic appeal unless subset views of the model are supported. When the description of the components of a model is stored in a common repository, some interconnection can be done behind the scenes. This is the approach taken in many workstation-based CASE offerings. Rather than trying to mix different dimensions on the same picture, the modeler integrates function and information models by means of the underlying dictionary descriptions of their objects.

Languages that capture and integrate more of the description of a business are beginning to emerge. We will take a brief look at one of them in the next chapter.

11.5 REFERENCES

[1]   Bachman, C. "Re-Engineering of Information Systems." Presentation made at San Francisco DAMA Day, San Francisco, Calif., December 7, 1988.

[2]   Freedman, D.H. "Canceled Flights," *CIO*, April 1989, pp. 49-54.

[3]   Bruce, T., J. Fuller, and T. Moriarty. "So You Want a Repository?" *Database Programming and Design*, Vol. 2, No. 5 (May 1989), pp. 60-69.

[4]   Winsberg, P. "Dictionary Standards: ANSI, ISO and IBM," *InfoDB*, Vol. 3, No. 4 (Winter 1988-1989).

[5]   Lefkovitz, H.C. *Draft Proposed American National Standards: Information Resource Dictionary System.* Wellesley, Mass.: QED Information Sciences, 1985.

[6]   "Information Resource Dictionary System (IRDS)—Technical Report X3.138-1986," Base Technical Committee X3H4-IRDS, Global Engineering Documents, 1986.

[7]   Ross, R. *Entity Modeling: Techniques and Application.* Boston, Mass.: Database Research Group, 1987.

12

OBJECTS AND DMT/2

The field of object-oriented systems analysis and design is becoming more than just an academic curiosity. Object-oriented database management systems, such as GemStone from Servio Corp., Versant from Versant Open Technology Corp., and Ontos from Ontologic, Inc., while still in a somewhat experimental period, are beginning to approach a point where they can be used for real business problems. The concept of combining function and data into object recognizes the fundamental tie between these aspects of the business model and could lead to more highly integrated systems.

12.1 OBJECTS, LOGIC, AND THE EXTENDED CONCEPTUAL SCHEMA

An *object* has both a data character and a function character. Think of it as an IDEF1X entity instance with a set of processes bound to it. The attributes of the entity instance represent the data properties of the object. The processes bound to the instance represent the active properties of the object, that is, what the object knows, does, or has done to it. In object-oriented terminology, these processes are called methods.

Objects communicate via defined protocols, each consisting of a set of messages. A *message* is a request for some property of an object. This property may be a data property (attribute) or an active property (method); it is important to note that the requestor does not need to know which kind of property—it simply requests the property.

Object classes are collections of objects (as IDEF1X entities, or more precisely entity types, are a collection of entity instances). Objects inherit the methods and protocols of their classes. For example, if an object class represents the customers of a business, each individual customer is represented in

276

the system as an object of the customer class. Some of these classes may represent aggregate objects, a concept that might be used to layer object diagrams much as is done today for a set of dataflow diagrams (DFDs).

Object classes can be organized into inheritance hierarchies similar to IDEF1X generalization hierarchies. Object classes in such hierarchies inherit the properties of the classes above them, including their protocols and methods.

Our current view of the conceptual schema (see Chapter 1) is that it is a description of the information that supports a business, and the rules that govern the behavior of that information. IDEF1X does a good job of describing the information structures and an adequate job of describing the rules. As we saw in Chapters 7 and 8, however, there are some business rules (generally complex constraints) that cannot be formally declared using the language. Verification that the conceptual schema is internally consistent (that is, that it does not contain conflicting assertions) can also become difficult and tedious as the models become large.

Work is under way to extend IDEF1X to describe objects and to use formal logic methods to state the assertions carried by the model. The conceptual schema then would become considerably more robust. Moreover, it could become possible to use expert-system approaches to draw logical inferences from the additional detail provided by the schema and to use rule-based processing engines to enforce the assertions in physical systems [1, 2]. The motivation is not simply to make IDEF1X object oriented. Rather, the motivation is to develop a language and technique (currently named DMT/2) that better address the development of integrated systems.

The transition from function orientation to data orientation requires that we shift our thought process from, How do I do this? to What information exists? To extend into the object and logic world requires that we shift again and begin to "think" like objects. We must start to ask, What am I? What do I know? What can I do? What can be done to me? What rules must I obey? Learning to think in this manner will involve another difficult transition.

It is not clear how the language extensions will finally appear, although they will likely evolve as a series of small steps, with IDEF1X remaining a compatible subset of the full language. The extended language is likely to have several types of models (similar to the current ERD, key based, and fully attributed types of IDEF1X models), with the project models used to specify all detail and the area models used to describe overall concepts. The material presented in the rest of the chapter is adapted from a paper by Bob Brown of the Data Base Design Group, and is used with permission [3].

12.2   DMT/2 MOTIVATION

To gain insight into DMT/2 as a specification language and technique for the future, we must first look back. Over the past fifteen years, we have seen database design evolve from being primarily concerned with pointer options and block sizes to today's full-scale model-building discipline. Although called data (or information) modeling for historical reasons, what the analyst actually does is focus on the business entity and model it directly. The analyst does not think of modeling the data as distinct from modeling the business entity. Similarly, program design has evolved to include structured analysis (Fig. 12.1).

Structured analysis helps us specify business functions and the computer programs that support them. Information modeling helps us specify business entities and the computer databases used to represent them. However, a gap now exists—between structured analysis and information modeling.

The future holds a continuation of the evolution toward system development through modeling. Extended modeling will subsume information modeling and replace much of structured analysis. There are two major additions to the information models: processes and rules.

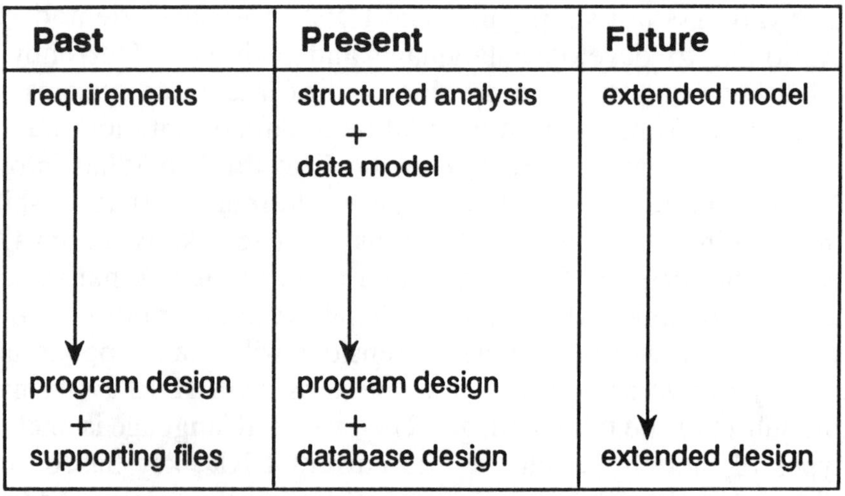

Past	Present	Future
requirements	structured analysis + data model	extended model
↓	↓	↓
program design + supporting files	program design + database design	extended design

Figure 12.1. Design Method Evolution.

Technically, the additions are based on the techniques of object-oriented and rule-based systems. That is, the concepts behind object-oriented and rule-based techniques are added to information modeling to give extended modeling. This allows us to more completely model the enterprise in a way that is consistent with advanced implementation techniques.

The fundamental objectives are unchanged: The models must be expressive and understandable enough for the user to work with, and at the same time, precise enough for the developer to use. Incorporating object-oriented and rule-based concepts simply allows these objectives to be better met.

DMT/2 will contain significant extensions in a number of areas: objects, specification language, constraints, domains, relationships, metaclasses, rules, views, and aggregate objects. In Sections 12.3 and 12.4, we will consider only objects, specification language, and rules (Note that the use of nonproportional typeface highlights DM/2 examples and syntax.). Even within these topics, important ideas such as object identity, inheritance, and conflict resolution are not covered. Instead, we will concentrate on the paradigm shift behind the object and rule extensions, illustrating them with examples based on the video store model introduced in Chapter 4.

12.3 OBJECT-ORIENTED MODELING

Object-oriented ideas have their roots in programming. But just as information modeling has moved beyond its roots in database, so the new modeling techniques will use object orientation in ways that go beyond its roots in programming. The essential insight of object orientation is to treat both the data about an entity and the processes about an entity as properties of that entity. An object perspective requires this critical shift in thinking—from considering *only* the data (of the entity) to considering *both* the data and the processes (of the object).

Treating data in this way is the fundamental principle of information modeling. Data is not considered ancillary to an application function; it is permanently tied to an entity. All data is data *about* some business entity. The new modeling techniques will treat process logic in the same way. Process logic does not exist only within the context of an application function, it is permanently tied to an entity (object). All processes are processes *about* some object. They are active properties (methods) of the object.

12.3.1 Object Subsumes Entity

The new modeling techniques can be seen as an evolution of information modeling. In information modeling, a working definition of *entity* is something like "a distinguishable person, place, or thing about which information is to be kept." Information is taken to mean attributes and relationships. Both are passive, used by and acted on by active processes. The extension of entity to object can be seen as expanding the notion of information to include active properties. More fundamentally, the passive entity becomes an active object—an intelligent actor with knowledge and actions. A working definition of *object* is "a distinct person, place, or thing with relevant knowledge or actions."

A passive property (attribute) is a fact that an object knows directly. An active property is an action taken by an object, or a fact known indirectly, by derivation. For example, in the video store example in Chapter 4, a movie may or may not have an available copy; this is something a movie *knows* indirectly, by derivation (based on the availability of its copies). Renting a movie is an active property of customers; this is something a customer *does*. A new movie rental record is created when a movie copy is rented to a customer; this is something that is *done to* the class of movie rental records.

The active properties of objects are what act on the passive properties of objects. There are no separate processes. The active properties make up what is called *behavior* in object-oriented terminology. In other words, what we have called an entity is just a special case of object. An entity is a degenerate object that doesn't know how to behave.

Although the new modeling techniques will be evolutionary for the data analyst, they will be revolutionary for the systems analyst. Focusing on process separate from data, as structured analysis does with DFDs, will be fundamentally inappropriate. Decomposition will still be useful to limit the scope of modeling, but the attempt to proceed top-down from high-level DFDs to low-level DFDs to mini-specifications to module structures to code must be abandoned.

12.3.2 Examples from the Video Store

In order to make these ideas more concrete, let's look at part of the video store model from Chapter 4: Video store customers rent movies. Actually, they request the movie by name, rent a copy of it if it is available, and receive an overdue notice if they do not return it in time. There are five objects involved: customer, movie, movie-copy, movie-rental-record, and overdue-notice.

The actions are

1. A customer rents any available copy of the requested movie.
2. A movie determines whether it has a copy available, and if so, which copy.
3. A movie copy determines if it is available.
4. A rental begins for a customer and copy of a movie.
5. A rental sends an overdue notice if it is late.

These actions can be considered active properties of the objects. The active properties can be shown along with the passive properties (attributes) in a revised diagram for the video store (see Fig. 12.2). It is similar to an IDEF1X diagram, but with some important differences. The diagram shows properties at both the class and instance level. The brackets above the boxes hold the properties applicable to the object class. Properties inside the boxes are applicable to object instances. Active properties are shown in boldface.

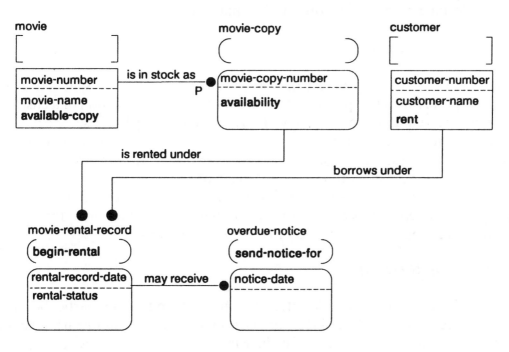

Figure 12.2. Object Relationships.

12.3.2.1 Instance properties

The `movie-name` attribute of `movie` is a passive property. It is an instance property because each instance of `movie` has its own value for `movie-name`. The `available-copy` property of `movie` is an active property. It is an instance property because each instance of `movie` has its own values for `available-copy`. Each instance of `movie` either has copies available for rent or it does not. Because it is derived, `available-copy` is an active property. A `movie` has an available copy if the `movie` is in stock as a `movie-copy` and if that `movie-copy` is available.

The `availability` property of `movie-copy` is an active, instance property. It is an instance property because each `movie-copy` either is available for rent or is not available. It is an active property because it is derived based on the `movie-rental-record` the `movie-copy` is rented under.

The `rent` property of `customer` is an active, instance property. It is an active property because it represents the customer *doing* the rental of a movie. It is an instance property because individual customers rent movies. Invoking the `rent` property for a `customer` causes (a representation of) the rental to take place (be recorded) for that customer.

12.3.2.2 Class properties

The `begin-rental` property of `movie-rental-record` is an active class property. It is an active property because it represents the action of a customer beginning a rental of a movie copy. It is a class property because `begin-rental` creates a new instance of `movie-rental-record` to record the fact that the `customer` has rented the `movie-copy`. It is up to the `movie-rental-record` class to create instances of `movie-rental-record`.

The `send-notice-for` property of `overdue-notice` is an active class property. It represents the action of sending an overdue notice for a rental record, creating a new instance of `overdue-notice`.

12.3.2.3 Object identity

In IDEF1X, entities are identified by their attributes, in particular, their primary keys. In DMT/2, objects are considered to have an intrinsic identity, represented by an object identifier invisible to the observer. A subset of the properties of an object usually must be unique according to the rules of the world being modeled. Some such unique set of properties, if any exist, is chosen as a primary uniqueness constraint. It is this set of properties that is shown above the dashed line in the box. The object identifiers are not shown in the diagram.

12.3.2.4 Relationships

In DMT/2, a relationship, although diagrammed with a line, is also an object. It is named by the participant and relationship names. A relationship has a property for each participant. Furthermore, each participant has a property for the other participant. The name of that participant property can be shown on the diagram as a name in parentheses following the relationship name. As with IDEF1X, there are relationship names in both directions. The default relationship name is none. The default participant property names are the participant object names. There are also cardinality, existence, and update rules for relationships, and these are essentially the same as in IDEF1X.

Figure 12.2 shows only forward relationship names and default participant property names. For example, the relationship labeled "is in stock as" indicates that `movie-copy` has a `movie` property. This is reminiscent of migrating keys in IDEF1X, but there are two important differences: First, the value of a property, such as `movie`, is an object identifier, not a primary key. Second, the participant properties are active properties, not passive (attributes) as in IDEF1X. If the default participant properties and both directions of the relationship name were shown in Fig. 12.2, the `movie` to `movie-copy` relationship would be labeled as

```
is in stock as (movie-copy) / is a copy of (movie)
```

Note that for each `movie-copy`, `movie` is a single-valued property. However, for each `movie`, `movie-copy` is a multi-valued property. A single-valued property, identifying a related object, can be used as a primary uniqueness constraint. If one is, the line for the relationship is solid. Hence, the line from `movie` to `movie-copy` in Fig. 12.2 is solid. The uniqueness constraint on `movie-copy` is on the two properties, `movie`, and `movie-copy-number`.

12.3.3 Property Definition

Active properties can be defined much like passive properties (attributes). The definition states the meaning of the property regardless of whether it is stored or derived (and without regard to how it is derived). During analysis or subsequent system evolution, what appeared at first to be a passive property may become an active property. As long as the property's meaning does not change, no references to the property need change. This strong separation of *what* from *how* is a characteristic advantage of object-oriented analysis. In object-oriented terminology, it is called *encapsulation*.

Notice also that the units of process attached to the objects are small—about the size of subroutines in functional design or structured programming. This fine-grained coupling of process and data is another distinctive characteristic of the object-oriented approach. It facilitates reuse by defining the processes in terms of the stable business entities instead of subordinating them to the application context. Discovering and stating this fine-grained coupling during analysis allows a smooth transition from analysis to design and implementation.

12.3.4 Message Patterns

The diagram we have just discussed, Fig. 12.2, shows the relationships among objects along with the class and object active and passive properties. These relationships are passive in that they represent object uniqueness and existence constraints. For example, although the detail is suppressed in the figure, the `movie-copy` object knows the identity of its parent `movie`. Likewise, `movie-rental-record` knows the identity of its parent `movie-copy` and `customer`, and so on. These passive relationships are maintained by active properties.

A second type of diagram will be used to show the dynamic relationships among objects created by message exchanges. Patterns of messages are similar to patterns of module calls in a functional design. For example, a simple diagram for the `rent` property of `customer` is shown in Fig. 12.3. When the `rent` property is invoked, these steps must occur: (1) `rent` must send a message to the `movie` object to interrogate the `available-copy` property (to determine if the movie has an available copy); (2) `movie` must, in turn, interact with `movie-copy` to find an available copy; and (3) `movie-copy` must interact with `movie-rental-record` to determine availability. If an available copy is found, the `rent` method must interact with the `movie-rental-record` class to invoke the creation of a new `movie-rental-record` object, that is, (4) `rent` must access the `begin-rental` property of `movie-rental-record`.

Figure 12.2 shows an object-relationship view of the extended conceptual schema. Figure 12.3 presents a second view of the schema, concentrating on

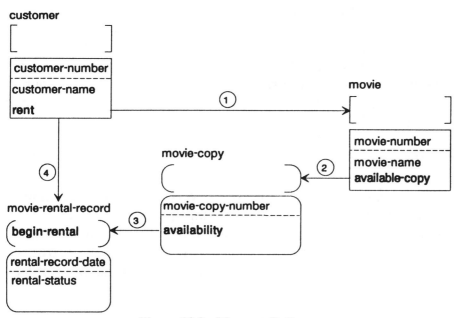

Figure 12.3. Message Patterns.

the processes (methods) and information flows (messages) rather than on the objects and relationships. The arrows show an object's access to a property of another object and represent the sending of messages (not the flow of information—information moves in the opposite direction). Some diagrams may display sequencing information (note the numbers 1, 2, and so on, along the message flow lines). A detailed message pattern diagram could show the parameters passed in the message, iteration, sequencing, and other embellishments reminiscent of structure charts in structured programming approaches. Typically, these views will be used to focus on a certain operation under consideration and will contain only the objects and properties of interest.

While Fig. 12.2 focuses primarily on the *what* aspect of the schema, Fig. 12.3 focuses on the *how*. These views roughly correspond to Zachman Framework data and function views, although the concepts of data and function have blurred a bit (the underlying meta-models for them have changed—see Appendix A). In time, a third view will emerge, representing the life cycle of an object. This view will be related to the relationship and message-pattern views, and might represent a modified *when* focus. Such a view could show, for example, that when an object is in a certain state and a given event occurs, certain messages will be sent to certain objects.

12.3.5 Specification Language

Complete specification of processes requires more than simply naming and defining the meaning of active properties. There must also be a way of specifying their derivation in terms of other objects and their properties. The specification language will be used to do this. It will also be used to state constraints and rules.

12.3.5.1 Messages

The specification language is simple, yet powerful. Like the relational calculus, it is based on predicate logic. In predicate logic, atomic formulae are combined into sentences using the logical connectives (*and, or, not*) and quantifiers (*forall, exists*). Each sentence is either true or false, depending upon the truth or falsity of the atomic formulae. In DMT/2, the atomic formulae are fundamentally of three forms:

```
Object
Object has Property
Object has Property Value
```

The first form is true if the object denoted by `Object` exists. The second form is true if the `Object` exists and the `Property` holds for it. The third form is true if the `Object` exists and the value of the specified `Property` is denoted by the specified `Value`. Syntactically, the specification language includes other message forms, but they are all ultimately defined in terms of the three fundamental forms.

In object-oriented terminology, the atomic formula is a message. Such a message is the *only* way a property value is accessible.

Some messages involving `movie` are given below. In the specification language, variable names begin with an uppercase letter. The variables are logical (mathematical) variables, not programming language variables. That is, a variable denotes a value, not a storage location.

If `Movie` identifies an instance of `movie`, the message

```
Movie has movie-name: Movie-name
```

is true if `Movie-name` is the value of the `movie-name` property of the `movie` identified by `Movie`. An alternate, equivalent syntactic form is

```
the movie-name of Movie is Movie-name
```

Suppose the instances of `movie` are represented by the sample instance table in Table 12.1. The first column holds object identifiers (*i1, i2*). These are not attributes but representations for intrinsic object identity. Some such representation is needed to specify the semantics of messages, but it is never necessary (nor possible) to actually use such representations in the specification language.

Table 12.1.
Object Sample Instance Table.

	movie-number	movie-name
i1	17	It's a Wonderful Life
i2	34	Miracle on 34th Street

With these instances, the following messages (atomic formulae) are all true.

```
i1 has movie-number: 17
the movie-number of i1 is 17
the movie with movie-number: 17 is i1
the movie-name of i2 is Movie-name
```

In the last message, the variable `Movie-name` is set to *Miracle on 34th Street* because it is that value that makes the atomic formula true.

Similarly, if `Copy` identifies an instance of `movie-copy`, the message

```
Copy has availability
```

is true if the identified movie copy is available.

If `Movie` is an instance of `movie`, the message

```
Movie has available-copy: Copy
```

is true if the identified movie has an available copy, `Copy`. An alternate, equivalent syntactic form is

```
the available-copy of Movie is Copy
```

12.3.5.2 Methods

The specification language can be used to specify the derivation of the `ava-ilable-copy` active property. For example, using a hypothetical syntax, a fragment of the definition of `movie` might be,

```
define movie
...
    Movie has available-copy: Copy if
        Movie 'is in stock as' Copy,
        Copy has availability.
```

This is semantically equivalent to

```
define movie
...
    the property
        available-copy: Copy
is true for movie instance Movie if
        Movie 'is in stock as' Copy,
        Copy has availability.
```

The comma between the two messages is the logical connective *and.* The message `Movie 'is in stock as' Copy` is an alternate syntactic form in the specification language. It is true if an instance of the `'is in stock as'` relationship has `movie Movie` as one participant and `movie-copy Copy` as the other participant.

Overall, the definition can be read to mean that if the message `Movie has available-copy: Copy` is sent to a `movie` instance of `Movie`, then that message is true if the message `Movie 'is in stock as' Copy` is true and the message `Copy has availability` is true.

All methods can be specified in this way. The result is a complete and precise specification of the derivation of active properties. The specifications are declarative, stating what must be true in order that the property hold (be true), not how to derive it. From the specification, code can be written or generated.

As a final example of the specification of active properties, a fragment of the definition of `customer` might be,

```
define customer
   ...
     Cust has rent: Movie-name if
          the movie with movie-name: Movie-name is Movie,
          the available-copy of Movie is Copy,
          the begin-rental of movie-rental-record
                  is [customer: Cust, copy: Copy ].
```

The hypothetical syntax is appropriate for a trained analyst (roughly as SQL is). A more English-like syntax will be appropriate for end users.

Including a precisely defined specification language provides another advantage: The DMT/2 model will be executable. With appropriate software tools, the specification language is a query language and the DMT/2 model is the prototype.

12.4 RULE-BASED MODELING

Rules form the second major area of extension over classic information modeling techniques such as IDEF1X. Rule-based ideas have their roots in artificial intelligence, specifically, in expert systems. However, their use in DMT/2 is not motivated by a desire to build expert systems, but by a desire to clearly and precisely state the rules of the enterprise.

12.4.1 Rules

The signal characteristic of a rule-based system is the separation of the statement of the rules from control over when they are invoked. In conventional systems, functions are specified in conformance to the rules with careful planning over the flow of control so that the functions that implement the rule will be executed when they should. Changing from function-driven analysis to object-oriented analysis does not in itself change this. Methods must be specified to enforce the rules and the flow of control must be planned so that messages are sent to invoke those methods at the right time. From this point of view, both process-driven specifications and object-oriented active properties are seen as ways to carry out rules. Both suffer from the same problem: They make the rules implicit. DMT/2 rule support allows stating the rule explicitly.

In general, a rule is a condition/action pair, as in the following example:

```
if a condition is true
then do some action.
```

In DMT/2, an explicit rule is simply declared; it does not have to be invoked by sending a message. The condition part is a query over object property values. The action part is a message send. Both are written in the specification language.

For example, the video store has a rule, "If a copy is late, then send an overdue notice." With explicit rule support, using a hypothetical syntax, the rule can be stated directly as follows:

```
define movie-rental-record
...
    if Rental-record has rental-status: late
    then overdue-notice does
        send-notice-for: Rental-record.
```

Without explicit rule support, one would have to define something like a check-for-overdue-copies method and specify that it should be invoked every day (the scan approach), or add logic to the methods that update the rental-status to send an overdue notice if needed under the rule. Both make the rule implicit in the methods defined to implement the rule. With explicit rule support, the rule is directly and precisely stated, clearly visible for concurrence and amenable to change. For example, the video store rule stated above could be elaborated on to include a grace period, or be sensitive to customer status, or demand for the movie. The rule could be further extended to send a copy of the notice to the store manager if there have been previous notices sent to the same customer, and so on.

12.4.2 Control

The control semantics are the same for every rule: The rule is evaluated whenever any property in its condition part changes value. Immediate evaluation represents an idealization, but it properly conveys the essential idea. In expert-systems terminology, such rules are called forward-chaining or data-driven rules.

The action taken by one rule may enable the conditions in another rule, resulting in a ripple of cause and effect. Nets of such rules have proven to be an effective way to incorporate knowledge into a system. Their effectiveness derives directly from the separation of rules from control. Explicitly stated rules allow a focus on knowledge, unencumbered (relatively) by computer systems concerns.

In an extension to the video store example, rules could be declared (with suitable additional object classes) to generate alternate movie suggestions if no copies of a requested movie are available. Such rules would begin to capture and exploit knowledge of the movie rental business.

12.5 TYPES OF MODELS

As with IDEF1X, several types of DMT/2 models are possible. The business planning model may look like an IDEF1X ERD supplemented by a description of the responsibilities of each object, that is, a high-level list of what the object knows, does, or has done to it. The distinction between a data property (attribute) and an active property (method) might be minimized. This model might contain classes, properties, and rules grouped into aggregates. As an example, consider the movie, movie-copy, and movie-rental-record objects in the video store. A description of their responsibilities as objects might read something like Fig. 12.4 (perhaps made a bit more English-like for the nontechnical audience). Note that the methods are named (for example, `begin-rental`), but are not yet described in any detail.

At the intermediate, integration level (roughly equivalent to the IDEF1X key based model), individual classes, properties, and rules might be selectively modeled, with only those most important for integration included. Active and passive properties would be distinguished, and the structure of the protocols would begin to be exposed. Figure 12.2 provides an example of such a model. Message patterns, such as that shown in Fig. 12.3, might also be included for selected operations.

At the level equivalent to the IDEF1X fully attributed model, all classes, relationships, properties, constraints, domains, rules, and events would be described in detail, using the specification language. The diagrams might show arguments and domains as well as property names. Detailed message-pattern diagrams might also be included. Below this level, physical solution models similar in concept to the Transformation and DBMS model types would be used.

As our specification languages become more powerful, we can expect to be able to apply the extended techniques to larger and more complex efforts. More powerful and sophisticated support tools are inevitable, but the extended language is still in its formative stage.

```
Class:  movie

Responsibilities:
     Know movie-name
     Know movie-rating
     Know movie-rental-rate
     Know availability of copies
     Know average-remaining-life of copies
               etc.


Class:  movie-copy

Responsibilities:
     Know general-condition
     Know remaining-life
     Know availability
               etc.


Class:  movie-rental-record

Responsibilities:
     Know rental-status
     begin-rental
     end-rental
               etc.
```

Figure 12.4. Object Responsibilities.

12.6 REFERENCES

[1]   Brown, R.G. "DMT/2 Overview," Oral presentation made at the DACOM User Forum, Laguna Del Rey, Calif., October 17, 1989.

[2]   _____. "The Data Engineering Quiz—Response," *Data Base Advisor,* October 1989, pp. 3-5.

[3]   _____. *The Video Store with DMT/2.* The Data Base Design Group, Inc., January 6, 1991.

PART THREE

Some time ago, a friend approached me with questions about software that might help him run his business. He had accumulated several accounting and database packages over the years and wanted to know how to use them to help keep track of things. He had some vague notions of sales tracking and accounts payable, but was having trouble figuring out how the various pieces of software might fit together.

Before he looked at software packages, he needed to know what his business looked like. Before he looked for solutions, he had to understand the problems. I suggested that we first draw a picture of his business, and only then decide which parts could be effectively addressed by a computer system. I gave him a quick idea of the concepts behind information modeling, and we proceeded from there.

The case study presented in Part Three evolved from those discussions. The analysis involves a real business, although liberties have been taken to illustrate certain modeling points. The objective of Part Three is to show you how the IDEF1X modeling technique has been applied in a real situation. By looking at a real model and the processes used to develop it, the concepts and ideas discussed in the rest of the text will become more real.

The case study, presented in three chapters and supported by one appendix, contains details of the key based model. Chapter 13 develops the business model, that is, a representation of the business to be supported by the eventual system. Chapter 14 develops the information system model. Chapter 15 describes the transformation of part of the information system model into a database design.

Review exercises are not included for this section of the book. You might, however, consider taking the case study further by preparing key based, fully attributed, and transformation models for parts of the entity relationship diagram not examined in Chapters 14 and 15.

13

MARKET BUSINESS MODEL

Monterey Foods Corporation, or the Monterey Market as it is known to its customers, is one of the most famous produce markets in the San Francisco Bay Area. It supplies fresh produce to some of the area's finest restaurants and is renowned for its variety and quality. If you live in northern California, and like fruits and vegetables, you have probably heard of it.

The Berkeley store was opened in 1961 by Tom and Mary Fujimoto. Two of their sons now operate the stores in Berkeley and Palo Alto. Bill takes care of much of the corporation's business and runs the store in Berkeley. Kenny runs the store in Palo Alto.

There is a lot to this business. The Berkeley store alone does over $6 million a year in gross revenue and employs about thirty people. On the average day, it carries more than four hundred varieties of produce and recycles more than a ton of cardboard boxes. If they don't have it, they will find it for you. This is not your run-of-the-mill mom-and-pop market.

In this chapter, we develop an overall entity relationship diagram for Monterey Foods. In terms of the Zachman Framework, this ERD provides a high-level Model of the Business. The objective of the case study is to show how the information model is developed, but in order to develop the model we must also understand the functions of the business. The functions provide a checklist that we use to guide our discussions of the data. Therefore, before we begin the discussion of the information model, it will help to review the major functions Monterey Foods performs.

13.1 FUNCTION MODEL

Function modeling techniques are just as important as information modeling techniques, and it is important to develop the function and information descriptions of the business at the same time. A list of functions provides overall context for the discussion of the data. Discussion of the data helps verify the function descriptions and uncovers new detail.

There are many ways to present a set of functions, including dataflow diagrams, activity diagrams, flow charts, and Hierarchical-Input-Process-Output (HIPO) diagrams. Here, we will use a modified Gane and Sarson style DFD to describe the interaction of the highest-level functions [1]. We use an indented list, rather than elaborate function diagramming techniques, for additional detail.

Figure 13.1 shows a dataflow diagram for Monterey Foods. The DFD contains the major functions of the business and the data that flows among these functions. In the DFD, functions are represented by rounded boxes, flows of data are represented by arrows, and external entities (sources and destinations of data) are represented by squares. Data stores—the places where data is stored by the functions—are represented by two parallel lines with the number and name of the data store written inside.

DFDs often contain many data stores. You will notice, however, that there is only one on the DFD in Fig. 13.1. Data stores represent *views* of stored data. At their lowest level of detail, information models contain all of the data in the data stores. Therefore, the data store in Fig. 13.1 *is* the information model we will develop in the case study.

Figure 13.2 lists the Monterey Foods business functions. The highest level functions—1.0, 2.0, and so on—correspond to functions in Fig. 13.1. In reality, Bill Fujimoto and I started not with what is shown in the figure but with a much shorter list of topics covering buying, selling, managing employees, accounting for the business, and so on. The list shown in the figure is closer to what we had midway through the effort. The functions marked with an asterisk (*) are not covered by the information model we will develop.

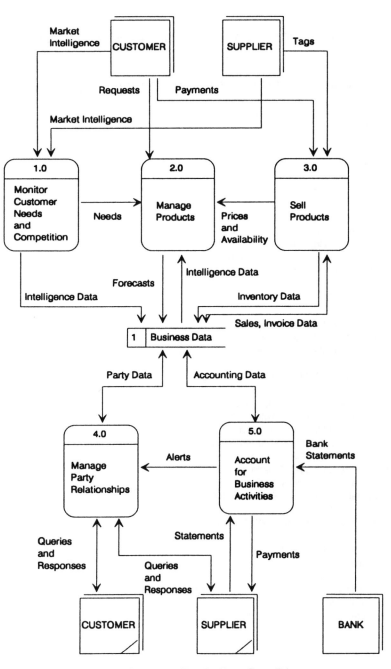

Figure 13.1. Monterey Foods Dataflow Diagram.

MONTEREY FOODS CORPORATION — BUSINESS FUNCTIONS

1.0   MONITOR CUSTOMER NEEDS AND COMPETITION

1.1   Monitor Customer Needs
1.2   Monitor Competitors *
1.3   Monitor Suppliers

2.0   MANAGE PRODUCTS

2.1   Forecast Demand
2.2   Track Availability
2.3   Track Competitors *
2.4   Determine Optimum Offerings
2.5   Project Buying Needs
2.6   Forecast Staffing Requirements
2.7   Project Advertising Needs *

3.0   SELL PRODUCTS

3.1   Purchase Products for Resale
3.2   Prepare Products for Sale
3.3   Sell Products to Customers

4.0   MANAGE PARTY RELATIONSHIPS

4.1   Manage Supplier Relationships
4.2   Manage Customer Relationships
          4.2.1   Set Up Customer Family
          4.2.2   Monitor Customer Family Status
          4.2.3   Monitor Customer Status
4.3   Manage Employee Relationships
4.4   Manage Advertiser Relationships *
4.5   Manage Accounting Relationships *

5.0   ACCOUNT FOR BUSINESS ACTIVITIES

5.1   Purchase Supplies *
5.2   Collect Charges
5.3   Pay Suppliers
5.4   Pay Employees *
5.5   Pay Taxes *
5.6   Interact with Regulatory Agencies *

Figure 13.2. Monterey Foods Business Functions.

13.2 ACQUIRING THE ENTITY RELATIONSHIP DIAGRAM

Although formal group sessions are needed in many modeling efforts, Bill was close enough to the business for us to work together directly throughout the entire effort. Therefore, all our sessions were two-person interviews. During our first meeting, Bill and I developed the entity relationship diagram in Fig. 13.3. This diagram is, in fact, a presentation-level ERD, since no attributes are included and since we did not capture formal definitions of the entities at the end of the session.

The interview that follows is close to the actual discussion that occurred in the first session. As you read the interview, remember that the purpose of the ERD is to get a wide view of the major information structures that are important to the business, not to capture all of the detail.

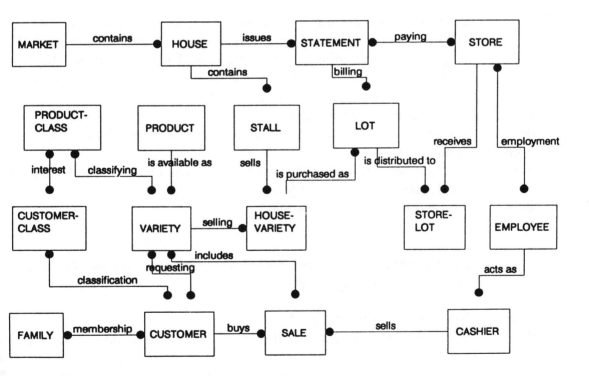

Figure 13.3. Monterey Foods Entity Relationship Diagram.

Tom: What we're going to do is draw a high-level picture of your business called an entity relationship diagram. It will represent the major things you deal with, called entities, and the relationships among the entities. Later, we will get into a more detailed model, where we also look at the information you keep about these entities.

          What I'm going to do is to ask you a bunch of questions and, as we go along, draw a diagram of what you tell me. Don't worry about reading it; I'll read it back to you to confirm that I understand what you said. I'm going to try to keep our discussion at a fairly high level, but I'll note details for us to follow up later. So bear with me if I leave some of what you say off the picture for now. It won't get lost. OK?

          (It's always a good idea to start with a clear purpose for the session. That way, the expectation levels of all participants are aligned.)

Bill: OK.

Tom: Let's start with the buying side of the business. I know you get up early every morning and go to the market. What goes on there?

Bill: Right. Every morning at around 2 A.M., I head for either the San Francisco or the Oakland produce market. Kenny usually goes to the other one so we have coverage at both.

Tom: So there are two MARKETs?

Bill: There are others, but those are the ones we generally use.

Tom: What's a MARKET?

Bill: It covers several city blocks and has a bunch of houses where we pick up the fruits and vegetables.

Tom: You mean like houses people live in?

Bill: No, wholesalers.

          (With MARKET and HOUSE, we had the beginnings of some definitions to be noted for future reference.)

Tom: You buy from the houses?

Bill: Each one has several stalls, and we pick up various items at the stalls.

          (This was a good point at which to confirm what we have gathered so far with a diagram. This had two purposes: to verify the information

and to show Bill I understood it. Figure 13.4 shows an initial attempt at a diagram.)

Tom: Let's draw a picture of that so I can see if I understand it. A MARKET <contains> many HOUSEs, and each HOUSE <contains> many STALLs. A STALL is only in one HOUSE, and a HOUSE is only in one MARKET.

Figure 13.4. Markets, Houses, and Stalls.

Bill: Right.
Tom: Is there anything bigger than a MARKET or smaller than a STALL?
Bill: No.
Tom: So you buy the products from the STALLs?
Bill: Yes.
Tom: Tell me about the products. Is that what we should call the things you buy from the stalls?
Bill: Yes. Well, actually, as you know, there are many varieties of almost everything. Lots of different kinds of mushrooms, lettuce, and so on.
Tom: Do you keep track of them at the variety level?
Bill: Sure.
Tom: So a PRODUCT <comes in> many VARIETYs, and you buy the varieties?
Bill: Yes.
Tom: You said you buy from the stalls not from the houses. Right?
Bill: Yes. Actually, the stalls write the tags, but we get the bills from the houses.
Tom: You get a TAG for each thing you buy?
Bill: No, we get a tag from each stall, and it has as many lines as there are lots. It is supposed to only have one lot per line, but sometimes it has more than one.

Tom: Let's put lines aside for later. Now, let's clarify a point and then add
          to our picture to see if I have it. When you buy a bunch of some-
          thing, ten crates of oranges or whatever, and they write up a tag, do
          you have a term for the "bunch"?

          (This was a point at which experience and judgment came into play.
          TAG, TAG-LINE, and detailed relationships to LOTs were emerging here,
          but it seemed that the overall concept of a LOT would capture the
          general idea of buying from the STALLs. Because I needed to confirm
          this with Bill, this was a good time to extend the diagram.)

Bill: We call it a lot.
Tom: OK. Here's the diagram.

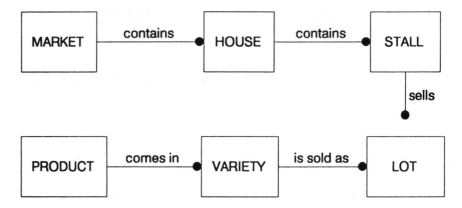

Figure 13.5. Products, Varieties, and Lots.

Tom: Do we need to keep track of which STALLs sell which VARIETYs, or
          do they all sell the same things?
Bill: We need to know. As a matter of fact, I spend a lot of time trying
          to find the best varieties and keep track of which houses have them,
          their prices, and so on. A big part of what I want to do is to keep
          track of what's available when and from whom, so I can know what
          stalls to visit in the morning and can gauge when I ought to be
          stocking up on things and when I should wait. A lot of this business
          is in the timing.
Tom: Then let's extend our diagram a bit. Shall we call a variety available
          from a stall a STALL-VARIETY?

Bill: I think of it more as a house variety.
Tom: Even though it comes from a STALL?
Bill: Yes.

(We had a definition here.)

Tom: That brings up a point. Can many stalls in the same house sell the
            same variety?
Bill: Yes.
Tom: But we still want to call a variety sold by a stall a HOUSE-VARIETY?
Bill: Yes.

*(Even though this seemed like a strange name, it was the one Bill
wanted to use. After all, it's his business.)*

Tom: OK. Here's the diagram.

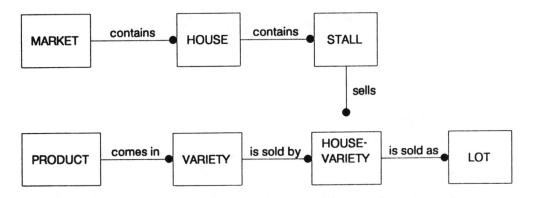

Figure 13.6. House Varieties.

Tom: We'll come back to this HOUSE-VARIETY when we get into more
            detail. Let's move on now. What happens to the lots after you buy
            them?

            *(Here, we needed to confirm the importance of HOUSE-VARIETY and
            note it as a major area to revisit.)*

Bill: Well, as you know, we have two stores. We load the lots onto the
            trucks, trying to split them so each store gets what it needs.

Tom: Then what?

Bill: When we get the trucks to the store, the stuff gets unloaded and put away. Some of it goes on the floor and some in the storage areas.

Tom: Do you ever break a single lot into two pieces, one for each store? Or does a single lot go to a single store?

Bill: Some of the time we divide them between the two stores, depending on which one needs what.

Tom: What happens as you divide the lots onto the trucks. Do you keep track of how they are broken down?

Bill: Not directly; we don't formally write it down there, but we know which lots go to each store.

Tom: OK. Let's extend the diagram again. Shall we call the part of a lot that goes to a store a STORE-LOT?

Bill: OK.

Figure 13.7. Store Lots.

(A definition.)

Tom: So the STORE LOTs go on the trucks and back to the stores. Do we need to keep track of scheduling for the trucks?

Bill: No. That's not as important as knowing what to buy. We only have two stores and six trucks.

Tom: What happens when a truck gets to the store?

Bill: We unload and distribute the stuff into various places in the store. Some of it goes into storage, in the cold box or back room, and some of it goes directly to the guys responsible for sections of the store. They put some away and prepare some to go onto the floor.

(We needed to slow down a bit here, since a lot of information was coming out at the same time. We needed to verify each piece and decide whether to explore it now or set it aside for later.)

Tom: Let's go through that a bit at a time. You're saying there are different sections of the store and that people are responsible for them?
Bill: Yes.
Tom: What shall we call these different sections? Sections? Areas?
Bill: Regions.
Tom: And the people responsible for them are employees?
Bill: Yes.
Tom: And the STORE LOTs are assigned to the people in the REGIONs?
Bill: Yes.

(REGIONs seemed important but would probably arise again as we moved into the detailed discussions of how Bill handled his inventory. However, they didn't seem to be the same level of importance as LOTs and STALLs, so they were noted for future investigation. The disposition of LOTs was also noted.)

Tom: Let's come back to this point later. I suppose once the produce is on the floor, it's sold to your customers?
Bill: Yes. Also, some of it spoils, and some of it we give away.
Tom: Do we need to keep track of the sales?
Bill: Yes, some of them, especially those made to groups, where we sometimes get bad checks. It would be nice to know what kind of customers are buying what and when, but they don't grow UPC scanning symbols into oranges yet. So any information we need to keep like that I have to set up directly in the registers. You know, a code for the thing. For example, I'm tracking a certain type of mushroom right now to see which cashiers are selling it, how much at a time, and so forth.
Tom: And to whom?
Bill: Not yet. That's harder to do.
Tom: Seems like a lot of trouble to go to for a mushroom.
Bill: It costs eighteen dollars a pound.
Tom: Oh.
Tom: Do we need to know who is running each register?
Bill: Yes.
Tom: OK. I'm going to make a note of this stuff about registers and regions and make sure we cover it later. But I'll leave it off the

diagram for now. At the moment, we're trying to get an overall look at all of the business in a fairly small picture.

Bill: OK.

(This is another example of a decision to lift the level of detail and note a topic to be explored later.)

Tom: Now let's turn to the accounts payable part of the business. Do you pay for the lots you buy each morning, or are you billed later?

Bill: We receive a statement once a month from each house, reconcile it to the tags we collected from the stalls during the month, and then make a payment.

Tom: So a statement . . . is that what we should call it?

(An obvious suggestion, and not too dangerous.)

Bill: Yes.

Tom: So a STATEMENT covers what you bought from a HOUSE. Is it itemized in any way?

Bill: There should be a line for each tag that was written.

Tom: And if I remember correctly, most of those TAGs are for single LOTs.

Bill: No. Tag lines correspond to the lots.

Tom: Do you receive a single statement, or do you get one for each store?

Bill: We get a single statement. But we need to be able to break it down by store so we can see how we are doing in each of them.

(There was a lot more material for definitions here, to be noted for future reference.)

Tom: I'm going to extend our picture again, but I'll leave out some of the detail about tags and lots. We will come back to this when we get to a lower level. Here is the picture. The new part says that a "HOUSE <issues> many STATEMENTs. A STATEMENT is <billing> for one or more LOTs." A LOT may appear on multiple statements (when you haven't paid for it during the statement period). Is that right?

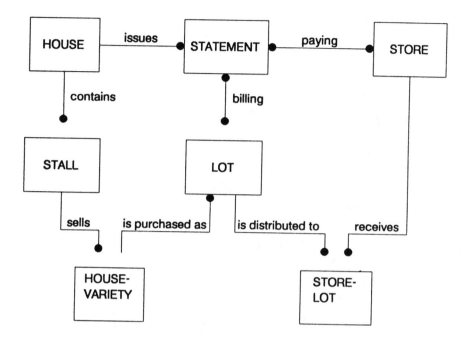

Figure 13.8. Statements.

(This was a clear blunder. Assumptions will get you every time.)

Bill: No. A tag is only on the statement for that month.

Tom: OK. I shouldn't assume. We'll take off the dot on the end near STATEMENT. Now it's one STATEMENT, many LOTs, but only one STATEMENT per LOT. Right?

Bill: Yes. That's right.

Tom: What happens when you sell the produce?

Bill: One of the cashiers rings up the sale, and the customer pays for it.

Tom: What's a . . .

Bill: Oh, yes . . . And sometimes a customer gives us a check which bounces. We've had some trouble with groups, buying groups, restaurants, and so on.

(This was the second time Bill had brought up the bad-check problem. We noted that it needed to be covered somewhere in the ERD.)

Tom: There are a couple of things here. Let's come back to the groups and the bounced checks. First, what's a CASHIER?

Bill: An employee who operates a cash register.

(A definition.)

Tom: Do we need to keep track of which CASH REGISTERs the EMPLOYEEs are operating?

Bill: Yes.

Tom: Can the same EMPLOYEE be both a CASHIER and responsible for some REGION?

Bill: No, not usually.

Tom: But sometimes?

Bill: I guess so. For example, I'm responsible for the entire store, which I guess is a region, and I sometimes operate a register during very busy times when I haven't projected the staffing requirements right.

Tom: Let's ignore the employee's responsibility for a region for now, but let's put in the cashiers. When a CASHIER makes a sale, what shall we call it. We'll add that too.

(Here were the regions again and more detailed relationships with employees. A judgment was needed on how much to include in the ERD. It was also a good time to verify our progress with another picture.)

Bill: A sale.

Tom: Here's the picture. It says that a STORE employs many EMPLOYEEs, and an EMPLOYEE is employed by many (in our case, one or two) STOREs. An EMPLOYEE <acts as> CASHIER, and a CASHIER <sells> SALEs. That last part may sound a bit funny at this point, but bear with me. So far so good?

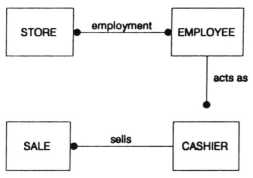

Figure 13.9. Cashiers and Sales.

Bill: Yes.

Tom: OK. When something is sold, I presume it's one of the varieties you have in the store.

Bill: Yes.

Tom: And I know from shopping at the store that a SALE can include many VARIETYs. If I buy apples, oranges, and lettuce, I pay once for the total not once for each item.

Bill: That would be a bit silly.

(That was safe. Now was another good time to verify.)

Tom: So here's our picture. SALE is now connected to the VARIETYs it includes. I've also added a CUSTOMER who is the buyer in the SALE. So we read this section as "A CASHIER <sells> to many CUSTOMERs, and a CUSTOMER <buys> from many CASHIERs (through SALEs). Each SALE <includes> many VARIETYs, and a VARIETY is included in many SALEs."

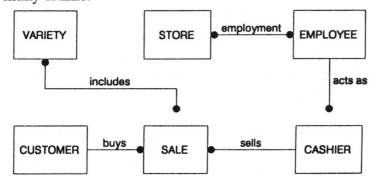

Figure 13.10. Sales to Customers.

Bill: That sounds right.

Tom: Let's get back to the groups and the bounced checks. Do you have a term for the groups?

(Now that SALE was on the diagram, it was a good time to return to the bad-check problem and see if the structure was important enough to add to the ERD.)

Bill: Well, we call them families, but I don't suppose that's a very good name, since they aren't families in the classical sense. You know, husband, wife, children.

Tom: You're right. It's not a very good name, since it might be a bit misleading. But as Humpty Dumpty once said, we can call it anything we want as long as we define it. Is there a better name that wouldn't confuse people?

Bill: The name family is what we use around the store, and most of our employees seem to know what it means.

Tom: Then if you are comfortable with it and people will recognize the term, let's use FAMILY. We can always change it later if we find a better term. You said that some customers belong to these families. I assume a FAMILY can contain many CUSTOMERs.

(Again, we used the name Bill used around his store, even if it was a bit strange. At the key based model level, we would look at this again, but it wasn't worth worrying about in this first session.)

Bill: Yes.

Tom: Can the same CUSTOMER belong to many FAMILYs?

Bill: Yes, over time that's possible. And, as a matter of fact, keeping track of whether a customer bounced a check in a previous family could help us a lot. We would not be likely to accept other checks from that customer in future families.

(It seemed like FAMILY would give us the hook for the bounced checks at a later time, so it was added to the ERD. It also looked like we were running out of topics, so it was a good time to summarize and prompt for new ideas.)

Tom: Again, let's leave the detail of bounced checks for later, but let's add
          the FAMILY so we have the major structures here. Looks like we
          have most of the picture. Here it is.

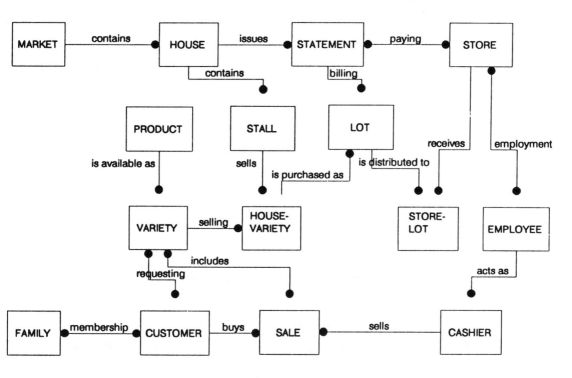

Figure 13.11. Partial ERD.

Bill: What about tracking what customers are interested in what varieties
          so I can make projections of what to buy?
Tom: We'll add the detail later, but let's get the important parts of that
          now. Do you want to keep track of which individual customers like
          which individual varieties?
Bill: Sometime that would be nice. But for now we can do it by type of
          customer and type of product.
Tom: Type of product or type of variety?
Bill: Variety.

(The purpose of this next step was to ensure Bill would accept the results of the session. It was intended to give him a feeling of "hands on.")

Tom: Here's a picture of that, I think. What should we call the group of customers?

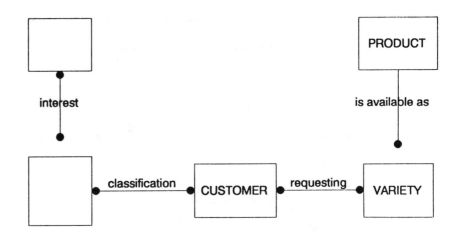

Figure 13.12. Groups of Customers.

Bill: How about a customer class.
Tom: OK. How about the group of varieties? Shall we call it a variety class?
Bill: No, let's call it a product class. Various groups or agencies have classifications for products we should use.
Tom: Do we include the PRODUCT in the class, or the VARIETY?
Bill: If we include the product, do all of its varieties get the same classification?

(Bill seemed to be catching on. We had more definitions here.)

Tom: Yes, that's what the structure would mean.
Bill: Then let's include the variety.
Tom: OK. Here's the diagram.

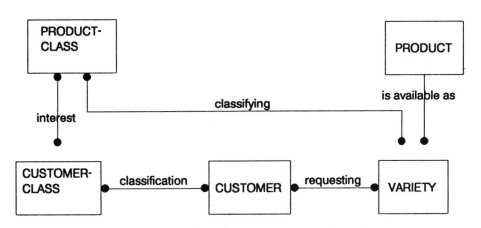

Figure 13.13. Product Classes.

Bill: One more thing here. Although we don't have a formal way to do
            it, we usually accept requests from customers to have certain things
            available for them at certain times. For example, if you wanted two
            hundred ears of white corn on a certain date, we could probably have
            it for you.

Tom: So customers may request certain varieties?

Bill: Yes.

Tom: This is another area we'll want to come back to. But let's indicate
            it this way for now. We'll put a relationship between VARIETY and
            CUSTOMER to represent the requesting of varieties by customers.

Bill: OK. But don't we need to have a box for the request so that we can
            record information about it?

            *(He was right. Putting a nonspecific relationship here was cheating a
            bit, but as long as we had noted the detail for later and were creating
            a high-level model for the purpose of communication and guidance for
            the later detailed work, it wasn't too bad a thing to do.)*

Tom: Yes, we do. We'll add that as we put more detail in our picture.

Bill: OK.

Tom: So here's the entire picture. It doesn't show a lot of detail yet, but
            it shows the major things we need to keep track of.

Bill: That's not a picture of my computer system. That's a picture of my
          business.
Tom: Right.
Bill: When do we add the detail?
Tom: We can start whenever you're ready.
Bill: How about tomorrow afternoon?
Tom: Fine. I'll get these rough pictures drawn up in a neater form and
          see you then.

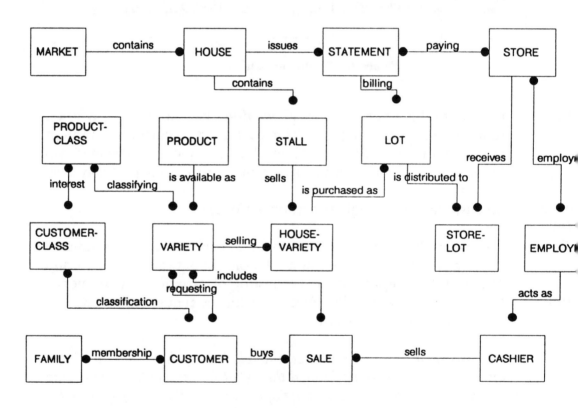

Figure 13.14. Complete ERD.

At the end of our session, we had acquired a model of the business. It is an
ERD for most of the market and corresponds to a model in the first row of
the IDEF1X model-type diagram in Chapter 3. That area is highlighted in
Fig. 13.15.

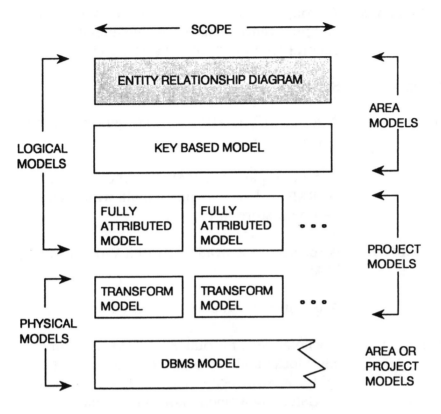

Figure 13.15. Area Entity Relationship Diagram.

13.3 ERD DEFINITIONS

After the interview, I prepared some definitions for Bill's review. We were now ready for the next phase, the creation of the key based model. At this point, however, the definitions were still rough. We waited until later to add examples and other clarifying information since we knew the model was likely to change as additional detail was uncovered. The rough definitions were as follows:

CASHIER: A job function in which an EMPLOYEE is assigned as the operator of a CASH-REGISTER. In this role, the EMPLOYEE is involved with SALEs to CUSTOMERs.

CUSTOMER: Someone who buys from a STORE.

CUSTOMER-CLASS: A grouping of CUSTOMERs formed to track buying trends and preferences. Each class includes a description of the general type of CUSTOMER to be included.

EMPLOYEE: Someone who works for a STORE.

FAMILY: A group of CUSTOMERs who generally act as a single buying entity.

HOUSE: A general part of a MARKET where produce is sold. A MARKET is like a shopping mall, with each HOUSE a department store in the mall.

HOUSE-VARIETY: A record of the availability of a VARIETY at a particular STALL.

LOT: A quantity of produce purchased as a unit.

MARKET: A wholesaler of produce. A MARKET can cover several city blocks and contains HOUSEs where the produce is sold. A MARKET is like a shopping mall, with each HOUSE a department store in the mall.

PRODUCT: A general classification of produce.

PRODUCT-CLASS: A grouping of VARIETYs formed to track buying trends and preferences. Each class includes a description of the general type of VARIETY to be included.

SALE: A record of a purchase by a CUSTOMER.

STALL: A specific location in a HOUSE where produce is sold. A STALL is like a department in a department store, where HOUSE is the store.

STATEMENT: An accounting for purchases from a HOUSE that is presented to Monterey Foods as a demand for payment of the associated bill.

STORE: One of the outlets of Monterey Foods.

STORE-LOT: A part of a LOT assigned to a particular STORE.

VARIETY: A specific type of PRODUCT. For example, if the PRODUCT is oranges, VARIETYs include valencia and navel.

13.4 REFERENCES

[1] Gane, C., and T. Sarson. *Structured Systems Analysis.* Englewood Cliffs, N.J.: Prentice-Hall, 1979.

14

MARKET KEY BASED MODEL

In Chapter 13, we completed an overall description of the functions and data of Bill's business. In this chapter, we will develop the key based model. To do this, we need to expand our model to include more detail. Whereas the purpose of the ERD is to get an overall summary of the business, the purpose of the key based model is to specify the business rules that will govern the automated system and the manual procedures that will surround it.

It is sometimes difficult to decide when a key based model is, in terms of the Zachman Framework, a Model of the Business or a Model of the Information System. The business model contains information structures that may not be implemented in the automated system, whereas the system model contains only automated information. The one we developed for the market was more a Model of the Information System (manual as well as automated), since it included entities and attributes that would not, at least initially, become part of the automated system. Even though our focus was on the automated system, we needed to include some of the information that would be managed outside that system.

In this chapter, we look first at the key based model—how it was acquired, how the separate parts (views) were integrated, and how it was presented. We then will look at prototyping, a technique for validating the model.

14.1 ACQUIRING THE KEY BASED MODEL

As is generally true, the key based model for the produce market was too large and complex to be formed in a single work session. Therefore, we needed to develop it in pieces. The first questions we had to ask were, What are the pieces? and, In what sequence shall we address them?

14.1.1 Choosing and Sequencing the Sessions

We decided to use the list of business functions (Fig. 13.2) as a guide. It is often useful to work backwards, beginning with functions that use the data in the model and proceeding to those that create the data. This process tends to focus attention on things we know we *will* need first, rather than on speculating about what we *might* need. If we are thorough in our exploration of functions that use the data, we can expect the ones that create the data to emerge naturally.

To help choose the sequence of analysis, we built a CRUD matrix (CRUD stands for Create, Replace, Use, Delete). This matrix mapped the business functions against the entities in the ERD and is shown as Fig. 14.1. At this point, there were no deletes in our matrix, since we were not yet concerned with how long business information was to be retained.

The functions involved in managing and selling products (Functions 2 and 3) appeared to need most of the entities in our ERD. Accounting for the activities of the business (Function 5) looked like it needed the remaining entities. We therefore scheduled view acquisition sessions to acquire the information needed to complete the key based model as follows:

Session 1:   Function 2 — Manage Products
Session 2:   Function 3 — Sell Products
Session 3:   Function 5 — Account for Business Activities
Session 4:   Function 1 — Monitor Customer Needs
Session 5:   Function 4 — Manage Party Relationships

14.1.2 Acquiring the Views

During our first session, we focused on the major products of the business; that is, the produce that was to be sold to the store's customers. From our CRUD matrix, we could see that the Manage Products function could touch on almost every entity in the ERD. We started with a general discussion of the MARKETs, PRODUCTs, VARIETYs, HOUSEs, and STALLs. Parts of the discussion follow:

Tom: When we developed the ERD, part of our diagram looked something like this. You'll notice the entity shapes are a bit different now, since we are going to add the data needed for each entity. I'll be asking you questions to draw out things like what identifies each entity and what the rules are that govern the relationships among them. Let's start with the HOUSE. How do you identify it?

BUSINESS FUNCTION	CASHIER	CUSTOMER	CUSTOMER-CLASS	EMPLOYEE	FAMILY	HOUSE	HOUSE-VARIETY	LOT	MARKET	PRODUCT	PRODUCT-CLASSIFICATION	SALE	STALL	STATEMENT	STORE	STORE-LOT	VARIETY
1.0 – MONITOR CUSTOMER NEEDS																	
1.1 - Monitor Customer Needs		U	C/U							U	C/U						U
1.3 - Monitor Suppliers						R	U	U	R	U	U		R	U	U		U
2.0 – MANAGE PRODUCTS																	
2.1 - Forecast Demand			U						U	U	U				C/U		U
2.2 - Track Availability							U	C/U	C/U	U	U		U				U
2.4 - Determine Optimum Offerings		U					U		U	U			U	U			U
2.5 - Project Buying Needs		U					U	U					U	U	U	U	U
2.6 - Forecast Staffing Requirements	U			U			U						U		U	U	
3.0 – SELL PRODUCTS																	
3.1 - Purchase Products for Resale							U	C	C	U	C		U				C
3.2 - Prepare Products for Sale							U								U	C	U
3.3 - Sell Products to Customers	U	U		U	U								C			U	U
4.0 – MANAGE PARTY RELATIONSHIPS																	
4.1 - Manage Supplier Relationships						C/R	U		C/R	C/R	U		C/R				C/U
4.2 - Manage Customer Relationships		C/R	U		C/U								U				
4.3 - Manage Employee Relationships	C/R			C/R													
5.0 – ACCOUNT FOR BUSINESS ACTIVITIES																	
5.2 - Collect Charges	R	U			U								C				
5.3 - Pay Suppliers							U		U	U					U	C/U	

Figure 14.1. CRUD Matrix.

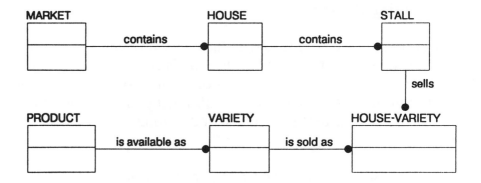

Figure 14.2. Starting Point.

Bill: What do you mean by "identify"?
Tom: Is there something like a number that is unique for each HOUSE?
Bill: We use the name.
Tom: Do two HOUSEs ever have the same name?
Bill: No.
Tom: Even if they are in different MARKETs?
Bill: That's right.
Tom: How about MARKETs? Do we identify them by names, too?
Bill: There might be two with the same name. I'd rather use a number.
Tom: OK. How about a STALL?
Bill: They have names too, but we generally think of them as John's at
         Oakland, or Joe's at San Francisco. Come to think of it, some have
         the same names.
Tom: In the same MARKET?
Bill: Yes, but not in the same HOUSE. Another thing about a STALL: We
         often think of them as Joe's Bananas or Hornworth's Mushrooms,
         their primary product, even though they sell many.

The discussion continued, and after a while we had developed the diagram
shown in Fig. 14.3. It seemed to have most of the data that we would need
to track availability (Function 2.2).

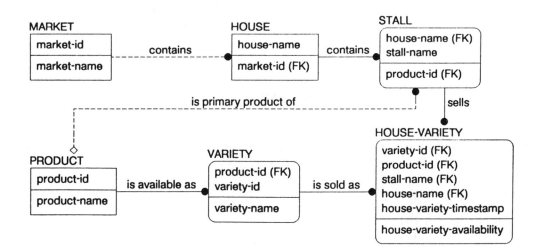

Figure 14.3. House Variety Details.

We then discussed Forecast Demand (Function 2.1) and ended up with the view in Fig. 14.4. This view also covered most of our Monitor Customer Needs (Function 1.1), although we still had not dealt with the needs of individual customers. Bill indicated that one of the easiest ways to track demand would be by tracking the interest classes of customers had in varieties of products. For instance, a certain ethnic group had a great interest in a specific type of mushroom for a few days each year just before one of their holidays. We knew that adding information about actual sales patterns in the store would be necessary in the long run, but we decided to leave that for later.

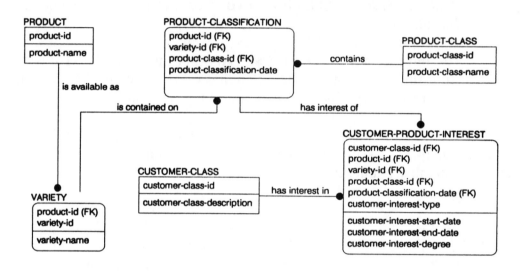

Figure 14.4.   Customer Interest.

Next, we turned to Determine Optimum Offerings (Function 2.4), Project Buying Needs (Function 2.5), and Forecast Staffing Requirements (Function 2.6). These looked as if they would bring in the selling function and most of its data, so we decided to move them into our session on selling, which was the next one on the list.

There were two more things to do before ending our session: First, we wrote rough definitions of the entities and attributes we had diagrammed so Bill could take them away and polish them up. Second, we reviewed the model (I read the business rules to Bill for verification) and added inversion entries, alternate keys, and a few more attributes. We could have deferred that step, but it was easy to do now. Basically, we just answered the questions, What other information do we want to keep about this entity? and What are the ways that we would like to look this up?

We then had our view for Session 1, as shown in Fig. 14.5.

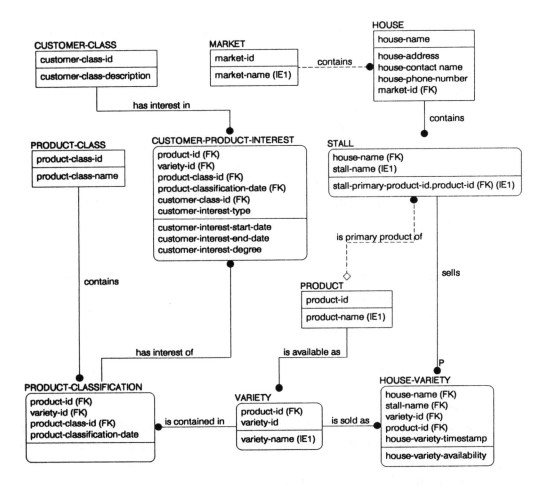

Figure 14.5. First Key Based View.

A few days later, we moved to the next business function, Sell Products (Function 3.0). Then other sessions provided more pieces of the model. It turned out that we did not need a separate session on Monitor Customer Needs (Function 1.0), since we found that it was covered as we discussed the parties involved in the business (Function 4.0).

14.1.3 Integrating and Validating the Views

Once we had acquired the pieces, some independently and some as extensions to parts of earlier views, it was time to put them together into a composite model and complete the definitions of all entities and attributes. The full composite and the definitions are in the supplementary material in Appendix F, and its five views are described in Section 14.1.4.

The original composite looked a bit different from the final model, especially because of two changes we decided to make. At the completion of our discussion of the selling function, we had the structure in Fig. 14.6 (for simplicity, I have left out the non-key attributes). It was apparent we were getting some pretty large composite keys in our model and therefore needed to ask whether the key structures actually represented *identification* assertions about the entities we needed to manage or simply represented *existence dependencies*. For example, it didn't seem reasonable to need a combination of fourteen attributes to identify an ASSIGNED-LOT.

As it turned out, the single attribute "lot-assignment-timestamp" would be sufficient to identify an ASSIGNED-LOT, since two LOTs would not be assigned at exactly the same time. We did, however, include three additional attributes as part of the key (the identifiers of the PRODUCT, the VARIETY, and the REGION), not so much as a specification of what needed to be present to identify the ASSIGNED-LOT but rather to cause those three key attributes to appear in DISPOSED-LOT and its categories. This first change was one made for convenience and represented a business decision on how ASSIGNED-LOTs would be identified.

For other entities in the view, in particular LOT and STORE-LOT, we asked the same question, What should the key really be? We decided not to change the keys of these entities even though we could find shorter identifiers. As you review the overall composite, look at the nonidentifying relationships; each reflects a conscious decision about the contribution of keys.*

---

*It is entirely proper to use some, but not all, inherited foreign keys as primary keys of a child entity. A contributed foreign key group, part of which becomes primary key attributes of the child and part of which does not, is often called a *split key*.

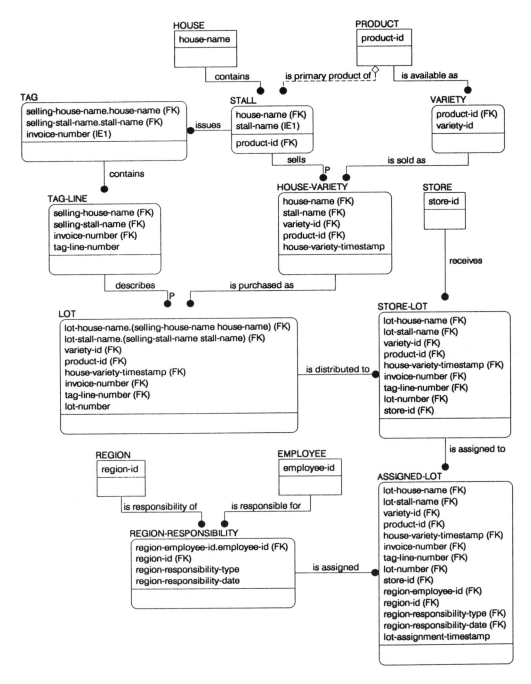

Figure 14.6. Large Compound Keys.

One additional area deserved some validation. When we acquired the view, we had said a SALE was identified by a "sale-timestamp". In looking at our structure for LOTs, we saw that a timestamp was also included for the AS-SIGNED-LOT and DISPOSED-LOT entities. Since a portion of a lot was disposed when a SALE occurred, it was clear that the timestamp for the SALE and the timestamp for the DISPOSED-LOT must hold the same value. So we used a unification assertion to make this statement. The result of this second change is shown in our model View 5 in the next section.

As you look at model View 5, notice the relationship between SALE and SOLD-LOT. This relationship carries our unification assertion. The relationship is *identifying* because the contributed foreign key of SALE is declared to be a constituent of the primary key of SOLD-LOT. In general, such identifying relationships are not allowed for categories—a category inherits its keys from its generic parent. This special case is, however, allowed in our extension to the unification assertion rules. The common base attribute is "timestamp" but you will not find it on the diagram. Rather, each occurrence of a timestamp in the model is based on (a data type of) the invisible attribute. You won't see such structures very often.

14.1.4 Views and View Descriptions

The key based model for Monterey Foods consisted of thirty-five entities and more than one hundred attributes.* Because of its size, the model was accom-panied by five subsets, called selective views. Each of these views has a description that translates the IDEF1X language into English and adds general discussion and examples to help the reader understand the information structure. The view descriptions are not intended to be exact statements of all the business rules captured by the model; rather, they provide a general summary of these rules.

View descriptions can be more or less elaborate than those prepared for this case study. The more complex (or abstract) the topic, the more useful the descriptions tend to be. There is no rule about how much detail or how many examples to include. As with all information modeling products, view descrip-tions must be tailored to the needs of their audiences.

---

*Throughout this case study, we are using the extended unification described in Chapter 8. The unification assertions that rely on these extensions are indicated by the symbol (*) on the composite model.

The five views and view descriptions for Monterey Foods follow.

VIEW 1: MARKETS AND PRODUCTS

A MARKET is a large area where buyers and sellers of produce come together to conduct business. A MARKET can cover several city blocks or a large area in a rural community. MARKETs are identified by a unique identifier but are often accessed by name.

MARKETs are sometimes associated with other MARKETs; for example, the Oakland produce market is affiliated with the San Francisco market. Relationships between MARKETs are recorded as MARKET-ASSOCIATIONs, with the kind of relationship designated by "market-association-type".

Each MARKET has one or more HOUSEs in which independent suppliers distribute their merchandise. The STALLs are independently operated, but are considered part of the larger HOUSE. It may be convenient to think of a MARKET as a shopping mall, with each HOUSE being a department store in the mall.

HOUSEs are identified by their names. Information recorded about a HOUSE includes its address and phone number, along with the name of a contact person. A HOUSE is divided into one or more STALLs where specific items of produce are sold. To continue the shopping center analogy, a STALL is like a department, such as automotive or kitchenware, in a large department store in the mall.

A PRODUCT is a particular type of produce, like oranges, apples, or lettuce. A VARIETY is a specific type of product, like valencia, navel, or mandarin oranges or iceberg, butter, or green-leaf lettuce. A primary class of product is designated for each STALL, but the STALL may sell many VARIETYs of this and other PRODUCTs. PRODUCTs and VARIETYs are identified by a unique identifier but are often accessed by name.

The availability of a VARIETY at a certain STALL is recorded as HOUSE-VARIETY. A set of HOUSE-VARIETYs is recorded for each stall, and each occurrence of HOUSE-VARIETY is further distinguished by a timestamp. This historical information can be used to analyze availability trends for certain VARIETYs and quality trends within individual STALLs.

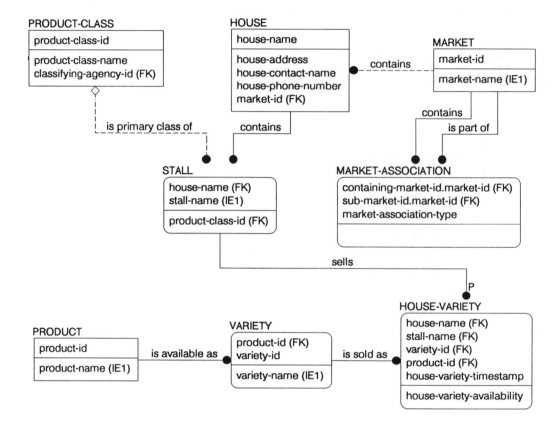

Figure 14.7. View 1: Markets and Products.

VIEW 2: CUSTOMERS AND CLASSIFICATIONS

A CUSTOMER is someone who buys from one of the STOREs. CUSTOMERs are identified by their names. CUSTOMER-CLASSs are established to track buying habits and preferences of various types of CUSTOMERs. Including a CUSTOMER in a CUSTOMER-CLASS is recorded as a CUSTOMER-CLASSIFICATION.

Various organizations, like trade organizations or chefs' organizations, have established classifications for produce. These are called PRODUCT-CLASSs, and the organizations that establish them are recorded as CLASSIFYING-AGEN-CYs. A CLASSIFYING-AGENCY may establish many PRODUCT-CLASSs.

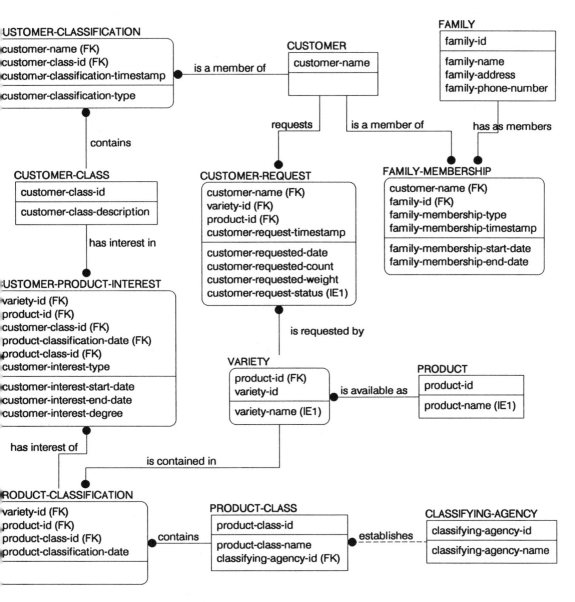

Figure 14.8. View 2: Customers and Classifications.

VARIETYs are included in the PRODUCT-CLASSs, with each linkage recorded as a PRODUCT-CLASSIFICATION. The interest of a particular type of CUSTOMER (a CUSTOMER-CLASS) in a specific VARIETY is recorded as a CUSTOMER-PRODUCT-INTEREST.

From time to time, a CUSTOMER will ask a STORE to obtain or reserve a certain item for purchase on a specific date or during a general time period. A specific request of this nature (as opposed to general interest in a PRODUCT or VARIETY) is recorded as a CUSTOMER-REQUEST.

Some CUSTOMERs are gathered into groups, called FAMILYs, to track group-buying and payment patterns. A FAMILY might represent a restaurant, with the CUSTOMERs being the buyers for the restaurant, or it might represent a buying CO-OP, with the CUSTOMERS being the members.

VIEW 3: THE STORE

A STORE is one of the two outlets of Monterey Foods. Each STORE has an identifier and a location. A STORE contains one or more REGIONs (general areas of the store, like the cold box and the outside area at the Berkeley store). A REGION is identified by a "region-id".

Each STORE also contains several CASH-REGISTERs (identified by "register--id"s) used to ring up sales.

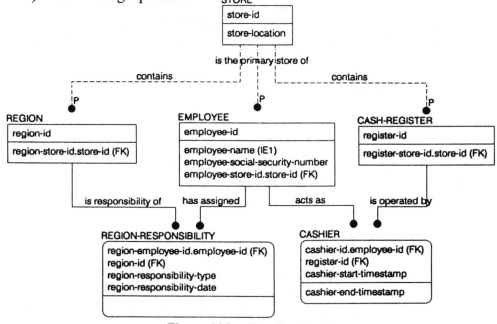

Figure 14.9. View 3: The Store.

Monterey Foods employs about fifty people. These are EMPLOYEEs. Each EMPLOYEE has one primary store in which he or she works. EMPLOYEEs are identified by "employee-id"s, but are often accessed by name. A "social-security-number" is recorded for each EMPLOYEE.

Store EMPLOYEEs may be assigned responsibilities for REGIONs in the STORE, and some may be assigned as operators of CASH-REGISTERs. The responsibility of an EMPLOYEE for a REGION is recorded as a REGION-RESPONSIBILITY. Assignment to a CASH-REGISTER is recorded as CASHIER (including the time and date on which the assignment begins and ends). An EMPLOYEE may be assigned to several different CASH-REGISTERs on a single day.

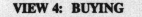

VIEW 4: BUYING

Produce is purchased from STALLs. When a purchase is made, the STALL issues a TAG containing an "invoice-number", a "tag-date", a "tag-number", and a total amount for the purchase ("tag-total-payable"). Produce is purchased in LOTs, with each LOT containing a description of what is purchased (product, variety, "lot-count", "lot-weight", "lot-unit-price", and so on). Each TAG contains one or more TAG-LINEs, one for each LOT that was part of the purchase.

Each LOT is supposed to appear on a single TAG-LINE, but sometimes a STALL will not follow this rule and will include several LOTs on a single line. Each LOT represents the purchase of exactly one HOUSE-VARIETY.

Once a LOT has been purchased, it is divided into one or more parts to be taken to the STOREs. A part of a LOT distributed to a STORE is designated as a STORE-LOT. Each STORE-LOT contains a "store-lot-count" or "store-lot-weight". Each STORE-LOT is further distributed to store employees with responsibility for REGIONs of the store. The assignments are recorded as ASSIGNED-LOTs.

Billing for purchases is done at the HOUSE rather than at the STALL level. Over time, a HOUSE issues many STATEMENTs, each of which includes a date and terms, along with a "statement-period" covered. Each STATEMENT may contain many STATEMENT-LINEs.

A STATEMENT-LINE generally corresponds to a single TAG, but at least one line on each STATEMENT is a total line and corresponds to no particular TAG. Each STATEMENT-LINE contains a "line-number", "line-type", and "line-amount".

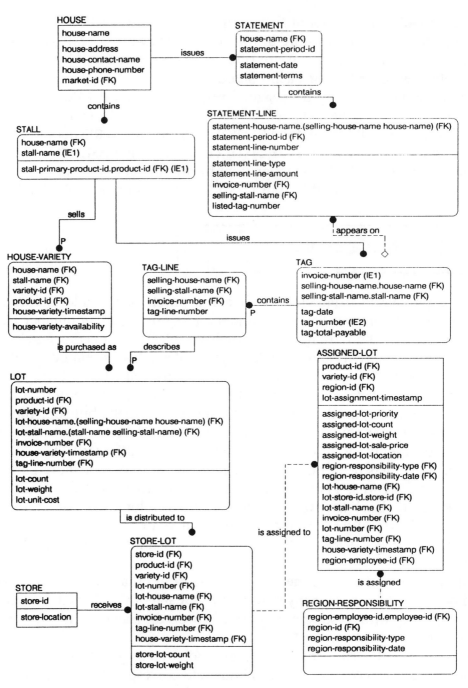

Figure 14.10. View 4: Buying.

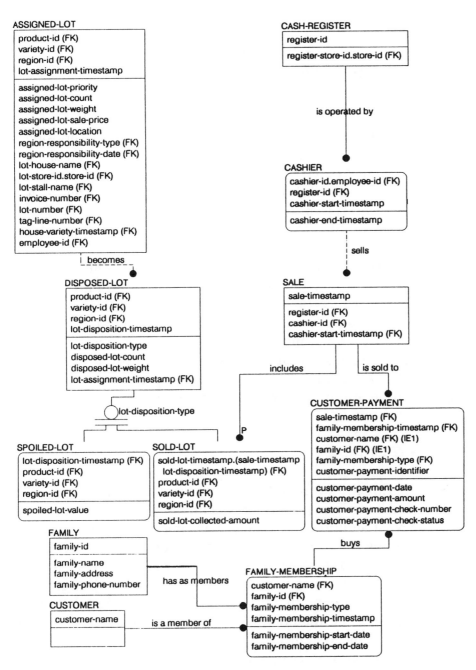

Figure 14.11. View 5: Selling.

VIEW 5: SELLING

A STORE-LOT is assigned to various EMPLOYEEs who have responsibility for various regions of the store (REGION-RESPONSIBILITYs). This assignment is recorded as an ASSIGNED-LOT. An ASSIGNED-LOT eventually becomes one or more DISPOSED-LOTs. Each DISPOSED-LOT disappears either as a result of a SALE (as a SOLD-LOT), or as a result of spoilage (as a SPOILED-LOT). A DISPOSED-LOT (either sold or spoiled) contains a time of disposition along with a count or weight disposed.

A CASHIER makes many SALEs. A SALE includes one or more SOLD-LOTs. Payments are received for SALEs made by the STORE, but only some are of the type that requires that records be kept of the history of the payment. Cash sales to individuals are simply recorded as such. Sales to FAMILYs, especially to restaurants, are tracked in more detail. Credit is sometimes extended to the FAMILY, and payments are often made by check. From time to time, a FAMILY or a CUSTOMER in the FAMILY will develop a pattern of bad checks; knowledge of this is useful in deciding whether to accept a check from a particular family member.

14.2 PROTOTYPING

As we were preparing the key based model, we were building lists of examples for each entity and had begun to test our structures with sample instance tables. To help decide what additional information we might need and to verify that what we had developed so far was correct, we decided to build a small proto-type of part of the database, using the model as a template. This would allow us to identify detailed requirements for that part, and allow Bill to get comfort-able with the concepts of relational tables (we had determined that our target technology would be some relational DBMS but had not yet chosen one).

The first part of the system Bill wanted to build was what he called the Product Database. This portion would establish the basic structure of products, varieties, stalls, and availability information and would be immediately useful for tracking and projecting buying patterns for the store. It also would be needed to support the next few functions, including tracking actual inventories and accounting for bills received from suppliers.

This area was therefore selected for the prototype. Bill set up some initial tables in a spreadsheet program, and imported them into a PC database package he had. During this stage, I got a phone call from Bill. He had been setting up products and varieties and was tying them to the stalls that sold them. He had about 500 varieties, 87 products, 5 markets, and 30 stalls and was trying to identify the primary product for each stall. In many cases, however, he seemed to find many primary products. For example, the wet vegetable stall in one of the houses sold many products, and none of them could be considered primary. There were other examples of the same problem.

Bill had uncovered an error in the model (see Fig. 14.6). A stall did not have a primary PRODUCT; it had a primary PRODUCT-CLASS. It was good to find this out now; in fact, finding errors in the data structure is one of the objectives of a prototype.

For the prototype, we added a column to the STALL table to hold a brief text description of the class, and revised the composite key based model, and its definitions. Selective View 1 in the previous section and the full model included at the end of this chapter contain this change.

Here are parts of some of our prototype tables.

MARKET

MARKET-ID	MARKET-NAME
MAR	MARIN COUNTY REGION
MEN	MENDICINO FARMING REGION
NAP	NAPA FARMING REGION
OAK	OAKLAND WHOLESALE MARKET
ORE	OREGON REGION
SDG	SAN DIEGO COUNTY REGION
SFT	SAN FRANCISCO TERMINAL MARKET
SON	SONOMA FARMING REGION
SSF	SOUTH SAN FRANCISCO MARKET

STORE

STORE-ID	STORE-NAME
B	MONTEREY FOODS BERKELEY
P	MONTEREY FOODS PALO ALTO

STALL

HOUSE-NAME	STALL-NAME	PRIM-PRD-CLASS
A & D PRODUCE	ALS ARTICHOKES	DRY VEGETABLES
B & C PRODUCE	RICCIS SPECIALTY	TROPICAL
D & R PRODUCE	KENS VEGGIE	VEGETABLES
D & R PRODUCE	TEDS FRUITS	FRUITS
FARMERS PRODUCE	EDDIES VEGETABLES	WET VEGETABLES
FARMERS PRODUCE	JOHNSONS VEGETABLES	VEGETABLES
FARMERS PRODUCE	LOUIES POTATOES	DRY VEGETABLES
FARMERS PRODUCE	SAMMYS MUSHROOMS	MUSHROOMS
FARMERS PRODUCE	SAMS TOMATOES	WET VEGETABLES
FARMERS PRODUCE	TONYS FRUIT	FRUITS
FARMERS PRODUCE	JONAH'S MELONS	FRUITS
GROWERS PRODUCE	CLARENCES FRUITS	FRUITS
GROWERS PRODUCE	DENNIS SPECIALTY	SPECIALTY
GROWERS PRODUCE	GLENNS VEGETABLE	VEGETABLES
GROWERS PRODUCE	HENRYS VEGETABLE	WET VEGETABLES
NATURES BOUNTY	NORMS SPECIALTY	SQUASH
SUNDANCE NATURAL FOODS	BILLS CITRUS	TROPICAL FRUIT
SUNDANCE NATURAL FOODS	SCOTT MILLER IMPORTS	TROPICAL FRUIT
WESTERN PRODUCE	FRANKS BANANAS	TROPICAL FRUIT

HOUSE

HOUSE-NAME	MARKET-ID	HOUSE-ADDRESS	HOUSE-PHONE
STAR ROUTE FARMS	MAR	95 OLEMA-BOLINAS RD BOLINAS CA 94924	415-868-1658
MUSHROOM CONNECTION	OAK	34233 ATTERIDGE PL FREMONT CA 94555	415-271-0188
A & D PRODUCE	OAK	216 FRANKLIN St OAKLAND CA 94607	415-452-4516
B & C PRODUCE	OAK	220 FRANKLIN St. OAKLAND CA 94607	415-444-5798
D & R PRODUCE	OAK	208 FRANKLIN St. OAKLAND CA 94607	415-451-2938
FARMERS PRODUCE	OAK	423 2nd St. OAKLAND CA 94607	415-444-6305
FUJII MELON	OAK	201 FRANKLIN St. OAKLAND CA 94607	415-451-5708
GROWERS PRODUCE	OAK	380 3rd St. OAKLAND CA 94607	415-834-5280
JOHN NAVAS PRODUCE	OAK	315 FRANKLIN St. OAKLAND CA 94607	415-832-5996
LAGORIO BROS	OAK	230 FRANKLIN ST. OAKLAND CA 94607	415-893-0411
SUN STATE PRODUCE	OAK	226 FRANKLIN St. OAKLAND CA 94607	415-451-1330
THE FELIX COHEN CO	OAK	300 FRANKLIN St. OAKLAND CA 94607	415-893-3981
WESTERN PRODUCE	OAK	323 FRANKLIN St. OAKLAND CA 94607	415-893-3716
NATURES BOUNTY THREE OAKS	ORE	23850 PEORIA RD HARRISBURG OR 97446	503-995-8208
SUNDANCE NATURAL FOODS	SDG	841 WOODSIDE LANE OLIVENHAIN CA 92024	619-727-9898

PRODUCT

ID	PRODUCT-NAME	ID	PRODUCT-NAME	ID	PRODUCT-NAME	ID	PRODUCT-NAME
APL	APPLES	COC	COCONUTS	LEK	LEEKS	POM	POMEGRANATES
ART	ARTICHOKES	COR	CORN	LEM	LEMONS	PSM	PERSIMMONS
ASP	ASPARAGUS	CRS	CRESS	LET	LETTUCE	PSN	PARSNIP
AVC	AVOCADOS	CUC	CUCUMBERS	LIM	LIMES	PTO	POTATOES
BAN	BANANAS	DAN	DANDELION	LMQ	LIMEQUATS	QUN	QUINCES
BEN	BEANS	END	ENDIVE	LOT	LOTUS ROOT	RAD	RADISH
BER	BERRIES	EPL	EGGPLANTS	MAN	MANGOES	RHU	RHUBARB
BET	BEETS	FEN	FENNEL	MEL	MELONS	RUT	RUTABAGAS
BRO	BROCCOLI	FIG	FIGS	MOL	MOLUNGA	SAL	SALSIFY
BRR	BROCCOLI RABE	FLW	FLOWERS	MSH	MUSHROOMS	SCA	SCALLIONS
BRS	BRUSSEL SPROUTS	GAR	GARLICS	NOP	NOPALES	SHL	SHALLOTS
BUR	BURDOCK	GIN	GINGER	OKR	OKRAS	SPN	SPINACH
CAB	CABBAGES	GPF	GRAPEFRUITS	ONI	ONIONS	SQU	SQUASH
CAC	CACTUS PEARS	GRN	GREENS	ORN	ORANGES	SWP	SWEET POTATOES
CAD	CARDOONS	GRP	GRAPES	PAF	PASSION FRUITS	TAR	TARO
CAR	CARROTS	GUA	GUAVAS	PAP	PAPAYAS	TOL	TOMATILLOS
CAU	CAULIFLOWERS	HER	HERBS	PAR	PARSLEY	TOM	TOMATOES
CEL	CELERY	HRS	HORSERADISH	PCH	PEACHES	TRN	TURNIPS
CHA	CHARDS	JIC	JICAMA	PEA	PEAS	WCH	WATERCHESTNUTS
CHI	CHICORY	KAL	KALES	PEP	PEPPERS	YAM	YAMS
CHY	CHOYS	KMQ	KUMQUATS	PER	PEARS	YUC	YUCCA
CIT	CITRONS	KOH	KOHLRABI	PIN	PINEAPPLES		
CLC	CELERIAC	KWI	KIWI	PLM	PLUMS		

VARIETY

VAR -ID	PRD -ID	VARIETY-NAME	VAR -ID	PRD -ID	VARIETY-NAME
ARB	APL	ARKANSAS BLACK	SPI	APL	SPITZENBURG
BAL	APL	BALDWIN	STA	APL	STARK SPLENDOR
BLW	APL	BLACK WINESAP	SWA	APL	SWAAR
CAB	APL	CAVILLE BLANC	WIN	APL	WINESAP
COX	APL	COX ORANGE PIPPIN	ARR	ART	JERUSALEM RED
CRB	APL	CRABAPPLE BC	ARW	ART	JERUSALEM WHITE
EMP	APL	EMPIRE	ARL	ART	LARGE
FJF	APL	FUJI FANCY	ARM	ART	MEDIUM
FJL	APL	FUJI LOOSE	ARS	ART	SMALL LOOSE
GAG	APL	GALA FANCY	ASJ	ASP	JUMBO
GWB	APL	GOLDEN DELICIOUS CAL BLUSHING	AST	ASP	STANDARD
GWG	APL	GOLDEN DELICIOUS CAL GILBERT	FLO	AVC	FLORIDA BOOTH
GWO	APL	GOLDEN DELICIOUS CAL ORGANIC	FUE	AVC	FUERTE
SDC	APL	GOLDEN DELICIOUS CRITERION	HSL	AVC	HASS LARGE
GWF	APL	GOLDEN DELICIOUS WASH FANCY	HSX	AVC	HASS LOOSE
GWS	APL	GOLDEN DELICIOUS WASH SMALL	HSS	AVC	HASS SMALL
JON	APL	JONATHAN	JIM	AVC	JIM BACON
LAD	APL	LADY APPLES	NEG	AVC	NEGRO
MBF	APL	MACINTOSH BC FANCY	ZUT	AVC	ZUTANO
MCL	APL	MACINTOSH CAL LOOSE	BUR	BAN	BURO
NOR	APL	NORTHERN SPY	CCM	BAN	CAVENDISH COMMERCIAL
PCL	APL	PIPPIN CAL LOOSE	COR	BAN	CAVENDISH ORGANIC
POF	APL	PIPPIN OREGON FANCY	DOM	BAN	DOMENICO
POL	APL	PIPPIN OREGON LOOSE	NAM	BAN	MANZANO
RCL	APL	RED DELICIOUS CAL LOOSE	PLN	BAN	PLANTAIN
RIO	APL	RED DELICIOUS IDAHO ORGANIC	RDX	BAN	RED LOOSE
RWF	APL	RED DELICIOUS WASH EX FANCY	RDS	BAN	RED STALK
RWJ	APL	RED DELICIOUS WASH JUMBO	BNB	BEN	BLUE LAKES
RWS	APL	RED DELICIOUS WASH SMALL	BNC	BEN	CHINESE YARD LONG
ROM	APL	ROME	BND	BEN	DRAGON TONGUE
SAS	APL	SASKATOON	BNV	BEN	FAVA
SIE	APL	SIERRA BEAUTY	BNF	BEN	FRENCH
BNI	BEN	ITALIAN	CHR	CHA	RED CHARD
BNK	BEN	KENTUCKY WONDER	CHR	CHI	GREEN RADDICHIO
BNL	BEN	LIMA	CHL	CHI	LOOSE LEAF
BNP	BEN	PURPLE	CHO	CHI	ORGANIC RADDICHIO
BNW	BEN	WINGED	CHD	CHI	RADDICHIO
BNY	BEN	YELLO WAX	CHT	CHI	TREVISO
CPG	BER	CAPE GOOSEBERRY	BBK	CHY	BABY BOK
CRG	BER	CRANBERRY ORGANIC	BOK	CHY	BOK
CRC	BER	CRANBERRY REGULAR	GAI	CHY	GAILON
HNC	BER	HUCKLEBERRY NORTH CASCADE	ONG	CHY	ONG
RSC	BER	RASPBERRY	TAT	CHY	TAT SOI
RSO	BER	RASPBERRY ORGANIC	YOW	CHY	YOW
STF	BER	STRAWBERRY FANCY	ETR	CIT	ETROG

VARIETY (continued)

STB	BER	STRAWBERRY FRAISES DES BOIS	FIN	CIT	FINGERED	
STZ	BER	STRAWBERRY NEW ZEALAND	CIL	CLC	LARGE	
STO	BER	STRAWBERRY ORGANIC	CIO	CLC	ORGANIC	
STS	BER	STRAWBERRY SMALL	MAT	COC	MATURE	
STM	BER	STRAWBERRY STEM	YOU	COC	YOUNG	
WHC	BER	WILD HUCKLEBERRY CALIFORNIA	CRB	COR	BABY	
BTC	BET	CHIOGGA	CRL	COR	BICOLOR	
BTG	BET	GOLD	CRY	COR	WHITE	
BT2	BET	LOOSE GOLD	CRY	COR	YELLOW	
BT1	BET	LOOSE RED	GAR	CRS	GARDEN	
BTA	BET	MINI CHIOGGA	WAT	CRS	WATERCRESS	
BTM	BET	MINI RED	SUC	CUC	ENGLISH	COMMERCIAL
BTW	BET	MINI WHITE	SUL	CUC	ENGLISH	LOOSE
BTR	BET	RED	SUF	CUC	ENGLISH	XF
BTT	BET	TOPS ONLY	SUJ	CUC	JAPANESE	
BRL	BRO	FLORETT	CUL	CUC	LARGE	
BRO	BRO	ORGANIC	SUM	CUC	LEMON	
BRR	BRO	REGULAR	SUD	CUC	PICKLE DILL	
RAB	BRR	SPROUTING	CUP	CUC	PICKLE SMALL	
BRF	BRS	FANCY	CUS	CUC	SMALL	
BRT	BRS	STALK	DNG	DAN	GREEN	
BUC	BUR	GOBO CALIFORNIA	ENF	END	BELGIAN	FANCY
BUH	BUR	GOBO HAWAIIAN	ENS	END	BELGIAN	SMALL
CBG	CAB	GREEN	EGB	EPL	BABY	
CAL	CAB	LACINADO	EGE	EPL	BABY JAPANESE	
CAP	CAB	NAPA	EGC	EPL	CHINESE	
CBR	CAB	RED	EGH	EPL	HAWAIIAN	
CBS	CAB	SALAD SAVOY	EGI	EPL	ITALIAN	LONG
CBV	CAB	SAVOY	EGD	EPL	ITALIAN	ROUND
CAR	CAC	RED	EGJ	EPL	JAPANESE	
CAY	CAC	YELLOW	EGL	EPL	LARGE	
ITA	CAR	ITALIAN	EGR	EPL	ROMA LONG	
CRX	CAR	LOOSE	EGS	EPL	SMALL	
CRM	CAR	MINI	EGT	EPL	THAI	
CRO	CAR	ORGANIC BUNCHED	FNB	FEN	BABY	
CRL	CAR	ORGANIC LOOSE	FNR	FEN	REGULAR	
CRR	CAR	RED	BRW	FIG	BROWN TURKEY	
CRG	CAR	REGULAR	FLB	FLW	BORAGE	
CRD	CAR	ROUND	FLC	FLW	CHIVE	
CRW	CAR	WHITE	FLJ	FLW	JOHNNY JUMP UP	
CLF	CAU	FLORETTS	FLM	FLW	MARIGOLDS	
CLA	CAU	LARGE	FLX	FLW	MIXED	
CLP	CAU	PURPLE	FLN	FLW	NASTURTIUMS	
CLR	CAU	ROMANESCO	FLP	FLW	PANSY	
CLS	CAU	SMALL	FLR	FLW	ROSES	
CLC	CEL	CHINESE	FLS	FLW	SAGE	
CLL	CEL	LARGE	GAC	GAR	CHINESE ROJA	
CLO	CEL	ORGANIC	GAE	GAR	ELEPHANT	
CLS	CEL	SMALL	GAD	GAR	ELEPHANT ROUND	
CHB	CHA	BABY	GAF	GAR	FANCY	
CHG	CHA	GREEN	GAS	GAR	SMALL	

etc.

HOUSE-VARIETY

HOUSE-NAME	STALL-NAME	VAR-ID	PRD-ID	H-VAR-TS	AVAIL
A & D PRODUCE	ALS ARTICHOKES	ARL	ART	12/19/89	P
A & D PRODUCE	ALS ARTICHOKES	ARL	ART	12/19/89	P
A & D PRODUCE	ALS ARTICHOKES	ARL	ART	12/20/89	A
A & D PRODUCE	ALS ARTICHOKES	ARL	ART	12/22/89	A
A & D PRODUCE	ALS ARTICHOKES	ARM	ART	12/18/89	P
A & D PRODUCE	ALS ARTICHOKES	ARS	ART	12/18/89	P
A & D PRODUCE	ALS ARTICHOKES	ARS	ART	12/21/89	A
A & D PRODUCE	ALS ARTICHOKES	ARS	ART	12/22/89	A
A & D PRODUCE	ALS ARTICHOKES	BNB	BEN	12/22/89	L
A & D PRODUCE	ALS ARTICHOKES	BNV	BEN	12/19/89	P
A & D PRODUCE	ALS ARTICHOKES	BNI	BEN	12/19/89	A
A & D PRODUCE	ALS ARTICHOKES	BNK	BEN	12/20/89	A
A & D PRODUCE	ALS ARTICHOKES	BNL	BEN	12/20/89	A
A & D PRODUCE	ALS ARTICHOKES	BNY	BEN	12/20/89	A
A & D PRODUCE	ALS ARTICHOKES	BRF	BRS	12/18/89	A
A & D PRODUCE	ALS ARTICHOKES	BRF	BRS	12/19/89	P
A & D PRODUCE	ALS ARTICHOKES	BRF	BRS	12/20/89	P
A & D PRODUCE	ALS ARTICHOKES	BRF	BRS	12/21/89	A
A & D PRODUCE	ALS ARTICHOKES	BRF	BRS	12/22/89	L
A & D PRODUCE	ALS ARTICHOKES	BRT	BRS	12/20/89	A
A & D PRODUCE	ALS ARTICHOKES	PRG	PEA	12/22/89	A
A & D PRODUCE	ALS ARTICHOKES	PRS	PEA	12/22/89	A
FARMERS PRODUCE	EDDIES VEGETABLES	BRR	BRO	12/18/89	P
FARMERS PRODUCE	EDDIES VEGETABLES	CBG	CAB	12/19/89	A
FARMERS PRODUCE	EDDIES VEGETABLES	CBR	CAB	12/18/89	A
FARMERS PRODUCE	EDDIES VEGETABLES	CBV	CAB	12/18/89	A
FAMRERS PRODUCE	EDDIES VEGETABLES	CBV	CAB	12/19/89	A
FARMERS PRODUCE	EDDIES VEGETABLES	CRX	CAR	12/18/89	A
FARMERS PRODUCE	EDDIES VEGETABLES	CRX	CAR	12/19/89	A
FARMERS PRODUCE	EDDIES VEGETABLES	CRG	CAR	12/19/89	A
FARMERS PRODUCE	EDDIES VEGETABLES	CLL	CEL	12/18/89	P
FARMERS PRODUCE	EDDIES VEGETABLES	CLS	CEL	12/18/89	P
FARMERS PRODUCE	EDDIES VEGETABLES	CRL	COR	12/18/89	L
FARMERS PRODUCE	EDDIES VEGETABLES	CRY	COR	12/18/89	L
FARMERS PRODUCE	EDDIES VEGETABLES	CBM	GRN	12/18/89	A
FARMERS PRODUCE	EDDIES VEGETABLES	CHM	GRN	12/18/89	A
FARMERS PRODUCE	EDDIES VEGETABLES	COL	GRN	12/18/89	A
FARMERS PRODUCE	EDDIES VEGETABLES	MST	GRN	12/18/89	A
FARMERS PRODUCE	EDDIES VEGETABLES	TUR	GRN	12/18/89	P
FARMERS PRODUCE	EDDIES VEGETABLES	KLG	KAL	12/18/89	A
FARMERS PRODUCE	EDDIES VEGETABLES	LT2	LET	12/18/89	A
FARMERS PRODUCE	EDDIES VEGETABLES	LTI	LET	12/19/89	A
FARMERS PRODUCE	EDDIES VEGETABLES	LRO	LET	12/18/89	A
FARMERS PRODUCE	EDDIES VEGETABLES	LT7	LET	12/18/89	A
FARMERS PRODUCE	EDDIES VEGETABLES	PAI	PAR	12/18/89	L
FARMERS PRODUCE	EDDIES VEGETABLES	PAR	PAR	12/18/89	L
FARMERS PRODUCE	EDDIES VEGETABLES	RTX	RUT	12/18/89	P
FARMERS PRODUCE	EDDIES VEGETABLES	SCR	SCA	12/18/89	P
FARMERS PRODUCE	EDDIES VEGETABLES	SPB	SPN	12/18/89	P
FARMERS PRODUCE	EDDIES VEGETABLES	TNB	TRN	12/19/89	P
FARMERS PRODUCE	EDDIES VEGETABLES	TNL	TRN	12/19/89	P

HOUSE-VARIETY (continued)

FARMERS PRODUCE	JOHNSONS VEGETABLE	BNB	BEN	12/21/89	L
FARMERS PRODUCE	JOHNSONS VEGETABLE	BNC	BEN	12/21/89	L
FARMERS PRODUCE	JOHNSONS VEGETABLE	BNV	BEN	12/21/89	L
FARMERS PRODUCE	JOHNSONS VEGETABLE	BNI	BEN	12/21/89	L
FARMERS PRODUCE	JOHNSONS VEGETABLE	BNK	BEN	12/21/89	L
FARMERS PRODUCE	JOHNSONS VEGETABLE	BNY	BEN	12/21/89	L
FARMERS PRODUCE	JOHNSONS VEGETABLE	CUP	CUC	12/21/89	L
FARMERS PRODUCE	JOHNSONS VEGETABLE	PP1	PEP	12/21/89	A
FARMERS PRODUCE	JOHNSONS VEGETABLE	PO3	PTO	12/21/89	P
FARMERS PRODUCE	JOHNSONS VEGETABLE	ON2	ONI	12/21/89	P
FARMERS PRODUCE	JOHNSONS VEGETABLE	ON6	ONI	12/21/89	P

TAG

HOUSE-NAME	STALL-NAME	INV-NUM	TAG-DATE	TAG-NUM	TAG-TOT
A & D PRODUCE	ALS ARTICHOKES	1	12/18/89	4202-05	172.00
A & D PRODUCE	ALS ARTICHOKES	2	12/19/89	4202-35	146.00
A & D PRODUCE	ALS ARTICHOKES	3	12/19/89	4202-37	108.00
A & D PRODUCE	ALS ARTICHOKES	4	12/20/89	4203-22	168.00
A & D PRODUCE	ALS ARTICHOKES	5	12/21/89	4204-25	101.00
A & D PRODUCE	ALS ARTICHOKES	6	12/22/89	4205-26	454.00
B & C PRODUCE	RICCIS SPECIALTY	35	12/18/89	436821	265.00
D & R PRODUCE	KENS VEGGIE	40	12/18/89	1135-18	485.00
FARMERS PRODUCE	EDDIES VEGETABLES	28	12/22/89	1883-42	456.75
FARMERS PRODUCE	EDDIES VEGETABLES	18	12/19/89	1886-29	249.00
FARMERS PRODUCE	EDDIES VEGETABLES	13	12/18/89	883-27	660.75
FARMERS PRODUCE	JOHNSONS VEGETABLES	22	12/20/89	1884.45	558.75
FARMERS PRODUCE	JOHNSONS VEGETABLES	27	12/21/89	1901-47	658.50

TAG-LINE

HOUSE-NAME	STALL-NAME	INV-NUM	LINE-NUM
A & D PRODUCE	ALS ARTICHOKES	1	1
A & D PRODUCE	ALS ARTICHOKES	1	2
A & D PRODUCE	ALS ARTICHOKES	1	3
FARMERS PRODUCE	EDDIES VEGETABLES	13	1
FARMERS PRODUCE	EDDIES VEGETABLES	13	2
FARMERS PRODUCE	EDDIES VEGETABLES	13	3
FARMERS PRODUCE	EDDIES VEGETABLES	13	4
FARMERS PRODUCE	EDDIES VEGETABLES	13	5
FARMERS PRODUCE	EDDIES VEGETABLES	13	6
FARMERS PRODUCE	EDDIES VEGETABLES	13	7
FARMERS PRODUCE	EDDIES VEGETABLES	13	8
FARMERS PRODUCE	EDDIES VEGETABLES	13	9
FARMERS PRODUCE	EDDIES VEGETABLES	13	10
FARMERS PRODUCE	EDDIES VEGETABLES	18	1
FARMERS PRODUCE	EDDIES VEGETABLES	18	2
FARMERS PRODUCE	EDDIES VEGETABLES	18	3
FARMERS PRODUCE	EDDIES VEGETABLES	18	4
FARMERS PRODUCE	EDDIES VEGETABLES	18	5

TAG-LINE (continued)

A & D PRODUCE	ALS ARTICHOKES	2	1
A & D PRODUCE	ALS ARTICHOKES	2	2
FARMERS PRODUCE	JOHNSONS VEGETABLE	27	1
FARMERS PRODUCE	JOHNSONS VEGETABLE	27	2
FARMERS PRODUCE	JOHNSONS VEGETABLE	27	3
FARMERS PRODUCE	JOHNSONS VEGETABLE	27	4
FARMERS PRODUCE	JOHNSONS VEGETABLE	27	5
FARMERS PRODUCE	JOHNSONS VEGETABLE	27	6
FARMERS PRODUCE	JOHNSONS VEGETABLE	27	7
FARMERS PRODUCE	EDDIES VEGETABLES	28	1
FARMERS PRODUCE	EDDIES VEGETABLES	28	2
FARMERS PRODUCE	EDDIES VEGETABLES	28	3
FARMERS PRODUCE	EDDIES VEGETABLES	28	4
FARMERS PRODUCE	EDDIES VEGETABLES	28	5
FARMERS PRODUCE	EDDIES VEGETABLES	28	6
FARMERS PRODUCE	EDDIES VEGETABLES	28	7
A & D PRODUCE	ALS ARTICHOKES	3	1
A & D PRODUCE	ALS ARTICHOKES	4	1
A & D PRODUCE	ALS ARTICHOKES	4	2
A & D PRODUCE	ALS ARTICHOKES	4	3
A & D PRODUCE	ALS ARTICHOKES	5	1
A & D PRODUCE	ALS ARTICHOKES	5	2
A & D PRODUCE	ALS ARTICHOKES	6	1
A & D PRODUCE	ALS ARTICHOKES	6	2
A & D PRODUCE	ALS ARTICHOKES	6	3
A & D PRODUCE	ALS ARTICHOKES	6	4
A & D PRODUCE	ALS ARTICHOKES	6	5

LOT

HOUSE-NAME	STALL-NAME	VAR-ID	PRD-ID	HVAR-TS	INV-NUM	LINE-NUM	LOT-NUM	LOT-COUNT	LOT-WT	UNIT-COST	LINE-AMOUNT
A & D PRODUCE	ALS ARTICHOKES	ARS	ART	12/18/89	1	1	1		40	1.33	38.00
A & D PRODUCE	ALS ARTICHOKES	ARM	ART	12/18/89	1	2	2	240		.40	95.00
A & D PRODUCE	ALS ARTICHOKES	BRF	BRS	12/18/89	1	3	3		90	.43	39.00
FARMERS PRODUCE	EDDIES VEGETABLES	CBV	CAB	12/18/89	13	1	101		270	.11	30.00
FARMERS PRODUCE	EDDIES VEGETABLES	KLG	KAL	12/18/89	13	2	102	72		.25	18.00
FARMERS PRODUCE	EDDIES VEGETABLES	CBR	CAB	12/18/89	13	3	103		90	.11	10.00
FARMERS PRODUCE	EDDIES VEGETABLES	CRY	COR	12/18/89	13	4	104	520		.26	134.00
FARMERS PRODUCE	EDDIES VEGETABLES	CRX	CAR	12/18/89	13	5	105		500	.14	70.00
FARMERS PRODUCE	EDDIES VEGETABLES	SPB	SPN	12/18/89	13	6	106		120	.38	45.00
FARMERS PRODUCE	EDDIES VEGETABLES	LRO	LET	12/18/89	13	7	107	144		.36	52.50
FARMERS PRODUCE	EDDIES VEGETABLES	LT2	LET	12/18/89	13	8	108	144		.36	52.50
FARMERS PRODUCE	EDDIES VEGETABLES	LT7	LET	12/18/89	13	9	109	120		.41	48.75
FARMERS PRODUCE	EDDIES VEGETABLES	CRY	COR	12/18/89	13	10	110	600		.33	200.00
FARMERS PRODUCE	EDDIES VEGETABLES	CBV	CAB	12/19/89	18	1	301		240	.25	60.00
FARMERS PRODUCE	EDDIES VEGETABLES	LTI	LET	12/19/89	18	2	302	144		.28	40.50
FARMERS PRODUCE	EDDIES VEGETABLES	CBG	CAB	12/19/89	18	3	303		270	.22	60.00
FARMERS PRODUCE	EDDIES VEGETABLES	CBV	CAB	12/19/89	18	4	304		135	.16	21.00
FARMERS PRODUCE	EDDIES VEGETABLES	CRX	CAR	12/19/89	18	5	305		500	.14	67.50
A & D PRODUCE	ALS ARTICHOKES	ARL	ART	12/19/89	2	1	4	120		.77	92.50
A & D PRODUCE	ALS ARTICHOKES	BRF	BRS	12/19/89	2	2	5		120	.45	54.00

LOT (continued)

HOUSE-NAME	STALL-NAME	VAR-ID	PRD-ID	HVAR-TS	INV-NUM	LINE-NUM	LOT-NUM				
FARMERS PRODUCE	JOHNSONS VEGETABLE	BNK	BEN	12/21/89	27	1	450		297	.37	110.`
FARMERS PRODUCE	JOHNSONS VEGETABLE	PO3	PTO	12/21/89	27	2	451		250	.54	135.`
FARMERS PRODUCE	JOHNSONS VEGETABLE	CUP	CUC	12/21/89	27	3	452		360	.11	40.`
FARMERS PRODUCE	JOHNSONS VEGETABLE	ON6	ONI	12/21/89	27	4	453		250	.36	90.`
FARMERS PRODUCE	JOHNSONS VEGETABLE	BNB	BEN	12/21/89	27	5	454		162	1.09	177.`
FARMERS PRODUCE	JOHNSONS VEGETABLE	ON2	ONI	12/21/89	27	6	455		250	.15	37.`
FARMERS PRODUCE	JOHNSONS VEGETABLE	PP1	PEP	12/21/89	27	7	456		162	.43	69.`
FARMERS PRODUCE	EDDIES VEGETABLES	LTI	LET	12/22/89	28	1	461	192		.28	54.`
FARMERS PRODUCE	EDDIES VEGETABLES	LRO	LET	12/22/89	28	2	462	144		.33	48.`
FARMERS PRODUCE	EDDIES VEGETABLES	LT7	LET	12/22/89	28	3	463	120		.46	55.`
FARMERS PRODUCE	EDDIES VEGETABLES	CBG	CAB	12/22/89	28	4	464		225	.18	40.`
FARMERS PRODUCE	EDDIES VEGETABLES	CBR	CAB	12/22/89	28	5	465		90	.18	16.`
FARMERS PRODUCE	EDDIES VEGETABLES	BRR	BRO	12/22/89	28	6	466		360	.41	146.`
FARMERS PRODUCE	EDDIES VEGETABLES	CRX	CAR	12/22/89	28	7	467		750	.13	97.`
A & D PRODUCE	ALS ARTICHOKES	BNV	BEN	12/19/89	3	1	6		120	.90	108.`
A & D PRODUCE	ALS ARTICHOKES	ARL	ART	12/20/89	4	1	7	120		.75	90.`
A & D PRODUCE	ALS ARTICHOKES	BRF	BRS	12/20/89	4	2	8		120	.43	52.`
A & D PRODUCE	ALS ARTICHOKES	BRT	BRS	12/20/89	4	3	9		60	.43	26.`
A & D PRODUCE	ALS ARTICHOKES	ARS	ART	12/21/89	5	1	11		40	.90	36.`
A & D PRODUCE	ALS ARTICHOKES	BRF	BRS	12/21/89	5	2	12		150	.43	65.`
A & D PRODUCE	ALS ARTICHOKES	ARL	ART	12/22/89	6	1	13	48		.75	36.`
A & D PRODUCE	ALS ARTICHOKES	ARS	ART	12/22/89	6	2	14		120	.90	108.`
A & D PRODUCE	ALS ARTICHOKES	PRG	PEA	12/22/89	6	3	15		120	.65	78.`
A & D PRODUCE	ALS ARTICHOKES	BRF	BRS	12/22/89	6	4	16		120	.43	52.`
A & D PRODUCE	ALS ARTICHOKES	PRS	PEA	12/22/89	6	5	17		150	.72	180.`

STORE-LOT

STORE -ID	HOUSE-NAME	STALL-NAME	VAR -ID	PRD -ID	HVAR-TS	INV- NUM	LINE -NUM	LOT- NUM	ST-L- COUNT	ST-L- WT
B	A & D PRODUCE	ALS ARTICHOKES	ARS	ART	12/18/89	1	1	1		40
P	A & D PRODUCE	ALS ARTICHOKES	ARM	ART	12/18/89	1	2	2	240	
B	A & D PRODUCE	ALS ARTICHOKES	BRF	BRS	12/18/89	1	3	3		45
P	A & D PRODUCE	ALS ARTICHOKES	BRF	BRS	12/18/89	1	3	3		45
B	FARMERS PRODUCE	EDDIES VEGETABLES	CBV	CAB	12/18/89	13	1	101		270
B	FARMERS PRODUCE	EDDIES VEGETABLES	KLG	KAL	12/18/89	13	2	102	72	
B	FARMERS PRODUCE	EDDIES VEGETABLES	CBR	CAB	12/18/89	13	3	103		90
B	FARMERS PRODUCE	EDDIES VEGETABLES	CRY	COR	12/18/89	13	4	104	260	
P	FARMERS PRODUCE	EDDIES VEGETABLES	CRY	COR	12/18/89	13	4	104	260	
P	FARMERS PRODUCE	EDDIES VEGETABLES	CRX	CAR	12/18/89	13	5	105		500
P	FARMERS PRODUCE	EDDIES VEGETABLES	SPB	SPN	12/18/89	13	6	106		120
P	FARMERS PRODUCE	EDDIES VEGETABLES	LRO	LET	12/18/89	13	7	107	144	
B	FARMERS PRODUCE	EDDIES VEGETABLES	LT2	LET	12/18/89	13	8	108	144	

It was apparent from our work with the prototype that entry of the day's TAGs would be one of the most critical points in the system. We could see that a simple method of recording the PRODUCT and VARIETY information written on the TAG was going to be needed, and noted this for our detailed design work.

At the end of our sessions, we had an IDEF1X area key based model covering most of the business. It corresponds to a model in the second row of the IDEF1X model type diagram shown in Chapter 3. That area is highlighted in Fig. 14.12. The full key based model is shown as Fig. 14.13.

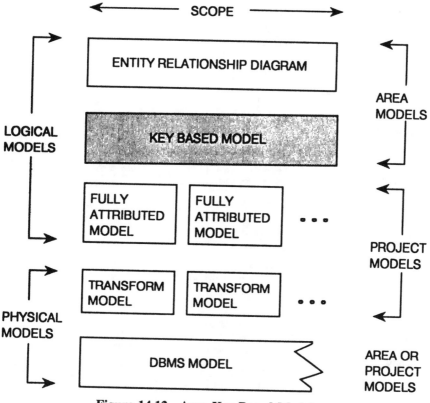

Figure 14.12. Area Key Based Model.

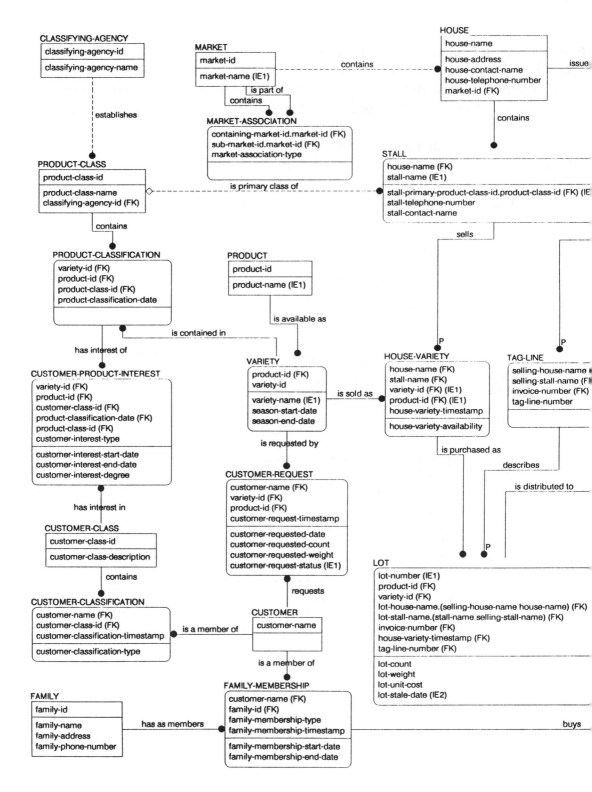

Figure 14.13. Full Key Based Model.

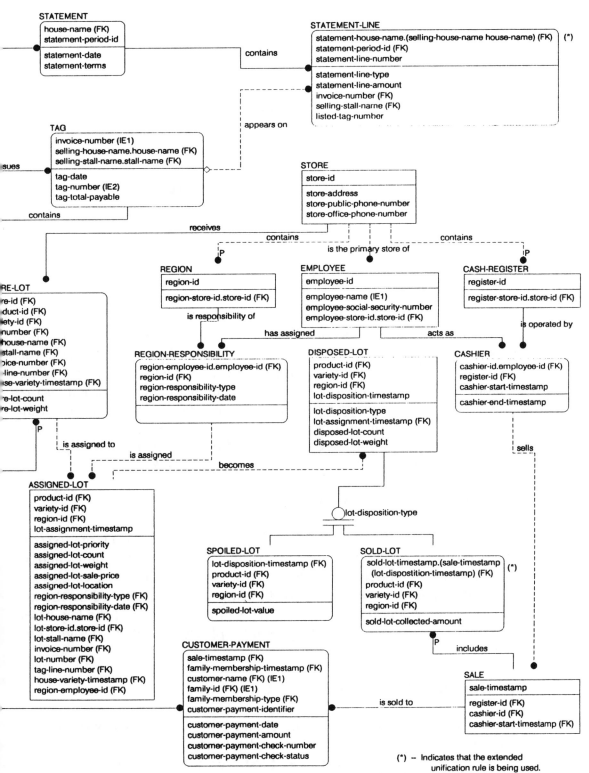

Figure 14.13. Full Key Based Model (continued).

15

MARKET DATABASE

In Chapter 14, we discussed the key based model for Monterey Foods. This chapter further develops a portion of that model, and shows the transformation of the detailed logical design into an initial physical design for the database.

The discussion starts with the fully attributed model (a Zachman Framework model of the information system), then examines logical transactions that represent projected access patterns against the data. We then substitute physical system names for entities and attributes and develop a set of relational tables. The transformation model developed during this process represents a Zachman Framework Technology Model for the market database.

15.1 FULLY ATTRIBUTED MODEL

The complete fully attributed model for Monterey Foods is too large to cover in this case study. It currently contains 62 entities and 263 attributes and, as do all requirements models, continues to grow as additional business rules and policies are included. The essence of the full model is captured by the key based model described in Chapter 13. We will use the part of the key based model covered by our prototype to prepare a physical database design. Our starting point is shown in Fig. 15.1.

15.1.1 Extending the Key Based Model

From our work on the key based model and prototype, we knew there were several areas we would need to review and extend. We started by examining the attributes that represented groups. First, we knew we would need to break the group attribute "house-address" into its constituents.

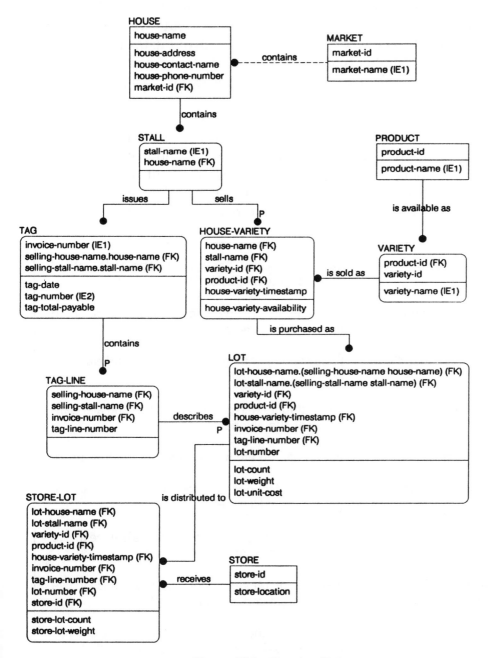

Figure 15.1. Starting Point.

Although we could have left it as a single attribute, we did the same for
"house-phone-number". We replaced the group attributes with their constituents, but retained the knowledge of the groupings in our data dictionary. Next,
we added a phone number and contact for each STALL and an address and
phone number for each STORE (the address replaced the original "store-loca-
tion" attribute).

Then, we undid much of what we had done with addresses, and thought
again about phone numbers. We discovered that each STORE had two phone
numbers and realized that all phone numbers we would need consisted of a
three-digit area code, a three-digit prefix, a four-digit suffix, and optionally,
a four-digit extension. We stepped outside the graphic language of the model
and recorded the attribute structure shown below in our data dictionary:

phone-area-code	base attribute with generic definition and standard physical characteristics
phone-number-prefix	base attribute with generic definition and standard physical characteristics
phone-number-suffix	base attribute with generic definition and standard physical characteristics
phone-number-extension	base attribute with generic definition and standard physical characteristics
phone-number	generic group attribute containing the four parts
house-phone-number	data type of "phone-number", with reference to use (to contact a HOUSE)
stall-phone-number	data type of "phone-number", with reference to use (to contact a STALL)
store-public-phone-number	data type of "phone-number", with reference to use (for general contact of a STORE)
store-office-phone-number	data type of "phone-number", with reference to use (a second semi-private number for a STORE)

Listing 15.1. Dictionary Entries.

This attribute structure did two things for us: First, without the base attributes, we were in danger of filling up the dictionary with multiple definitions of what a prefix or a suffix was (we would have needed to define the terms in each definition—that is, "store-phone-prefix", "house-phone-prefix", "stall-phone-prefix", and so on). Forming a common set of base attributes allowed us to define the terms only once, then reference them as needed. Second, by defining each use of a phone number by reference to a standard base, we ensured that the physical representations of all phone numbers would be the same, regardless of what the phone numbers were used for.

We also made a choice about how much detail to include in our fully attributed model diagram. We decided not to worry about manipulating the constituents of phone numbers; we would think of these numbers as groups, at least until we got to the most detailed level of our design and began the transformation to the physical database. Therefore, in the diagram, we defined each occurrence as a use of a "phone-number" rather than as the four separate attributes "whatever-area-code", "whatever-prefix", "whatever-suffix", and "whatever-extension".

At this point, we discovered that there are no phone extension numbers in the Berkeley store. There are extension phones, but they do not have separate numbers. This required that we change some attribute names and modify our definition structure. We added "phone-number" (without an extension) and "extended-phone-number" (with extension) group attributes to the dictionary. The details are in the supplementary material in Appendix F. Figure 15.2 provides a summary of how the definitions are structured. The "extended-phone-number" attribute was established so that we could change our definition linkages and break "telephone-number"s directly into their constituents if needed.

We created a similar structure for the constituents of an "address". Figure 15.3 shows the definition structure. We referred to the super-group that contained all the constituent attributes as "address". We now had the ability to be specific in our model about a type of address without needing to list constituents each time. That is, we could refer to a "street-address" when we needed number and street, "po-box-address" if we needed only a post office box number, or "address" if we needed to accommodate an address of either type. With the changes to phone numbers and addresses, the HOUSE, STALL, and STORE entities now appeared as in Fig. 15.4.

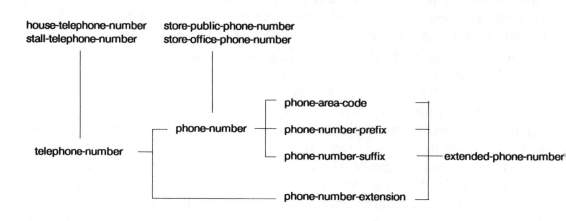

Figure 15.2. Phone Number Definition Structure.

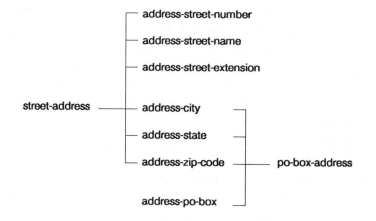

Figure 15.3. Address Definition Structure.

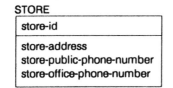

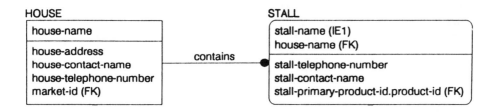

Figure 15.4. Group Attributes.

We moved on from our examination of groups and began looking for additional attributes. We looked at PRODUCT, VARIETY, and HOUSE-VARIETY. We could not think of additional attributes for PRODUCT or VARIETY. For HOUSE-VARIETY, we decided to designate the pair of attributes "product-id" and "variety-id" as an inversion entry, since we would be using this combination as part of a standard query—that is, Which HOUSE-VARIETYs are at a certain level of availability?

We then looked at TAG, TAG-LINE, and LOT. We examined real tags and verified that the few attributes we had would support them. For LOT we added the attribute "lot-stale-date" (a date by which a LOT should be sold or discarded) so that our system could prompt us with inventory that should be moved soon. We examined STORE and STORE-LOT, and verified we had the needed attributes. We added a "P" to the relationship between LOT and STORE-LOT (each LOT needs to be distributed to at least one STORE) and designated an additional inversion entry for STORE-LOT.

These changes gave us our preliminary fully attributed model for the buying function of the store. It is shown in Fig. 15.5 and corresponds to a model in the third row of the IDEF1X model type diagram in Chapter 3. That area is highlighted in Fig. 15.6. Before we could consider it final, we needed to document the access patterns that would occur, and again test to see that the model could hold all required information. We also needed to add anticipated entity instance volumes. This led us to the next step, documenting logical transactions.

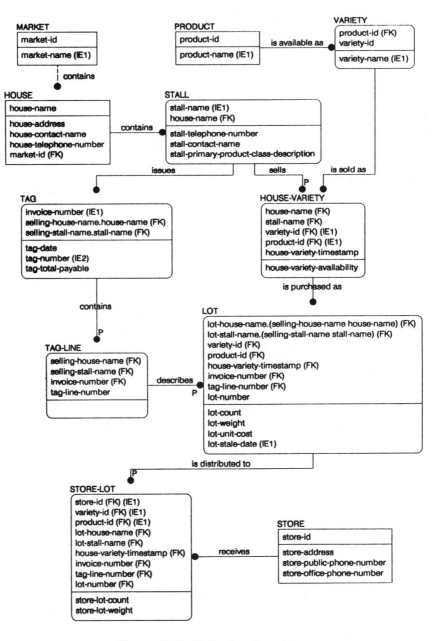

Figure 15.5. Fully Attributed Model.

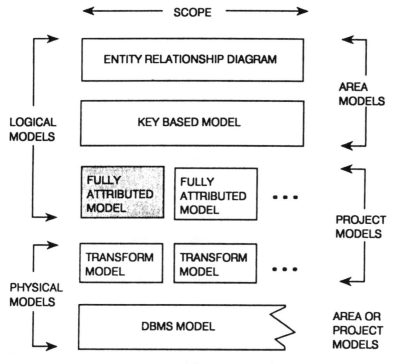

Figure 15.6. Project Fully Attributed Model.

15.1.2 Logical Transactions

Logical transactions represent discrete units of work performed against the database. A screen interaction or a set of batch-processing activities that accomplish a specific task are examples of a logical transaction. For our buying function, we developed a set of the most common transactions. Transactions to set up reference data (stalls, varieties, and so on) would be infrequent and were not included in the initial set. We knew there would also be ad-hoc query transactions with frequencies and access requirements that would be difficult to anticipate in advance and that we would likely have to do some physical system tuning as these patterns became evident.

Our initial transaction list is shown in Fig. 15.7. Detailed transaction descriptions and entity instance volumes follow in Listings 15.2 and 15.3. From this information, we could see that entry of TAG-LINEs would be a part of TAG entry, and that each TAG-LINE entry could in turn create an instance of HOUSE-VARIETY. We knew from our prototype that the entry of a TAG-LINE would often involve the look-up of the correct identifiers for the key constituents (identifiers of the PRODUCT, VARIETY, and so on), so we decided to consider these queries as part of our transaction set. The list of logical transactions is structured to reflect the sequence of actions that would need to be performed.

```
Enter a TAG
        Query a HOUSE
        Query a STALL
        Enter a TAG-LINE
                Enter a HOUSE-VARIETY
                        Query a PRODUCT
                        Query a VARIETY
                Enter a LOT
Assign a STORE-LOT
Prepare an availability list
Prepare an availability trend report
Prepare a list of inventory acquired by a STORE
```

Figure 15.7. Logical Transactions.

If we had been using a structured analysis and design technique for describing the functional part of the system, the set of transactions in Fig. 15.7 would be similar to the description of the lowest-level processes in the decomposition diagrams (some of the query transactions might represent the edits being performed).

Logical Transaction Descriptions

Transaction:	Enter a TAG
Sub-Transactions:	Query a STALL
	Query a HOUSE
	Enter a TAG-LINE
Frequency:	100 per day, within a span of two hours.
Peak Transaction Rate:	1 per minute
Response Time Required:	< 3 seconds
Entity Instances Created:	TAG
	(TAG-LINE)
Entity Instances Replaced:	None
Entity Instances Used:	STALL (access by primary key)
Entity Instances Deleted	None

Transaction:	Query a HOUSE
Sub-Transactions:	None
Access Key:	"house-name" (partial)
Frequency:	700 per day, within a span of two hours.
Peak Transaction Rate:	7 per minute
Response Time Required:	< 2 seconds
Entity Instances Created:	None
Entity Instances Replaced:	None

Entity Instances Used:	HOUSE
Entity Instances Deleted:	None

Transaction:	Query a STALL
Sub-Transactions:	None
Access Key:	"stall-name" (partial)
Frequency:	700 per day, within a span of two hours.
Peak Transaction Rate:	7 per minute
Response Time Required:	< 2 seconds
Entity Instances Created:	None
Entity Instances Replaced:	None
Entity Instances Used:	STALL
Entity Instances Deleted:	None

Transaction:	Enter a TAG-LINE
Sub-Transactions:	Enter a HOUSE-VARIETY
	Enter a LOT
Frequency:	700 per day, within a span of two hours.
Peak Transaction Rate:	7 per minute
Response Time Required:	< 1 second
Entity Instances Created:	TAG-LINE
	(HOUSE-VARIETY)
	(LOT)
Entity Instances Replaced:	None
Entity Instances Used:	TAG (access by primary key)
Entity Instances Deleted:	None

Transaction:	Enter a HOUSE-VARIETY
Sub-Transactions:	Query a PRODUCT
	Query a VARIETY
Frequency:	700 per day, within a span of two hours.
Peak Transaction Rate:	7 per minute
Response Time Required:	< 1 second
Entity Instances Created:	HOUSE-VARIETY
Entity Instances Replaced:	None
Entity Instances Used:	STALL (access by primary key)
	VARIETY (access by primary key)
	(PRODUCT)
	(HOUSE)
Entity Instances Deleted:	None

Transaction:	Query a PRODUCT
Sub-Transactions:	None
Access Key:	"product-name" (partial)
Frequency:	700 per day, within a span of two hours.
Response Time Required:	< 2 seconds
Peak Transaction Rate:	7 per minute
Entity Instances Created:	None
Entity Instances Replaced:	None
Entity Instances Used:	PRODUCT
Entity Instances Deleted:	None

Transaction:	Query a VARIETY
Sub-Transactions:	None
Access Key:	"variety-name" (partial)
Frequency:	700 per day, within a span of two hours.
Response Time Required:	< 2 seconds
Peak Transaction Rate:	7 per minute
Entity Instances Created:	None
Entity Instances Replaced:	None
Entity Instances Used:	VARIETY
Entity Instances Deleted:	None

Transaction:	Enter a LOT
Sub-Transactions:	None
Frequency:	700 per day, within a span of two hours.
Response Time Required:	< 1 second
Peak Transaction Rate:	7 per minute
Entity Instances Created:	LOT
Entity Instances Replaced:	None
Entity Instances Used:	TAG-LINE (access by primary key)
	HOUSE-VARIETY (access by primary key)
Entity Instances Deleted:	None

Transaction:	Assign a STORE-LOT
Sub-Transactions:	None
Frequency:	1000 per day, within a span of two hours.
Response Time Required:	< 1 second
Peak Transaction Rate:	10 per minute
Entity Instances Created:	STORE-LOT
Entity Instances Replaced:	None
Entity Instances Used:	LOT (access by primary key)
	STORE (access by primary key)
Entity Instances Deleted:	None

Transaction:	Prepare an availability list
Sub-Transactions:	None
Frequency:	1 per day
Peak Transaction Rate:	1 per day
Response Time Required:	< 2 minutes
Entity Instances Created:	None
Entity Instances Replaced:	None
Entity Instances Used:	HOUSE-VARIETY (access by a range of "house-variety-timestamp"s) (search) (1000).
	For each,
	VARIETY (access by primary key)
	PRODUCT (access by primary key)
	STALL (access by primary key)
	HOUSE (access by primary key)
	MARKET (access by primary key)
Entity Instances Deleted:	None

Transaction:	Prepare an availability trend report
Sub-Transactions:	None
Frequency:	4 per month
Peak Transaction Rate:	1 per day
Response Time Required:	< 5 minutes
Entity Instances Created:	None
Entity Instances Replaced:	None
Entity Instances Used:	HOUSE-VARIETY (access by a range of "house-variety-timestamp"s) (search) (20,000). For each selected, VARIETY (access by primary key) PRODUCT (access by primary key) STALL (access by primary key) HOUSE (access by primary key) MARKET (access by primary key)
Entity Instances Deleted:	None

Transaction:	Prepare a list of inventory by STORE
Sub-Transactions:	None
Frequency:	4 per month
Peak Transaction Rate:	1 per day
Response Time Required:	< 5 minutes
Entity Instances Created:	None
Entity Instances Replaced:	None
Entity Instances Used:	STORE-LOT (access by "store-id", range of "house-variety-timestamp"s) (search). For each selected, VARIETY (access by primary key) PRODUCT (access by primary key)
Entity Instances Deleted:	None

Listing 15.2. Logical Transactions.

Entity Instance Volumes

Entity:	HOUSE
Occurrences:	200
Growth Rate:	25 per year
Retention Period:	10 years

Entity:	HOUSE-VARIETY
Occurrences:	500,000
Growth Rate:	700 per day
Retention Period:	3 years

Entity:	LOT
Occurrences:	42,000
Growth Rate:	700 per day
Retention Period:	60 days

Entity:	MARKET
Occurrences:	20
Growth Rate:	5 per year
Retention Period:	10 years

Entity:	PRODUCT
Occurrences:	200
Growth Rate:	20 per year
Retention Period:	10 years

Entity:	STALL
Occurrences:	100
Growth Rate:	10 per year
Retention Period:	10 years

Entity:	STORE
Occurrences:	2
Growth Rate:	1 per 5 years
Retention Period:	10 years

Entity:	STORE-LOT
Occurrences:	84,000
Growth Rate:	1,400 per day
Retention Period:	60 days

Entity:	TAG
Occurrences:	30,000
Growth Rate:	100 per day
Retention Period:	1 year

Entity:	TAG-LINE
Occurrences:	42,000
Growth Rate:	700 per day
Retention Period:	60 days

Entity:	VARIETY
Occurrences:	5,000
Growth Rate:	100 per year
Retention Period:	10 years

Listing 15.3. Entity Instance Volumes.

15.2 TRANSFORMATION

The pattern of logical transaction access against the model was used to help us determine whether to denormalize the structure for physical system performance and decide where to create indices for rapid access to an entity instance by other than its primary key. Our experience with the prototype told us how much we should expect the people who eventually would operate the system to remember about the identifiers of products, varieties, stalls, and so on. For our small section of the model, the denormalization issue was not too difficult (only a few revisions were felt to be needed here). The "what can I remember" issue was more interesting.

We knew from our prototype that during the entry of a TAG, the operator of the system would need to know, or quickly be able to find, the keys of the STALL, HOUSE, PRODUCT, and VARIETY listed on the TAG. We envisioned an entry screen that looked something like Fig. 15.8.

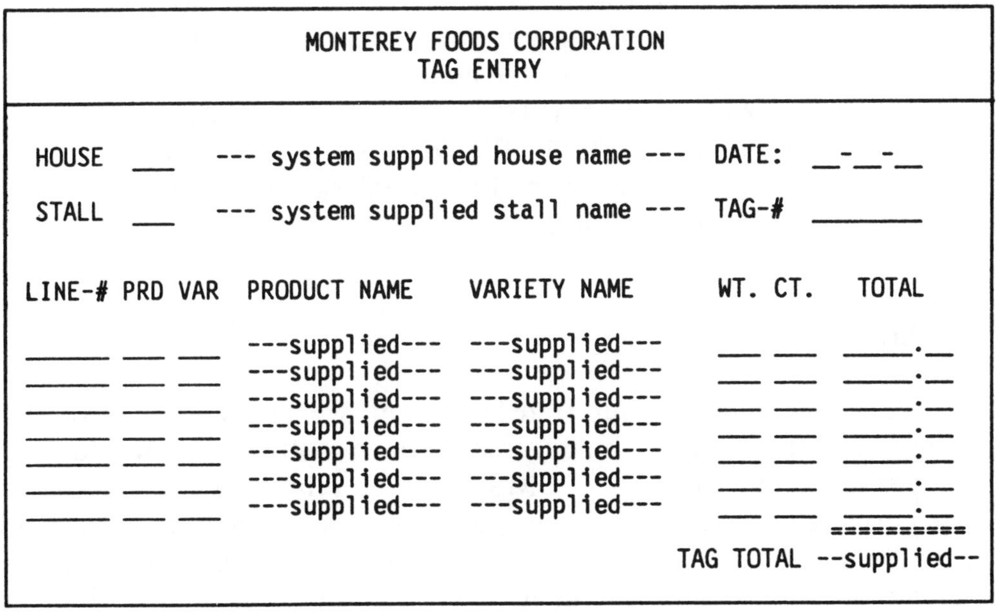

```
┌─────────────────────────────────────────────────────────────────┐
│                   MONTEREY FOODS CORPORATION                      │
│                          TAG ENTRY                                │
├─────────────────────────────────────────────────────────────────┤
│                                                                   │
│  HOUSE  ___    --- system supplied house name ---  DATE:  __-__-__│
│                                                                   │
│  STALL  ___    --- system supplied stall name ---  TAG-# _____  │
│                                                                   │
│  LINE-# PRD VAR  PRODUCT NAME    VARIETY NAME      WT. CT.  TOTAL  │
│                                                                   │
│  _____ __ __   ---supplied---  ---supplied---    __ __  ____.__   │
│  _____ __ __   ---supplied---  ---supplied---    __ __  ____.__   │
│  _____ __ __   ---supplied---  ---supplied---    __ __  ____.__   │
│  _____ __ __   ---supplied---  ---supplied---    __ __  ____.__   │
│  _____ __ __   ---supplied---  ---supplied---    __ __  ____.__   │
│  _____ __ __   ---supplied---  ---supplied---    __ __  ____.__   │
│  _____ __ __   ---supplied---  ---supplied---    __ __  ____.__   │
│                                                   ==========      │
│                                       TAG TOTAL  --supplied--     │
└─────────────────────────────────────────────────────────────────┘
```

Figure 15.8. Tag Entry Screen.

Remembering the identifiers of HOUSE and STALL would not be too hard; there were only about thirty HOUSEs and a hundred STALLs, and the person doing the entry of the TAGs would be dealing with them every day. We therefore decided that a printed list of HOUSEs and STALLs would be sufficient for looking up identifiers when necessary. We felt that the same approach might work for PRODUCTs. Although there would eventually be hundreds of PRODUCTs, a list would probably work well. For VARIETY, however, we needed another approach since there could eventually be thousands in the database.

Providing a query to look up a VARIETY by its "variety-name" was only a partial solution, since some names are obscure and the operator might not be able to remember a name well enough to enter it exactly as it was known to the database. Our look-up query would have to be able to deal with misspellings and situations in which the entire name was not known.

We needed an indexing capability that would let us find a VARIETY whose name was only partially known. We chose a Soundex [1] algorithm to derive a look-up key (inversion entry) for each VARIETY. Now our entry operator could enter the correct keys of PRODUCT, HOUSE, and STALL (using the reference lists as needed) and guess at the name of the VARIETY until the system found the right one. This might work. We also thought we could present a list of VARIETYs of the PRODUCT that was entered or show the previous day's HOUSE-VARIETYs for the PRODUCT as a way to let the operator narrow the search or chose the VARIETY from a list. A possible help screen for VARIETY is shown in Fig. 15.9. We considered this to be an adequate approach for the moment and returned to the job of transforming our logical model into a set of physical tables.

15.2.1 Physical System Names

Before we could complete our transformation, we needed to make some decisions about the database management system software we would use to build the system. We knew the DBMS would be relational (we are going to use a generic database from here on, which may look remarkably like IBM's DB2, although this is not the DBMS we actually used). This would constrain the length of the physical system names we could assign for entities and attributes. Unlike the names used in the business model, which can be up to 65 characters long, table and column names would be limited to 18 characters. This meant that we would have to assign abbreviated names.

```
┌─────────────────────────────────────────────────────────────────────┐
│                     MONTEREY FOODS CORPORATION                        │
│                      HOUSE VARIETY HELP                               │
├─────────────────────────────────────────────────────────────────────┤
│                                                                       │
│  HOUSE   xxx    --- system supplied house name -----                  │
│  STALL   xxx    --- system supplied stall name -----                  │
│  PROD    xxx    --- system supplied product name ---                  │
│                                                                       │
│  VARIETY        --- system supplied variety name ---      KEY: xxxxx   │
│                 _____                 │
│                                                                       │
│                                                                       │
│  PAST HOUSE VARIETIES (chose one)                                     │
│                                                                       │
│  --- supplied variety name ---       --- supplied variety name ---    │
│  --- supplied variety name ---       --- supplied variety name ---    │
│  --- supplied variety name ---       --- supplied variety name ---    │
│  --- supplied variety name ---       --- supplied variety name ---    │
│  --- supplied variety name ---       --- supplied variety name ---    │
│  --- supplied variety name ---       --- supplied variety name ---    │
│                                                                       │
└─────────────────────────────────────────────────────────────────────┘
```

Figure 15.9. House Variety Help Screen.

We developed a set of abbreviation conventions and assigned physical system names to each entity and attribute. We also developed the physical descriptions for attributes and recorded them in terms of the DBMS data type for a column. (We refer to the DBMS data type as format to make a clear distinction between this and the IDEF1X data type).

As we were assigning formats, we had to make a choice about whether to store addresses and phone numbers as long character strings, or break them down into their constituents. Our dictionary entries recorded the groupings we had discovered earlier. We decided to include addresses and phone numbers as character strings for the first version of our database, but knew this meant we could not operate on the parts of the group directly. For example, answering a question such as, What HOUSEs are in California? would be difficult. We would need to use an application program to parse the character strings into their constituents if we needed to operate directly on the constituents.

We also asked ourselves whether each STALL had a separate phone number or whether all STALLs in a HOUSE used extensions of the HOUSE phone number. We decided we could not require that all STALLs use extensions of the phone number for the HOUSE. (If we had, we could simply have included an "extension" attribute in STALL and recorded the phone number in the HOUSE.) We were satisfied with our model, and ready to begin the physical design for the database.

15.2.2 Transformation Model

The transformation model is an IDEF1X picture of the physical database design. It includes system control and access information as well as the business data from the fully attributed model. In preparing the transformation model, our first step was to add our Soundex inversion entry attribute to the VARIETY entity (although we did not intend to implement it in the first version of our database). For good measure, we added Soundex attributes to the PRODUCT and HOUSE entities with the idea that this type of look-up capability might be useful in the future.

Next, we re-drew our fully attributed model using the physical system names we had assigned. We left off the notation that recorded role name extensions (the part that referenced the base or unified attribute names) and derived the model shown in Fig. 15.10, which is an IDEF1X diagram of our initial physical table design.

Bill and I continued to work with the detail shown in Fig. 15.10. However, to keep things to a reasonable size, we will drop the STORE and STORE-LOT entities from our case study from this point forward. You may wish to add them back as an exercise.

Next, we needed to decide what denormalization might be in order. We had already introduced some by storing the name of the primary PRODUCT-CLASS as an attribute of STALL, but we had been forced to do so by our decision to leave PRODUCT-CLASS outside our initial development scope. For each of the business rules in the model, we now needed to ask whether it was worth the cost of enforcing the rule in the system. If it was, we needed also to decide if we would ask the DBMS to enforce the rule or have the application code do it, and whether we should do the enforcement in real-time or look for violations, and repair them after-the-fact. Many of the business rules are embodied by the relationships.

The relationships from MARKET to HOUSE, HOUSE to STALL, and PRODUCT to VARIETY represented paths we would often use to answer ad-hoc queries, and declared fundamental relationships among the tangible things the business dealt with. It seemed reasonable to expect a relational DBMS to be

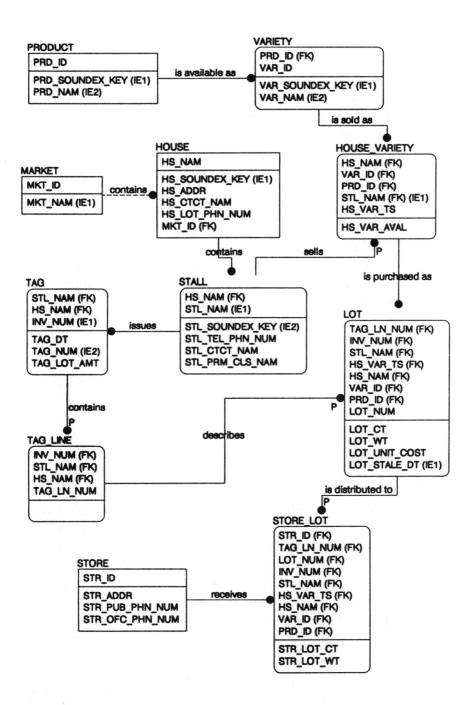

Figure 15.10. Physical System Names.

able to manage these relationships. Since the insert and delete activity against them would not be very high (in comparison to the activity against tables involved in the entry of TAGs), we decided to use the referential integrity enforcement capability of the DBMS to manage these relationships. We decided never to allow null foreign keys on insert (or update), and to restrict all deletes. This would prevent us from entering basic data that violated the structural rules of the business model and from accidentally deleting, say, all knowledge of everything ever connected with a MARKET by simply deleting that MARKET.

When we looked at HOUSE_VARIETY and its connections to HOUSE and to VARIETY, we asked whether it was practical to record every occurrence of a VARIETY at a HOUSE (even if we had not purchased it that day) and where that information would come from if we had no TAG that included it. We also envisioned a query (What has ever been available?) that might run for a very long time. Our investigation of how TAG entry would have to be done had also told us that it might be convenient to have a smaller table in which to look up the keys of the various entities.

Therefore, we made a minor change in our database model. We broke out the pair of attributes "house-variety-timestamp" and "house-variety-availability" into their own entity. This allowed us to keep a separate list (HOUSE_ VARIETY) of everything that had ever been available at a STALL (which would help our queries) while still allowing us to record availability information on a daily basis.

As we thought about the answers we would like to obtain from our database, we discovered there were at least two things we would like to know about the availability of VARIETYs. The first we had covered—tracking what was available from which STALLs. The second was a variation on the first—it would be convenient to know the approximate periods during the year when certain VARIETYs were generally available; where didn't matter.

Although we believed we could derive this data at any time by reviewing the history of varieties, we decided to store two pieces of derived data. We added a "season-start-date" and a "season-end-date" attribute to the VARIETY entity. We could have placed these attributes in our new HOUSE_VARIETY entity but decided we did not care about that level of precision; generally knowing when the season started and ended would be sufficient.

Figure 15.11 shows these changes. The symbols next to the relationships (for instance, the (R) below the relationship between MARKET and HOUSE) are a convenient extension to IDEF1X that is sometimes used to record the delete rules that govern the relationships. (As we saw in Chapter 8, insert and replace rules are directly stated by the IDEF1X relationship types.)

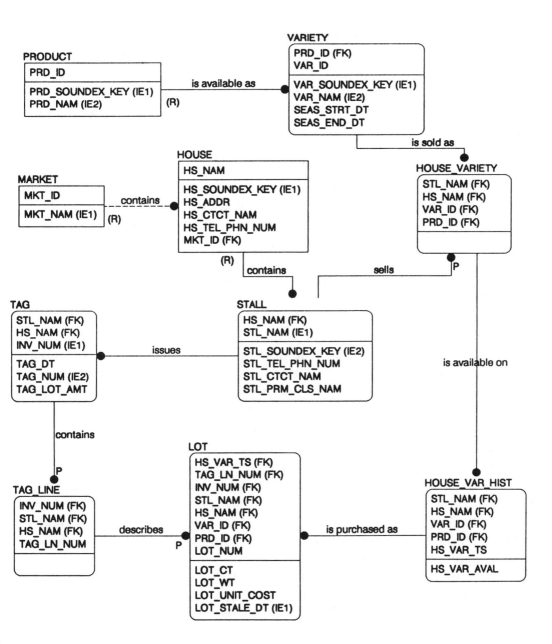

Figure 15.11.   Some Derived Data.

We continued to add the delete rule symbols to our diagram. For VARIETY, we decided to restrict deletes to prevent the accidental deletion of a VARIETY (along with all of its history). For STALL, however, we decided to allow the delete to cascade and remove any dependent HOUSE_VARIETYs and their history. This delete could begin only if there were no TAGs connected to the STALL. We also decided to cascade the deletion of HOUSE_VAR_HIST, TAG, and TAG_LINE. This would mean that whenever we wanted to delete a STALL from our database, we would first have to delete all of its TAGs, but the STALL, along with all of its connected information, could then be deleted with a single action.

TAG_LINE and LOT had originally appeared in our model to represent things that were identified separately and to allow multiple LOTs to be included on a TAG_LINE on the rare occasion when this occurred. Most of the time, however, there would be exactly one LOT for each TAG_LINE. We decided it was not worth the expense to support the one in a thousand exception. TAG_LINE and LOT were therefore merged into a single entity, with the TAG_LINE name. When we encountered the occasional multi-lot line, we would artificially introduce individual lines for each lot. We had changed the business rule, but it was worth it.

Next, we had to decide what to do with HOUSE_VAR_HIST. It contributed "house-variety-timestamp" ("hs_var_ts") to TAG_LINE, and we realized that all we would know was the date, not the time of day. Therefore, we replaced the timestamp with a new "house-variety-date". We also decided that since we knew a "tag-date" attribute for each TAG, we would break the direct connection to HOUSE_VAR_HIST. Again, we had changed a business rule (our model now allowed a TAG_LINE for a variety for which we had no HOUSE_VAR_HIST). The transformation model now approximated the business model (we could still track availability) without directly involving the TAG_LINEs.

The final transformation model is shown in Fig. 15.12. We actually had two versions of it—the one shown and one with the full names of the tables (entities) and columns (attributes). The one showing full names would be useful to people not dealing directly with the column names. The one showing physical system names was for the techies.

At the end of our sessions, we had an IDEF1X project transformation model for our small section of the business. It corresponds to a model in the fourth row of the IDEF1X model type diagram in Chapter 3. That area is highlighted in Fig. 15.13.

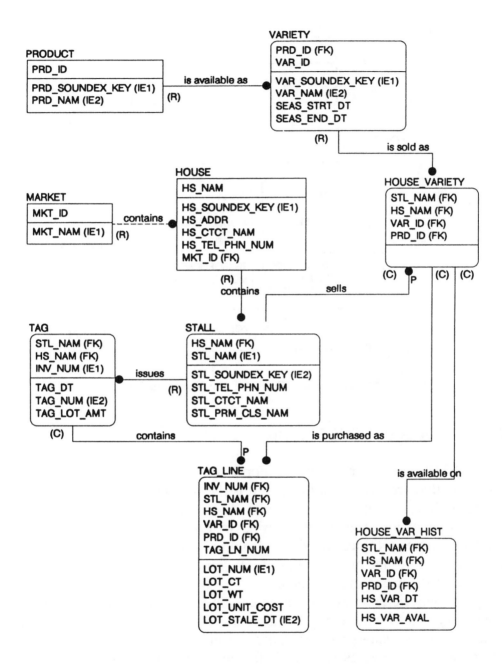

Figure 15.12.   Transformation Model.

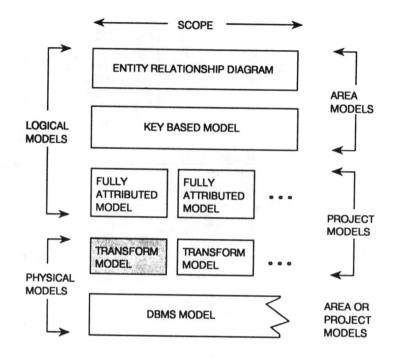

Figure 15.13.   Project Transformation Model.

15.3   DATABASE GENERATION

The DBMS model for Monterey Foods is described by the data definition language that creates the database. It is the first section of the DBMS model in the bottom row of Fig. 15.13 and will grow as the database is extended to cover other major areas of the business. Each entity in the transformation model becomes a table, and each attribute becomes a column. Primary and foreign keys are declared for each table, and referential integrity constraints are declared for each relationship.

The generic table create statements in Listing 15.4 were produced using the model as a source. Unique indices are declared for the primary keys, and other indices are established to represent inversion entries. We will conclude the case study here, as to take it farther would lead us into the world of physical system tuning, a topic best left for another time.

Table Create Statements

```
CREATE TABLE MARKET
(
MKT_ID                  INTEGER             NOT NULL,
MKT_NAM                 VARCHAR(40)         NOT NULL,
PRIMARY KEY (MKT_ID)
);

CREATE UNIQUE INDEX X_MARKET
    ON MARKET (MKT_ID);

CREATE INDEX XN_MARKET
    ON MARKET (MKT_NAM);

CREATE TABLE HOUSE
(
HS_NAM                  VARCHAR(40)         NOT NULL,
HS_SOUNDEX_KEY          INTEGER             NOT NULL,
HS_ADDR                 VARCHAR(40)         NOT NULL,
HS_CTCT_NAM             VARCHAR(40)         NOT NULL,
HS_TEL_PHN_NUM          CHARACTER(14)       NOT NULL,
MKT_ID                  INTEGER             NOT NULL,
PRIMARY KEY (HS_NAM),
FOREIGN KEY (MKT_ID)
    REFERENCES MARKET
    ON DELETE RESTRICT
);

CREATE UNIQUE INDEX X_HOUSE
    ON HOUSE (HS_NAM);

CREATE INDEX SX_HOUSE
    ON HOUSE (VAR_SOUNDEX_KEY);

CREATE TABLE STALL
(
HS_NAM                  VARCHAR(40)         NOT NULL,
STL_NAM                 VARCHAR(40)         NOT NULL,
STL_SOUNDEX_KEY         INTEGER             NOT NULL,
STL_TEL_PHN_NUM         CHARACTER(14)       NOT NULL,
STL_CTCT_NAM            VARCHAR(40)         NOT NULL,
STL_PRM_CLS_NAM         VARCHAR(40)         NOT NULL,
PRIMARY KEY (HS_NAM, STL_NAM),
FOREIGN KEY (HS_NAM)
    REFERENCES HOUSE
    ON DELETE RESTRICT
);

CREATE UNIQUE INDEX X_STALL
    ON STALL (HS_NAM, STL_NAM);

CREATE INDEX SX_STALL
    ON STALL (STL_SOUNDEX_KEY);

CREATE INDEX NX_STALL
    ON STALL (STL_NAM);
```

Listing 15.4.   Table Create Statements for the Market Database.

```
CREATE TABLE PRODUCT
(
PRD_ID                 CHARACTER(3)      NOT NULL,
PRD_SOUNDEX_KEY        INTEGER           NOT NULL,
PRD_NAM                VARCHAR(40)       NOT NULL,
PRIMARY KEY (PRD_ID)
);

CREATE UNIQUE INDEX X_PRODUCT
    ON PRODUCT (PRD_ID);

CREATE INDEX SX_PRODUCT
    ON PRODUCT (PRD_SOUNDEX_KEY);

CREATE INDEX NX_PRODUCT
    ON PRODUCT (PRD_NAM);

CREATE TABLE VARIETY
(
PRD_ID                 CHARACTER(3)      NOT NULL,
VAR_ID                 CHARACTER(3)      NOT NULL,
VAR_SOUNDEX_KEY        INTEGER           NOT NULL,
VAR_NAM                VARCHAR(40)       NOT NULL,
SEAS_STRT_DT           DATE              NOT NULL,
SEAS_END_DT            DATE              NOT NULL,
PRIMARY KEY (PRD_ID, VAR_ID),
FOREIGN KEY (PRD_ID)
    REFERENCES PRODUCT
    ON DELETE RESTRICT
);

CREATE UNIQUE INDEX X_VARIETY
    ON VARIETY (PRD_ID, VAR_ID);

CREATE INDEX SX_VARIETY
    ON VARIETY (VAR_SOUNDEX_KEY);

CREATE INDEX NX_VARIETY
    ON VARIETY (VAR_NAM);

CREATE TABLE HOUSE_VARIETY
(
PRD_ID                 CHARACTER(3)      NOT NULL,
VAR_ID                 CHARACTER(3)      NOT NULL,
STL_NAM                VARCHAR(40)       NOT NULL,
HS_NAM                 VARCHAR(40)       NOT NULL,
PRIMARY KEY (PRD_ID, VAR_ID, STL_NAM, HS_NAM),
FOREIGN KEY (STL_NAM, HS_NAM)
    REFERENCES STALL
    ON DELETE CASCADE,
FOREIGN KEY (PRD_ID, VAR_ID)
    REFERENCES VARIETY
    ON DELETE RESTRICT
);
```

Listing 15.4. Table Create Statements for the Market Database (continued).

```
CREATE UNIQUE INDEX X_HOUSE_VARIETY
    ON HOUSE_VARIETY (PRD_ID, VAR_ID, STL_NAM, HS_NAM);


CREATE INDEX LX_HOUSE_VARIETY
    ON HOUSE_VARIETY (VAR_ID, STL_NAM);


CREATE TABLE HOUSE_VAR_HIST
(
VAR_ID                 CHARACTER(3)      NOT NULL,
STL_NAM                VARCHAR(40)       NOT NULL,
PRD_ID                 CHARACTER(3)      NOT NULL,
HS_NAM                 VARCHAR(40)       NOT NULL,
HS_VAR_DT              DATE              NOT NULL,
HS_VAR_AVAL            CHARACTER(1)      NOT NULL,
PRIMARY KEY (VAR_ID, STL_NAM, PRD_ID, HS_NAM, HS_VAR_DT),
FOREIGN KEY (VAR_ID, STL_NAM, PRD_ID, HS_NAM)
    REFERENCES HOUSE_VARIETY
    ON DELETE CASCADE
);


CREATE UNIQUE INDEX X_HOUSE_VAR_HIST
    ON HOUSE_VAR_HIST (VAR_ID, STL_NAM, PRD_ID, HS_NAM, HS_VAR_DT);


CREATE TABLE TAG
(
SEL_HS_NAM             VARCHAR(40)       NOT NULL,
SEL_STL_NAM            VARCHAR(40)       NOT NULL,
INV_NUM                VARCHAR(12)       NOT NULL,
TAG_DT                 DATE              NOT NULL,
TAG_NUM                INTEGER           NOT NULL,
TAG_TOT-AMT            DECIMAL(6,2)      NOT NULL,
PRIMARY KEY (SEL_HS_NAM, SEL_STL_NAM, INV_NUM),
FOREIGN KEY (SEL_HS_NAM, SEL_STL_NAM)
    REFERENCES STALL
    ON DELETE RESTRICT
);


CREATE UNIQUE INDEX X_TAG
    ON TAG (SEL_HS_NAM, SEL_STL_NAM, INV_NUM);


CREATE INDEX LN_TAG
    ON MARKET (INV_NUM);


CREATE INDEX TN_TAG
    ON MARKET (TAG_NUM);
```

Listing 15.4.   Table Create Statements for the Market Database (continued).

```
CREATE TABLE TAG_LINE
(
LOT_HS_NAM              VARCHAR(40)      NOT NULL,
LOT_STL_NAM            VARCHAR(40)      NOT NULL,
PRD_ID                 CHARACTER(3)     NOT NULL,
VAR_ID                 CHARACTER(3)     NOT NULL,
INV_NUM                VARCHAR(12)      NOT NULL,
TAG_LN_NUM             INTEGER          NOT NULL,
LOT_NUM                INTEGER          NOT NULL,
LOT_CT                 INTEGER          NOT NULL,
LOT_WT                 DECIMAL(6,2)     NOT NULL,
LOT_UNIT_COST         DECIMAL(5,3)     NOT NULL,
LOT_STL_DT            DATE             NOT NULL,
PRIMARY KEY
    (LOT_HS_NAM, LOT_STL_NAM, PRD_ID, VAR_ID, INV_NUM, TAG_LN_NUM),
FOREIGN KEY (PRD_ID, VAR_ID, LOT_STL_NAM, LOT_HS_NAM)
    REFERENCES HOUSE_VARIETY
    ON DELETE CASCADE,
FOREIGN KEY (LOT_HS_NAM, LOT_STL_NAM, INV_NUM)
    REFERENCES TAG
    ON DELETE CASCADE
);

CREATE UNIQUE INDEX X_TAG_LINE
    ON TAG_LINE (LOT_HS_NAM, LOT_STL_NAM,
    PRD_ID, VAR_ID, INV_NUM, TAG_LN_NUM);

CREATE INDEX LN_TAG_LINE
    ON TAG_LINE (LOT_NUM);

CREATE INDEX LS_TAG_LINE
    ON TAG_LINE (LOT_STL_DT);
```

Listing 15.4.   Table Create Statements for the Market Database (continued).

15.4 REFERENCES

[1]   Roughton, K.G., and D.A. Tyckoson. "Browsing with Sound: Sound-Based Codes and Automated Authority Control," *Information Technology and Libraries,* Vol. 4, No. 2 (June 1985), pp. 130-36.

APPENDICES

Eight appendices supplement the main body of the text. Appendices A, B, and C support Part One. Appendix A includes a more detailed discussion of John Zachman's Framework. Appendix B discusses the markets and needs served by a data administration function. Appendix C provides hints on conducting effective information modeling sessions.

Detailed information supporting Parts Two and Three is included in Appendices D and E. Appendix D contains a listing of referential integrity rules that can be stated with IDEF1X constructs, and sample SQL queries that will detect data integrity violations in a relational database. Appendix E describes two commercial products available for preparing IDEF1X models. Appendix F contains additional detail supporting the case study.

Appendix G reviews the information modeling language introduced in 1990 by IBM for use with its Repository Manager product. It describes the language and provides translations between the IBM and IDEF1X languages. Finally, answers to selected review exercises are provided in Appendix H.

Having gotten this far, you are now well on your way to becoming a practicing information modeler. The Glossary that follows Appendix H provides a final tool.

APPENDIX A

ZACHMAN'S FRAMEWORK

Chapter 2 introduced John Zachman's "Framework for Information Systems Architecture" as a context for our discussion of information modeling. The Framework first appeared publicly at an IBM Guide session in 1986, when it was described in an early working paper [1], and gained wide recognition in 1987 when that paper became the basis for an article in the *IBM Systems Journal* [2].

Zachman's Framework is simple, but extremely powerful. Its power is seen in attempts to extend it. This short Appendix provides additional thoughts about the Framework in general and a few considerations to keep in mind when applying and extending the work.

A.1 ZACHMAN'S FRAMEWORK

The Framework is not an active thing. What it does is force us to think clearly. Simply stated, the Framework is a context to help us think about and communicate our understanding of how information systems need to be designed and developed, not necessarily in methodological terms but in conceptual terms.

A.1.1 Labels for the Rows and Columns

The original rows and columns of the Framework were described in Chapter 2, and are shown in Fig. A.1. When "thinking" with the Framework, it must be clear what its rows and columns represent. Each cell (row/column intersection) represents a view of the final product (an architectural representation) as seen by a class of stakeholders in the development of the system. The rows represent viewpoints or perspectives, and although such architectural represen-

INFORMATION SYSTEMS ARCHITECTURE—A FRAMEWORK

	DATA	FUNCTION	NETWORK
OBJECTIVES/ SCOPE	List of Things Important to the Business Entity = Class of Business Thing	List of Processes the Business Performs Process = Class of Business Process	List of Locations in Which the Business Operates Node = Business Location
MODEL OF THE BUSINESS	e.g., Entity Relationship Diagram Ent. = Business Entity Rel. = Business Rule	e.g., Data Flow Diagram Proc. = Bus. Process I/O = Bus. Resource (including info.)	e.g., Logistics Network Node = Business Unit Link = Bus. Relationship (Org., Product, Info.)
MODEL OF THE INFORMATION SYSTEM	e.g., Data Model Ent. = Data Entity Rel. = Data Rel.	e.g., Function Diagram Proc. = Appl. Functions I/O = User Views (set of Data Elements)	e.g., Distributed Sys. Arch. Node = I/S Function (Processor, Storage, etc.) Link = Line Char.
TECHNOLOGY MODEL	e.g., Data Design Ent. = Segment/Row Rel. = Pointer/Key	e.g., Structure Chart Proc. = Computer Functions I/O = Screen/Device Formats	e.g., System Arch. Node = Hardware/Sys. Software Link = Line Specs.
DETAILED REPRESEN- TATIONS	e.g., Data Design Description Ent. = Fields Rel. = Addresses	e.g., Program Description Proc. = Language Stmts. I/O = Control Blocks	e.g., Network Architecture Node = Addresses Link = Protocols
FUNCTIONING SYSTEM	e.g., DATA	e.g., FUNCTION	e.g., COMMUNICATIONS

Figure A.1. Zachman Framework.

tations are normally developed as a progression (from owner to designer to builder), Zachman cautioned against confusing rows with levels of detail:

> A significant observation regarding these architectural representations is that each has a different *nature* from the others. They are not merely a set of representations, each of which displays a level of detail greater than the previous one. Level of detail is an independent variable, varying *within* any one architectural representation. [3]

This text uses the following terms to label the rows, columns, and cells: A row is a *perspective*. A perspective reflects an area of interest or responsibility of a class of stakeholders. Each perspective describes the same product. This is consistent with the concept of owners' views, designers' views, and builders' views. That is, the perspective is different depending on whom you are. A *view* spans part of a cell, a full cell, or more than one cell *in the same row*. A view can be provided for any perspective, can be broad or narrow in scope (the subject area covered), and can be presented at any appropriate level of detail. A view satisfies the need of an individual or function for a description of something with emphasis appropriate to that individual or function.

Information included about a view can be divided into two parts and includes the following.

View Descriptive Information

- Perspective (what kind of viewer is served by the view)
- What the view shows (focus)
- The technique or language used to describe the view (for example, IDEF1X for a data view, IDEF0 or dataflow diagram for a function view)
- Level of detail (high to low)
- Scope (narrow to broad)
- Expected use (how the view is to be used)
- User (who is expected to use it)
- Boundary assumptions (assumptions made about how this view integrates with other views)

View Administrative Information

- How the view was developed
- Whom to contact for change management

- State (how complete it is and how certain it is)
- Constituents (for example, diagrams, glossaries, trends, critical success factors)

The notion of scope for a view suggests the notion of focus. As an analogy, think about photography and what we focus on when we take a picture (view) from a certain perspective. When we take a picture of an automobile, are we focusing on its parts (bill of materials), how it runs (processes), its shape (spatial relationships), or are we trying to cover several of these in the same picture? In photography, as in architecture, it is hard to focus on several things at once.

A *focus* is represented by a Framework column. We focus on data with data models, on function with function models, and on networks with network models. Eventually, we will focus on various aspects of objects with object models.

A view cannot span rows in the Framework, although it can span columns (it can be wide or narrow in focus). Views can, however, be transformed into other views. A *transform* maps a view from one perspective into a view from another perspective. A transform spans rows, whereas a view spans columns.

Finally, the Framework is a context for providing various views of an enterprise. The Framework supports multiple views, which focus on aspects of the final product important to different audiences, and which are created from the viewers' perspectives. The Framework provides the context for everyone to communicate about the enterprise in a language accepted and understood by all.

A.1.2 Framework Extensions

At least three aspects of Zachman's Framework are actively being extended. First, the original Framework is specified as "A Framework for *Information Systems* Architecture," so it is natural to speculate about what should happen to the names and descriptions of rows and columns as the Framework is extended to cover manual as well as automated portions of a system. Second, extending the concepts to consider types of systems other than information systems is useful. Finally, it is natural to attempt to fill in the blanks Zachman left in the *IBM Systems Journal* article and explore the who, when, and why.

Extensions to cover the manual portion of a system require that the concept of data, function, and location expand. Function needs to include manual as well as automated functions. Location needs to accommodate physical locations as well as machine addresses. Data is still data, but the *what* might include physical (tangible) things as well as intangible (data) things.

It may be best to simply use the labels *what, how, where, who, when,* and *why* for the columns, but even this might be too constraining, since it might lead us to believe there are only six focuses. There may be more (or less) depending on how we wish to view the world. As soon as some label is attached (like *data* for the *what*), thinking may be constrained.

Extending the Framework to cover the manual as well as automated portions of a system requires some revisions to the labels for the rows. Objectives/Scope and Model of the Business remain appropriate labels for the first two rows. If we define "system" to include the manual part as well as the automated part, Model of the Information System might simply become Model of the System. Since people and other types of resources (raw materials and knowledge, for example) are involved, Technology Model might become Resource-Constrained Model. Detailed Representations remains an appropriate name, but it is difficult to know what to do with the last row.

The bottom row in the Framework is a bit of an enigma. To some, it represents the final product itself, the *thing*. To others, it remains a *representation* of the final product. If it is a representation, there may be one more perspective to recognize, the perspective of the operators of the system (their view may be distinctly different from the views of the owners, designers, and builders). If it is the thing itself, then Functioning System remains an appropriate name.

Choosing good labels for Framework rows and columns is more important than we might suspect. It may seem obvious that each row and column label should have a clear definition, but few people will take the time to study a glossary, and most will try to use their own definitions for terms. One of the strongest features of Zachman's Framework is that it uses an analogy and terms that are familiar to many different types of people (owners, designers, and builders).

A.1.3 Notion of Completeness

When we use the Framework to guide our thinking, we must be clear on whether we consider the Framework to completely cover all architectural representations of a system. In other words, are all aspects of a system described by the three (or six) focuses? If the Framework is *complete,* addition of a column must result in the removal of aspects covered by the new column from all other columns. For example, if we were to add a Rules column, all "rules" would need to be removed from other columns; the other columns would need to be redefined so that there would be no overlap in coverage.

If, on the other hand, we consider the Framework *incomplete*, and are not striving to place an aspect of a system in exactly one column, new columns can be added whenever convenient. In addition, the columns might vary by row in the Framework.

A.1.4 Rules for Extensions

A simple representation of an extended Framework is shown in Fig. A.2. It is based on a hand-drawn diagram introduced by John Zachman in March 1991. Although it remains a Framework for describing automated information systems, it has been extended to cover the three remaining columns. It is still viewed as tentative since "there is not a lot of precedence out there (at least in the information community) for the cells in the 'other three' columns. . .

Therefore, these cells are going to be a lot more hypothetical and a lot less empirical than the first three columns." [4]

There are some clear rules for adding rows and columns and interpreting what each cell represents. The fundamental principle is that the Framework is a context, not an active thing. Each view is, as Zachman puts it, "a representation of the final product from the perspective of the . . ." (fill in the blank). Thus, each new row must represent a new perspective and each new column must represent a new focus.

The following rules were developed with John Zachman's help in early 1991:

1.   *Columns have no order.*

     There is no specific order to the columns of the Framework. Each is relevant to some type of architectural description, and it is up to the user to determine which should be included or emphasized in any given situation.

2.   *Each column has a base model (that can be defined and shown with different cell content from cell to cell vertically). The meta-entities in the base model are constant within a column.*

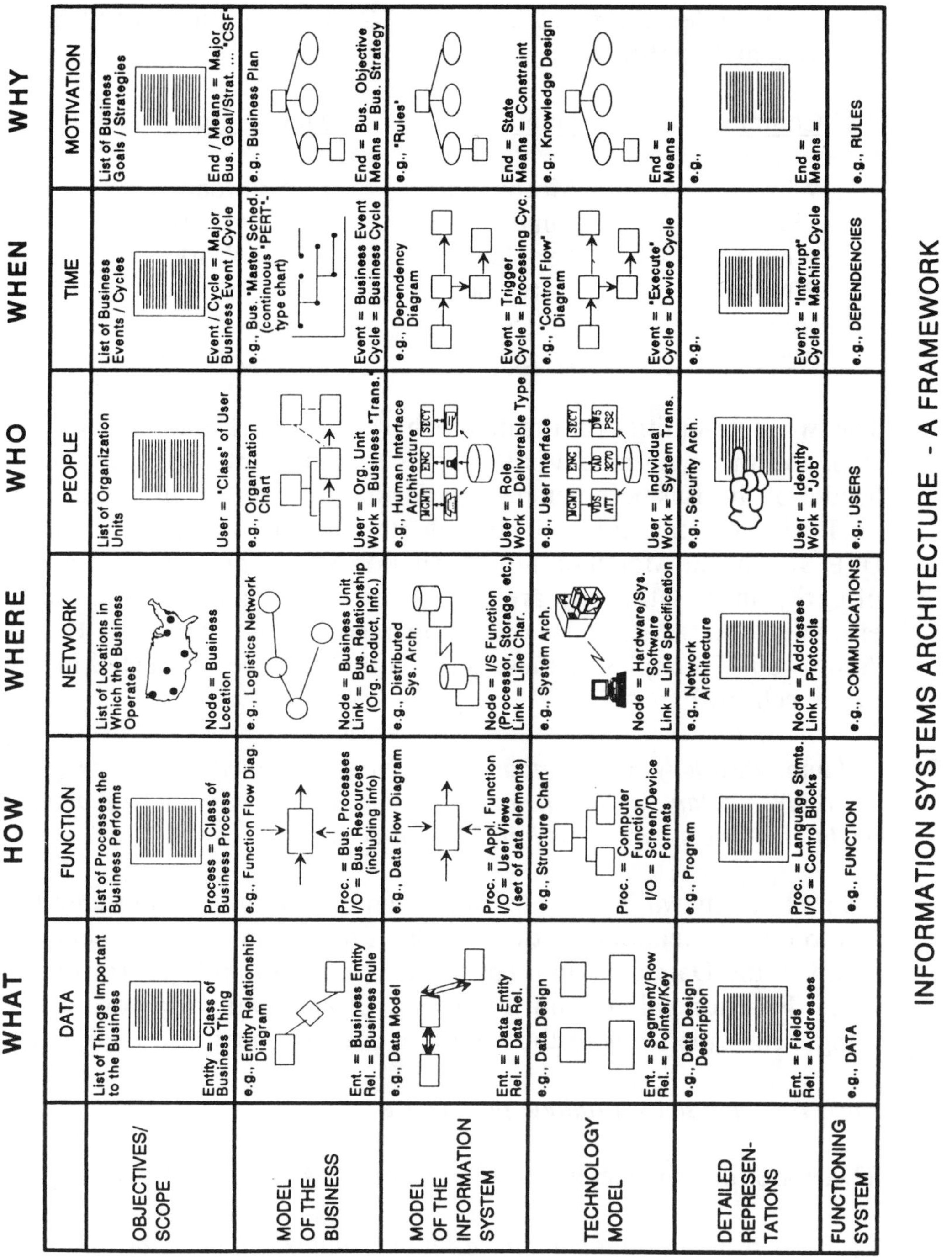

	WHAT DATA	HOW FUNCTION	WHERE NETWORK	WHO PEOPLE	WHEN TIME	WHY MOTIVATION
OBJECTIVES/ SCOPE	List of Things Important to the Business Entity = Class of Business Thing	List of Processes the Business Performs Process = Class of Business Process	List of Locations in Which the Business Operates Node = Business Location	List of Organization Units User = 'Class' of User	List of Business Events / Cycles Event / Cycle = Major Business Event / Cycle	List of Business Goals / Strategies End / Means = Major Bus. Goal/Strat. .... 'CSF'
MODEL OF THE BUSINESS	e.g., Entity Relationship Diagram Ent. = Business Entity Rel. = Business Rule	e.g., Function Flow Diag. Proc. = Bus. Processes I/O = Bus. Resources (including Info)	e.g., Logistics Network Node = Business Unit Link = Bus. Relationship (Org. Product, Info.)	e.g., Organization Chart User = Org. Unit Work = Business 'Trans.	e.g., Bus. 'Master Sched.' (continuous 'PERT'-type chart) Event / Cycle = Major Business Event / Cycle	e.g., Business Plan End = Bus. Objective Means = Bus. Strategy
MODEL OF THE INFORMATION SYSTEM	e.g., Data Model Ent. = Data Entity Rel. = Data Rel.	e.g., Data Flow Diagram Proc. = Appl. Function I/O = User Views (set of data elements)	e.g., Distributed Sys. Arch. Node = I/S Function (Processor, Storage, etc.) Link = Line Char.	e.g., Human Interface Architecture User = Role Work = Deliverable Type	e.g., Dependency Diagram Event = Trigger Cycle = Processing Cyc.	e.g., 'Rules' End = Bus. Objective Means = Bus. Strategy
TECHNOLOGY MODEL	e.g., Data Design Ent. = Segment/Row Rel. = Pointer/Key	e.g., Structure Chart Proc. = Computer Function I/O = Screen/Device Formats	e.g., System Arch. Node = Hardware/Sys. Software Link = Line Specification	e.g., User Interface User = Individual Work = System Trans.	e.g., 'Control Flow' Diagram Event = 'Execute' Cycle = Device Cycle	e.g., Knowledge Design End = State Means = Constraint
DETAILED REPRESEN-TATIONS	e.g., Data Design Description Ent. = Fields Rel. = Addresses	e.g., Program Proc. = Language Stmts. I/O = Control Blocks	e.g., Network Architecture Node = Addresses Link = Protocols	e.g., Security Arch. User = Identity Work = 'Job'	e.g., Event = 'Interrupt' Cycle = Machine Cycle	e.g., End = Means =
FUNCTIONING SYSTEM	e.g., DATA	e.g., FUNCTION	e.g., COMMUNICATIONS	e.g., USERS	e.g., DEPENDENCIES	e.g., RULES

INFORMATION SYSTEMS ARCHITECTURE - A FRAMEWORK

Figure A.2. Extended Framework.

For the extended Framework in Fig. A.2, the base models contain the following meta-entities.

Column	Name	Meta-Entities
Why	Motivation	End / Means
When	Time	Event / Cycle
Who	People	User / Work
Where	Network	Node / Link
How	Function	Process / Input-Output
What	Data	Entity / Relationship

The two meta-entities for the data (what) column are entity and relationship, and the meta-model is ENTITY <relationship> ENTITY. For the Model of the Business perspective, instances of entity and relationship are Business Entity and Business Rule (for example, PERSON <uses> ADDRESS). For the Model of the Information System perspective, instances of entity and relationship are Data Entity and Data Relationship (for example, PERSON <has use of address recorded as> ADDRESS-USAGE). And so on. Examples of these meta-entity instances are listed in many of the cells in Fig. A.2.

3. *Columns are totally nonredundant, but there is an extractive relationship (that is, complementary extractions at similar levels of detail may be represented by different meta-entities within different cells).*

No meta-entity will appear in more than one column. Nonredundancy has to do with mapping between cells. For example, the concept of an Entity in the Data column maps to the concept of an Input (or Output) in the Function column, but Input/Output and Entity are not the same thing. This rule leads to the notion of completeness discussed earlier.

4. *Each row represents a unique perspective.*

These are the perspectives of the owners, designers, and builders.

5. *Each cell is unique and contains a set of primitives (that is, the lowest level of description of the components of the base model).*

Examples of primitives for the cell at the intersection of the Function column and Model of the Information System row might be Create, Replace, Use, Delete, or Make, Move, Store, Validate. Examples of primitives for the Data column (same row) might be CUSTOMER, PRODUCT, and CONTRACT.

6. *Representations pictured in cells are examples only, not recommendations for specific technologies or techniques.*

Many techniques are available for presenting the model represented by a cell, and the Framework says nothing about which technique should be used. For example, business models for the Data column can be presented using IDEF1X, many variants of the Chen style, Bachman, Information Engineering, NIAM, MERISE, or some other graphic presentation technique. Each of these techniques has its advantages and disadvantages. Although one presentation technique may serve multiple cells in the same column, its peculiar advantages and disadvantages may lend it best to use in a given cell.

7. *The composite of all cell models in a row represents a complete description of the system from the perspective of that row.*

This rule directly leads to the notion of completeness discussed earlier.

8. *The logic of the Framework is recursive.*

This final rule is in a preliminary state. The basic concept is that the meta-model of a product is the model of the enterprise that develops that product. If the product is an airplane, the meta-model for building airplanes is the model of the airplane manufacturing business. If the product is an information system, that is, an enterprise or portion of an enterprise, the meta-model for building information systems is the model of the information systems organization.

The Framework will continue to evolve. For example, we will eventually need to address object-oriented systems and techniques. This may lead to some changes in the what and how columns, and will bring to the surface the issue of what to do with rules.

WHAT   HOW   WHEN

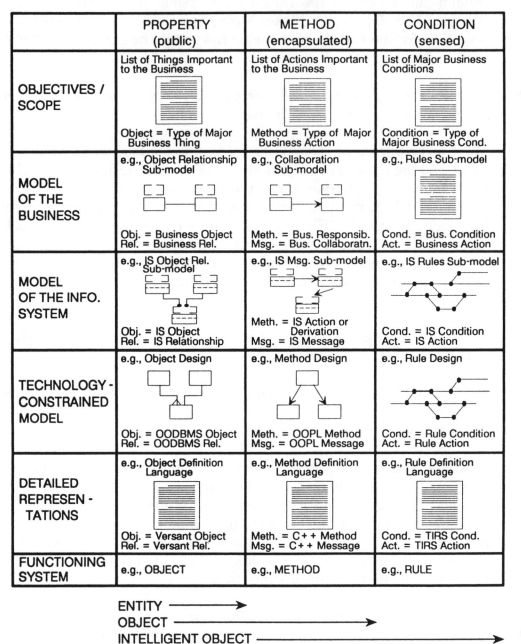

	PROPERTY (public)	METHOD (encapsulated)	CONDITION (sensed)
OBJECTIVES / SCOPE	List of Things Important to the Business Object = Type of Major Business Thing	List of Actions Important to the Business Method = Type of Major Business Action	List of Major Business Conditions Condition = Type of Major Business Cond.
MODEL OF THE BUSINESS	e.g., Object Relationship Sub-model Obj. = Business Object Rel. = Business Rel.	e.g., Collaboration Sub-model Meth. = Bus. Responsib. Msg. = Bus. Collaboratn.	e.g., Rules Sub-model Cond. = Bus. Condition Act. = Business Action
MODEL OF THE INFO. SYSTEM	e.g., IS Object Rel. Sub-model Obj. = IS Object Rel. = IS Relationship	e.g., IS Msg. Sub-model Meth. = IS Action or Derivation Msg. = IS Message	e.g., IS Rules Sub-model Cond. = IS Condition Act. = IS Action
TECHNOLOGY - CONSTRAINED MODEL	e.g., Object Design Obj. = OODBMS Object Rel. = OODBMS Rel.	e.g., Method Design Meth. = OOPL Method Msg. = OOPL Message	e.g., Rule Design Cond. = Rule Condition Act. = Rule Action
DETAILED REPRESEN - TATIONS	e.g., Object Definition Language Obj. = Versant Object Rel. = Versant Rel.	e.g., Method Definition Language Meth. = C++ Method Msg. = C++ Message	e.g., Rule Definition Language Cond. = TIRS Cond. Act. = TIRS Action
FUNCTIONING SYSTEM	e.g., OBJECT	e.g., METHOD	e.g., RULE

ENTITY ⟶
OBJECT ⟶
INTELLIGENT OBJECT ⟶

Figure A.3. Object-Oriented Framework.

A.1.5 Framework Revisions for Objects

Chapter 12 provided an overview of object-oriented concepts, and the evolution of IDEF1X into an Object/Rule modeling language. Object orientation is not specifically addressed by Zachman's Framework. The Framework, however, can accommodate objects and rules, that is, with suitable translation of terms, object concepts can be mapped into Framework cells.

Recall the three views of a DMT/2 model described in Chapter 12. The first view focuses on object properties, and the relationships that exist among the objects. It describes what the system is made of (objects). The second view focuses on object methods, and the exchange of messages. It describes how the system works (methods). A third view can be expected to focus on certain types of rules, that is, conditions and the actions that follow from them. It describes when things happen. We can think of these three views as describing what, how, and when in the object-oriented paradigm.

The meta-models for the Framework columns can be restated in object-oriented terms. The meta-model of *what* (entity + relationship) becomes object + relationship. The meta-model of *how* (process + input/output) becomes method + message. The meta-model of *when* (event + span) can be replaced with the model of a timing rule, that is, condition + action invocation.

The result is shown in Fig. A.3, on the preceding page. The examples shown in the cells are taken from DMT/2 (for the technology-independent rows) and sample object and expert system products (for the technology-dependent rows).

The figure shown in A.3 is not intended to be complete, and is probably not entirely correct, but it shows how the underlying principles of the Framework can help us to understand object orientation. It shows how we might view object orientation in concepts we are already familiar with, those of the Framework. Figure A.3 demonstrates that object/rule modeling, like that emerging in DMT/2, can be considered a single integrated technique for developing internally synchronized views spanning more than a single column (in this case, three).

A.2 REFERENCES

[1]   Zachman, J.A. "A Framework for Information Systems Architecture," Report No. GU320-2785, International Business Machines Corporation, Los Angeles, Calif., 1986. (Released by IBM's Los Angeles Scientific Center at 1986 Guide Conference.)

[2]   ____. "A Framework for Information Systems Architecture," *IBM Systems Journal,* Vol. 26, No. 3 (1987), pp. 276-92.

[3]   ____. loc. cit., p. 281.

[4]   ____. "Introduction and Framework Extensions," Presented at *A Framework for Information Systems Architecture Conference,* Washington, D.C., March 25, 1991.

APPENDIX B

DATA ADMINISTRATION

Chapter 2 introduced an important discipline referred to as information management. An organization sometimes formalizes the practice of information management in a function called data administration (DA). This Appendix discusses how data administration can understand and meet the needs of a business. It first looks at the needs of the various markets for information management services, then focuses on the functions performed by DA and how they meet these needs.

B.1 NEEDS OF A BUSINESS

A data administration function must operate as a business within its host organization. Like any business, DA must configure its products and services around different markets. To do so effectively, DA must first understand the needs of each market. This section outlines a generic set of markets and their needs (see Fig. B.1). Markets and needs vary, so you will have to develop your own list. But you can use this material as a starting point.

B.1.1 Business Client Needs

Business clients often need help planning for future developments and identifying requirements they can forward to an internal system development organization or outside vendor. They must also consider the current state of their business and systems (what is often called *situation analysis*) and identify future automation alternatives. Business clients often need to reconcile data coming from a diverse set of current systems and extract meaningful business information from that data.

B.1.2 Application Development Needs

Application developers often are called upon to help the business develop requirements and strategies for information systems. They must design function and data structures that satisfy requirements, generate data layouts and control blocks to include in application programs, manage change in their applications, and create appropriate documentation. They must test everything. In many cases, application developers must analyze old systems and bring documentation up to date. They must understand the general capabilities and specific details of software packages being considered for use, and build interfaces between new packages and existing environments.

B.1.3 Database Administration Needs

A database administrator (DBA) needs a great deal of information to design long-lasting databases. All objects in the business and database models need precise definitions. Data volumes, transaction response times, and access patterns need to be specified, and the business model needs to be transformed into a technology model of the database. Databases need to be installed and versions adequately controlled. Access privileges must be granted, monitored, and maintained.

B.1.4 Systems Programming Needs

Systems programmers who install new hardware and new releases of operating systems and shop utilities need good documentation and access to an inventory to manage change. They need to know what software releases are operating where, what licenses exist, and so on. They also need to develop and administer standards for the use of general purpose utilities and the general structure of jobs that will run on the machines.

B.1.5 Telecommunications Needs

The telecommunications function must manage networks and devices, know what is running where, get broken things fixed quickly, and introduce change in an orderly and controlled way. Again, standards, good documentation, and good configuration management and change control information are needed. Advance information on future requirements is essential, so appropriate communication facilities are available when and where needed.

B.1.6 Data Processing Operations Needs

Data processing operations staff who keep the information systems running day after day rely heavily on up-to-date operational and exception processing documentation. When something goes wrong, they need to solve problems quickly. They also need to assess the impact of changes in the processing environment and control these changes in an orderly manner. Service level requirements (hours of operation, time to recovery, and so on) need to be specified early in the development of a new system so the operating environment can be prepared to satisfy them.

B.1.7 Audit Needs

Auditors (both those concerned with business audits and those concerned with EDP systems and operations) need to determine whether systems are operating correctly and whether they conform to specific organizational policy and generally accepted accounting practices. To do so, they need documentation of functions, data, and the requirements the systems are intended to satisfy, as well as the ability to retrieve, summarize, and reconcile this documentation.

B.2 DATA ADMINISTRATION PRODUCTS (FUNCTIONS)

Figure B.1 summarizes the markets and needs just discussed. The general areas of opportunity for DA are represented by the rows in the figure. This section briefly reviews each area in terms of the opportunity, the applicable method, the tools, and the value DA can add. As we discussed in Chapter 2, some type of information model can help in most areas.

B.2.1 Education

Everyone needs education now and then, including occasional refreshers as knowledge and techniques evolve. Chapter 2 provided a general structure for education in information management. Two major contributions data administration can make are to help the organization find a structure for this education and to prepare and deliver the training.

NEEDS	Business Clients	Application Development	Database Administration	Systems Programming	Telecommunications	Data Processing Operations	Audit
EDUCATION	X	X	X	X	X	X	X
BUSINESS PLANNING SUPPORT	X						
BUSINESS REQUIREMENTS ANALYSIS	X	X					
DATABASE REQUIREMENTS DEFINITION	X	X	X				
REQUIREMENTS DOCUMENTATION	X	X	X				X
LOGICAL AND PHYSICAL DESIGN		X	X				
DATABASE GENERATION			X				
"COPY CODE" GENERATION		X					
DATA OBJECT STANDARDIZATION		X	X				
EXISTING SYSTEM AND "PACKAGE" ANALYSIS		X	X				
SYSTEM DOCUMENTATION	X	X	X			X	X
INVENTORY/CHANGE MANAGEMENT		X	X	X	X	X	X
STANDARDS/POLICY ENFORCEMENT				X	X	X	X
SPEED	X	X	X	X	X	X	X

Figure B.1. Data Administration Opportunities.

B.2.2 Business Planning Support

A business needs to plan its current and future activities. It must understand how its current information management environment is configured and how well that environment is positioned for the future. It must also determine how profitable its current products and services are, and how changes in the current manual and automated systems can improve that profitability.

The challenge for data administration is to focus the business on its information needs and make it aware of how important it is to manage that information. The process of information planning described briefly in Chapter 2 can help with both short-term tactical planning and long-term strategic planning.

B.2.3 Business Requirements Analysis and Database Requirements Definition

Techniques are needed to quickly and accurately identify business requirements for new or revised systems and translate these requirements into specifications for application processes and databases. Necessary tools and techniques include planning methods, modeling tools, and a repository that stores the results of the analysis. The DA function has a major responsibility to develop and apply the methods and manage the tools and repository.

B.2.4 Requirements Documentation

Good documentation of the requirements for a new or modified system is critical to the success of a development effort. By helping to prepare this documentation, DA can build its alliance with the business and application development community. The models, data object definitions, and information planning processes discussed in this text are focused on ensuring the quality of system requirements.

Requirements documents are needed by those who ensure that systems are developed and operated correctly as well as by those who initially develop the systems. Auditors need access to good documentation of requirements as well as documentation of solutions.

B.2.5 Logical and Physical Design

Data administration can help the application development function prepare logical (technology-independent) and physical (technology-dependent) designs for needed systems. Because of its involvement in many efforts over an extended period of time, DA often can bring examples of solutions from other efforts to these discussions. Using previous solutions can drastically reduce development cycles, but this must be done with extreme care so as not to preempt the real requirements.

B.2.6 Database and Copy-Code Generation

The goal of our efforts is a system that satisfies stated requirements. Database administrators need to design and generate the database, and programmers need to have views into it (for example, file layouts stored as copy library members).

The primary tool to support database documentation and generation is the data dictionary, with its "structures out" capabilities. When properly configured, the dictionary can store the definition of a database, generate the statements needed to establish the database, and generate the sections of application programs that describe the data. DA needs to find or develop tools and techniques to rapidly transform information models (requirements) into database specifications (solutions) and then to make the results available to DBA and application programmers.

B.2.7 Data Object Standardization

One of the major benefits of information modeling is standardization of the definitions and uses of data objects. This is because, over time, the same business fact (for example, data element) can become part of separate systems, often under different names. Without centralized knowledge represented by information models and dictionary definitions, application developers have trouble finding this redundant and probably out-of-sync data, and the business has trouble using it.

Identifying such data and tying it together is a DA function. This activity involves a great deal of manual data analysis with a data dictionary used to record results. Developing standard object names and tying various manifestations of a data object to the standard are areas where value can be delivered.

It takes time for the value of standardization to be recognized. A base of standard definitions must be put in place before the organization can draw on them. In time, a significant amount of dictionary work must be distributed to other organizational units, under the coordination of the DA function. At the beginning, DA can deliver perceived value by helping to define and document existing data.

B.2.8 Existing System and Package Analysis

Organizations that recognize the need for a data administration function have existing data processing environments. Many existing systems are poorly documented, providing an opportunity for short-term DA contributions to an organization. Creating inventories of existing systems, databases, data elements, and so on, in the form of data dictionary definitions and reverse-engineered models, is often the place where DA must begin its efforts, and is an area in which to demonstrate short-term value.

The techniques applied to documenting existing systems can be applied to analyzing software packages being considered as alternatives to in-house solutions. These techniques are discussed in Chapter 10.

B.2.9 Systems Documentation and Inventory / Change Management

The needs of various parties for good systems documentation can provide DA with opportunities to deliver value in many forms. Documenting current systems and packages was discussed above in Section B.2.8. Providing a way to record operating documentation for data processing and business operations and making the documentation available when needed is another area of focus for DA. The data dictionary is a major tool for these functions.

A dictionary can be used as a DBMS to record application descriptions, release levels, responsible parties, exception procedures, and so on, even if the dictionary has not been populated with the detailed descriptions of functions, databases, data elements, and the like. The dictionary can become an on-line runbook. In time, the dictionary, or its future incarnation as a repository, will become the vehicle for managing change. Much work is being done in this area by standards organizations and vendors.

B.2.10 Standards / Policy Enforcement

The DA function can help develop and enforce standards meeting the needs of such areas as data processing operations, systems programming, telecommunications, and audit. It must also provide standards for dictionary use and for techniques like information modeling.

B.2.11 Speed

Each function we have discussed is directed at speeding the development process while ensuring the consistency and integrity of the various documentation views. Standards assist with the latter. Reuse of information developed in direct project support (models, object definitions, standard names, and so forth) assist with the former. The idea of building from inventory rather than building from scratch each time is not new. It takes a long time, however, to develop the inventory.

B.2.12 Summary

Table B.1 summarizes the functions, tools, and education areas that emerge from this discussion of markets and needs. Data administration can generally be cast in the role of the provider of an information management environment, an educator, and a consultant and helper in development of business systems.

Table B.1.
DA Responsibilities.

FUNCTIONS

- Data Object Standardization
- Information Modeling Supporting
  - Requirements Definition
  - Logical and Physical Design
  - Database Generation
  - Current Systems Inventory Management
- Data Analysis and Definition
- Data Dictionary Population
- Data Dictionary Administration
  - Standards Development / Quality Assurance
  - Security Administration
- Business Planning Support
- Application Planning and Design Support
- Education

TOOLS

- Data Dictionary (Repository, Encyclopedia)
- Modeling
  - Mainframe-based
  - Workstation-based
- Cross Model Validation
- Reverse Engineering

EDUCATION AREAS

- Information Management / Modeling
- General Application Development
- Data Dictionary
- Change Management

Figure B.2 presents the major data administration functions as overlays to the Zachman Framework introduced in Chapter 2. Opportunities for adding value exist in all areas.

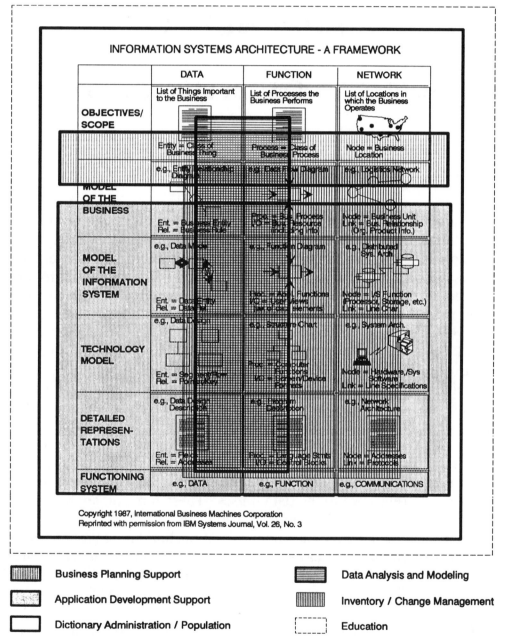

Figure B.2. DA Functions.

APPENDIX C

INFORMATION MODELING SESSIONS

Small modeling efforts can be completed by work groups, and in some larger efforts, much of an information model can be constructed from material gathered outside formal sessions. Large modeling efforts, however, require formal sessions in which business and technical professionals meet to develop the model. When formal sessions are used, there are effective participant roles, session rules, and process steps that can be used to acquire and validate a model view. These roles, rules, and steps are described in this Appendix. Keep in mind, however, that in practice, roles often blur, and experienced modelers do not necessarily follow the formal steps rigorously.

This discussion assumes that at least the high-level functions of the business (or system, depending on the type of model being constructed) have already been determined. In practice, it is often advisable to combine the function and data analysis sessions. When this is done, a series of steps that examine the functions can be interwoven with the data steps so a general flow of data through the functions can be understood and each function can be described with reference to the data it uses. These function analysis steps are listed in the summary at the end of Section C.4.

There is no set length for a modeling session, but three to four hours often seems to be optimum. Full-day sessions can be effective, but must be carefully orchestrated. Shorter sessions may be used for reviews, but often do not allow a team to get fully into an analysis task. Groups tend to lose their effectiveness in marathon sessions lasting several days.

Conducting good modeling sessions, like conducting good meetings of any kind, depends on preparation and real-time facilitation techniques. Modeling sessions should be facilitated sessions. This means that they should be scheduled well in advance, carefully planned to cover focused material, and orchestrated so desired results are achieved [1].

C.1 SESSION PLANNING

The first step in conducting a series of modeling sessions is to plan for them. Make sure the project scope and required level of detail are clearly specified. Choose a sequence of discussion topics that introduces general structure first, then fills in details. For example, if the effort involves developing a billing system, discuss the involved parties (customers, suppliers, employees, and so on) and things for which billing is to be done (for example, products, accounts, or transactions) before discussing detailed accounting rules.

The next step is to select participants and assign them roles for each session. Participants and roles may change from session to session. The same business participants may not attend all sessions, but if the proper expertise cannot be committed for a session on a certain date, reschedule the session. Much time and energy go into planning and conducting sessions, and it is important that the needed business experts be present.

Arranging the proper facilities is more important than it might first seem. Find a room that is large enough for people to spread out and be comfortable. Make sure that sufficient drawing surfaces are available (white boards, blackboards, flip charts, and so on). If there will be a series of sessions, try to schedule the same location for each. The continuity of environment will be helpful. If possible, ensure that the meeting location is away from the day-to-day business. You don't want your business experts disappearing every five minutes to take care of some minor emergency.

If possible, arrange for the use of a copy board—a large white board (at least 3 feet by 5 feet), which will print an 8-1/2 by 11-inch photocopy of what is drawn on it. Using such a board relieves scribes of a significant burden and improves the accuracy of session notes.

For each session, make sure there is an agenda that clearly specifies the objective of the session and lists the activities to be conducted. Make sure the agenda includes frequent breaks.

C.2 SESSION ROLES

The following participant roles are effective in getting the most out of a modeling session: The *facilitator* is the session guide. He or she is responsible for arranging the meetings and facilities, providing follow-up documentation, and intervening when necessary to keep the session on track. The *information modeler* is responsible for leading the group through the process of developing and validating the model. This person develops the model in front of the group by asking questions that bring out the important details and by then recording the structure for all to see. It is often possible (although somewhat difficult) for the same person to play both facilitator and modeler roles.

The *data analyst* records the definitions of all entities and attributes that make up the model. *Subject matter experts* provide the business knowledge needed to construct the model. They are business people, not systems people; it is their business that is being analyzed.

The *manager,* either from the systems or business community, participates in the sessions as facilitator or subject matter expert and makes any decisions needed to keep the process moving. The manager breaks ties, but only when absolutely necessary. When the manager cannot attend all sessions, the facilitator identifies issues requiring action by the manager and tables them for resolution later. *Observers* attend the sessions to learn. They do not participate in the discussions.

Whenever function and data modeling are done at the same time, it is important to include a *process modeler* and a *process analyst* with responsibilities similar to those of the information modeler and data analyst but with respect to the functions being explored.

C.3 SESSION RULES

It is important to have clear session rules, agreed to by all participants. Rules should be reviewed at the start of each session, and either reconfirmed or modified. Rules represent a contract between the facilitator and session participants. Session rules are not often invoked, but having them focuses the group on the work at hand, and allows the facilitator a nonthreatening way to intervene when things are bogging down (for example, by saying, "We agreed earlier that we would discuss only requirements, not solutions, during this session. Do we want to stick with that rule, or shall we change it?").

Here are a few rules you might want to adopt:

1. **Stick to the rules.**

   The first rule is to stick to the rules. Rules can be changed by the group at any time, but as long as a rule is in force, it should be observed.

2. **Keep to the agenda.**

   The agenda focuses the discussion. The group should confirm the agenda at the start of each session, and then agree to stick to it. The group can change the agenda at any time.

3. **Develop requirements, not solutions.**

   The objective of most modeling sessions is to uncover and document requirements. However, many people, especially application developers, find it easier to discuss solutions than requirements. Confirming this rule at the start of a session reminds participants why they are there, and invoking it during discussions can bring a modeling session back on track if it has wandered into solution discussions.

4. **Table interesting but useless discussions.**

   During a modeling session, side topics often arise (for example, yesterday's billing problem) that participants find fascinating to discuss. Some of these discussions are interesting, but may not be useful in meeting the objectives of the session. Invoking this rule can cut off side discussions and allow the session to continue toward its objective. (Rule 4 is sometimes called the rule of "Interesting but not useful.")

5. **Practice professionalism.**

   Disagreements often arise during modeling sessions. People see things differently, and often have different needs and objectives. Disagreements can be handled professionally, by allowing the discussion to work its way out, or can degenerate to unprofessional behavior. Reminding participants that they are professionals and should be able to resolve disputes in nonhostile ways is important. There are better ways to conduct a discussion than calling someone a jerk (either verbally or nonverbally).

6.   Leave baggage outside.

The table outside the door is a place to leave unneeded baggage. A title can often be such baggage (all participants in the session must have an equal voice). Leaving your title outside the door can be an effective way to ensure that everyone speaks equally. While you're at it, leave your ego there as well.

C.4 SESSION STEPS

The exact sequence of session steps will vary according to the type of model being developed. For example, developing a key based model requires a discussion of keys, but developing an entity relationship diagram does not require such a discussion since keys are not included in the ERD. Here are a set of generic session steps that can be tailored to a specific session:

1.   Review and validate the function.

In this initial step, the function or closely related group of functions is discussed to ensure it is understood well enough by the session participants to proceed with an information model. When the information model is being prepared from an existing set of function descriptions, this step is a context-setting activity that makes sure everyone is thinking about the same problem.

If the information modeling session is part of a larger session that is exploring both function and data, this step corresponds to a high-level review and description of the function to be examined.

2.   List the data objects.

While the function is being discussed (Step 1), the modeler listens for data objects (entities, attributes, and relationships) and writes their names on a large surface visible to all session participants. No attempt is made to create the diagram at this point or to distinguish among different data object types. An experienced modeler will be able to identify most of the relevant data objects from listening to the discussion of the function and asking questions as the discussion proceeds.

3. Classify the data objects.

Based on feedback from the participants, the modeler determines whether the data objects listed in Step 2 are entities, attributes, or relationships. Questions that begin with, Can you tell me more about a (whatever)? and What's a (whatever)? work well.

4. Diagram the data objects.

The information modeler next draws a diagram of the entities and attributes identified in Step 3. Here the modeler is seeking to collect the attributes under their respective entities. Some of the names of the entities and attributes may change based on the interaction between the group and the modeler. Leading questions for the modeler should include, Which entity on our list contains this attribute? and How many times does this attribute occur for this entity?

5. Add the relationships.

The modeler adds the relationships from the list of data objects developed in Step 3. New relationships may be identified during this process, and the type of relationship (identifying or not) may change in Step 6. Depending on the type of model being developed, nonspecific (many-to-many) relationships may be broken into pairs of one-to-many relationships to an intervening associative entity. Leading questions include, How many of (this) are related to (that)? and Must (this) exist if (that) does?

6. Identify and add keys.

As we have discussed, primary keys are attributes or groups of attributes chosen as the unique identifiers of entities. The evolving diagram is now adjusted to include the keys. As keys are identified, relationship types are confirmed or changed. Alternate keys and inversion entries may also be found and added to the diagram. Important questions to ask are, What are the ways in which (this) can be identified?, How will you chose to identify (this)? and When you want to know about (this), what information will you have to allow you to find it? This step is skipped entirely if the model is not intended to be a key based or fully attributed model.

7.   Define the entities and attributes.

A definition is obtained for each entity and attribute in the diagram. If definitions emerged during the earlier steps, it is the responsibility of the data analyst(s) to have listened for them and written them down in preparation for this formal definition activity. As modeling teams work together, a style of signaling between the modeler and the data analyst may develop in which the modeler alerts the data analyst that a definition is being given. Often, the modeler may have helped the data analyst get these earlier definitions by inserting appropriate pauses in the process or by asking questions such as, What do you mean by (whatever)?

Sometimes, it is sufficient to get general definitions for final wording outside the session. At other times, it is important to create the formal definition as a group activity.

8.   Review normalization.

For a key based or fully attributed model, this step verifies that the model is as close to third normal form (or higher) as can be achieved during the session. More importantly, it ensures that the model carries the correct business rules. Experienced modelers usually discuss the model with session participants so as to directly lead to a technically normalized model. When the modeler is not as experienced or the resulting structure is quite complex, after-the-fact review and normalization may be needed. How far to push the technical aspects of normalization during the sessions depends on the interest and tolerance of the group, but verification of the business rules is essential.

9.   Rename for clarity.

During Steps 7 and 8, a more precise understanding of the entities, attributes, and relationships that have emerged from the early steps is usually achieved. The normalization step may have introduced new structures and clarified the meaning or intent of others. It is a good idea at this point to examine the names of the entities and attributes to see that they carry a good sense of what the data objects represent. In practice, the names of the entities and attributes are likely to change several times during the sessions, and this step is a formal confirmation that these data objects have good names.

10. Confirm definitions.

Either after the completion of Step 9 or in parallel with it, the definitions of all entities and attributes are reviewed a final time. Whether this step is taken is up to the data analyst.

C.4.1 Session Steps Summary

Figure C.1 lists the steps for a modeling session. When function is being addressed in the same setting, a similar series of steps can be used to discover and record the functions that operate on the data in the information model. These function steps are listed beside the data steps in the figure.

Function objects correspond to processes, dataflows, external sources and destinations of data, and so on. The concept of function normalization is not as formal as data normalization, but seeks to eliminate redundant function and gather similar functions into general utilities that can be combined as needed to form a complete process. Function normalization also includes the balancing of levels of dataflow diagrams—that is, ensuring that all dataflows entering and leaving a process are reconciled with the flows entering and leaving its constituent processes.

	DATA	FUNCTION
1.	Review and validate the function.	Review the function.
2.	List the data objects.	List the function objects.
3.	Classify the data objects.	Classify the function objects.
4.	Diagram the data objects.	Diagram the processes.
5.	Add the relationships.	Add the dataflows.
6.	Identify and add keys.	Add the external sources and sinks.
7.	Define the entities and attributes.	Define all function objects.
8.	Review normalization.	Review normalization.
9.	Rename for clarity.	Rename for clarity.
10.	Confirm definitions.	Confirm definitions.

Figure C.1. Session Steps.

C.5 FORMING A MODEL FROM THE VIEWS

Constructing a complete model from individual views is called *composition* and is normally a matter of integrating and reconciling the views gathered during the modeling sessions. Different composition techniques are used, depending on how these sessions are conducted. In large projects in which several modelers are involved and many sessions occur over a short period of time, there may be little alternative to acquiring independent data views function by function and integrate them later. In other cases, a complete model can be constructed by using each session to add to an emerging composite.

There are advantages and disadvantages to each of these methods: Extending an existing model may prejudice discussions if the participants believe their input is constrained by the existing work (which may still be in a state of flux). The resulting views, however, are automatically consistent since any differences among viewpoints are resolved on the fly.

Acquiring separate views in separate sessions has the appearance of completing the model more quickly while not prejudicing the discussions. Sometimes, however, the separately acquired views will not integrate well, thus requiring another round of reconciling sessions. If the session participants have built up a feeling of ownership for certain constructs or definitions, it may take a lot of backtracking to get the pieces to fit together.

C.6 VALIDATION AND STRESS TESTS

Once a view or set of views has been acquired, it must be validated with the subject-matter experts who created it and with others who must understand and use it. A formal process of reading the model back to the participants can be used for validation. Sample instance tables can help explain the resulting model or point out areas where there are remaining issues.

Depending on the objectives of a modeling effort, it is sometimes useful to test the resilience of the model, that is, its ability to withstand changes in the functions of the business. A model representing a set of business requirements can never be considered final, as requirements will change in time. A model is stronger if it can accommodate change. How much change is one of the questions that needs to be answered when the objectives of the effort are set.

Changing the requirements and seeing how this requires changes to the model is a way to understand its resilience and is sometimes referred to as a *stress test*. We cannot reasonably expect that a model designed, say, for a commodity trading firm would easily accommodate a change in the focus of the business toward the manufacture of pogo sticks, but it might be reasonable to expect the model to enable the introduction of new trading products without requiring extensive revision.

C.7 REFERENCES

[1]   Doyle, M., and D. Straus. *How to Make Meetings Work.* New York: Playboy Paperbacks, 1976.

APPENDIX D

IRD RULE SUMMARY

As we saw in Chapter 8, delete rules govern what will happen in a database when an entity instance is deleted. Insert and replace rules govern what will happen when an instance is added or changed, and are explicitly stated in the model. They are stated by the relationship types and cardinality. Most delete rules cannot be stated without extension of the language.

For insert, an instance can be added only if all referenced foreign keys match existing instances in the referenced entities, unless the relationship explicitly states otherwise (for example, the diamond on a nonidentifying relationship indicating that the foreign key or keys may be null). A replace is, in effect, an insert of an instance with the same primary key (overriding all attributes of the old instance), so it is governed by the insert rules.

This Appendix provides a complete description of the insert and delete rules for IDEF1X relationships. It lists the insert rules stated by the relationships, and specifies the delete rule options. In physical systems, these rules must be enforced either by the database management system, or by the application code that maintains the content of the database. Taken together, they are commonly referred to as *referential integrity* rules.

The Appendix also discusses ways to detect violations of constraints (business rules) in relational systems when the capabilities of the DBMS are not used to enforce the constraints. Violations are detected by queries that check the content of the database.

D.1 IRD RULE SUMMARY—IDENTIFYING RELATIONSHIPS

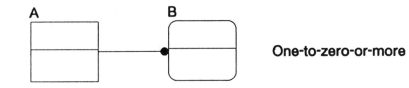

One-to-zero-or-more

Insert

Entity A   No constraints.
Entity B   No B may be inserted without a parent A.

Delete

Entity A
    Cascade: Delete all Bs for which the deleted A is the parent.
    Restrict: Do not allow a delete of A if there are Bs for which
                  it is parent.
Entity B   No constraints.

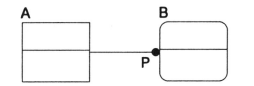

One-to-one-or-more

Insert

Entity A   The insert of an A must be accompanied by the insert
                  of at least one B for which A is the parent.
Entity B   No B may be inserted without a parent A.

Delete

Entity A
    Cascade: Delete all Bs for which the deleted A is the parent.
    Restrict: Do not allow a delete of A (since there will be at
                  least one B for which it is parent).

Entity B
    Cascade: Delete the parent A if the deleted B is the only child of A (note that this is a cascade *up* the relationship).

    Restrict: Do not allow a delete of B if there are no other Bs with the same parent A.

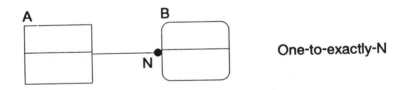

                                                        One-to-zero-or-one

Insert

Entity A   No constraints.

Entity B   No B may be inserted without a parent A or if there exists a B with the same parent A.

Delete

Entity A

    Cascade: If it exists, delete the B for which the deleted A is the parent.

    Restrict: Do not allow a delete of A if there is a B for which it is the parent.

Entity B   No constraints.

A   B

N   One-to-exactly-N

Insert

Entity A   The insert of an A must be accompanied by the insert of exactly N Bs for which A is the parent.

Entity B   No B may be inserted without inserting a parent A and N-1 additional Bs with the same parent.

Delete

Entity A
  Cascade: Delete all Bs for which the deleted A is the parent.
  Restrict: Do not allow a delete of A.
Entity B
  Cascade: Delete the parent A and all other Bs for which A is the parent (note that this is a cascade up and back down the same relationship).
  Restrict: Do not allow a delete of B.

D.2 IRD RULE SUMMARY—NONIDENTIFYING RELATIONSHIPS

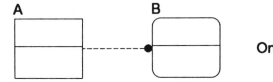

One-to-zero-or-more

Insert

  Entity A   No constraints.
  Entity B   No B may be inserted without a parent A.

Delete

  Entity A
    Cascade: Delete all Bs for which the deleted A is the parent.
    Restrict: Do not allow a delete of A if there are Bs for which it is parent.
  Entity B   No constraints.

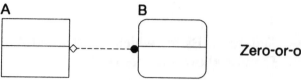

Insert

Entity A   No constraints.
Entity B   No B may be inserted without a parent A, unless the foreign key of A is set to null in B.

Delete

Entity A
  Cascade: Delete all Bs for which the deleted A is the parent.
  Restrict: Do not allow a delete of A if there are Bs for which it is parent.
  Set Null: In all Bs where A is the parent, set the foreign key of A to null.
Entity B   No constraints.

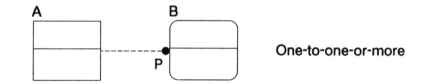

Insert

Entity A   The insert of an A must be accompanied by the insert of at least one B for which A is the parent.
Entity B   No B may be inserted without a parent A.

Delete

Entity A
  Cascade: Delete all Bs for which the deleted A is the parent.
  Restrict: Do not allow a delete of A (since there will be at least one B for which it is parent).

Entity B
    Cascade: Delete the parent A if the deleted B is the only child of A.
    Restrict: Do not allow a delete of B if there are no other Bs with the same parent A.

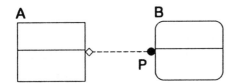

Zero-or-one-to-one-or-more

Insert

Entity A   The insert of an A must be accompanied by the insert of at least one B for which A is the parent.

Entity B   No B may be inserted without a parent A unless the foreign key of A in B is set to null.

Delete

Entity A
    Cascade: Delete all Bs for which the deleted A is the parent.
    Restrict: Do not allow a delete of A (since there will be at least one B for which it is parent).
    Set Null: In all Bs where A is the parent, set the foreign key of A to null.

Entity B
    Cascade: If the foreign key of A in B is not null, delete the parent A if the deleted B is the only child of A, else delete the B.
    Restrict: Do not allow a delete of B if there are no other Bs with parent A and the foreign key of A in B is not null.
    Set Null: If the foreign key of A in B is not null, delete the B, else, delete the B and, if the deleted B is the only child of A, delete the A.

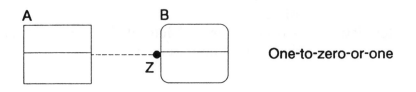

One-to-zero-or-one

Insert*

Entity A	No constraints.
Entity B	No B may be inserted without a parent A, or if there exists a B with the same parent A.

Delete

Entity A
    Cascade: If it exists, delete the B for which the deleted A is the parent.

    Restrict: Do not allow a delete of A if there is a B for which it is the parent.

Entity B   No constraints.

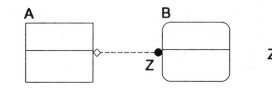

Zero-or-one-to-zero-or-one

Insert*

Entity A	No constraints.
Entity B	No B may be inserted with a parent A if there exists a B with the same parent A. Any B may, however, be inserted if the foreign key of A is set to null in B.

---

*In any (zero-or-) one-to-zero-or-one relationship, the contributed foreign key must be an alternate key of the receiving entity.

Delete

Entity A
    Cascade: If it exists, delete the B for which the deleted A is the
                  parent.
    Restrict: Do not allow a delete of A if there is a B for which
                  it is the parent.
    Set Null: If there is a corresponding B, set the foreign key of
                  A in the corresponding B to null.
Entity B   No constraints.

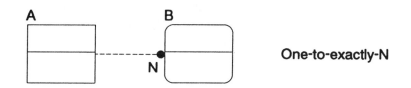

One-to-exactly-N

Insert

Entity A   The insert of an A must be accompanied by the insert
                  of exactly N Bs for which A is the parent.
Entity B   No B may be inserted without inserting a parent A
                  and N-1 additional Bs with the same parent.

Delete

Entity A
    Cascade: Delete all Bs for which the deleted A is the parent.
    Restrict: Do not allow a delete of A.
Entity B
    Cascade: Delete the parent A and all Bs for which A is the
                  parent.
    Restrict: Do not allow a delete of B.

Zero-or-one-to-exactly-N

Insert

Entity A   The insert of an A must be accompanied by the insert
                    of exactly N Bs for which the A is the parent.

Entity B   No B may be inserted without a inserting a parent A
                    and N-1 additional Bs with the same parent unless the
                    key of A is set to null in B.

Delete

Entity A
    Cascade: Delete all Bs for which the deleted A is the parent.
    Restrict: Do not allow a delete of A.
    Set Null: In all Bs where A is the parent, set the foreign key
                    of A to null.

Entity B
    Cascade: If the foreign key of A in B is not null, delete the
                    parent A and all Bs for which A is the parent, else
                    delete the B.
    Restrict: Do not allow a delete of B.
    Set Null: Delete the B, and, in all Bs where A is the parent, set
                    the foreign key of A to null.

D.3 IRD RULE SUMMARY—COMPLETE CATEGORY RELATIONSHIPS

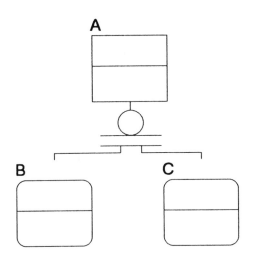

Insert

Entity A	The insert of an A must be accompanied by the insert either a B or a C with the same key as A, and a category discriminator in A with the correct value.
Entity B	No B may be inserted without inserting a parent A with a category discriminator with the correct value, and ensuring the absence of a C with the same key.
Entity C	No C may be inserted without inserting a parent A with a category discriminator with the correct value, and ensuring the absence of a B with the same key.

Delete

Entity A
Cascade:	Delete the category instance for which the deleted A is parent.
Restrict:	Do not allow a delete of A.

Entity B
Cascade:	Delete the parent A along with the category B.
Restrict:	Do not allow a delete of B.

Entity C
    Cascade: Delete the parent A along with the category C.
    Restrict: Do not allow a delete of C.

D.4 IRD RULE SUMMARY—INCOMPLETE CATEGORY RELATIONSHIPS

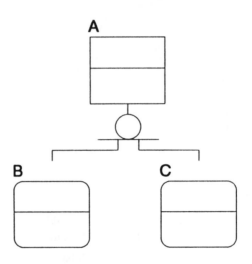

Insert

Entity A
    The insert of an A may be accompanied by the insert either a B or a C with the same key as A, and a category discriminator in A with a value designating a B or a C, or may occur without the insert of a B or C, and with a discriminator indicating that neither B nor C is present.

Entity B
    No B may be inserted without inserting a parent A with a category discriminator with the correct value, and ensuring the absence of a C with the same key.

Entity C
    No C may be inserted without inserting a parent A with a category discriminator with the correct value, and ensuring the absence of a B with the same key.

Delete

Entity A
    Cascade: Delete the category instance for which the deleted A is parent.
    Restrict: Do not allow a delete of A.
Entity B
    Cascade: Delete the parent A along with the category B.
    Restrict: Do not allow a delete of B.
    Set Null: Do not delete A, but change the category discriminator to indicate that neither B nor C is present.
Entity C
    Cascade: Delete the parent A along with the category C.
    Restrict: Do not allow a delete of C.
    Set Null: Do not delete A, but change the category discriminator to indicate that neither B nor C is present.

D.5 CONSTRAINTS

Throughout this book, we have discussed constraint statements that can and cannot be made with the IDEF1X language. Constraint statements in the model represent business rules governing the behavior of the data structure. We found situations (for example, the Boolean constraints and complex category existence constraints discussed in Chapters 7 and 8) in which an adjunct to the graphic language is an appropriate recording mechanism. The first part of this Appendix summarized existence and identification constraints statements that can be specified with identifying, nonidentifying, and category relationships.

The relationship constraints (identifying, nonidentifying, and category) are often referred to as *referential integrity* constraints. Some relational database management systems have evolved to the point where internal functions can be invoked to prevent database activity that would violate specific constraints. Examples include the primary key and foreign key referential assertions that can be declared when creating a set of DB2 tables (in Release 2.1 and beyond).

Some constraints can be enforced in real-time by the RDBMS, and some must be enforced by application function. Enforcing referential integrity or other constraints in real-time is, however, expensive in terms of performance of the system. There can be situations in which the only realistic alternative for ensuring the quality of the data is to detect (and resolve) violations after the fact. Perhaps the DBMS does not include the required functionality, or its use is determined to have too large an impact on performance, or it is judged too difficult to write the code in the application programs to enforce the constraints.

General referential integrity support is spelled out in the SQL standard. Primary and foreign key assertions declared in a model can be directly declared to some RDBMSs. Chapter 8 provided examples of DB2 data definition language statements, which will declare and enforce the primary and foreign keys and SQL queries that would find violations of the integrity constraints as an alternative to asking the DBMS to enforce them.

The general queries for detecting referential integrity violations are given below. They are taken from the manual that describes an early version of the IDEF1X modeling tool developed by The Data Base Design Group [1], and are used with permission of the author. Similar queries can be developed to find situations in which inter-attribute dependencies are violated (for example, to find invalid combinations of attribute values). You can also create queries to detect invalid relationship combinations (that is, situations in which relationships must exist together, in which some cannot exist if others do, and so on).

D.5.1 Primary Key

For every table with an unenforced primary key, rows are selected for which the primary key values are equal.

```
SELECT *
FROM tablename
GROUP BY primary key columnames
HAVING COUNT(*) > 1;
```

D.5.2 Alternate Key

For every unenforced alternate key, rows with duplicate alternate key values are selected. An alternate key value in which any constituent is null is not considered equal to any other alternate key value, even if all non-null values agree. Notice that for this query to work, the GROUP BY clause must place any row having a null value in any grouping column in a separate group. Some RDBMSs do this, and some do not.

```
SELECT *
FROM tablename
GROUP BY alternate key columnames
HAVING COUNT(*) > 1;
```

D.5.3 Foreign Key

For every unenforced foreign key, child table rows are selected for which no
parent table row exists with a primary key value equal to the foreign key value.
If any constituent of the foreign key is null, the parent need not exist. In
general, the foreign key constituent may be a role name.

```
SELECT child primary key columnames,
        'MISSING parent tablenames',
        child foreign key columnames
  FROM child tablename
 WHERE NOT EXISTS
        (SELECT *
         FROM parent tablename
         WHERE child role name-1 = parent key name-1
           AND child role name-2 = parent key name-2
               . . .
           AND child role name-n = parent key name-n
        )
   AND child role name-1 IS NOT NULL
   AND child role name-2 IS NOT NULL
               . . .
   AND child role name-n IS NOT NULL;
```

If the child role name is the same as the parent key name, each is qualified
with its table name.

D.5.4 Category

In the following set of queries, it is assumed that the value of the category
discriminatory in the generic parent is equal to a value called "categoryshortta-
blename" or "category(-n)shorttablename".

Taken together, the checks verify that a category row exists if and only
if a generic row exists with a discriminator value equal to the "shorttablename"
of the category. Rows in violation are selected.

D.5.4.1 Missing generic parent

This is a foreign key check. Since the foreign key in the category is the primary key and all foreign key constituents are not null, there is no need to check for null values.

```
SELECT category primary key columnnames,
       'MISSING generic tablename'
FROM category tablename
WHERE NOT EXISTS
       (SELECT *
        FROM generic tablename
        WHERE category role name-1 = generic key name-1
          AND category role name-2 = generic key name-2
             . . .
          AND category role name-n = generic key name-n
       );
```

If the category role name is the same as the generic key name, each is qualified with its table name.

D.5.4.2 Bad discriminator

```
SELECT category primary key,
       'has generic disc',
          generictablename.discriminatorname
FROM categorytablename, generictablename
WHERE category role name-1 = generic key name-1
  AND category role name-2 = generic key name-2
        . . .
  AND category role name-n = generic key name-n
  AND generictablename.discriminatorname <> 'categoryshorttablename'
```

If the category role name is the same as the generic key name, each is qualified with its table name.

D.5.4.3 *Missing category*

```
SELECT generic primary key,
    'MISSING category',
    generictablename.discriminator
FROM generic, category-1, category-2, ... category-n
WHERE (generictablename.discriminator = 'category-1shorttablename'
    AND NOT EXISTS
      (SELECT *
       FROM category-1
       WHERE category-1 role name-1 = generic key name-1
         AND category-1 role name-2 = generic key name-2
          . . .
         AND category-1 role name-n = generic key name-n
      )
    )
    OR
    (generictablename.discriminator = 'category-2shorttablename'
     AND NOT EXISTS
       (SELECT *
        FROM category-2
        WHERE category-2 role name-1 = generic key name-1
          AND category-2 role name-2 = generic key name-2
           . . .
          AND category-2 role name-n = generic key name-n
       )
    )
    OR
    . . .
    OR
    (generictablename.discriminator = 'category-nshorttablename'
     AND NOT EXISTS
       (SELECT *
        FROM category-n
        WHERE category-n role name-1 = generic key name-1
          AND category-n role name-2 = generic key name-2
           . . .
          AND category-n role name-n = generic key name-n
       )
    )
);
```

If the category role name is the same as the generic key name, each is qualified
with its table name.

D.6 REFERENCES

[1]   The Data Base Design Group. *ADAM 1.6 User Guide,* 4th ed., June 1985.

APPENDIX E

COMMERCIAL PRODUCT SUPPORT FOR IDEF1X

Automated support is essential for preparing an information model of any reasonable size. Examples can be created with pencil and paper, but real models quickly grow beyond the size where they can be maintained that way. This Appendix therefore describes two commercial products, Leverage and ERwin, that support the development of large IDEF1X models.

E.1 LEVERAGE

The Leverage product [1] is available from D. Appleton Co. (DACOM) of Manhattan Beach, California, and is the public version of the IDEF1X support tool originally developed by The Data Base Design Group [2] and Bank of America. The 2.2 version available when this text was prepared supports IDEF1X information modeling and IDEF0 activity modeling. This is primarily a mainframe tool that operates in various environments, including IBM MVS and DEC VAX computers.

E.1.1 Product Functions

Host Leverage, the mainframe component, is not an interactive product. Rather, information models are described in *structured modeling language* (SML), and activity models are described in a similar language called *activity modeling language* (AML). The model descriptions are processed in batch mode.

Figure E.1 provides an example of a view described in DACOM's SML. It represents the video store model introduced in Fig. 4.1. A more extensive example is given with the case study supplementary material in Appendix F.

```
VIEW MOVIE-RENTAL-STORE

    GENERAL INFORMATION
        SHORT-NAME RENTAL
        LEVEL KB

    STRUCTURE

        ENTITY MOVIE
            KEY
                MOVIE-NUMBER
            ENDK
            ALTERNATE KEY 1
                MOVIE-NAME
            ENDA
            MOVIE-RATING
            MOVIE-RENTAL-RATE
        ENDE

        ENTITY MOVIE-COPY
            KEY
                MOVIE "is in stock as" P
                MOVIE-COPY-NUMBER
            ENDK
            REMAINING-LIFE
            RENTAL-RATE
        ENDE

        ENTITY CUSTOMER
            KEY
                CUSTOMER-NUMBER
            ENDK
            INVERSION ENTRY 1
                CUSTOMER-NAME
            ENDI
            CUSTOMER-STATUS-CODE
            CUSTOMER-ADDRESS
        ENDE

        ENTITY EMPLOYEE
            KEY
                EMPLOYEE-NUMBER
            ENDK
            INVERSION ENTRY 1
                EMPLOYEE-NAME
            ENDI
            HIRE-DATE
            SALARY
            EMPLOYEE-ADDRESS
        ENDE
```

```
        ENTITY MOVIE-RENTAL-RECORD
           KEY
              CUSTOMER "borrows under" P
              MOVIE-COPY "is rented under"
              RENTAL-RECORD-DATE
           ENDK
           RENTAL-DATE
           DUE-DATE
           PAYMENT-AMOUNT
           PAYMENT-DATE
           PAYMENT-STATUS
           OVERDUE-CHARGE
        ENDE

        ENTITY RECORD-INVOLVEMENT
           KEY
              MOVIE-RENTAL-RECORD "has involvement of" P
              EMPLOYEE "is involved with"
              INVOLVEMENT-TIMESTAMP
           ENDK
           INVOLVEMENT-TYPE
        ENDE

        ENTITY OVERDUE-NOTICE
           KEY
              MOVIE-RENTAL-RECORD "may receive"
           ENDK
*          EMPLOYEE "listed on"
           NOTICE-TEXT
        ENDE

     ENDS

 ENDV
```

Figure E.1. Video Store View SML.

Relationships between entities are declared by stating the parent entity name
followed by a relationship verb phrase and optional cardinality and existence
assertions. If a relationship is declared inside the key structure of the entity
(the area between the words KEY and ENDK(EY)), the relationship is identifying. If it is declared outside the key structure, it is nonidentifying. A required
nonidentifying relationship is declared by including the NONULL assertion after
the relationship declaration. For example, the relationship between OVERDUE-
NOTICE and EMPLOYEE could be made mandatory by replacing the statement
marked with the asterisk in Fig. E.1 with the one shown in Fig. E.2.

EMPLOYEE "listed on" NONULL

Figure E.2. Mandatory Nonidentifying Relationship SML.

Host Leverage contains its own internal glossary for recording definitions of
the entities and attributes in the model and for recording data type relationships (group and role name declarations) among attributes. In future versions,
it is expected that Leverage will be able to use an external repository to store
these definitions.

The following general classes of function are provided by the Host
Leverage product; as you read them, refer to Fig. E.3.

1. Create Graphs and Reports

Graphs (model diagrams) and reports are produced as requested. Graphs
can be presented in several forms (for example, showing all keys or
suppressing those contributed by other entities). Reports contain lists and
definitions of entities and attributes, cross reference information (use of
attributes in various entities), relationship descriptions, and so on. A
business-rules report is available for converting the model into a set of
declarative statements that describe the relationships among entities. A
wide range of output devices is supported, including laser printers and
plotters. Placement, however, is automatic and the user has no control
over the location of objects on the information model graphs. The ability
to chose the location of model objects is important for small models, but
automatic placement can be helpful for large ones.

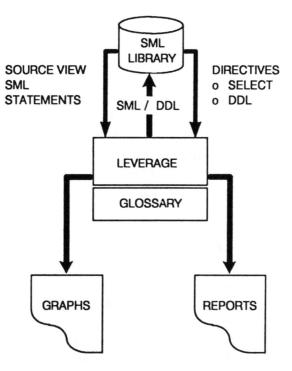

Figure E.3. Leverage Product.

2. Selective Viewing

A *selective view* is a subset of a larger *source view* (model). The ability to extract small pieces of a model and diagram each separately can be extremely helpful with real IDEF1X models. Unlike the small examples shown throughout this text, real models can contain hundreds of entities. Ten to twenty entities on a single diagram is about as much as anyone can easily deal with in graphic form. The composite case study model in Part Three of this text, for example, contains 35 entities, which is more than you normally will want to see in one detailed view.

The extraction of a selective view from a source view is controlled by a set of *select statements* provided to Leverage along with the source. The resulting view contains the selected entities and others which, in the source view, either contribute keys to or inherit keys from the selected entities. These additional entities are referred to as *shadow entities* and can be included in or excluded from the graphs produced from the selective view. When the shadow entities are included on the graph, they appear with dashed rather than solid outlines.

3. Compose

Composition is the merging of two views to create a composite view. The Leverage product will merge a set of views to create a composite. In doing so, it will attempt to identify and reconcile differences among the views. The compose function is also used to invoke normalization and quality assessment functions on a view.

4. Schema Generation

A key based or fully attributed information model can be transformed into a DBMS model for DB2, Oracle, or VAX RDB. Category structures can be automatically collapsed, with all category attributes encased in the generic parent. Technology-specific names for entities and attributes and physical representations of the attributes are described by a set of *DDL directives*. Leverage uses the source view and the directives to create a new view and a set of data definition language statements that will create the relational tables and indices. Graphing the view results in a diagram in which the database element names can be substituted for the original entity and attribute names. The graph looks a bit different from normal IDEF1X graphs but represents the original design specified in the source view.

As an option, a set of SQL queries can be generated to check the integrity of the physical database. These queries can be useful for after-the-fact detection of referential integrity violations in cases in which the DBMS is not or cannot be used to enforce the assertions made in the source model.

Host Leverage is accompanied by two products for the 80x86 workstation environment. Personal Leverage is a customization of the Excelerator product from Intersolv, formerly Index Technology, and supports both IDEF0 activity models and IDEF1X information models. A special version of the ERwin product (see below) is offered by DACOM under the name ModelPro and is a significant improvement over the data model graphics capabilities of the Personal Leverage alternative.

E.1.2 Normalization Support

Leverage provides full support for normalization of IDEF1X models. Although the normalization algorithm is proprietary, it can generally be described as one that looks at the assertions made in a model and points out errors discovered through analysis of an extended form of functional dependencies [3]. The following errors can be found:

1. Multiple use of the same name.

    Leverage will find cases in which multiple entities contain the same attribute and that attribute is not a contributed foreign key.

2. Unification into a group.

    Leverage will find situations in which an attribute is declared in an entity and is also part of a group attribute in the same entity. In such situations, Leverage will replace the group attribute with its constituents. The hidden unification situations described in Chapter 9 are found by this normalization function and pointed out to the modeler.

3. Elimination of multiple relationships.

    Whenever Leverage discovers multiple paths to the same fact, it will attempt to eliminate all but one of the paths by changing relationship structures. Most situations in which relationships are modified by the product point to the need to inspect the assignment of role names carefully to see that the proper assertions are being made.

Leverage reports all situations in which changes were made for the purpose of normalization, along with its reasons for making the changes. It is the responsibility of the modeler to review these reports to ensure that the changes are appropriate and to make revisions to the model structure to resolve errors and remove any changes deemed inappropriate.

The Leverage product also contains a quality assessment function that will inspect a model and point out possible unification problems and other modifications that might strengthen the model. Fourteen tests are provided, including analysis of multiple relationships among category structures, discovery of entities with identical keys, discovery of multiple key migration paths, and discovery of unnamed and cyclic relationships. These assessments can be of considerable help when the models become large. With experience, finding and resolving errors in small models is not too difficult. Finding them in models containing hundreds of entities and relationships can be a difficult endeavor.

E.2 ERWIN

ERwin is an interactive modeling tool that operates under Microsoft Windows in an 80x86-based computer [4]. Versions are also available for the Apple Macintosh. The product is offered by Logic Works, Inc., of Princeton, New Jersey and is available in three versions: ERwin, ERwin/SQL, and ERwin/ERX. IDEF1X diagrams are created by point-and-click interactive methods on the PC. Most of the IDEF1X figures in this book were prepared using ERwin.

E.2.1 Product Functions

ERwin is more than a drawing package; it knows the rules of IDEF1X and enforces them in the construction of diagrams. It is much newer than Leverage, and is positioned as a cooperative product for the Leverage environment.

ERwin provides a full range of reports and diagram views. Reports include entity and attribute lists, cross references, definitions, and so on. Several different views of a model diagram are supported:

1. Attribute Level

    All entities, attributes, relationships, foreign keys, role names, and so on, are displayed in the diagram. Options at this level allow you to suppress certain information as needed (for example, display primary keys only, do not show relationship cardinality or verb phrases). Most of the figures in the text are presented at this level.

2. Entity Level

    In an entity-level view, only the names of the entities are displayed. The name of each entity is placed inside the entity shape, and all of the attributes are removed. This level can be useful in presenting high-level summaries of the model.

The IDEF1X standard for presentation of entity-level diagrams is to place the entity name at the top of the shape (as in the key based levels). ERwin's treatment of this level must therefore be considered a dialect of IDEF1X, but it is effective in practice. The case study ERD presented in Chapter 12 (Fig. 12.2) is an example of a model presented in this way.

3.   Definition Level

A diagram produced at the definition level looks at first like an attribute-level model. Entity names appear at the top of the entity shape, and all relationship information can be displayed. The detail inside the entity shape (the primary key and data attributes) is, however, replaced with a short definition of the entity. This level is primarily intended for presentation purposes.

4.   Physical Schema Level

A diagram produced at this level also looks like an attribute-level model. All relationship information can be displayed and database-level names (usually short abbreviations) replace the full entity and attribute names. Database field sizes can optionally be included on the diagram. This type of diagram is intended to support physical database design activities and represents the Transformation Model described in Chapter 3. Figure 15.12 presents an example of a model presented at this level.

ERwin has its own internal glossary in which entities and attributes may be defined. In time, it is expected that this internal glossary will be linked to an external repository of definitions. The import/export file format available in ERwin/ERX is a step in this direction.

The special version of ERwin marketed by DACOM under the name ModelPro can be used to create SML for use with the Leverage product and to import a view (SML and initial graph placement) from Leverage for revision or presentation in the PC environment.

DDL for relational products (IBM's DB2, SQLBase from Gupta Technologies, the Microsoft SQL Server, Sybase, Oracle, and INGRES) can also be generated directly by ERwin. ERwin/ERX will also convert a set of relational table create statements into an ERwin model, as a starting point for reverse-engineering, or simply documenting a database.

ERwin provides some support for normalization, but versions available when this text was prepared do not contain a full normalization algorithm. The areas described in Sections E.2.2 and E.2.3 are addressed. When using an interactive modeling tool, you may find these features helpful in preventing normalization errors from occurring in the first place.

E.2.2 First Normal Form Support

In an information model, ERwin cannot know that a name you assign to an attribute represents a list of things. For example, ERwin is happy to accept "childrens-names" as an attribute name in the first example in Chapter 9. Therefore, it does not directly guarantee that every model is in first normal form. (The same is true for DACOM's Leverage.)

E.2.3 Second and Third Normal Form Support

In an IDEF1X model, each entity and attribute is identified by its name. ERwin will accept any name for an entity or attribute, with the following exceptions:

- No entity may have the same name as any other entity.

- ERwin will flag a second use of an entity name (depending on a user-selectable option).

- ERwin will, as an option, flag a second use of an attribute name, unless that name is a role name. When role names are assigned, the same name for an attribute may be used in different entities as long as the role names chain back to a common base attribute.

- ERwin will let you bring a foreign key into an entity more than once without giving it a role name each time, but it will assume that unification should be performed.

If you reconstruct the examples in Chapter 9 using ERwin, you will find, for example, that once "spouse-address" has been defined as an attribute of SPOUSE (Fig. 9.8), you cannot also define it as an attribute of CHILD unless the "unique name" function is disabled. This follows from our single occurrence of a name rule.

By preventing multiple use of the same name, ERwin leads you to put each single fact in exactly one place. There may still be other second and third normal form errors if an attribute is placed incorrectly (improper functional dependencies), but no algorithm will find this without additional knowledge of these attribute dependencies.

By unifying the multiple occurrence of foreign keys not given separate role names, ERwin reminds you to think about what the structure represents. If the same foreign key occurs twice in the same entity, there is a business question to ask: Can these be the keys of two separate instances of another entity being recorded here, or do both of the keys represent the same instance?

E.3 REFERENCES

[1]   The Leverage product is available from D. Appleton Company, Inc., 225 S. Sepulveda Blvd., Manhattan Beach, CA 90266.

[2]   The software has recently been re-acquired by The Data Bsase Design Group with the intention of developing and marketing IDEF1X-based products. The company can be contacted at 441 Via Lido Nord, Newport Beach, CA 92663.

[3]   Brown, R., and D. Stott Parker, Jr. "Laura: A Formal Data Model and Her Logical Design Methodology," *Proceedings of the Ninth International Conference on Very Large Data Bases,* Florence, Italy, October 31-November 2, 1983.

[4]   The ERwin product is available from Logic Works, Inc., 601 Ewing St., Suite B-7, Princeton, NJ 08034.

APPENDIX F

CASE STUDY SUPPLEMENTARY MATERIAL

This Appendix includes the full key based model for the Monterey Foods case study (Fig. F.1) along with a glossary of entity and attribute definitions. Definitions for the fully attributed model segment discussed in Part Three are complete to the degree that they are consistent with the level of detail of the corresponding model; the remaining areas of the model are not taken to that level of detail.

Entity definitions generally contain a description of the entity, an example or two, and additional comments where appropriate. Entity instance occurrence volumes, growth rates, and retention periods are recorded where known. Attribute definitions include the normal description, comments, and examples sections; a domain declaration; and physical system characteristics including a relational column name and format. Consistent abbreviation conventions are used to turn the attribute's full name into its column name.

When an attribute is based on (a role name for) another attribute, its values must come from the same domain as the base, and its physical representation must be the same as the base. IDEF1X refers to this as an attribute being a data type of a base attribute. The relationship is indicated by naming the base attribute in the data type entry for the role named attribute and, as needed, constraining its domain in the Domain entry.

Group attributes are recorded in a similar way. "Group" names the constituents, and "domain" is used as needed to constrain allowed combinations of constituent values. Some of the group attributes are included because they specify constraints on the values of certain combinations of attributes. For example, if either a count or weight but not both is to be recorded, a group attribute is used to declare this exclusivity. Since IDEF1X does not specify a systematic way to record constraints, this style is used. Other methods of declaring constraints can also be used.

Structured modeling language for the Leverage product described in Appendix E is included following the entity and attribute definitions.

F.1 KEY BASED MODEL ENTITY DEFINITIONS

ASSIGNED-LOT

Description:	A record of the assignment of a portion of a STORE-LOT to a person responsible for it.
Comment:	ASSIGNED-LOTs are tracked under REGION-RESPONSIBILITYs.

CASH-REGISTER

Description:	An electro-mechanical device used to record SALEs.
Comment:	A single CASH-REGISTER is associated with a check-out line.

CASHIER

Description:	A job function in which an EMPLOYEE is assigned as the operator of a CASH-REGISTER.
Comment:	In this role, the EMPLOYEE is involved with SALEs to CUSTOMERs.
Example:	EMPLOYEE Judy is assigned to CASH REGISTER 123 from 1:00 October 17 to 5:30 October 17.

CLASSIFYING-AGENCY

Description:	An organization or individual that establishes a method for classifying produce.
Example:	American Vegetable Association, the management of Monterey Foods.

CUSTOMER

Description:	Someone who buys from a STORE.
Example:	Allen Campbell, George Smith

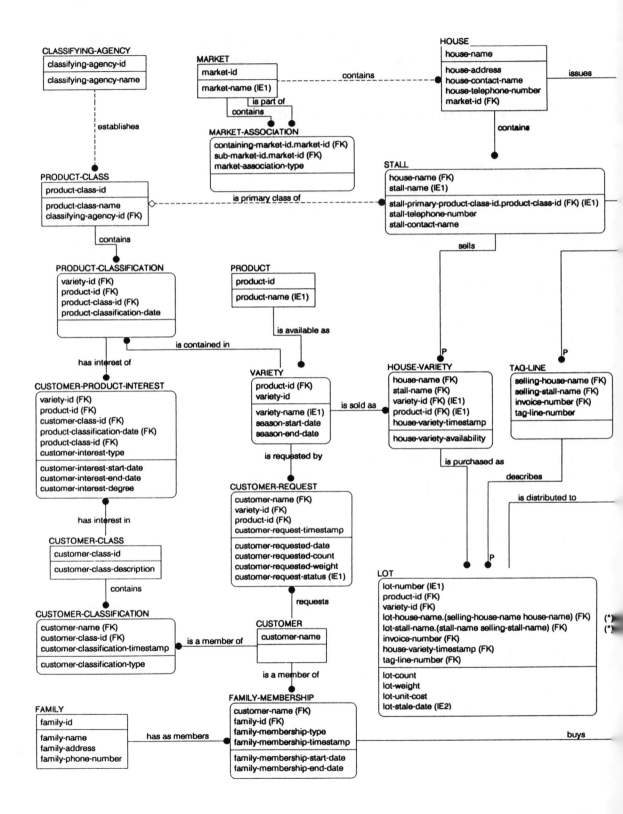

Figure F.1. Full Key Based Model for Monterey Foods.

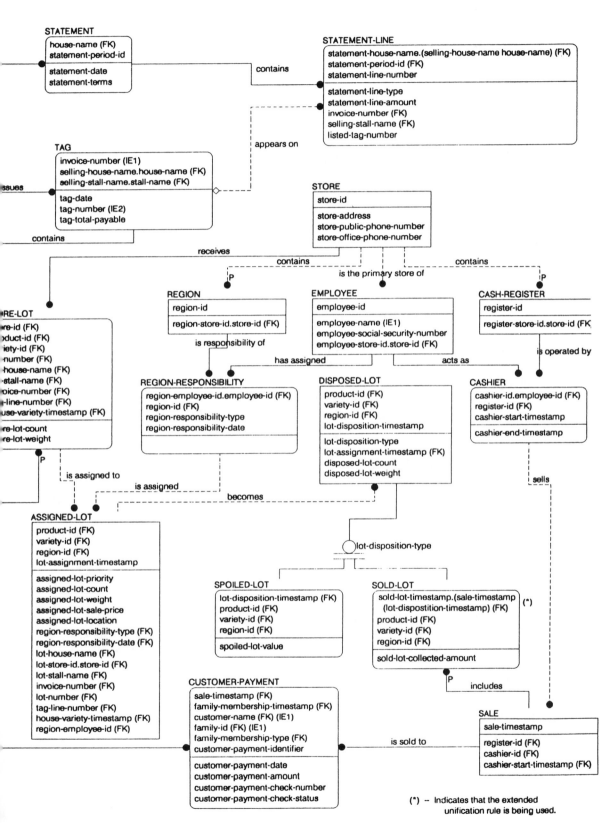

Figure F.1.   Continued.

CUSTOMER-CLASS

Description: A grouping of CUSTOMERs formed to track buying trends and preferences.
Comment: Each class includes a description of the general type of CUSTOMER to be
                included.
Example: Berkeley Gourmands.

CUSTOMER-CLASSIFICATION

Description: A record of the inclusion of a CUSTOMER in a CUSTOMER-CLASS.
Example: Customer Alvyn is included in the Berkeley Gourmand class.

CUSTOMER-PAYMENT

Description: A record of a CUSTOMER's payment for a SALE.
Comment: Records are not currently kept for all SALEs, only those made by check or
                on credit.

CUSTOMER-PRODUCT-INTEREST

Description: A record of the level of interest a CUSTOMER-CLASS has in a particular
                PRODUCT-CLASSIFICATION.
Comment: These records assist in planning availability of specialty items throughout
                the year.

CUSTOMER-REQUEST

Description: A record of a specific request by a CUSTOMER for a certain VARIETY.
Comment: The request includes the availability date and amount requested.
Example: Helen has requested three crates of Washington Apples for availability on
                July 10.

DISPOSED-LOT

Description: A record of the disposition of a part of an ASSIGNED-LOT.
Comment: The lot is disposed either because it is sold or because it spoils.
Example: 800 pounds of pumpkins were discarded on November 4, 1989.

EMPLOYEE

Description: Someone who works for a STORE.
Example: Judy Fujimoto.

FAMILY

Description: A group of CUSTOMERs who generally act as a single buying entity.
Example: Clancy's Restaurant.

FAMILY-MEMBERSHIP

Description: A record of the inclusion of a CUSTOMER in a FAMILY.
Example: Allen Campbell is a buyer for Clancy's Restaurant.

HOUSE

Description: A general part of a MARKET where produce is sold.
Comment: A MARKET is like a shopping mall, with each HOUSE a department store in the mall. A HOUSE can also represent a farm, where the MARKET represents the farming region.
Instances: 200
Growth: 25 per year
Retention: 10 years

HOUSE-VARIETY

Description: A record of the availability of a VARIETY at a particular STALL.
Example: Cherry tomatoes were available from John's, Oakland, on September 12. Quality was fair, price was $14 per crate.
Instances: 500,000
Growth: 700 per day
Retention: 3 years

LOT

Description: A quantity of produce purchased as a unit.
Instances: 42,000
Growth: 700 per day
Retention: 60 days

MARKET

Description: A wholesaler of produce.
Comment: A MARKET can cover several city blocks and contains HOUSEs where the produce is sold. A MARKET is like a shopping mall, with each HOUSE a department store in the mall. A MARKET can also cover a geographic region, like Sonoma County.
Example: San Francisco Produce Market, Northern California.
Instances: 20
Growth: 5 per year
Retention: 10 years

MARKET-ASSOCIATION

Description: A record of a relationship between one MARKET and another.
Example: The Bay Area MARKET contains the San Francisco MARKET.

PRODUCT

Description: A general classification of produce.
Example: Apples, Oranges, Greens, Flowers, Potatoes.
Instances: 200
Growth: 20 per year
Retention: 10 years

PRODUCT-CLASS

Description: A grouping of VARIETYs formed to track buying trends and preferences.
Comment: Classes are established by CLASSIFYING-AGENCYs. Each class includes a description of the general type of VARIETY to be included.
Example: Fruits, Nuts, Vegetables, Dry Vegetables, Wet Vegetables.

PRODUCT-CLASSIFICATION

Description: A record of the inclusion of a VARIETY in a PRODUCT-CLASS.
Example: Butter Lettuce is included in the Wet Vegetables class.

REGION

Description: A part of the STORE.
Example: Cold box, Center Island, Outside.

REGION-RESPONSIBILITY

Description: A record of the assignment to an EMPLOYEE of responsibility for a REGION.

Comment: Responsibilities include stocking produce for sale, keeping inventories and projecting buying requirements.

Example: Tony has primary responsibility for the Center Island on September 17.

SALE

Description: A record of a purchase by a CUSTOMER.

SOLD-LOT

Description: A record of a VARIETY sold to a CUSTOMER as part of a SALE.

Comment: A SOLD-LOT is a type of DISPOSED-LOT.

Example: 3 pounds of navel oranges were included in the sale timestamped 15JUL890-9451292.

SPOILED-LOT

Description: A portion of an ASSIGNED-LOT discarded due to spoilage.

Comment: A SPOILED-LOT is a type of DISPOSED-LOT.

Example: 800 pounds of pumpkins were discarded on November 4, 1989.

STALL

Description: A specific location in a HOUSE where produce is sold.

Comment: A STALL is like a department in a department store, where HOUSE is the store. A STALL is often known by the primary class of product that it sells.

Instances: 100

Growth: 10 per year

Retention: 10 years

STATEMENT

Description: An accounting for purchases from a HOUSE that is presented to Monterey Foods as a demand for payment of the associated bill.

STATEMENT-LINE

Description: A part of a STATEMENT that describes a purchase made by Monterey Foods.

STORE

Description:	One of the outlets of Monterey Foods.
Instances:	2
Growth:	1 per 5 years
Retention:	10 years

STORE-LOT

Description:	A part of a LOT assigned to a particular STORE.
Example:	50 cases from a certain lot of oranges were assigned to Berkeley on July 12, 1988.
Instances:	84,000
Growth:	1,400 per day
Retention:	60 days

TAG

Description:	A record of a purchase by the store issued by a STALL.
Comment:	A TAG is written for each purchase and often has separate lines for multiple LOTs.
Entity:	TAG
Instances:	30,000
Growth:	100 per day
Retention:	1 year

TAG-LINE

Description:	A section of a TAG that describes a purchase by Monterey Foods.
Comment:	TAGs are supposed to list only one LOT per line, but sometimes they have several. In the market system, a separate (artificial) line will be inserted for each LOT when multiple LOTs are included in a single line on the original TAG.
Instances:	42,000
Growth:	700 per day
Retention:	60 days

VARIETY

Description:	A specific type of PRODUCT.
Example:	If the PRODUCT is oranges, VARIETYs include valencia and navel.
Instances:	5000
Growth:	100 per year
Retention:	10 years

F.2 KEY BASED MODEL ATTRIBUTE DEFINITIONS

address

Description:	A place at which someone can be contacted.
Comment:	This is a group attribute established for two purposes. First, it is used in high-level models to leave a place mark for future extension. Second, it explodes into the constituents of all types of addresses and is used in low-level models to distinguish between a situation in which a generic (able to accommodate any kind) as opposed to specific type of address is needed.
	It is clear that only some combinations of cities, states, and zip codes are allowable. This additional detail may be needed at some point.
Example:	A street address or a post office box.
Col Name:	addr
Group:	address-po-box
	address-street-number
	address-street-name
	address-street-extension
	address-city
	address-state
	address-zip-code

address-city

Description:	A part of an address containing the name of a city.
Example:	Berkeley
Domain:	Any nonblank character string up to length 30.
Col Name:	addr_city
Format:	VARCHAR (30)

address-po-box

Description:	A part of an address containing a post office box number.
Example:	122
Domain:	Any positive integer, or null (designated by the value zero).
Col Name:	addr_po_box
Format:	INTEGER

address-state

Description:	A part of an address containing an abbreviation for a state.
Example:	CA
Domain:	Any valid postal state code.
Col Name:	addr_state
Format:	CHARACTER (2)

address-street-extension

Description: A part of an address containing an extension to a number and street.
Example: Apt. 304
Domain: Any character string, or null (designated by all blanks).
Col Name: addr_st_ext
Format: VARCHAR (10)

address-street-name

Description: A part of an address containing the name of a street.
Example: Hopkins St.
Domain: Any character string, or null (designated by all blanks).
Col Name: addr_st_name
Format: VARCHAR (30)

address-street-number

Description: A part of an address containing a number on a street.
Example: 1334A
Domain: Any character string starting with a number, or null (designated by all blanks).
Col Name: addr_st_num
Format: VARCHAR (30)

address-zip-code

Description: A part of an address containing a zip code.
Example: 94710, 94710-3366
Comment: Two forms of zip code are recognized, standard 5-digit codes and their 9-digit extensions. At some point, it may be advisable to drop the second format, add a "zip-route-code" attribute to represent the additional 4 digits, and form an "extended-zip-code" as a group attribute that contains both parts of the 9-digit code.
Domain: Any valid postal zip code.
Col Name: addr_zip_cd
Format: 1:   DECIMAL (5,0)
                 2:   DECIMAL (9,0)

assigned-lot-amount-constraint

Description:	A group attribute formed to declare the composite domain of the attributes "assigned-lot-count" and "assigned-lot-weight".
Group:	assigned-lot-count assigned-lot-weight
Domain:	One of the constituents must be null, and one must be not null.

assigned-lot-count

Description:	A count of the number of pieces in the ASSIGNED-LOT.
Comment:	The size of a lot is recorded either as "assigned-lot-count" or as "assigned-lot-weight".
Domain:	Any positive integer, or null (designated by the value zero).
Col Name:	asg_lot_ct
Format:	INTEGER

assigned-lot-location

Description:	A text description of the physical location (within a REGION) of the ASSIGNED-LOT.
Comment:	Not often used.
Example:	Cold box B lower rear.
Domain:	Any nonblank character string up to length 60, or null (designated by all blanks).
Col Name:	asg_lot_loc
Format:	VARCHAR (60)

assigned-lot-priority

Description:	A specification of how quickly an ASSIGNED-LOT should be sold.
Comment:	The priority is an indication of the remaining life expectancy of the AS-SIGNED-LOT.
Domain:	H/M/L (High / Medium / Low).
Col Name:	asg_lot_prty
Format:	CHARACTER (1)

assigned-lot-sale-price

Description:	The price at which items in the lot will be offered for sale.
Comment:	If an assigned-lot-weight is included, the price is per pound. If an assigned-lot-count is included, the price is per item.
Example:	0.89 (per pound), 0.39 (each).
Domain:	Valid decimal numbers in the range of 0.01 to 99.999.
Col Name:	asg_lot_prc
Format:	DECIMAL (5,3)

assigned-lot-weight

Description:	A measure of the weight of the ASSIGNED-LOT, stated in pounds.
Comment:	The size of a lot is recorded either as "assigned-lot-count" or as "assigned-lot-weight".
Domain:	Valid decimal numbers in the range of 0.01 to 9999.99 or null (designated by the value zero).
Col Name:	asg_lot_wt
Format:	DECIMAL (6.2)

cashier-end-timestamp

Description:	The date and time at which a CASHIER assignment ends.
Example:	17OCT8917040000
Domain:	Any valid time and date after 1/1/89 or null (designated by zero) if the CASHIER is still assigned.
Col Name:	csh_end_ts
Data Type:	timestamp

cashier-id

Description:	The identifier of the EMPLOYEE who is serving as CASHIER.
Data Type:	employee-id
Col Name:	csh_id

cashier-start-end-constraint

Description:	A group attribute formed to declare the composite domain of the attributes "cashier-start-timestamp" and "cashier-end-timestamp".
Group:	cashier-start-timestamp cashier-end-timestamp
Domain:	When recorded, the end timestamp must be later than the start timestamp, but by no more than 5 hours.

cashier-start-timestamp

Description: The date and time at which a CASHIER assignment begins.
Example: 17OCT8916300000
Domain: Any valid time and date after 1/1/89.
Col Name: csh_strt_ts
Data Type: timestamp

classifying-agency-id

Description: The unique identifier of a CLASSIFYING-AGENCY.
Domain: Any positive integer.
Col Name: cls_agcy_id
Format: INTEGER

classifying-agency-name

Description: The primary name by which the CLASSIFYING-AGENCY is known to the
                managers of Monterey Foods.
Domain: Any nonblank character string up to length 60.
Col Name: cls_agcy_nm
Format: VARCHAR (60)

containing-market-id

Description: The identifier of a MARKET that contains another MARKET.
Domain: Any valid "market-id".
Col Name: cnt_mkt_id
Data Type: market-id

customer-class-description

Description: A general description of the CUSTOMER-CLASS.
Example: Berkeley Gourmands.
Domain: Any nonblank character string up to length 40.
Col Name: cst_cls_dsc
Format: VARCHAR (40)

customer-class-id

Description: The unique identifier of a CUSTOMER-CLASS.
Domain: Any positive integer.
Col Name: cst_cls_id
Format: INTEGER

customer-classification-timestamp

Description: The date and time at which the CUSTOMER was assigned to the class.
Domain: Any valid time and date after 1/1/89.
Col Name: cst_cls_ts
Data Type: timestamp

customer-classification-type

Description: A specification of a type of membership of a CUSTOMER in a CUSTOM-
                  ER-CLASS.
Domain: F: Full membership in the class (** needs
                  clarification **).
                  L: Limited membership in the class (** needs clarification **).
Col Name: cst_cls_typ
Format: CHARACTER (1)

customer-interest-degree

Description: A measure of the strength of interest exhibited by the class.
Domain: H/M/L   (High / Medium / Low).
Col Name: cst_int_deg
Format: CHARACTER (1)

customer-interest-end-date

Description: The date on which the interest ends.
Comment: The year is not included since interest is assumed to be cyclic and continue
                  from year to year. Format is MMMDD.
Domain: Valid month / day combinations.
Col Name: cst_int_strt_dt
Format: CHARACTER (5)

customer-interest-start-date

Description: The date on which the interest begins.
Comment: The year is not included since interest is assumed to be cyclic and continue
                  from year to year. Format is MMMDD.
Domain: Valid month / day combinations.
Col Name: cst_int_end_dt
Format: CHARACTER (5)

customer-interest-start-end-constraint

Description:	A group attribute formed to declare the composite domain of the attributes "customer-interest-start-date" and "customer-interest-end-date".
Group:	customer-interest-start-date
	customer-interest-end-date
Domain:	The end date must be later than the start date.

customer-interest-type

Description:	A code indicating the type of interest exhibited by the class.
Domain:	G: General interest.
	H: Holiday interest.
	S: Seasonal interest.
Col Name:	cst_int_typ
Format:	CHARACTER (1)

customer-name

Description:	The name by which the CUSTOMER is known to the store.
Domain:	Any nonblank character string up to length 40.
Col Name:	cst_nam
Format:	VARCHAR (40)

customer-payment-amount

Description:	The amount of the payment.
Example:	$13.47
Domain:	Valid decimal numbers in the range of 0.01 to 9999.99.
Col Name:	cst_pmt_amt
Format:	DECIMAL (6,2)

customer-payment-check-number

Description:	The number of a check accepted as payment.
Example:	3155
Domain:	Any positive integer, or null (designated by the value zero).
Col Name:	cst_pmt_ck_num
Format:	INTEGER

customer-payment-check-status

Description:	The status of the check (collected, bounced, and so on).
Comment:	The status moves to "C" (cleared) on day 15 if no other status change is recorded.
Domain:	A: Accepted, not deposited.
	B: Deposited, not cleared.
	C: Cleared.
	R: Returned.
	S: Resubmitted.
	Z: Written off.
Col Name:	cst_pmt_ck_stat
Format:	CHARACTER (1)

customer-payment-date

Description:	The date of a customer payment.
Example:	21JAN1989
Domain:	Valid dates after 1/1/89.
Col Name:	cst_pmt_dt
Format:	DATE

customer-payment-identifier

Description:	The unique identifier of a CUSTOMER-PAYMENT.
Domain:	Any positive integer.
Col Name:	cst_pmt_id
Format:	INTEGER

customer-request-amount-constraint

Description:	A group attribute formed to declare the composite domain of the attributes "customer-requested-count" and "customer-requested-weight".
Group:	customer-requested-count
	customer-requested-weight
Domain:	One of the constituents must be null, and one must be not null.

customer-request-status

Description:	A code that specifies the status of a CUSTOMER-REQUEST.
Domain:	F: Filled.
	O: Overdue / outstanding.
	P: Pending.
	W: Withdrawn.
Col Name:	cst_req_stat
Format:	CHARACTER (1)

customer-request-timestamp

Description:	The date and time of the receipt of the CUSTOMER-REQUEST.
Domain:	Any valid time and date after 1/1/89.
Col Name:	cst_req_ts
Data Type:	timestamp

customer-requested-count

Description:	The amount requested, stated as an item count.
Comment:	Either "customer-requested-count" or "customer-requested-weight" are recorded for each request.
Example:	22 (pieces).
Domain:	Any positive integer, or null (designated by the value zero).
Col Name:	cst_req_ct
Format:	INTEGER

customer-requested-date

Description:	The date on which the CUSTOMER has requested the item.
Example:	24DEC1989
Domain:	Valid dates after 1/1/89.
Col Name:	cst_req_dt
Format:	DATE

customer-requested-weight

Description:	The amount requested, stated as a weight in pounds.
Comment:	Either "customer-requested-count" or "customer-requested-weight" are recorded for each request.
Example:	12.25 (pounds).
Domain:	Valid decimal numbers in the range of 0.01 to 9999.99 or null (designated by the value zero).
Col Name:	cst_req_wt
Format:	DECIMAL (6.2)

disposed-lot-amount-constraint

Description:	A group attribute formed to declare the composite domain of the attributes "disposed-lot-count" and "disposed-lot-weight".
Group:	disposed-lot-count disposed-lot-weight
Domain:	One of the constituents must be null, and one must be not null.

disposed-lot-count

Description:	The amount disposed, stated as an item count.
Comment:	Either "disposed-lot-weight" or "disposed-lot-count" are recorded for each DISPOSED-LOT.
Example:	128 (pieces).
Domain:	Any positive integer, or null (designated by the value zero).
Col Name:	dsp_lot_ct
Format:	INTEGER

disposed-lot-weight

Description:	The amount disposed, stated as a weight in pounds.
Comment:	Either "disposed-lot-weight" or "disposed-lot-count" are recorded for each DISPOSED-LOT.
Example:	12.8 (pounds).
Domain:	Valid decimal numbers in the range of 0.01 to 9999.99 or null (designated by the value zero).
Col Name:	dsp_lot_wt
Format:	DECIMAL (6.2)

employee-id

Description:	The unique identifier of an EMPLOYEE.
Domain:	Any positive integer.
Col Name:	emp_id
Format:	INTEGER

employee-name

Description:	The name by which an EMPLOYEE is known to Monterey Foods.
Domain:	Any nonblank character string up to length 40.
Col Name:	emp_nm
Format:	VARCHAR (40)

employee-social-security-number

Description:	The social security number of the EMPLOYEE.
Comment:	May be null for employees without a social security number.
Domain:	Valid decimal numbers in the range of 1 to 999999999, or null (designated by the value zero).
Col Name:	emp_ssn
Format:	DECIMAL (9,0)

employee-store-id

Description:	The identifier of the STORE to which the EMPLOYEE is assigned.
Comment:	An EMPLOYEE can work for both STOREs but has one designated as the primary STORE.
Domain:	Valid "store-id".
Col Name:	emp_str_id
Data Type:	store-id

extended-phone-number

Description:	A public system phone number, including a possible extension number at which someone or some thing can be contacted.
Comment:	This is a group attribute established to contain the constituents of all types of telephone numbers, including those needing extensions, and provides a way to distinguish between a situation in which a generic (able to accommodate any kind) as opposed to specific type of phone number is needed.
	It is clear that only certain combinations of area code, prefix, and suffix are allowable. This additional detail may eventually be needed.
Example:	(415) 555-1212 Ext. 3253
Col Name:	ext_phn_num
Group:	phone-area-code
	phone-number-prefix
	phone-number-suffix
	phone-number-extension

family-address

Description:	The mailing address of the FAMILY.
Comment:	** This group needs to be broken into its constituents in the fully attributed model. **
Example:	123 4th Street, Berkeley, CA 94703.
Domain:	Any valid character string up to length 120.
Col Name:	fam_addr

family-id

Description:	The unique identifier of a FAMILY.
Domain:	Any positive integer.
Col Name:	fam_id
Format:	INTEGER

family-membership-end-date

Description:	The date on which a CUSTOMER's association with a FAMILY ends.
Example:	20JAN989
Domain:	Valid dates or null when the membership still exists.
Col Name:	fam_mbr_end_dt
Format:	DATE

family-membership-start-date

Description:	The date on which a CUSTOMER's association with a FAMILY begins.
Example:	01NOV989
Domain:	Valid dates.
Col Name:	fam_mbr_strt_dt
Format:	DATE

family-membership-start-end-constraint

Description:	A group attribute formed to declare the composite domain of the attributes "family-membership-start-date" and "family-membership-end-date".
Group:	family-membership-start-date family-membership-end-date
Domain:	The end date, if not null, must be later than the start date.

family-membership-timestamp

Description:	A timestamp representing the entry time for the membership record.
Domain:	Any valid time and date after 1/1/89.
Col Name:	fam_mbr_ts
Data Type:	timestamp

family-membership-type

Description:	A specification of the type of relationship between the CUSTOMER and the FAMILY.
Domain:	B: Buyer for the establishment represented by the FAMILY. G: General membership, no specific type recorded. M: Manager of the establishment represented by the FAMILY. O: Owner of the establishment represented by the FAMILY.
Col Name:	fam_mbr_typ
Format:	CHARACTER (1)

family-name

Description:	The name by which the FAMILY is known to Monterey Foods.
Domain:	Any nonblank character string up to length 40.
Col Name:	fam_nam
Format:	VARCHAR (40)

family-phone-number

Description:	A telephone number for the FAMILY.
Example:	(415) 555-1212 Ext. 2453
Domain:	Any valid character string up to length 24.
Col Name:	fam_phon
Data Type:	extended-telephone-number

house-address

Description:	The mailing address of the HOUSE.
Example:	123 4th Street, Berkeley, CA 94703
Domain:	Any valid address, either a street address or a post office box.
Col Name:	hs_addr
Data Type:	address

house-contact-name

Description:	The name of an individual generally used as a contact at a HOUSE.
Domain:	Any nonblank character string up to length 40 or null (designated by all blanks).
Col Name:	hs_ctct_nam
Format:	VARCHAR (40)

house-name

Description:	The primary name by which a HOUSE is known to the store.
Domain:	Any nonblank character string up to length 40.
Col Name:	hs_nam
Format:	VARCHAR (40)

house-phone-number

Description: A telephone number for the HOUSE.
Comment: This key based model attribute was replaced by "house-telephone-number" in the fully attributed model.
Example: (415) 555-1212 Ext. 2453
Domain: Any valid character string up to length 24.
Col Name: hs_phon
Format: VARCHAR (24)

house-telephone-number

Description: A telephone number used for general communication with a HOUSE.
Example: (415) 555-1212 Ext. 3253
Domain: Any valid telephone number, possibly with an extension.
Col Name: hs_tel_phn_num
Data Type: extended-telephone-number

house-variety-availability

Description: A code indicating the degree of availability of the variety.
Domain: A: Average.
                L: Limited.
                N: None.
                P: Plentiful.
                Z: Overstocked.
Col Name: hs_var_avail
Format: CHARACTER (1)

house-variety-date

Description: A date on which a HOUSE-VARIETY is available.
Domain: Any valid date after 1/1/89.
Col Name: hs_var_dt
Format: DATE

house-variety-timestamp

Description: A timestamp for the recording of the HOUSE-VARIETY.
Comment: ** This attribute is obsolete. It has been replaced by "house-variety-date". **
Domain: Any valid time and date after 1/1/89.
Col Name: hs_var_ts
Data Type: timestamp

invoice-number

Description:	An identifier of a TAG.
Comment:	This identifier is assigned by the STALL, which issues the TAG. It is not necessarily unique.
Domain:	Any nonblank character string up to length 12.
Col Name:	inv_num
Format:	VARCHAR (12)

listed-tag-number

Description:	A HOUSE's identifier of a TAG listed on a STATEMENT-LINE.
Comment:	This should match an "invoice-number" on some TAG, but, since it is provided by the HOUSE, is not guaranteed to.
Domain:	Any nonblank character string up to length 12.
Col Name:	inv_num
Format:	VARCHAR (12)

lot-amount-constraint

Description:	A group attribute formed to declare the composite domain of the attributes "lot-count" and "lot-weight".
Group:	lot-count
	lot-weight
Domain:	One of the constituents must be null, and one must be not null.

lot-assignment-timestamp

Description:	A timestamp for an ASSIGNED-LOT.
Domain:	Any valid time and date after 1/1/89.
Col Name:	lot_asg_ts
Data Type:	timestamp

lot-count

Description:	A count of the number of pieces in the LOT.
Comment:	The size of a LOT is recorded either as an approximate "lot-count" or as a "lot-weight". This size is often understated to account for expected spoilage.
Domain:	Any positive integer, or null (designated by the value zero).
Col Name:	lot_ct
Format:	INTEGER

lot-disposition-timestamp

Description:	A timestamp for a DISPOSED-LOT.
Domain:	Any valid time and date after 1/1/90, or null if the LOT has not yet been "disposed."
Col Name:	lot_dsp_ts
Data Type:	timestamp

lot-disposition-type

Description:	A code specifying the type of disposition of a DISPOSED-LOT.
Domain:	1: Sold.
	2: Spoiled.
Col Name:	lot_dsp_typ
Format:	DECIMAL (1,0)

lot-house-name

Description:	The "house-name" for the HOUSE from which the LOT was purchased.
Comment:	This attribute plays an extended unification role in the model.
Domain:	Valid "house-name".
Col Name:	lot_hs_nam
Data Type:	selling-house-name, house-name

lot-number

Description:	An identifier of a LOT.
Domain:	Any positive integer.
Col Name:	lot_num
Format:	INTEGER

lot-stale-date

Description:	A date by which a LOT should be sold or discarded.
Comment:	This attribute is used to prompt for disposal of aging inventory.
Domain:	Any valid date that is later than the "tag-date" for the LOT.
Col Name:	lot_stale_dt
Format:	DATE

lot-stall-name

Description:	The "stall-name" for the STALL from which the LOT was purchased.
Comment:	This attribute plays an extended unification role in the model.
Domain:	Valid "stall-name".
Col Name:	lot_stl_nam
Data Type:	selling-stall-name, stall-name

lot-unit-cost

Description:	A unit cost for the constituents of a LOT.
Comment:	The cost is recorded as a cost either per item or per pound.
Domain:	Any positive integer, or null.
Col Name:	lot_un_cost
Format:	DECIMAL (5.3)

lot-weight

Description:	A measure of the weight of the LOT, stated in pounds.
Comment:	The size of a LOT is recorded either as an approximate "lot-count" or as a "lot-weight". This size is often understated to account for expected spoilage.
Domain:	Valid decimal numbers in the range of 0.01 to 9999.99 (designated by the value zero).
Col Name:	lot_wt
Format:	DECIMAL (6.2)

market-association-type

Description:	A code that specifies the type of relationship between two MARKETs.
Domain:	I: The second MARKET is included as part of the first.
	O: The second MARKET is owned by the first.
Col Name:	mkt_asc_typ
Format:	CHARACTER (1)

market-id

Description:	The unique identifier of a MARKET.
Domain:	Any positive integer.
Col Name:	mkt_id
Format:	INTEGER

market-name

Description: The primary name by which a MARKET is known to Monterey Foods.
Domain: Any nonblank character string up to length 40.
Col Name: mkt_nam
Format: VARCHAR (40)

phone-area-code

Description: A part of a telephone number consisting of a 3-digit code identifying a
                telephone company calling area.
Example: 415
Domain: Any valid telephone area code. Codes are listed in telephone directories
                issued by phone companies.
Col Name: phn_area_cd
Format: DECIMAL (3,0)

phone-number

Description: A public system phone number at which someone or some thing can be
                contacted.
Comment: This is a group attribute established to contain the constituents of a tele-
                phone number that does not include an extension, and provides a way to
                distinguish between a situation in which a generic (able to accommodate any
                kind) as opposed to a specific type of phone number is needed.
                     It is clear that only certain combinations of area code, prefix, and suffix
                are allowable. This additional detail may eventually be needed.
Example: (415) 555-1212
Col Name: phn_num
Group: phone-area-code
                phone-number-prefix
                phone-number-suffix

phone-number-extension

Description: A part of an telephone number consisting of a 4-digit code identifying a
                single telephone or group of telephones that is individually addressable
                within a single telephone number.
Example: 3253
Domain: Any valid extension recognized for a specific telephone number. Extensions
                are not normally listed in telephone directories issued by phone companies
                but are supplied by the users of the phone numbers.
Col Name: phn_ext
Format: DECIMAL (4,0)

phone-number-prefix

Description: A part of an telephone number consisting of a 3-digit code identifying a telephone company calling area within an area code.
Example: 555
Domain: Any valid telephone company prefix for the area code. Prefixes are listed in telephone directories issued by phone companies.
Col Name: phn_pfx
Format: DECIMAL (3,0)

phone-number-suffix

Description: A part of an telephone number consisting of a 4-digit code identifying a single telephone company service to some address or group of addresses. Combined with the prefix, the resulting number will cause a bell to ring on an installed telephone or will connect to an extension service that will complete the call when supplied with a valid extension.
Example: 1212
Domain: Any valid telephone company suffix for a designated prefix and area code. Suffixes are listed in detailed phone number entries in telephone directories issued by phone companies.
Col Name: phn_sfx
Format: DECIMAL (4,0)

po-box-address

Description: A type of address designating a location within a post office facility to which mail may be sent.
Example: PO Box 122, Berkeley, CA 94710
Comment: It is clear that only some combinations of cities, states, and zip codes are allowable. This additional detail may be needed at some point. Private carriers, such as Federal Express and UPS, will not deliver to a PO Box.
Col Name: po_box_addr
Group: address-po-box
                address-city
                address-state
                address-zip-code

product-class-id

Description: The unique identifier of a PRODUCT-CLASS.
Domain: Any positive integer.
Col Name: prod_cls_id
Format: INTEGER

product-class-name

Description: The primary name by which Monterey Foods refers to a PRODUCT-CLASS.
Example: Summer vegetables.
Domain: Any nonblank character string up to length 40.
Col Name: prd_cls_nam
Format: VARCHAR (40)

product-classification-date

Description: The date of inclusion of a VARIETY in a PRODUCT-CLASS.
Example: 01JAN1989
Domain: Valid dates.
Col Name: prd_cls_dt
Format: DATE

product-id

Description: The unique identifier of a PRODUCT.
Domain: Any nonblank 3-character string.
Col Name: prd_id
Format: CHARACTER (3)

product-name

Description: The primary name by which a PRODUCT is known to Monterey Foods.
Example: Apple, Orange
Domain: Any nonblank character string up to length 40.
Col Name: prd_nam
Format: VARCHAR (40)

region-employee-id

Description: The "employee-id" of the EMPLOYEE who holds responsibility for the REGION.
Domain: Valid "employee-id".
Col Name: reg_emp_id
Data Type: employee-id

region-id

Description: The unique identifier of a REGION.
Domain: Any positive integer.
Col Name: reg_id
Format: INTEGER

region-responsibility-date

Description:	The date on which the EMPLOYEE is responsible for the REGION.
Comment:	EMPLOYEEs may be responsible for different regions on different days.
Domain:	Valid dates after 1/1/90.
Col Name:	reg_rsp_dt
Format:	DATE

region-responsibility-type

Description:	A specification of the type of responsibility an EMPLOYEE has for a REGION.
Domain:	P: Primary responsibility for the REGION.
	S: Secondary responsibility. This EMPLOYEE is accountable to the "Primary".
Col Name:	reg_rsp_typ
Format:	CHARACTER (1)

region-employee-id

Description:	The "employee-id" of the EMPLOYEE who holds responsibility for the REGION.
Domain:	Valid "employee-id".
Col Name:	reg_emp_id
Data Type:	employee-id

region-store-id

Description:	The "store-id" of the STORE that contains the REGION.
Domain:	Valid "store-id".
Col Name:	reg_str_id
Data Type:	store-id

register-id

Description:	The unique identifier of a CASH-REGISTER.
Domain:	Any nonblank character string up to 10 characters.
Col Name:	rg_id
Format:	CHARACTER (10)

register-store-id

Description:	The identifier of a CASH-REGISTER assigned to a STORE.
Domain:	Any valid "register-id".
Col Name:	rg_str_id
Data Type:	register-id

sale-timestamp

Description:	The date and time of a SALE.
Comment:	This attribute identifies the SALE. No two SALEs may occur at exactly the same time. The "sale-timestamp" is the same as the "lot-disposition-time-stamp" for each SOLD-LOT included in the SALE.
Domain:	Any valid time and date after 1/1/90.
Col Name:	sale_ts
Data Type:	timestamp

selling-house-name

Description:	The "house-name" for the HOUSE from which the LOT is purchased.
Domain:	Valid "house-name".
Col Name:	sel_hs_nam
Data Type:	house-name

selling-stall-name

Description:	The "stall-name" for the STALL from which the LOT is purchased.
Domain:	Valid "stall-name".
Col Name:	sel_stl_nam
Data Type:	stall-name

sold-lot-collected-amount

Description:	The amount (in dollars and cents) collected for a SALE.
Domain:	Valid decimal numbers in the range of 0.01 to 9999.99.
Col Name:	sal_lot_col_amt
Format:	DECIMAL (6.2)

sold-lot-timestamp

Description:	A timestamp reflecting the date and time of the SALE that resulted in the SOLD-LOT.
Comment:	This attribute plays an extended unification role in the model.
Col Name:	sal_lot_col_amt
Data Type:	lot-disposition-timestamp, sale-timestamp

spoiled-lot-value

Description:	The value of the SPOILED-LOT stated in dollars and cents.
Domain:	Valid decimal numbers in the range of 0.01 to 9999.99.
Col Name:	spl_lot_val
Format:	DECIMAL (6.2)

stall-contact-name

Description:	The name of an individual who is the primary contact for the STALL.
Example:	Joe, Lenny
Domain:	Any nonblank character string up to length 40.
Col Name:	stl_ctct_nam
Format:	VARCHAR (40)

stall-name

Description:	The primary name by which a STALL is known to the store.
Comment:	This is the primary identifier of the STALL.
Example:	Joe's, Lenny's
Domain:	Any nonblank character string up to length 40.
Col Name:	stl_nam
Format:	VARCHAR (40)

stall-primary-product-id

Description:	The identifier of the primary PRODUCT of the STALL.
Comment:	A STALL may be known by its major product, although it may sell several. ** Attribute is obsolete. It has been replaced by "stall-primary-product-class-id". **
Example:	Beans, Flowers
Domain:	Any valid "product-id".
Col Name:	stl_prm_prd_id
Data Type:	product-id

stall-primary-product-class-id

Description:	The identifier of the primary PRODUCT-CLASS of the STALL.
Example:	Wet Vegetables, Flowers
Domain:	Any valid "product-class-id".
Col Name:	stl_prd_cls_id
Data Type:	product-class-id

stall-primary-product-class-name

Description:	The name of the primary PRODUCT-CLASS of the STALL.
Comment:	This attribute is a physical system derived attribute.
Example:	Wet Vegetables, Flowers
Domain:	Any "product-class-name".
Col Name:	stl_prd_cls_nam
Data Type:	product-class-name

stall-telephone-number

Description:	A telephone number used for general communication with a STALL.
Comment:	This can often be the number of the HOUSE plus an extension specific to the STALL.
Example:	(415) 555-1212 Ext. 3253
Domain:	Any valid telephone number, possibly with an extension.
Col Name:	stl_tel_phn_num
Data Type:	telephone-number

statement-date

Description:	The date of a STATEMENT.
Domain:	Valid dates after 1/1/89.
Col Name:	stmt_dt
Format:	DATE

statement-house-name

Description:	The "house-name" for the HOUSE from which the STATEMENT is received.
Comment:	This attribute plays an extended unification role in the model.
Domain:	Valid "house-name".
Col Name:	stmt_hs_nam
Data Type:	selling-house-name, house-name

statement-line-amount

Description:	The amount listed on a line on a STATEMENT (STATEMENT-LINE).
Domain:	Any positive number between 0 and 99,999.99.
Col Name:	stmt_ln_amt
Format:	DECIMAL (7,2)

statement-line-number

Description:	The identifier of a line on a STATEMENT STATEMENT-LINE).
Domain:	Any positive integer between 1 and 999.
Col Name:	reg_id
Format:	INTEGER

statement-line-type

Description:	A specification of the type of STATEMENT-LINE.
Domain:	D: Statement detail line.
	S: Statement subtotal line.
	T: Statement total line.
Col Name:	stmt_ln_typ
Format:	CHARACTER (1)

statement-period-id

Description:	The identifier of the period represented by the statement.
Comment:	This field is supplied by the HOUSE that issues the STATEMENT.
Domain:	Any nonblank character string up to length 12.
Col Name:	stmt_prd_id
Format:	VARCHAR (12)

statement-terms

Description:	A description of the payment and discount terms of the STATEMENT.
Example:	2-10 net 30 (2% discount for payment within 10 days, full payment (net) required within 30 days).
Domain:	Any nonblank character string up to length 40.
Col Name:	stl_trms
Format:	VARCHAR (40)

store-id

Description:	The unique identifier of one of the STOREs.
Domain:	B: Berkeley.
	P: Palo Alto.
Col Name:	str_id
Format:	CHARACTER (1)

store-location

Description:	A text description of the location of the STORE.
Example:	Berkeley, Palo Alto
Domain:	Any nonblank character string up to length 20.
Col Name:	str_loc
Format:	VARCHAR (20)

store-lot-amount-constraint

Description:	A group attribute formed to declare the composite domain of the attributes "store-lot-count" and "store-lot-weight".
Group:	store-lot-count store-lot-weight
Domain:	One of the constituents must be null, and one must be not null.

store-lot-count

Description:	A count of the number of pieces in the STORE-LOT.
Comment:	The size of a lot is recorded either as "store-lot-count" or as "store-lot-weight".
Domain:	Any positive integer, or null (designated by the value zero).
Col Name:	str_lot_ct
Format:	INTEGER

store-lot-weight

Description:	A measure of the weight of the STORE-LOT, stated in pounds.
Comment:	The size of a lot is recorded either as "store-lot-count" or as "store-lot-weight".
Domain:	Valid decimal numbers in the range of 0.01 to 9999.99 (designated by the value zero).
Col Name:	str_lot_wt
Format:	DECIMAL (6.2)

store-office-phone-number

Description:	A phone number used for general communication with a STORE's office.
Comment:	This number is not generally given to the public, but is used by suppliers.
Example:	(415) 555-1111
Domain:	Any valid telephone number for a STORE.
Col Name:	str_ofc_phn_num
Data Type:	phone-number

store-public-phone-number

Description:	A phone number given to the public as a way to contact the STORE.
Example:	(415) 526-6049
Domain:	Any valid telephone number for a STORE.
Col Name:	str_pub_phn_num
Data Type:	phone-number

street-address

Description:	A type of address designating the location of a non-post office facility to which mail may be sent.
Example:	1334A Hopkins Street, Apt. 304, Berkeley, CA 94702
Col Name:	str_addr
Group:	address-street-number
	address-street-name
	address-street-extension
	address-city
	address-state
	address-zip-code

sub-market-id

Description:	The identifier of a MARKET contained in or associated in some other way with another MARKET.
Domain:	Any valid "market-id".
Col Name:	sub_mkt_id
Data Type:	market-id

tag-date

Description:	The date on which the TAG was written.
Domain:	Valid dates after 1/1/89.
Col Name:	tag_dt
Format:	DATE

tag-line-number

Description:	An identifier of an individual entry (line) on the TAG.
Domain:	Any positive integer.
Col Name:	tag_ln_num
Format:	INTEGER

tag-number

Description:	The unique identifier of a TAG.
Comment:	This identifier is assigned by Monterey Foods.
Domain:	Any positive integer.
Col Name:	tag_num
Format:	INTEGER

tag-total-payable

Description:	The total amount payable for purchases represented by the TAG, stated in dollars and cents.
Domain:	Valid decimal numbers in the range of 0.00 to 9999.99.
Col Name:	tag_tot_amt
Format:	DECIMAL (6.2)

telephone-number

Description:	A public system phone number, including a possible extension number at which someone or some thing can be contacted.
Comment:	This is a group attribute established to contain a group phone number plus an extension, and provides a way to distinguish between a situation in which a generic (able to accommodate any kind) as opposed to a specific type of phone number is needed.
Example:	(415) 555-1212 Ext. 3253
Col Name:	tel_phn_num
Group:	phone-number
	phone-number-extension

timestamp

Description:	A recording of the date and time.
Comment:	This attribute is established as a base for definition of all timestamps in the model. Each separate timestamp (for example, "sale-timestamp" or "lot-disposition-timestamp") is declared to be a data type of this common base. Each then acquires the physical format and, unless otherwise specified, the domain of timestamp.
Example:	17OCT198915041079
Format:	TIMESTAMP
Domain:	Any valid date and time expressed as DDMMMYYYYHHMMSSHH.

variety-id

Description:	The unique identifier of a VARIETY.
Domain:	Any nonblank character string of length 6.
Col Name:	var_id
Format:	CHARACTER (3)

variety-name

Description: The name by which the VARIETY is known to Monterey Foods.
Comment: Valencia (orange), navel (orange)
Domain: Any nonblank character string up to length 40.
Col Name: var_nam
Format: VARCHAR (40)

F.3 LEVERAGE STRUCTURED MODELING LANGUAGE FOR THE KEY BASED MODEL

VIEW MONTEREY-FOODS-KEY-BASED-MODEL

```
GENERAL INFORMATION
    SHORT NAME MARKETKB
    LEVEL KB

STRUCTURE

    ENTITY CLASSIFYING-AGENCY
        KEY
            CLASSIFYING-AGENCY-ID
        ENDK
        CLASSIFYING-AGENCY-NAME
    ENDE

    ENTITY PRODUCT-CLASS
        KEY
            PRODUCT-CLASS-ID
        ENDK
        CLASSIFYING-AGENCY "establishes" NONULL
        PRODUCT-CLASS-NAME
    ENDE

    ENTITY MARKET
        KEY
            MARKET-ID
        ENDK
        INVERSION ENTRY 1
            MARKET-NAME
        ENDI
    ENDE
```

```
ENTITY MARKET-ASSOCIATION
    KEY
        MARKET "contains"
            ROLE CONTAINING-MARKET-ID FOR MARKET-ID
        MARKET "is part of"
            ROLE SUB-MARKET-ID FOR MARKET-ID
        MARKET-ASSOCIATION-TYPE
    ENDK
ENDE

ENTITY HOUSE
    KEY
        HOUSE-NAME
    ENDK
    MARKET "contains" NONULL
    HOUSE-ADDRESS
    HOUSE-CONTACT-NAME
    HOUSE-TELEPHONE-NUMBER
ENDE

ENTITY PRODUCT
    KEY
        PRODUCT-ID
    ENDK
    INVERSION ENTRY 1
        PRODUCT-NAME
    ENDI
ENDE

ENTITY VARIETY
    KEY
        PRODUCT "is available as"
        VARIETY-ID
    ENDK
    INVERSION ENTRY 1
        VARIETY-NAME
    ENDI
    SEASON-START-DATE
    SEASON-END-DATE
ENDE

ENTITY PRODUCT-CLASSIFICATION
    KEY
        VARIETY "is contained in"
        PRODUCT-CLASS "contains"
        PRODUCT-CLASSIFICATION-DATE
    ENDK
ENDE
ENTITY STALL
    KEY
        HOUSE "contains"
        STALL-NAME
    ENDK
```

```
        PRODUCT-CLASS "is primary class of"
            ROLE STALL-PRIMARY-PRODUCT-CLASS-ID
              FOR PRODUCT-CLASS-ID
        INVERSION ENTRY 1
            STALL-NAME
        ENDI
        STALL-CONTACT-NAME
        STALL-TELEPHONE-NUMBER
    ENDE

    ENTITY HOUSE-VARIETY
        KEY
            STALL "sells" P
            VARIETY "is sold as"
            HOUSE-VARIETY-TIMESTAMP
        ENDK
        INVERSION ENTRY 1
            PRODUCT-ID
            VARIETY-ID
        ENDI
        HOUSE-VARIETY-AVAILABILITY
    ENDE

    ENTITY STATEMENT
        KEY
            HOUSE "issues"
            STATEMENT-PERIOD-ID
        ENDK
        STATEMENT-DATE
        STATEMENT-TERMS
    ENDE

    ENTITY STATEMENT-LINE
        KEY
            STATEMENT "contains"
                ROLE STATEMENT-HOUSE-NAME FOR HOUSE-NAME
            STATEMENT-LINE-NUMBER
        ENDK
        STATEMENT-LINE-TYPE
        STATEMENT-LINE-AMOUNT
        TAG "appears on"
            ROLE STATEMENT-HOUSE-NAME FOR SELLING-HOUSE-NAME
        LISTED-TAG-NUMBER
    ENDE

    ENTITY TAG
        KEY
            STALL "issues"
(*)               ROLE SELLING-HOUSE-NAME FOR HOUSE-NAME
(*)               ROLE SELLING-STALL-NAME FOR STALL-NAME
            INVOICE NUMBER
        ENDK
        TAG-DATE
```

```
                    TAG-TOTAL-PAYABLE
                    INVERSION ENTRY 1
                        INVOICE NUMBER
                    ENDI
                    INVERSION ENTRY 2
                        TAG-NUMBER
                    ENDI
                ENDE

                ENTITY TAG-LINE
                    KEY
                        TAG "contains"
                        TAG-LINE-NUMBER
                    ENDK
                ENDE

                ENTITY LOT
                    KEY
                        LOT-NUMBER
                        TAG-LINE "describes" 1
(*)                         ROLE LOT-HOUSE-NAME FOR SELLING-HOUSE-NAME
(*)                         ROLE LOT-STALL-NAME FOR SELLING-STALL-NAME
                        HOUSE-VARIETY "is purchased as"
(*)                         ROLE LOT-HOUSE-NAME FOR HOUSE-NAME
(*)                         ROLE LOT-STALL-NAME FOR STALL-NAME
                    ENDK
                    INVERSION ENTRY 1
                        LOT-NUMBER
                    ENDI
                    LOT-COUNT
                    LOT-WEIGHT
                    LOT-UNIT-COST
                    INVERSION ENTRY 2
                        LOT-STALE-DATE
                    ENDI
                ENDE

                ENTITY STORE
                    KEY
                        STORE-ID
                    ENDK
                    STORE-ADDRESS
                    STORE-PUBLIC-PHONE-NUMBER
                    STORE-OFFICE-PHONE-NUMBER
                ENDE

                ENTITY STORE-LOT
                    KEY
                        STORE "receives"
                        LOT "is distributed to"
                    ENDK
                    STORE-LOT-WEIGHT
                    STORE-LOT-COUNT
                ENDE
```

```
ENTITY REGION
    KEY
        REGION-ID
    ENDK
    STORE "contains"
        ROLE REGION-STORE-ID FOR STORE-ID
ENDE

ENTITY EMPLOYEE
    KEY
        EMPLOYEE-ID
    ENDK
    INVERSION ENTRY 1
        EMPLOYEE-NAME
    ENDI
    EMPLOYEE-SOCIAL-SECURITY-NUMBER
    STORE "is the primary store of"
        ROLE EMPLOYEE-STORE-ID FOR STORE-ID
ENDE

ENTITY CASH-REGISTER
    KEY
        REGISTER-ID
    ENDK
    STORE "contains"
        ROLE REGISTER-STORE-ID FOR STORE-ID
ENDE

ENTITY CASHIER
    KEY
        CASH-REGISTER "is operated by"
        EMPLOYEE "acts as"
        CASHIER-START-TIMESTAMP
    ENDK
    CASHIER-END-TIMESTAMP
ENDE

ENTITY REGION-RESPONSIBILITY
    KEY
        REGION "has assigned"
        EMPLOYEE "responsible for"
            ROLE REGION-EMPLOYEE-ID FOR EMPLOYEE-ID
        REGION-RESPONSIBILITY-TYPE
        REGION-RESPONSIBILITY-DATE
    ENDK
ENDE
```

```
ENTITY ASSIGNED-LOT
    KEY
        PRODUCT-ID
        VARIETY-ID
        REGION-ID
        LOT-ASSIGNMENT-TIMESTAMP
    ENDK
    STORE-LOT "is assigned to" NONULL
    REGION-RESPONSIBILITY "is assigned" NONULL
    ASSIGNED-LOT-PRIORITY
    ASSIGNED-LOT-COUNT
    ASSIGNED-LOT-WEIGHT
    ASSIGNED-LOT-SALE-PRICE
    ASSIGNED-LOT-LOCATION
ENDE
ENTITY SALE
    KEY
        SALE-TIMESTAMP
    ENDK
    CASHIER "sells" NONULL
ENDE
ENTITY DISPOSED-LOT
    KEY
        LOT-DISPOSITION-TIMESTAMP
        PRODUCT-ID
        VARIETY-ID
        REGION-ID
    ENDK
    ASSIGNED-LOT "becomes" NONULL
    DISPOSED-LOT-COUNT
    DISPOSED-LOT-WEIGHT
    LOT-DISPOSITION-TYPE
    GENERALIZATION BY LOT-DISPOSITION-TYPE OF
        SOLD-LOT
        SPOILED-LOT
    ENDG
ENDE
ENTITY SPOILED-LOT
    CATEGORY BY LOT-DISPOSITION-TYPE
        OF DISPOSED-LOT
    SPOILED-LOT-VALUE
ENDE
ENTITY SOLD-LOT
    CATEGORY BY LOT-DISPOSITION-TYPE
        OF DISPOSED-LOT
(*)     ROLE SOLD-LOT-TIMESTAMP
(*)         FOR LOT-DISPOSITION-TIMESTAMP
    SALE P "includes" NONULL
(*)         ROLE SOLD-LOT-TIMESTAMP
(*)             FOR SALE-TIMESTAMP
ENDE
```

```
ENTITY CUSTOMER
    KEY
        CUSTOMER-NAME
    ENDK
ENDE


ENTITY CUSTOMER-CLASS
    KEY
        CUSTOMER-CLASS-ID
    ENDK
    CUSTOMER-CLASS-DESCRIPTION
ENDE

ENTITY CUSTOMER-CLASSIFICATION
    KEY
        CUSTOMER-CLASS "contains"
        CUSTOMER "is a member of"
        CUSTOMER-CLASSIFICATION-TIMESTAMP
    ENDK
    CUSTOMER-CLASSIFICATION-TYPE
ENDE

ENTITY CUSTOMER-REQUEST
    KEY
        VARIETY "is requested by"
        CUSTOMER "requests"
        CUSTOMER-REQUEST-TIMESTAMP
    ENDK
    CUSTOMER-REQUEST-DATE
    CUSTOMER-REQUEST-COUNT
    CUSTOMER-REQUEST-WEIGHT
    INVERSION ENTRY 1
        CUSTOMER-REQUEST-STATUS
    ENDI
ENDE

ENTITY CUSTOMER-PRODUCT-INTEREST
    KEY
        PRODUCT-CLASSIFICATION "has interest of"
        CUSTOMER-CLASS "has interest in"
        CUSTOMER-INTEREST-TYPE
    ENDK
    CUSTOMER-INTEREST-START-DATE
    CUSTOMER-INTEREST-END-DATE
    CUSTOMER-INTEREST-DEGREE
ENDE
```

```
    ENTITY FAMILY
        KEY
            FAMILY-ID
        ENDK
        FAMILY-NAME
        FAMILY-ADDRESS
        FAMILY-PHONE-NUMBER
    ENDE

    ENTITY FAMILY-MEMBERSHIP
        KEY
            FAMILY "has as members"
            CUSTOMER "is a member of"
            FAMILY-MEMBERSHIP-TYPE
            FAMILY-MEMBERSHIP-TIMESTAMP
        ENDK
        FAMILY-MEMBERSHIP-START-DATE
        FAMILY-MEMBERSHIP-END-DATE
    ENDE

    ENTITY CUSTOMER-PAYMENT
        KEY
            FAMILY-MEMBERSHIP "buys"
            SALE "is sold to"
            CUSTOMER-PAYMENT-IDENTIFIER
        ENDK
        CUSTOMER-PAYMENT-DATE
        CUSTOMER-PAYMENT-AMOUNT
        CUSTOMER-PAYMENT-CHECK-NUMBER
        CUSTOMER-PAYMENT-CHECK-STATUS
        INVERSION ENTRY 1
            CUSTOMER-NAME
            FAMILY-ID
        ENDI
        INVERSION ENTRY 2
            CUSTOMER-NAME
        ENDI
        INVERSION ENTRY 3
            FAMILY-ID
        ENDI
    ENDE

    ENDS

  ENDV
```

NOTE: THE LINES MARKED WITH AN ASTERISK (*) REPRESENT EXTENSIONS
       OF THE STANDARD IDEF1X UNIFICATION ASSERTIONS.

APPENDIX G

IBM'S REPOSITORY MODELING LANGUAGE

In June 1990, IBM released the first public version of its Repository Manager (RM) product. The repository is a super data dictionary and is the cornerstone of the emerging IBM AD/Cycle application development environment [1]. The RM release includes a description of the information modeling technique, one similar to IDEF1X, used to define the structure of information to be managed in the repository environment [2].

This Appendix provides a brief overview of the IBM modeling constructs. It compares basic IDEF1X modeling constructs to their IBM equivalents, where they exist, and to approximations using IBM constructs where there is no direct translation between the languages.

To begin, here is the video store model introduced in Chapter 4 (Fig. 4.1) drawn with the IBM notation. Figure G.1 shows an approximate translation* that has the same shape as the IDEF1X model. Figure G.2 shows another translation that takes advantage of the IBM concept of a relationship participating in a relationship. The remainder of this Appendix describes the constructs used in the video store model as well as others available in the IBM modeling language.

G.1 IBM ENTITY TYPES

As with IDEF1X, an *entity type* in the IBM language represents a collection of entities. Throughout this book, we substituted the terms *entity* and *instance*

---

*This first translation is not entirely correct since the IBM language does not allow a dependent entity with two parents. The MOVIE_RENTAL_RECORD and RECORD_INVOLVEMENT entities violate this rule.

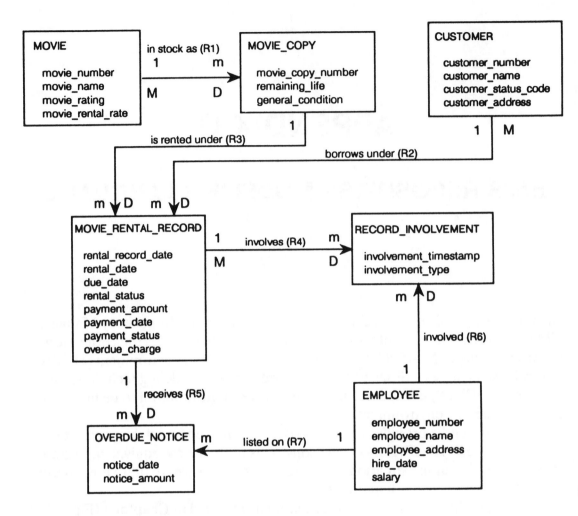

Legend: The relationship types shown above have
alphanumeric identifiers that correspond to these names:

(R1) MOVIE_is_in_stock_as_MOVIE_COPY
(R2) CUSTOMER_borrows_under_MOVIE_RENTAL_RECORD
(R3) MOVIE_COPY_is_rented_under_MOVIE_RENTAL_RECORD
(R4) MOVIE_RENTAL_RECORD_has_involvement_of_RECORD_INVOLVEMENT
(R5) MOVIE_RENTAL_RECORD_may_receive_OVERDUE_NOTICE
(R6) EMPLOYEE_is_involved_with_RECORD_INVOLVEMENT
(R7) EMPLOYEE_listed_on_OVERDUE_NOTICE

Figure G.1. IBM Video Store Model, Version 1 Approximation.

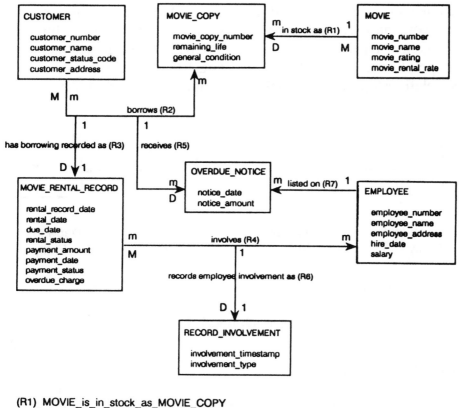

(R1) MOVIE_is_in_stock_as_MOVIE_COPY
(R2) CUSTOMER_borrows_MOVIE_COPY
(R3) CUSTOMER_has_borrowing_recorded_as_MOVIE_RENTAL_RECORD
(R4) MOVIE_RENTAL_RECORD_involves_EMPLOYEE
(R5) CUSTOMER_receives_OVERDUE_NOTICE
(R6) MOVIE_RENTAL_RECORD_records_employee_involvement_as_RECORD_INVOLVEMENT
(R7) EMPLOYEE_listed_on_OVERDUE_NOTICE

Figure G.2. IBM Video Store Model, Version 2.

for *entity type* and *entity,* but the concepts are identical. Thus, an IBM entity type is an IDEF1X entity and an IBM entity is an IDEF1X entity instance. The IBM and equivalent IDEF1X notation for independent and dependent entities is shown in Fig. G.3. Recall that with IDEF1X, the shape of an entity distinguishes between identification independence and identification dependence ("square" boxes and "roundy" boxes). In the IBM language, identification dependence is designated by placing the letter D beside the relationship that contributes to the dependent entity's identification.

Unlike an IDEF1X dependent entity, an IBM dependent entity type can have only one parent. That parent, however, can be a relationship type. This allows an entity type to be identification dependent on more than one parent entity type. For example, MOVIE_RENTAL_RECORD in Fig. G.2 is dependent on the relationship between CUSTOMER and MOVIE_COPY.

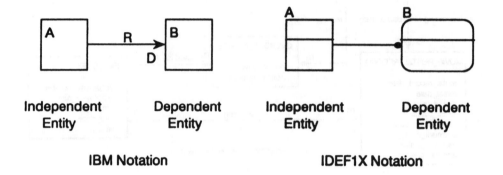

IBM Notation   IDEF1X Notation

Figure G.3. Independent and Dependent Entities.

G.2 IBM ATTRIBUTES

As with IDEF1X, an attribute in the IBM language represents a property or characteristic of the entity type. Attributes, however, cannot be designated as foreign keys, alternate keys, or inversion entries. Other techniques are used to declare these properties.

G.3 IBM ENTITY KEYS

Except for dependent entities, IBM entity keys consist of only one attribute. The key attribute is the first one listed for the entity. All IBM independent entities are identified by their own keys. IBM dependent entity keys are qualified (in the repository, not in the graphic notation) by the keys of the dependent entity's parents. These parent foreign keys are not shown in the diagram.

Keys can be system assigned and displayed as such in the model (that is, SYSTEM_KEY *). System assigned keys are surrogates. IBM models look very much like IDEF1X models in which all relationships are nonidentifying, and all keys are either single entity attributes or surrogate keys.

Figure G.4 shows how IBM entity keys are displayed. The IBM constructs are shown at the left and the equivalent IDEF1X constructs are shown at the right.

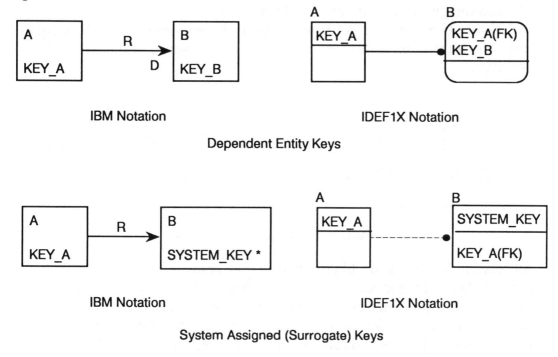

Figure G.4. Primary Keys.

G.4 IBM RELATIONSHIP TYPES

Unlike the IDEF1X relationship, an IBM relationship type represents a *thing* that can be directly involved in another relationship type. The IBM relationship type line is not the same as the solid or dashed line used in IDEF1X to represent a relationship. It is more like a diamond (the relationship symbol) in a Chen style model. An IBM relationship type represents a pairing of the keys of the two participating entity types (or relationship types). It is an IDEF1X associative entity that contains only primary key attributes and in which each primary key attribute is a foreign key.

IBM relationship types do not cause primary key attributes of a parent (called the *source* of the relationship) to migrate to a child (called the *target*). The child entity does not contain the foreign key attribute(s). As you will see in the comparison summaries below, IDEF1X can, by using associative entities to represent all relationships, be forced to emulate the IBM constructs. However, many of the constructs that represent the relationship as an associative entity are semantically equivalent in IDEF1X to simpler constructs that take advantage of the migration of foreign keys.

Figure G.5 compares an IBM relationship type with its IDEF1X equivalent. The translation is further specified by the *properties* of the IBM relationship type.

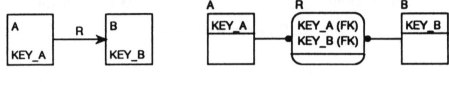

Figure G.5. Simple Relationships.

All relationship types are binary, that is they connect exactly two constructs. Either or both of these constructs may themselves be relationships. Figure G.6 shows the five possibilities. All relationship types are also *directed;* that is, there is a *from* direction and a *to* direction. Each relationship type has a separate name for each direction (for example, "uses" and "is used by"). These are called the *primary name* and the *inverse name.* Note that in Fig. G.6 the arrowhead does *not* represent the many end of the relationship (either or both ends can be many). It simply indicates the direction in which to read the relationship.

G.5 IBM RELATIONSHIP PROPERTIES

The IBM language contains a formal notion of relationship instance as well as of entity instance. A relationship instance connects the key attributes of the two entity or relationship instances. Each relationship type has four properties: Instance Control, Mandatory, Controlling, and Ordered Set. Together, the Instance Control and Mandatory properties form the concept of cardinality found in IDEF1X. The Controlling and Ordered Set properties have no direct IDEF1X equivalents.

Entity Type to Entity Type

Entity Type to Self (Recursive Relationship)

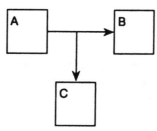

Entity Type to Relationship Type

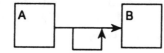

Relationship Type to Self (Recursive Relationship)

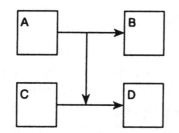

Relationship Type to Relationship Type

Figure G.6. Binary Relationships.

G.5.1 Instance Control Property

The Instance Control property specifies how many instances of the relationship may exist between the source and the target. The symbols 1 or m are placed at each end of the relationship and have the meanings shown in Fig. G.7.

```
           1          1
     ------------------->
```

A single instance of the source may be related to a single instance
of the target (thus, there may be at most one instance of the
relationship type).

```
           1          m
     ------------------->
```

A single instance of the source may be related to zero, one, or more
instances of the target (thus, there may be many instances of the
relationship type).

```
           m          1
     ------------------->
```

Zero, one, or more instances of the source may be related to at
most one instance of the target (thus, there may be many instances
of the relationship type).

```
           m          m
     ------------------->
```

Zero, one, or more instances of the source may be related to zero,
one, or more instances of the target (thus, there may be many
instances of the relationship type).

Figure G.7. Instance Control Property.

G.5.2 Mandatory Property

For a relationship instance to exist, an instance of the source and an instance
of the target to which the relationship instance connects must also exist (for
either not to exist would be equivalent to saying something is connected to
nothing). The Mandatory property of the relationship type specifies whether
a relationship instance must exist if either or both the source and target
instances exist. In IDEF1X, the concept of "mandatory" is represented by the
1 and P symbols at the many end of the relationship and the absence of a
diamond at the one end of a nonidentifying relationship.

   If a relationship type is mandatory for its source, an instance of the source
can exist only if an instance of the relationship type also exists. To specify
"mandatory for source," the symbol M is placed at the end of the relationship
type next to the source. If a relationship type is mandatory for its target, an
instance of the target can exist only if an instance of the relationship type also
exists. To specify "mandatory for target," the symbol M is placed at the end

of the relationship type next to the target. The notation and its meaning are summarized in Fig. G.8.

```
                        -------------------->
```

Instances of source and target may exist independently.

```
                        -------------------->
                                  M
```

An instance of the target may exist only if an instance of the relationship type also exists. Thus, the source instance must exist for the target instance to exist.

```
                        -------------------->
                          M
```

An instance of the source may exist only if an instance of the relationship type also exists. Thus, there must also exist at least one target instance for the source instance to exist.

```
                        -------------------->
                          M         M
```

An instance of the source may exist only if an instance of the relationship type also exists. An instance of the target may exist only if an instance of the relationship type also exists. Thus, an instance of the target must exist for each instance of the source, and vice versa.

Figure G.8. Mandatory Property.

G.5.3 Controlling Property

The Controlling property is used to state delete rules. Figure G.9 shows the first delete rule: cascade. Placing the Controlling property symbol (C) at the target end of a relationship specifies that the target instance is to be deleted when the relationship instance is deleted. Therefore, deleting a source instance will cascade down to the target, since the removal of a source instance will cause removal of all relationship instances for which it is the source. Placing the symbol at the source end of the relationship specifies that the source instance is to be deleted when the relationship instance is deleted. Deleting a target instance, therefore, will cascade up to the source.

Cascade down is a meaningful rule. Cascade up is a bit questionable and specifies that deletion of a target entity instance should result in the deletion of its source entity instance. What to do with remaining target instances also dependent on the deleted source entity instance is left unspecified.

Figure G.9. Cascade Delete Rule.

Figure G.10 shows the second delete rule, set null. The absence of the controlling property at the target of a relationship type coupled with the absence of the mandatory property at its target emulates a set null delete rule. In this situation, if the source entity instance is deleted, the relationship instance will also be deleted. The absence of the controlling property on the target entity type means that the target entity instance will remain. The absence of the mandatory property on the target entity type for the relationship says that this is proper; that is, the target entity instance may exist without a relationship instance and therefore without a source entity instance.

```
1                  m
-------------------->
```

Figure G.10. Set Null Delete Rule.

The third delete rule, restrict, is shown in Fig. G.11 and is accomplished via a combination of contradictions. It looks like the emulation of set null except that the mandatory property is present for the target of the relationship type. An attempt to delete a source entity instance where a relationship instance exists, would require that the relationship instance also be deleted, resulting in a target entity instance without the required relationship instance. Since this is not allowed (the relationship is mandatory on the target), the delete is, in effect, restricted.

```
          1              m
          --------------------->
                         M
```

Figure G.11. Restrict Delete Rule.

The presence or absence of the Controlling property specifies a delete rule. Without an extension such as that introduced in Chapter 15 (Figs. 15.11 and 15.12), IDEF1X cannot state delete rules.

G.5.4 Ordered Set Property

The Ordered Set property determines a retrieval sequence for multiple target entity instances associated with the same source instance. It has little to do with a logical data structure. Rather, it is a convenience that helps in the construction of IBM external schemas, called logical views. There is no IDEF1X equivalent for the Ordered Set property.

G.6 IBM TO IDEF1X MODEL TRANSLATIONS— INDEPENDENT ENTITIES

When only the Instance Control and Mandatory properties are used in IBM models, direct translation into the IDEF1X language is possible. Figures G.12 through G.14 show these translations. The IBM constructs are shown at the left and the IDEF1X constructs are shown at the right.*

For one-to-many relationships, there are two semantically equivalent IDEF1X translations. If the IBM model being translated contains a structure in which a relationship is itself the source or target of another relationship, the first alternative must be used (the relationship is represented by the associative entity R) so the participation can be shown. If the IBM relationship does not participate in another relationship, the second (simpler) alternative can be used.

---

*Alternate keys are not shown in the IDEF1X diagrams in the figure. They are implied by the 1 and Z cardinality declarations.

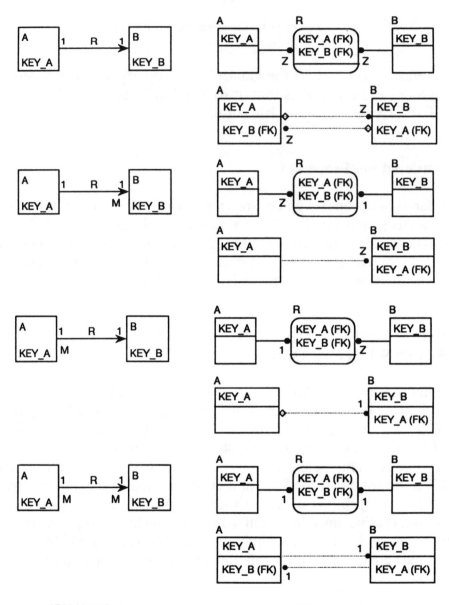

IBM Notation   IDEF1X Notation

Figure G.12.   One-to-One Relationships.

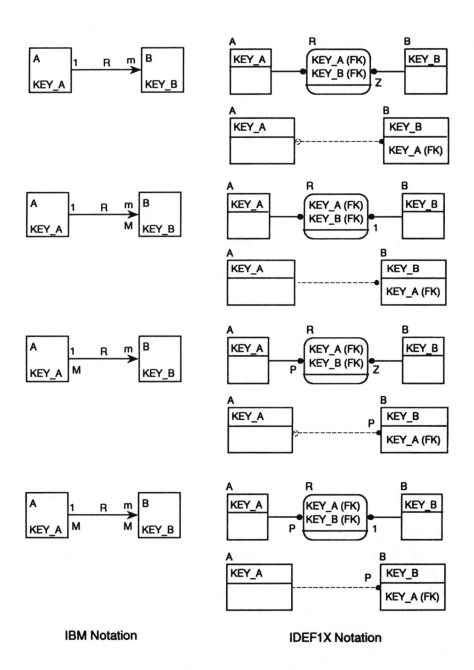

IBM Notation   IDEF1X Notation

Figure G.13.   One-to-Many Relationships.

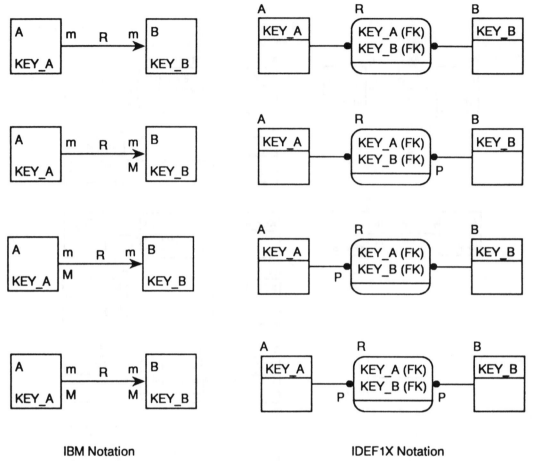

IBM Notation   IDEF1X Notation

Figure G.14. Many-to-Many Relationships.

G.7 IBM TO IDEF1X MODEL TRANSLATIONS—DEPENDENT ENTITIES

Like IDEF1X, the IBM language includes the notion of a dependent entity—one that inherits part of its key from another entity. Unlike IDEF1X, an IBM dependent entity may have only one identifying parent. This parent can, however, be a relationship type, allowing multiple parent entities to contribute to the key of a dependent entity. The D symbol designates a dependent entity, and implies a source Instance Control property of 1, a target Mandatory property of M, and a target Controlling property of C.

Figure G.15 shows the translation from the IBM notation for dependent entities to the IDEF1X notation. In the figure, the IDEF1X construct must include the entity R if we wish to emulate an entity with a two-part primary key, with each part a foreign key. The figure includes the last two constructs for completeness only; although they can be drawn, they have no valid meaning.

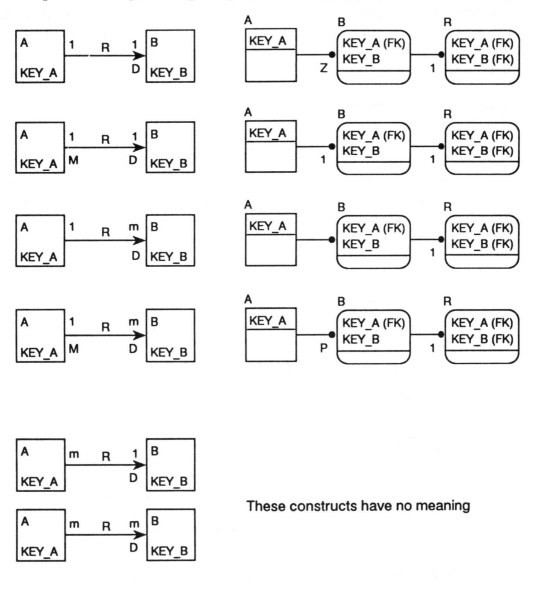

These constructs have no meaning

IBM Notation   IDEF1X Notation

Figure G.15. Dependent Entities.

G.8 GENERALIZATION HIERARCHIES

The IBM modeling language does not contain a graphic construct for a generalization hierarchy. Rather, a set of one-to-one relationship types must be established between an entity type that serves as a generic parent and others that serve as categories. Because the entity types are not treated as a complete hierarchy, neither the inheritance property of a generalization hierarchy nor the existence constraints asserted by the IDEF1X structure (for example, exclusive or) are evident in the IBM graphics. The IBM language emulation of a generalization hierarchy is equivalent to describing the structure in IDEF1X as a set of one-to-zero-or-one ("is a Z") relationships (see Chapter 7, Section 7.2.2).

Figure G.16 shows an example of an IBM language emulation of a generalization hierarchy. The IBM notation is shown at the left with the IDEF1X notation at the right. Unlike the IDEF1X construct, in the IBM language, a key may be assigned to a category that is not the key of the generic parent.

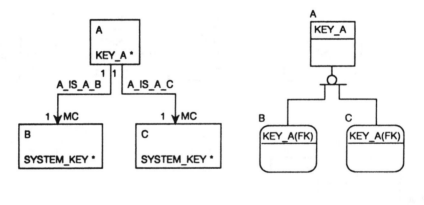

IBM Notation   IDEF1X Notation

Figure G.16. Generalization Hierarchies.

G.9 ALTERNATE KEYS AND INVERSION ENTRIES

The IBM language supports alternate identification of entities differently from IDEF1X. Alternate keys cannot be directly shown in an entity type. Rather, a separate entity type must be added to hold the alternate key, with a one-to-one relationship to the entity type identified by the alternate key. Figure G.17 shows this construct.

In Fig. G.17, the IDEF1X diagram at the right indicates that a CUSTOMER has SSN as an alternate key. Both the primary key and the alternate key are shown in the CUSTOMER entity. The IBM diagram at the left contains two entity types: The CUST_SSN entity type and the CUST_SSN_CUSTOMER_L relationship type are required to specify that a CUSTOMER has a SSN that serves as an alternate key. The use of the separate entity type and the relationship type ending in L (for link) follows the IBM conventions.

Note that as in IDEF1X, the IBM alternate key may be null. The IBM diagram, however, also seems to say that a CUST_SSN entity instance may exist without a corresponding CUSTOMER entity instance. This appears to mean that an alternate key may exist for which there is no corresponding entity instance.

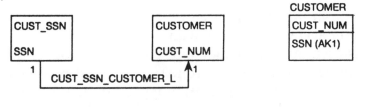

IBM Notation   IDEF1X Notation

Figure G.17. Alternate Keys.

Inversion entries in IDEF1X are something of a physical world compromise, and represent access indexes for an entity. They can be emulated in the IBM language by a structure similar to that in Fig. G.17. If we wish to declare that SSN is an inversion entry for CUSTOMER, we can place an m (rather than a 1) at the CUSTOMER end of the relationship type.

G.10 CONSTRAINTS, POLICIES, AND NOTES

Policies in the IBM modeling language are used to state and enforce constraints. For example, the emulation of an IDEF1X generalization hierarchy (Fig. G.16) is completed by declaring a policy that ensures that for each entity A there is exactly one entity B or one entity C but not neither or both. Policies are used to declare business rules that cannot be stated with the graphic language and to ensure that the data held in the repository database adheres to the declared constraints.

Four types of policies are specified: *Derivation policies* are used to assign values to attributes. *Integrity policies* are used to ensure that attributes take values only from specified domains (the domain is declared by the integrity policy). *Security policies* are used to protect against unauthorized processing or access. *Trigger policies* make it possible to automatically call functions based on the state of the data.

Policies can be stated in IDEF1X with notes. The main difference between the IBM and IDEF1X standards is that IBM policies are stated in a machine-interpretable language, REXX.* IDEF1X notes can also be stated in a machine-interpretable language, but the language is not specified as it is for IBM; free-form English is more commonly used.

G.11 AGGREGATION TYPES

An aggregation type in the IBM repository modeling language represents a template for a query against repository data. It is not a modeling construct; it is an access construct. An aggregation type consists of a root entity type (or root) together with zero or more subordinate entity and relationship types collected into a tree structure. Aggregation types can be used by tools that access repository data, including an extended version of IBM's Query Management Facility product [3].

G.12 STRENGTHS AND WEAKNESSES

The IBM repository modeling language is quite powerful. It is intended to be an active language in that the models represent the business rules that control repository data objects, and provide the basis for defining tool interfaces at the conceptual rather than physical level. To fully judge the capabilities of the language, however, requires that we separate the language itself from its use with the IBM Repository Manager product.

Although specifically designed to support the repository, the IBM language can also be used to prepare business models. In a single business, it is possible to use the IBM language to define repository information structures and some other language, like IDEF1X, to define business information structures. Deciding whether to use the IBM language in a business situation requires that

---

*Restructured EXtended eXecutor.

we understand its strengths and weaknesses. Some of these are covered below, using IDEF1X for comparison.

G.12.1 Strengths of the IBM Language

- IBM language, including its policy capability, is sufficiently robust to state most business information requirements. All necessary entity and relationship types are provided, as are the required cardinality properties and insert/replace/delete rules. Support for IRD rules is stronger in the IBM language than in basic IDEF1X.

- IBM policies allow the formal definition of many complex constraints not directly declarable in the graphic language. This formality is stronger than the informal IDEF1X notes.

- The IBM models are a bit more readable than IDEF1X models, especially in the area of relationships among relationships. For example, in Fig. G.2, we can clearly see that a CUSTOMER receives zero or more OVERDUE_NO-TICEs (the relationship name for R5 tells us this directly). Compare this to Fig. 4.1, the IDEF1X video store version. In the IDEF1X version, we can still see that a CUSTOMER may receive OVERDUE-NOTICEs, but this may not be as obvious since we need to read through the MOVIE-RENTAL-RECORD to see it.

G.12.2 Weaknesses of the IBM Language

- The IBM language was developed specifically for the IBM Repository Manager product. It may not be adopted by other vendors. If you are not a user of the IBM products, it is not clear that the new language has sufficient benefits to replace other available languages used to develop business information models.

- The IBM language does not explicitly support foreign keys in entities and does not require unique attribute names. It is therefore difficult to see how formal normalization support can be provided for IBM models as it is for IDEF1X models.

- The IBM language forces the extensive use of surrogate keys. Because foreign keys are not present in IBM entities, the role name and unification (common ancestor) assertions described in Chapters 8 and 9 cannot be made. Recall the dilemma encountered in Fig. 9.21, the transaction example. In that figure, the use of surrogate keys led to a situation in which an incorrect business rule appeared to be stated by the graphics, requiring a separate constraint statement (as a note) to ensure that the correct rule was recorded.

- The choice of the REXX language for policies appears to limit the language to IBM environments. Policies described in REXX code may be somewhat difficult to discuss with business clients who are not REXX programmers.

- The IBM language is not well suited for describing some detailed models in the Zachman Model of the Information System row (models in which foreign keys are used extensively to describe business rules) and cannot be used for models in the Technology Model row. IDEF1X is stronger here in that it can be used both for technology independent (Model of the Information System) and technology dependent (Technology Model) descriptions. Adopting the IBM language for describing business and information system models therefore requires that another language be chosen for the Technology Model row.

- Composite keys are not supported by the IBM language. All IBM entity keys consist of a single attribute. A business decision to identify an entity by a multipart key cannot be directly supported by the IBM language.

G.13 ANALYSIS

Although they are just beginning to emerge, repositories, especially IBM's, will change the market and technical direction for languages like IDEF1X and the products that support it. Information modeling languages will be judged by the degree to which they subsume or are compatible with directions of IBM and other major vendors. Long term, most organizations will look only to these major vendors to provide integration platforms like the repository but will look elsewhere for the best tools and techniques to plug into that development environment.

IBM's Repository Manager contains various functions and capabilities, one of which allows information models to be defined, instantiated, and populated. The modeling language is a combination of entity relationship modeling plus three extensions: relationships to relationships, policies (for constraint enforcement), and aggregation types. Relationships to relationships are a matter of taste. Policies are a precursor to object-oriented methods and rules. Aggregation types are important to physical access to the repository, but their meaning as a modeling construct is obscure.

The repository includes a limited concept of "object" but is not truly "object oriented" as objects are defined on top of the information model and are not part of the modeling language itself. The IBM repository modeling language will evolve along with the repository product. As Segawa, the architect of RM wrote, "We continue to work on extending the conceptual view data modeling constructs to be semantically richer. . . . The concepts of entity, entity aggregation, and object will continue to converge, with eventual integration with the general concepts of entity generalization." [4]

G.14 REFERENCES

[1]   IBM Corporation. *Repository Manager/MVS: General Information,* Document No. GC26-4608-0, 1989.

[2]   IBM Corporation. *Repository Manager/MVS: Repository Modeling Guide,* Document No. GC26-4619, 1990.

[3]   IBM Corporation. *Query Management Facility: Accessing Repository Data,* Document No. SC26-4579-0, 1990.

[4]   Segawa, J.M. "Repository Manager Technology," *IBM Systems Journal,* Vol. 29, No. 2 (1990).

APPENDIX H

ANSWERS TO SELECTED REVIEW EXERCISES

H.1 CHAPTER 1

1.1 Q. What is a database?

A. The minimum answer is "an organized collection of data values."

1.3 Q. Which schema does information modeling address?

A. Information modeling primarily addresses the *conceptual schema,* although it can be used to some degree to define *internal* (relational table definition) and *external schemas* (views in relational systems).

1.5 Q. Are there schemas for function as well as for data? If so, what are they?

A. Yes. These are often represented as logical dataflow diagrams, flow charts, program language statements, and object code. The separation of internal, conceptual, and external representations is not as well defined for function as it is for data.

1.6 Q. Why are schemas threatening? Whom do they threaten?

A. There are no precise answers to this. Some database analysts and designers find schemas threatening because they require an engineering (rather than artistic) approach to design and because, apparently, some control is given up by the designer.

H.2 CHAPTER 2

2.1 Q. For each of the following system development products, processes, and tools, identify the cells of the Zachman Framework in which they are most commonly represented.

PRODUCTS

A	Preliminary Requirements	F	Application Software / Job Control Language
B	Initial System Solutions	G	Area Information Models
C	Detailed Requirements	H	Project Information Models
D	Functional Specifications	I	Physical Database Specifications
E	Hardware / Software Specifications	J	Design Templates

A.

INFORMATION SYSTEMS ARCHITECTURE - A FRAMEWORK

	DATA	FUNCTION	NETWORK
OBJECTIVES/ SCOPE	List of Things Important to the Business	List of Processes the Business Performs	List of Locations in which the Business Operates
MODEL OF THE BUSINESS	Entity = Class of Business Thing e.g., Entity Relationship Diagram Ent. = Business Entity Rel. = Business Rule	Process = Class of Business Process e.g., Data Flow Diagram Proc. = Busi. Process I/O = Bus. Resources (including Info.)	Node = Business Location e.g., Logistics Network Node = Business Unit Link = Bus. Relationship (Org., Product Info.)
MODEL OF THE INFORMATION SYSTEM	e.g., Data Model Ent. = Data Entity Rel. = Data Rel.	e.g., Function Diagram Proc. = Appl. Functions I/O = User Views (set of data elements)	e.g., Distributed Sys. Arch. Node = I/S Function (Processor, Storage, etc.) Link = Line Char.
TECHNOLOGY MODEL	e.g., Data Design Ent. = Segment/Row Rel. = Pointer/Key	e.g., Structure Chart Proc. = Computer Functions I/O = Screen/Device Formats	e.g., System Arch. Node = Hardware/Sys. Software Link = Line Specifications
DETAILED REPRESEN- TATIONS	e.g., Data Design Description Ent. = Fields Rel. = Addresses	e.g., Program Description Proc. = Language Stmts I/O = Control Blocks	e.g., Network Architecture Node = Addresses Link = Protocols
FUNCTIONING SYSTEM	e.g., DATA	e.g., FUNCTION	e.g., COMMUNICATIONS

A, G		C, D, H		F	
B		E, I		J	

PROCESSES

K   System Development Life Cycle
L   Business Systems Planning
M   Functional Analysis
N   Information Modeling
O   Structured Design
P   Structured Programming
Q   Prototyping
R   Project Planning and Control

A.

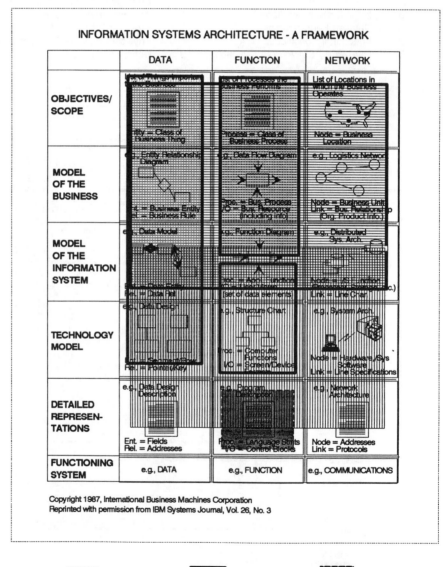

INFORMATION SYSTEMS ARCHITECTURE - A FRAMEWORK

 K, R   M   P

L   N   Q

 O

TOOLS

S   Activity / Function Modeling
T   Information Modeling
U   Data Dictionary / Repository
V   Programming
W   Prototyping
X   Source Code Library Maintenance
Y   Project Planning and Control
Z   Reverse Engineering
1   Re-Engineering
2   Editors
3   Compilers

A.

INFORMATION SYSTEMS ARCHITECTURE - A FRAMEWORK

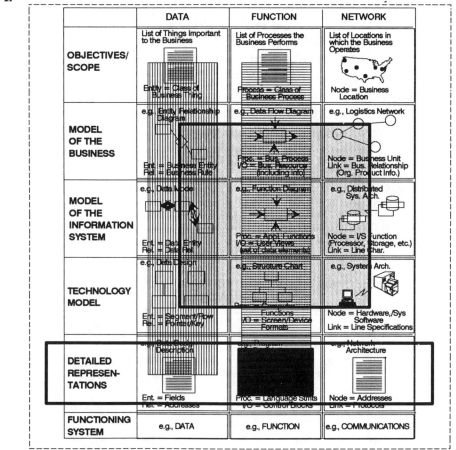

Copyright 1987, International Business Machines Corporation
Reprinted with permission from IBM Systems Journal, Vol. 26, No. 3

2.3 Q.   Two white spots on a black background are provide as *data*. What is a context that will turn this data into *information?* Hint: It is the night of April 18, 1775, in Boston, Massachusetts.

     A.   The context is the steeple of the Old North Church. The *information* is "The British are coming by sea."

2.5 Q.   Why is it important to develop architectures starting at the top of the Zachman Framework and working down?

     A.   Each row represents a transformation of the requirements stated in the row above into a representation that is closer to the final product. Without the requirements represented by the architectures in the previous row, assumptions have to be made in order to complete the architectures in the current row. For example, without the preceding architectures, builders need to make design assumptions, and designers need to make business requirements assumptions. Any assumptions we make are liable to cost us.

H.3 CHAPTER 3

3.2 Q.   Identify the row(s) of the Zachman Framework supported by each of the IDEF1X model types.

     A.

Model Type	Zachman Framework Row
Entity Relationship Diagram	Objectives / Scope Model of the Business
Key Based Model	Model of the Business Model of the Information System
Fully Attributed Model	Model of the Information System
Transformation Model	Technology Model
Database Management System Model	Detailed Representations Functioning System

3.3 Q. What factors influence how well information modeling benefits are realized?

A. This exercise is intended to stir up discussion. Here are some things to consider:

1. *Objective:* Why is the model being created? Is it going to be used for the design of a system, or is it simply "part of the methodology"? Is it to be a strategic or a tactical model? Is this to be a reverse-engineering effort, or is it top-down?

2. *Expectations:* What are they? Are they in alignment with what can be expected from the type of effort being conducted? For example, if you are preparing a reverse-engineered model without the benefit of business input, it is not likely that the model can represent a clear vision of future business requirements.

3. *Scope:* How large is the area being studied? The amount of effort necessary tends to change the nature of the benefits. A small effort may benefit from the design rigor brought by the process of modeling, but it is not likely to yield the type of process benefits obtained in modeling sessions for very large projects.

4. *Rigor:* Will the modeling process follow all the way from initial requirements to physical database design, or will it be used in early stages only? Benefits tend to diminish as the rigor is diminished.

5. *Culture:* Does the organization considering developing a model tend to spend a lot of time in the analysis and design phases of system development, or does it tend to go to the "solution" early?

6. *Skill:* How experienced are the people charged with preparing the model?

7. *Automation:* Is an automated tool used to manage the models?

8. *Schedule:* Do you have the time needed to prepare a model? Will modeling be followed by a physical design activity that uses the model as a statement of requirements (or is logical design being done in parallel with the physical design)?

9. *Point of Entry:* When is the modeling to begin? Is it too late (see Fig. 3.8)?

H.4 CHAPTER 4

4.2 Q. Name and define the three main building blocks of an IDEF1X model.

A. Entities, attributes, and relationships. The minimum definitions are given in the glossary and are repeated here.

ENTITY   any distinguishable person, place, thing, event, or concept about which information is kept.

ATTRIBUTE   a property of an entity.

RELATIONSHIP   a connection between two entities in which each primary key attribute of the parent entity becomes a foreign key attribute of the child entity.

4.3 Q. Classify each of the following as an entity, entity instance, attribute, or relationship.

A. animal   entity, entity instance
    vegetable   entity, entity instance
    mineral   entity, entity instance
    cabbage   entity instance
    dog   entity, entity instance
    the dog named Spot   entity instance

selling	relationship
car engine type	attribute
car type	attribute
car door	entity, entity instance
salesperson	entity
employee	entity
John—the salesperson	entity instance
Sally—the employee	entity instance

This is a bit of a trick question since many of the objects can be different model components in different types of models.

4.5 Q. Why can no part of a primary key be null? Show, with a sample instance table, an example of what would happen if this were allowed.

A. An entity instance is uniquely identified by its primary key. In the sample instance table, the values of three attributes (k1, k2, and k3) must be known in order to identify the instance. If the combination of k1, k2, and k3 for two instances of the entity is the same, the two instances must be the same. Otherwise, how could we tell them apart?

Null can have several meanings, but the two most common are "not applicable" and "not known." If we claim that a primary key should not contain attributes on which others are not *functionally dependent,* we cannot say something is dependent on something else that *is not there* (not applicable). Also, how can we use a primary key attribute to distinguish between two different instances when it is not applicable for either or both?

If we claim that to distinguish between instances we must have a unique key, it might seem like we could handle the "not known" situation. In the first eleven instances in our sample instance table, we still have unique keys, even though some contain nulls (indicated by the —). We simply don't know the key attribute value for certain instances, but we know everything else about the instances (for example, that in the tenth instance, the values of a1 and a2 are 90 and 09).

Suppose we find another instance with values B0 and 0B for a1 and a2 and want to assign the key, but we don't know the value for k2. For this new instance, we know that the value of k2 cannot be 1 because we would have a duplicate (1.1.1 already exists), and we know that this instance is distinct from our new instance because its a1 and a2 values are different. The value of k2 may be 2, 3, or some other value.

We also know the value of k2 for the new instance must be different from the value of k2 in the ninth instance (even though we don't know what that value is) because the a1 and a2 values, again, are different.

Therefore, we know that the twelfth instance is distinct from the tenth, *but we cannot add it to the table because it cannot be uniquely identified.*

ENTITY

k1	k2	k3	a1	a2
0	0	0	00	00
0	0	1	10	01
0	1	0	20	02
0	1	1	30	03
1	0	0	40	04
1	0	1	50	05
1	1	0	60	06
1	1	1	70	07
1	1	--	80	08
1	--	1	90	09
--	1	1	A0	0A
1	--	1	B0	0B

4.7 Q.   Review the following diagram and write down what it says.

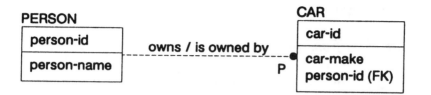

A.   A PERSON owns one or more CARs.
     A CAR is owned by (exactly) one PERSON (at any one time).

4.11 Q.   Write down the business rules stated by these three diagrams. What
          are the differences?

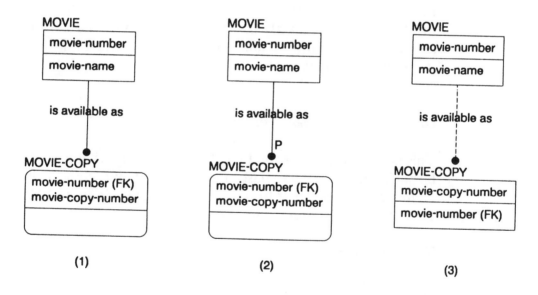

A.   First structure:

Rules:

Each MOVIE is available as zero, one, or more MOVIE-COPYs. A
MOVIE-COPY is a copy of exactly one MOVIE. A MOVIE-COPY cannot

exist and cannot be identified unless the MOVIE exists and the identity of the MOVIE is known. A MOVIE can exist for which there are no copies.

Differences from other structures:

The identifier of a MOVIE-COPY contains the identifier of a MOVIE. Thus, unlike the third structure, "movie-copy-number" must be unique only within a MOVIE. Unlike the second structure, a MOVIE can be included in the database even if there are no copies.

Second structure:

Rules:

Each MOVIE is available as one or more MOVIE-COPIES. A MOVIE-COPY is a copy of exactly one MOVIE. A MOVIE-COPY cannot exist and cannot be identified unless the MOVIE exists and the identity of the MOVIE is known. A MOVIE cannot exist for which there are no copies.

Differences from other structures:

This is the same as for the first structure, except that no MOVIE can be included in the database unless at least one copy of it is also included. It is different from the third structure in that a MOVIE can exist for which there are no copies.

Third structure:

Rules:

Each MOVIE is available as zero, one, or more MOVIE-COPYs. A MOVIE-COPY is a copy of exactly one MOVIE. A MOVIE-COPY cannot exist unless the MOVIE exists. A MOVIE-COPY can be identified even if the identity of the MOVIE is not known. A MOVIE can exist for which there are no copies.

Differences from other structures:

The identifier of a MOVIE-COPY does not contain the identifier of a MOVIE, but the MOVIE's identifier is known for each copy. Like the first structure and unlike the second structure, a MOVIE can be included for which there are no copies. Unlike the first structure, "movie-copy-number" must be unique for all MOVIE-COPYs, even if they are copies of different MOVIEs.

H.5 CHAPTER 5

5.2 Q. Provide good names for the following:

a) A record of a request by a customer to purchase a product that is not in stock.

A. UNFILLED-PURCHASE-REQUEST
OPEN-CUSTOMER-PRODUCT-PURCHASE-REQUEST
OPEN-PURCHASE-ORDER

b) A record of a request by a customer to purchase a product that was not originally in stock, but that was acquired and delivered to the customer.

A. FILLED-PURCHASE-REQUEST
FILLED-CUSTOMER-PRODUCT-PURCHASE-REQUEST
FILLED-PURCHASE-ORDER
CLOSED-PURCHASE-REQUEST
CLOSED-CUSTOMER-PRODUCT-PURCHASE-REQUEST
CLOSED-PURCHASE-ORDER

An alternate answer to a and b is

PURCHASE-REQUEST
CUSTOMER-PRODUCT-PURCHASE-REQUEST
PURCHASE-ORDER

with the addition of an attribute to designate whether the order is open or closed and an attribute to specify whether the merchandise had to be back ordered.

c) Something that is mechanical and generally is used to transport people or things from one place to another.

A.   VEHICLE
     MECHANICAL-TRANSPORT-MECHANISM

d) A building in which one or more people can or do live.

A.   RESIDENCE
     HABITATION

e) A record of a relationship between a mazerkaf and a quantu.

A.   MAZERKAF-QUANTU-ASSOCIATION

5.4   Q.   Name and define the associative entities in the following diagrams.

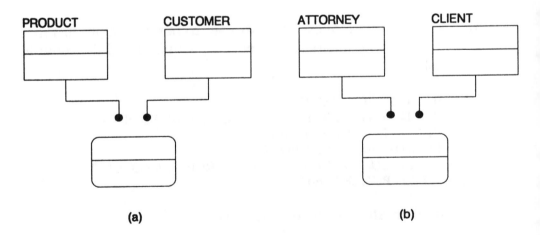

(a)   (b)

A.   These names could be almost anything, which is the message of the exercise. The same structure can support any number of business rules. The only rule evident in either structure is that there is a many-to-many relationship between the two independent entities.

Note that the associative entity structure supports grouping as well as the types of relationships we might infer from the names of the independent entities. We might, for example, speculate that the associative entity in Fig. 5.4a should be called SALE. Solely from Fig. 5.4a, however, we could also claim that a CUSTOMER is formed as a group of PRODUCTs.

5.6   Q.   Write definitions and domain specifications for the following attributes:

   c.   account-currency-code
   d.   account-balance
   e.   account-balance-currency-code

A.   There is no one correct answer for each. Poor answers, however, should be recognizable. Here are some that are okay.

Note: In examples c and e, the objective is to show that another attribute ("currency-code") needs to be defined, with the definition of its use as "account-currency-code" based on the new "currency-code" attribute. In example d, the objective is to show that the definition of "account-balance" should reference the definition of the CURRENCY entity.

CURRENCY

Description:	A medium of exchange issued by a government.
Example:	US Dollars
	French Francs
	Hong Kong Dollars

currency-code

Description:	A code that uniquely identifies a CURRENCY.
Domain:	The coding system is specified by the International Standards Organization in publication 3166-1981.
Col Name:	cur_code
Format:	CHARACTER (3)

c.   account-currency-code

Description: The "currency-code" that specifies the CURREN-
CY in which amounts are denominated for the
ACCOUNT.
Col Name: acct_cur_code
Data Type: "currency-code"

d.   account-balance

Description: A count of how much of a CURRENCY is held in
the ACCOUNT.
Comment: The value of the balance cannot be known with-
out knowing the CURRENCY involved.   This
CURRENCY is identified by the attribute "ac-
count-balance-currency-code".
Domain: Any number from -999,999,999.999999 to 999,
999,999.999999
Col Name: acct_bal
Format: DECIMAL(15,6)

e.   account-balance-currency-code

Description: A "currency-code" that designates the CURREN-
CY in which the "account-balance" is denominat-
ed.
Comment: The value of the balance cannot be known without knowing the CURRENCY involved.   The
amount of the balance is identified by the attribute "account-balance".
Col Name: acct_bal_cur_code
Data Type: "currency-code"

H.6 CHAPTER 6

6.2 Q. Some modeling languages do not have separate graphic symbols for relationships that have no attributes and relationships that have attributes. IDEF1X uses different symbols for these situations. What are the different symbols?

   A. A relationship without attributes is shown as a solid or dashed line, with a dot on one end. It is the IDEF1X *identifying or nonidentifying relationship* symbol seen in key based and fully attributed models. A relationship with attributes is normally shown as an *associative entity.* In entity relationship diagrams, the *nonspecific relationship* (the solid line with dots on both ends) also signifies a relationship with attributes, since it will need to be replaced with an associative entity as the model is transformed into a key based model.

6.4 Q. Create a model from the following list of attributes:

   - salesperson-id
   - customer-id
   - salesperson-name
   - territory-sales-target
   - order-customer-id
   - territory-salesperson-id
   - customer-name
   - territory-name
   - customer-rating
   - order-number
   - territory-id
   - order-status
   - quota
   - order-salesperson-id
   - size

   A. Not enough information is given for a single answer. Here is an example of one that will accommodate the attributes. The relationship types (identifying or not, mandatory or not) could however be different, and associative entities could be used to represent some of them. Also note the difficulty of placing the attributes that do not have clear names. The attribute "quota" is not too difficult to place (we assume salespeople have them), but "size" could be an attribute of any of the four entities. The "size" attribute is left out of the solution.

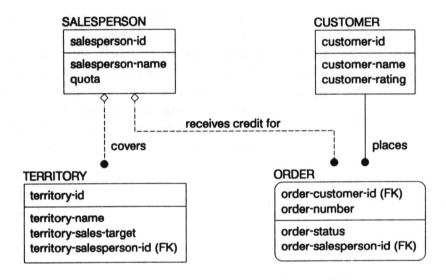

6.6 Q. For each of the following diagrams, explain why the primary key of entity A must be an alternate key of entity B.

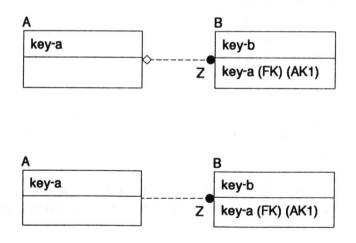

A. In the case of the mandatory relationship, every instance of entity B will contain a foreign key to a matching instance of entity A. The foreign key, "key-a", is unique for each instance of entity B since each instance of entity A can have at most one corresponding instance of entity B. The cardinality is one to zero-or-one. Therefore, "key-a" is an alternate key for entity B.

In the case of the optional relationship, "key-a" will be unique in entity B as long as it is not null. Unlike primary keys, alternate keys (by definition) are allowed to be null. Therefore, "key-a" is an alternate key for entity B.

H.7 CHAPTER 7

7.2 Q. What is lost in substituting a mandatory nonidentifying "is a Z" relationship for a category relationship?

A. 1. Inheritance of the attributes and relationships of the generic parent.
    2. Boolean constraint (and/or) support.

7.3 Q. Create a model based on the following business rules:

- An account can be a deposit account and, at the same time, a loan account. There are no other types of accounts.

- An account can have a loan balance if it is a loan and can have a deposit balance if it is a deposit account.

- There are at least three types of deposit accounts: checking accounts, savings accounts, and time deposits.

- There are exactly two types of loan accounts: credit lines and term loans.

- A term loan has a due date and can be either secured or unsecured.

- Secured loans require collateral, and the type of collateral must be known. One possible type of collateral is a time deposit. A time deposit may be used as collateral for at most one secured loan.

- A credit line may provide overdraft protection for any number of checking accounts.

- A credit line has a credit limit.

- The amount of available credit for a credit line must be known.

- A savings account can receive automatic transfers from only one checking account, but the same checking account can be the transfer source for any number of savings accounts.

- A savings account can be the source of automatic payments for any number of credit lines.

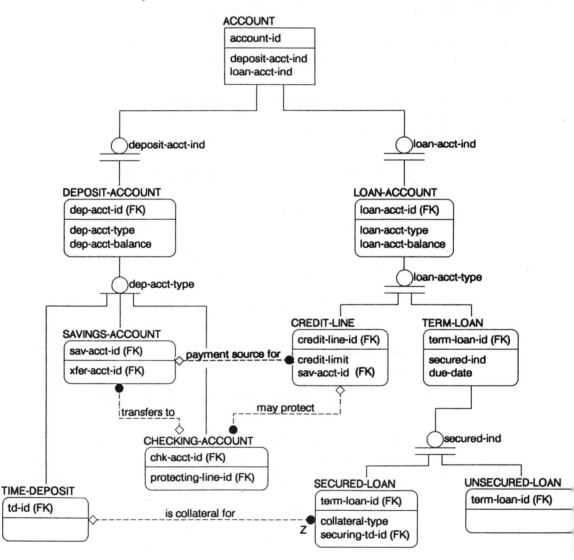

H.8 CHAPTER 8

8.1 Q. Draw a Venn diagram showing the intersection of the domains of
"base-tran-id", "oper-tran-id", "term-tran-id", and "tran-id" in Fig. 8.9.
Draw a second diagram to represent the actual instances for a single
TERMINAL and a single OPERATOR under the assumption that the
terminal and operator share at least some common privileges. Draw
a third diagram showing this second case but with the unification
assertion dropped and having both the "oper-tran-id" and "term-tran-
id" present in the TRANSACTION entity (see Fig. 8.8).

A.

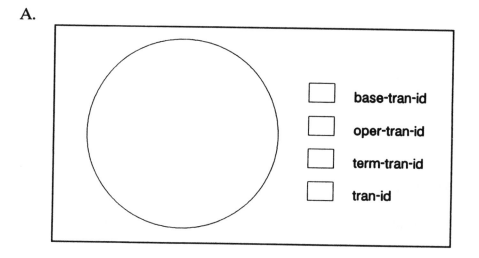

The first diagram is a single circle. The domains of the four attributes are the same (unless there are some transactions that no terminals or operators will ever be allowed to perform).
        The first diagram shown is for the original unification assertion.
Without the assertion, "tran-id" would include all of "oper-tran-id"
and all of "term-tran-id", not just the intersection of the two, as
shown in the second diagram.

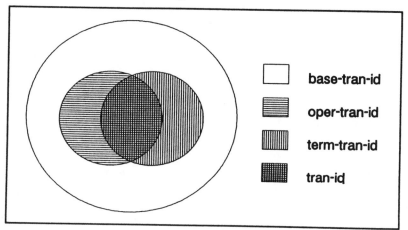

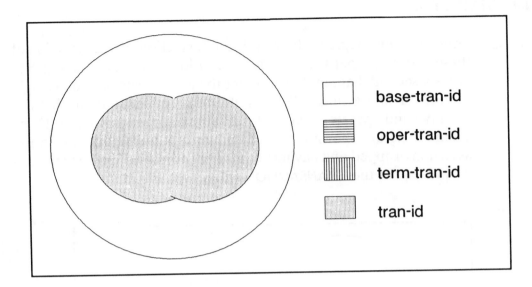

H.9 CHAPTER 9

9.2 Q.   What, if any, are the technical errors in these diagrams?

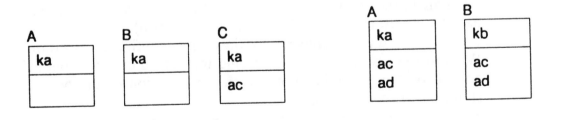

A. There is nothing technically wrong with either diagram. There are, however, some questions that need to be asked. For example:

   a. Since entities A, B, and C have identical keys, are they the same entity? If not, why not? Since attribute ac is determined by knowing ka, must an instance of entity C with key ka exist whenever an instance with that key exists in either entity A or entity B?

   b. Entities A and B have exactly the same attributes. Are they the same entity? If they really are the same entity, is it possible to combine them and designate either ka or kb as the primary key and let the other be an alternate key?

9.4 Q. What, if any, are the technical errors in this diagram? What revisions must be made to remove the errors?

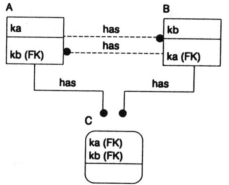

A. The error is that there can be two ways to know about the relationship between entity A and entity B. The logic used to find and resolve the error is as follows:

The primary key of A is ka.
The key ka uniquely determines kb, since kb is a foreign key in entity A.
For each instance of entity C, there is exactly one instance of entity A, and this instance of entity A contains kb.
Therefore, the attribute kb should not be part of the key of entity C, because it can be determined by looking at entity A.

After removing the redundant attribute from the key of entity C, the
model would look like this:

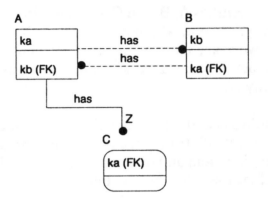

From the perspective of entity A, there are still two ways to know
the value of kb: Look at the foreign key kb in the instance of
entity A, or look at an instance of entity B with the foreign key
ka identifying the original instance of entity A.

From the original diagram, we know there can only be one instance
of entity B for each instance of entity A. The new diagram can
therefore be changed as follows:

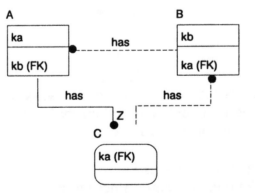

Now, for an instance of entity B, we still can find the corresponding
instance of entity A (via the path through entity C). We can also
find exactly one instance of entity A and one instance of entity B for
each instance of entity C. The assertion that there may or may not
be an instance of entity C for each pair of A/B instances also holds.

This is one of two solutions. The other is a mirror image. Note however, that the entire structure might collapse into a single entity (call it A) with one primary key (ka) and one alternate key (kb), since there are no data attributes in entity C. Trying to truly and precisely untangle such cases led to the data sub-field of dependency theory. Unfortunately, so many assumptions need to be made, and the reasoning becomes so tortuous that, in practice, *syntactic* analysis of this sort is usually assisted with *semantic* analysis of the structure. Strictly formal syntactic analysis is only an aid.

9.6 Q. What, if any, are the technical errors in this diagram? What revisions must be made to remove the errors?

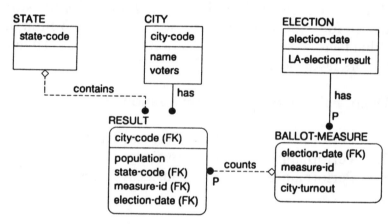

A. There are no technical errors in the diagram, but now we can see some business rule errors. The diagram makes the following questionable assertions (among others):

1. The only way we can know the state that contains a city is via election results.
2. The only true election result we can record is for the city of LA.
3. City turnout is not determined by city. It is the same for all cities.
4. The population of a city within a state depends on the result of a ballot measure in an election (this may not be so far from the truth).

5. The number of voters in a city is the same for all elections.
6. All ballot measures taken anywhere are determined by election results in the city of LA. (Again, this may not be so far from the truth.)

This is an example of semantic (as opposed to syntactic) analysis. There are no syntactic inconsistencies or redundancies, but there are many semantic errors. Good English can be used to argue an untruth. That does not mean that there is no value in using good English—without it one would simply not know what was being said. It is no different with IDEF1X.

9.8 Q. When a fully normalized information model is transformed into a design for a physical database, some denormalization often occurs. What factors favor denormalization for the physical database? What factors favor normalization?

A. Denormalization   Normalization

1. Performance   1. Business Rules
2. Performance   2. Business Rules
3. Performance   3. Business Rules

H.10 CHAPTER 10

10.2 Q. What are the potential benefits of reverse engineering?

A. A picture of where we are now can be developed. That picture can be the basis for discussion of where we want to be. See Section 10.2.2 for additional benefits.

10.3 Q. What are the potential risks of reverse engineering?

A. A picture of where we are now can be misinterpreted to be a picture of where we want to be. Such a model is based, to a large degree, on assumptions.

10.4 Q. Why is a reverse-engineered model not necessarily a model of what you want? What is required to make it so?

A. Such a model is based, to a large degree, on assumptions. These assumptions must be removed.

GLOSSARY

ACCESS METHOD

a utility function, normally provided by a computer operating system, that allows an application function to store and retrieve data on some external media.

ACCESS PATH

a specification of the primary key, alternate key, and inversion entry attributes that will be used to obtain instances of the entity.

ACCESS PATTERN

a specification of the sequence in which a logical transaction creates, replaces, uses, and deletes instances of entities.

ACCESS RATE

a specification of the frequency with which instances of an entity will be accessed.

AGGREGATION

the process of combining several objects into a new object.

ALIAS

1) another name for something, used in a different context; 2) another name for an object, usually one that is common throughout a business area.

ALTERNATE KEY

a candidate key that has not been chosen as the primary key.

ANCESTOR

an entity that provides a primary key attribute to another entity; can be the parent of the subject entity, a parent of one of its parents, and so on.

AREA INFORMATION MODEL

an information model that covers a broad business area, and that usually is larger than the business chooses to address with a single automation project.

ASSERTION   a statement that something is either true or false.

ASSOCIATIVE ENTITY   an entity that inherits its primary key from two or more other entities (those that are associated).

ATTRIBUTE   a property of an entity.

BASE ATTRIBUTE   an attribute for which a role name is assigned.

BUSINESS RULE   a policy of the business; can contain one or more assertions representing constraints on the behavior of the business.

BUSINESS VIEW   a subset of an entity relationship diagram; normally represents one or more major business functions.

CANDIDATE KEY   an attribute or group of attributes that might be chosen as a primary key.

CARDINALITY   a statement of the number of entity instances that may or must participate at each end of a relationship.

CASCADE   a procedure to ensure that the deletion of an entity instance causes the simultaneous deletion of all other entity instances dependent on it for existence.

CATEGORY   *see* CATEGORY ENTITY.

CATEGORY DISCRIMINATOR   an attribute that determines to which category a generic parent instance belongs.

CATEGORY ENTITY   a subset of the instances of an entity (referred to as a generalization entity, or generic parent) that share common attributes or relationships distinct from other subsets. This is the entity below the category discriminator symbol in any level of a generalization hierarchy. The category entity inherits all of the properties of the generic parent.

CATEGORY HIERARCHY   *see* GENERALIZATION HIERARCHY.

CHARACTERISTIC ENTITY   a group of attributes that occurs many times for an entity, and is not directly identified by any other entity; a dependent entity with only one identifying parent.

CHILD ENTITY   the entity to which a relationship contributes a foreign key; found on the many end of the relationship.

COMMON ANCESTOR   an entity that contributes primary keys to another entity along two or more relationship paths.

COMPOSITE DOMAIN   a constraint over the values of a group of attributes, declaring the permissible constituent value combinations.

COMPOSITE KEY   a primary key that contains two or more attributes, possibly foreign keys.

COMPOSITE MODEL   an information model formed by combining and resolving differences among a group of other information models.

COMPOSITION   the process of forming an information model from smaller information models.

COMPOUND KEY   *see* COMPOSITE KEY.

CONCEPTUAL SCHEMA   the middle level of the ANSI/SPARC Three Schema Architecture, in which the structure of data is represented in a form independent of any physical storage or external presentation format.

CONCEPTUAL VIEW   *see* CONCEPTUAL SCHEMA.

CONSTITUENT   an attribute that is a part of a group attribute.

CONSTRAINT   a rule that determines a valid state of the data.

CRUD MATRIX   a matrix mapping functions against data entities, and showing which functions Create, Replace, Use, and Delete (CRUD) instances of the entities.

DATA   individual values and their meanings.

DATA ADMINISTRATION   a business function responsible for identifying, documenting, and modeling business information requirements, and for maintaining the business' set of data definitions and standards.

DATA ADMINISTRATOR (DA)   a person who is part of the data administration function.

DATA ANALYST   a person skilled in data analysis and definition techniques.

DATA AREA   the area inside the entity shape that lies *below* the line that divides the shape.

DATA ATTRIBUTE   *see* NON-KEY ATTRIBUTE.

DATABASE   an organized collection of data values.

DATABASE ADMINISTRATION   a business function responsible for designing, implementing, and maintaining physical databases.

DATABASE ADMINISTRATOR (DBA)   a person who is part of the database administration function.

DATABASE MANAGEMENT SYSTEM (DBMS)   a computer application that manages the storage of data, and presents it to application programs in a form independent of its storage.

DATABASE MANAGEMENT SYSTEM MODEL   a specification of the detailed structure of the database that includes the Transformation Model, and any other information needed to describe the intended use of the database management system.

DATA DEFINITION LANGUAGE (DDL)   the language used to declare the data structure to a DBMS.

DATA DICTIONARY   an early version of an Information Resource Dictionary System; generally oriented at storing the physical definitions of databases, data elements, and so on.

DATA ELEMENT   the physical system representation of one or more attributes.

DATAFLOW DIAGRAM   a diagram that describes the processes and information flows required to complete some function.

DATA MANIPULATION LANGUAGE   the language with which an application program or a system user instructs the DBMS to perform operations on the database.

DATA MODEL	*see* INFORMATION MODEL.
DATA OBJECT	a term used to refer to either an entity or an attribute.
DATA TYPE	1) an attribute for which the domain has been declared as a subset of the domain of another attribute, and for which a role name has been assigned; 2) the physical representation of an attribute in a relational DBMS.
DEFINITION DEPENDENCY	an undesirable situation in which the definition of an attribute depends on the value of some other attribute.
DENORMALIZATION	the intentional transformation of a model to a lower-level normal form; normally done to tune a database toward a particular type of physical access.
DEPENDENT ENTITY	an entity that depends on one or more other entities for its identification (that is, its primary key contains foreign keys).
DERIVED ATTRIBUTE	an attribute whose value can be determined from the values of other attributes.
DESCENDENT	an entity that is identification-dependent on one or more other entities; a dependent entity is said to be a descendent of each entity or entities that provides the foreign key or keys.
DETERMINANT	an attribute or group attribute on which some other attribute is fully functionally dependent.
DISTRIBUTION MODEL	a model that shows how function and data are distributed over a series of separate machines.
DOMAIN	a set of values that an attribute may take.
ENTITY	a distinguishable person, place, thing, event, or concept about which information is kept.
ENTITY INSTANCE	*see* INSTANCE.
ENTITY INSTANCE VOLUME	an estimate of the number of instances that an entity can be expected to have.

ENTITY RELATIONSHIP DIAGRAM (ERD)   an information model that shows the major entities and relationships that support a wide business area.

ENTITY TYPE   *see* ENTITY.

EXISTENCE CONSTRAINT   an assertion made in an information model that an instance of an entity may not exist without the simultaneous existence of an instance of some other entity with the latter said to be existence-dependent on the former.

EXTERNAL SCHEMA   the outside level of the ANSI/SPARC Three Schema Architecture, in which views of information are represented in a form convenient for the users of the information; a description of the structure of data as seen by the user of a system.

FACILITATOR   a person whose declared role is to guide a meeting toward its objective.

FISH HOOK   *see* RECURSIVE RELATIONSHIP.

FOREIGN KEY   a primary key of a (parent) entity that is contributed to another (child) entity across a relationship.

FORWARD ENGINEERING   the conversion of a system's logical design into a functioning system.

FULLY ATTRIBUTED MODEL   a third (or higher) normal form information model that includes all entities, attributes, relationships, and integrity rules needed by a single automation project; contains entity instance volumes, access paths, access rates, and expected transaction access patterns against the data structure.

FUNCTIONAL DEPENDENCY   given an entity E, attribute B of E is functionally dependent on attribute A of E if and only if each value of A in E has associated with it precisely one value of B in E (at any one time).

GENERALIZATION   the inference of a general, common structure from a set of known facts.

GENERALIZATION ENTITY   *see* GENERIC PARENT.

GENERALIZATION HIERARCHY

a hierarchical grouping of entities that share common characteristics, possibly including a common set of attributes and/or relationships. At each level in the hierarchy, the entities are specific types or kinds of the higher-level entity.

GENERIC PARENT

the entity at the top of any level of a generalization hierarchy.

GROUP ATTRIBUTE

an attribute that is a collection of other attributes called constituents.

HOMONYM

1) a word that is like another in sound and perhaps in spelling, but with a different meaning; 2) a name that is or sounds the same or nearly the same for two different objects.

IDENTIFICATION DEPENDENCE

a characteristic of an entity that inherits one or more primary key attributes from another entity.

IDENTIFYING RELATIONSHIP

a relationship in which all primary key attributes of the parent entity become part of the primary key of the child entity.

INDEPENDENT ENTITY

an entity that does not depend on any other for its identification.

INDEX

a file containing pairs of data values and record locations; speeds retrieval of records based on the values of specified fields.

INFORMATION

data in a context.

INFORMATION MODEL

a specification of the data structures and business rules needed to support a business area.

INFORMATION MODELER

a person skilled in the practice of preparing information models.

INFORMATION MODELING

a technique for describing information structures and for capturing information requirements, policies, and rules.

INFORMATION REPOSITORY

a knowledge base that integrates an enterprise's business information and application portfolio.

INFORMATION RESOURCE
DICTIONARY SYSTEM (IRDS)

an application that controls access to an information repository, and provides facilities for recording, storing, and processing descriptions of an organization's significant data and data processing resources.

INHERITANCE

a quality in which all properties of a generic parent become properties of its category entities.

INSTANCE

a single occurrence of an entity.

INTEGRITY

a property of an information model or database in which all assertions hold. *See also* INTEGRITY CONSTRAINT, REFERENTIAL INTEGRITY.

INTEGRITY CONSTRAINT

a statement in an information model that specifies one or more assertions.

INTEGRITY RULE

a rule that specifies a valid state of a database.

INTERNAL SCHEMA

the inside level of the ANSI/SPARC Three Schema Architecture, in which views of information are represented in a form specific to the database management system used to store the information; a description of the physical structure of data.

INVERSION ENTRY

an attribute or group of attributes that will frequently be used to access the entity but may not result in finding exactly one instance.

IRD RULE

a business rule that specifies a constraint for inserting, replacing, or deleting instances of an entity.

KEY

see PRIMARY KEY, ALTERNATE KEY, FOREIGN KEY.

KEY AREA

the area inside the entity shape that lies *above* the line that divides the shape.

KEY ATTRIBUTE

see PRIMARY KEY ATTRIBUTE.

KEY BASED MODEL

a third normal form information model that describes the major data structures that support a wide business area, including all entities and primary keys along with sample attributes.

LOCAL VIEW

a subset of a fully attributed model; normally represents one or more logical transactions.

LOGICAL TRANSACTION

a transaction that accomplishes a single logical function.

META-DATA

data that describes other data.

META-MODEL

a model that describes other models.

MIGRATION

a movement of a primary key from the parent entity to a child entity across a relationship.

NONIDENTIFYING RELATIONSHIP

a relationship in which the primary key of the parent entity does not become part of the primary key of the child entity.

NON-KEY ATTRIBUTE

an attribute that has not been chosen as part of the primary key of the entity.

NONSPECIFIC RELATIONSHIP

a presentation style relationship in which no foreign keys are contributed, and in which many of one entity are related to many of another entity; allowable only in entity relationship diagrams.

NONULL

not allowed to be null.

NORMALIZATION

a process of removing inaccurate, inconsistent, and/or overly complex assertions from an information model.

NULL

having no value. An attribute can have a null value for many reasons—for example, the value is unknown, or the value is inapplicable.

NULLIFY

a process that sets a foreign key of an entity to null.

OBJECT

1) *see* DATA OBJECT; 2) in object-oriented approaches, a distinct person, place, or thing with relevant knowledge or actions.

PARENT ENTITY

the entity from which a relationship contributes a foreign key; found on the one end of the relationship.

PRIMARY KEY

an attribute or group of attributes that has been chosen as the unique identifier of the entity.

PRIMARY KEY ATTRIBUTE
an attribute that, either by itself or in combination with other primary key attributes, will form the primary key.

PROJECT INFORMATION MODEL
an information model that describes a portion of an overall data structure intended for support by a single automation project.

PROPAGATION
see MIGRATION.

RE-ENGINEERING
the rebuilding of a system to address new requirements, involving forward engineering from a logical design for the new system, and sometimes involving reverse engineering of the requirements of an existing system.

RECURSIVE RELATIONSHIP
a nonidentifying relationship in which the same entity is both the parent and the child.

REFERENTIAL INTEGRITY
a guarantee that all assertions covering a set of relationships are true. A database satisfies referential integrity if and only if it contains no unmatched foreign key values.

RELATIONAL MODEL
a model of information in which data is represented as tables, with records stored as rows of the table, and data elements stored as columns of each row.

RELATIONSHIP
a connection between two entities in which each primary key attribute of the parent entity becomes a foreign key attribute of the child entity.

REPOSITORY
a software tool for management of data and information that provides a mechanism for storing and processing descriptions of information and data processing resources.

RESTRICT
a process to ensure that deletion of an entity instance will not occur unless there are no other entity instances dependent on it for existence.

REVERSE ENGINEERING
the inference and documentation, to a specified level of detail and business generalization, of models of data and information structures, and business rules, under-

	lying one or more current or proposed data processing systems.
ROLE NAME	a new name for a foreign key attribute or group of foreign key attributes that defines the role it plays in the child entity. Its domain must be a subset (which can include the entire set) of the domain of the foreign key.
SAMPLE INSTANCE TABLE	a graphic example of an entity in which a table is used to show sample instances as rows in the table, with sample attributes shown as columns.
SCHEMA	a representation of the structure of data.
SEMANTICS	a meaning in language.
STORAGE VIEW	*see* INTERNAL SCHEMA.
STRESS TEST	an examination of the degree of change that will be required in an information model as the business functions that it supports are changed.
STRUCTURED QUERY LANGUAGE (SQL)	a data definition and manipulation language developed for use in relational database management systems.
SUB-TYPE	*see* CATEGORY.
SUB-TYPE HIERARCHY	*see* GENERALIZATION HIERARCHY.
SUBJECT MATTER EXPERT	a person with detailed knowledge of a certain topic (subject).
SUPER-TYPE	*see* GENERIC PARENT.
SURROGATE KEY	a single meaningless attribute assigned as the primary key for an entity.
SYNONYM	1) a word with the same or nearly the same meaning as another word; 2) another name for a thing that already has a name.
SYNTAX	the specification of the structure of a language.

TABLE   a collection of records arranged such that each record is a row and each field in the record is a column. In a relational database, an IDEF1X entity is represented as a table.

THIRD NORMAL FORM   a product of normalization in which every non-key attribute of the entity (a) depends on the entity's key, (b) depends on the whole of the key, and (c) does not depend on any key or non-key attribute of any other entity.

TRANSFORMATION MODEL   a transformation of a fully attributed information model into a structure that is appropriate for the expected access patterns and the database management system chosen for implementation.

UNIFICATION   the merging of two or more foreign key attributes into a single foreign key attribute based on the assertion that the values of the original foreign key attributes must be identical.

UNIQUE INDEX   an index that identifies a path to a single record.

USER VIEW   1) a subset of a key based model, normally representing one or more business functions; 2) *see* EXTERNAL SCHEMA.

VERB PHRASE   a description of a relationship intended to convey a sense of the business rule that governs the relationship; constructed such that reading the relationship from the parent to the child yields a meaningful sentence (for example, parent entity <verb phrase> child entity).

VIEW   a subset of an information model.

VIEW DESCRIPTION   a natural language description of the entities, attributes, relationships, and business rules described by a view.

INDEX

IDEF1X NOTATION CONVENTIONS

ENTITY NOTATION

ENTITY-NAME

key-area
data-area

Independent entity
Depends on no other
for its identification

ENTITY-NAME

key-area
data-area

Dependent entity
Depends on other(s)
for its dentification

ATTRIBUTE NOTATION

attribute (FK)

Foreign Key
Primary key of another entity
contributed by a relationship

role-name.attribute (FK)

Role name
New name for foreign key
connoting its use

attribute (AKn)

Alternate key
Alternate unique identifier
of the entity

attribute (IEn)

Inversion entry
Non-unique access identifier
of the entity

group.(c1,c2,c3)

Group attribute
Attribute is a group containing
the listed constituents

attribute (fk1 fk2 fk3) (FK)

Unified foreign key
Listed foreign keys are unified
to a single foreign key attribute

CATEGORY NOTATION

GENERIC PARENT

category-discriminator

CAT-1   **CAT-2**

Each category entity represents a
subset of the instances of the generic
parent, and inherits the attributes
and relationships of that parent

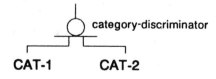
Complete
All categories shown

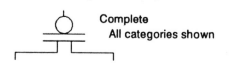
Incomplete
Not all categories shown